D0713482

GOOD MEAT

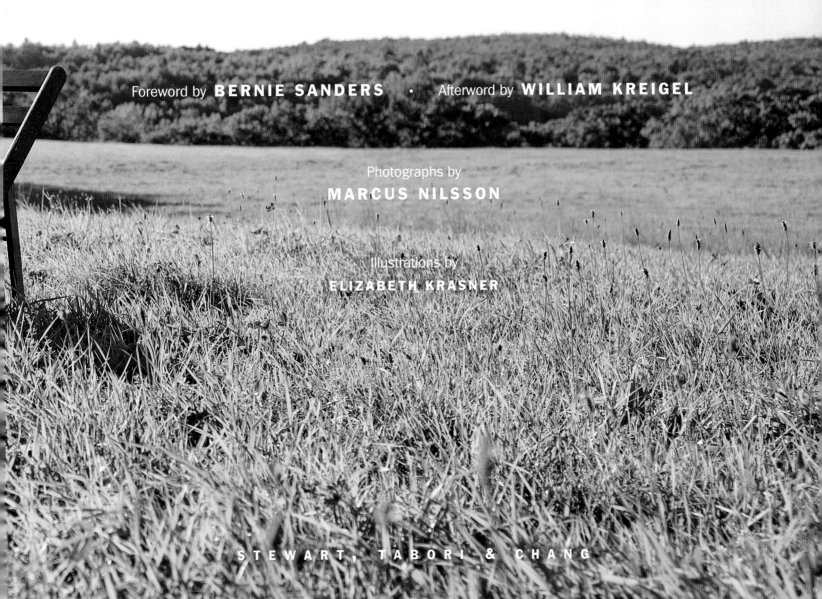

GOOD MEAT

The Complete Guide to Sourcing and Cooking Sustainable Meat

✳ WITH MORE THAN 200 RECIPES ✳

Deborah Krasner

Foreword by **BERNIE SANDERS** · Afterword by **WILLIAM KREIGEL**

Photographs by
MARCUS NILSSON

Illustrations by
ELIZABETH KRASNER

STEWART, TABORI & CHANG

Published in 2010 by Stewart, Tabori & Chang
An imprint of ABRAMS

Text copyright © 2010 Deborah Krasner
Photographs copyright © 2010 Marcus Nilsson
Illustrations copyright © Elizabeth Krasner

All rights reserved. No portion of this book may
be reproduced, stored in a retrieval system, or
transmitted in any form or by any means, mechanical,
electronic, photocopying, recording, or otherwise,
without written permission from the publisher.

Library of Congress Cataloging-in-Publication Data

Krasner, Deborah.
   Good meat : the complete guide to sourcing and
cooking sustainable meat / Deborah Krasner.
      p. cm.
   Includes bibliographical references and index.
   ISBN 978-1-58479-863-7 (alk. paper)
1. Cookery (Meat) 2. Cookery (Poultry) 3. Sustainable
living–United States. 4. Meat industry and trade–
Environmental aspects–United States.
I. Title.
   TX749.K68 2010
   641.6'6–dc22   2009047925

This one—number seven—is for Michael

Editor: Luisa Weiss/Natalie Kaire
Designer: Susi Oberhelman
Production Manager: Tina Cameron

The text of this book was composed in
Plymouth and Farnham

Printed and bound in U.S.A.
10 9 8 7 6 5 4 3 2 1

Stewart, Tabori & Chang books are available
at special discounts when purchased in quantity
for premiums and promotions as well as
fundraising or educational use. Special editions
can also be created to specification. For details,
contact specialsales@abramsbooks.com or
the address below.

115 West 18th Street
New York, NY 10011
www.abramsbooks.com

"Husbandry is the name of all the practices that

sustain life by connecting us conservingly to our places

and our world; it is the art of keeping tied all

the strands in the living network that sustains us."

Wendell Berry

ACKNOWLEDGMENTS

This book is deeply rooted in my life in Vermont for the past twenty-odd years and reflects the values I've learned here. It is a privilege to be part of a community that honors farmers who grow good food.

Many of those farmers have given me information, opened their farms to me, and provided meat and/or animal husbandry advice. These include Rod Hewitt, Lucas Fletcher, Ping Ting, and Asa Goodband. Some of my sources for local meats include Fowl Mountain Farm and Rabbitry, who raise rabbit and pheasant; Martha Miller of Dwight Miller Orchard, who raises pastured chicken; and Judy Sopenski of Not Your Ordinary Farm, who raises lamb. I have also learned from Bekah Murchison of Fair Winds Farm, who hosted the poultry-processing workshop; and Lili Bookwalter of Ledgewood Farm Icelandics, who breeds the lambs I raise for meat.

Four authors have influenced much of my thinking over the last few years: Wendell Berry, who has written so movingly about place, agriculture, personal responsibility, and sustainability; Eric Schlosser, who illuminated the connections between industrial food and factory farming; Michael Pollan, whose writing introduced me to Joel Salatin and taught so many of us about feedlot beef; and Barbara Kingsolver, who, along with her family, walks the walk.

During the process of writing this book, a number of people read parts of the manuscript and offered their help. I am most grateful to Michael Gourlay, owner of Hardwick Beef, for reading the beef chapter, making suggestions and comments, and getting me some of the harder-to-source beef cuts I needed. Thank you as well to Shannon Hayes for reading the lamb chapter and commenting most helpfully.

Adam Tiberio was invaluable in helping me create the cut sheet guides that offer consumers a logical series of choices, primal by primal. Jake Dickson, of Dickson's Farmstand Meat, graciously allowed us to photograph Adam in the shop, breaking down meat to illustrate this book.

Chef's Choice gave me a meat slicer and sausage grinder, and both were extremely useful pieces of equipment in the creation of this book. KitchenAid has long been a great source of support, and I am glad once again to acknowledge their help with equipment large and small.

My friend Jessie Haas and her parents, Bob and Pat Haas, have offered country wisdom born of their long experience raising, cooking, and eating their own meat.

My valiant recipe testers have been incredible, cooking carefully at home and letting me know what works and what is confusing. I, of course, tested every recipe as I developed it, often repeatedly. But these testers took the printed recipes and tried them again with their own grass-fed and pastured meats, letting me know where they felt the writing or the dish needed help. Their e-mails have given me belly laughs, anxiety, joy, and thankfulness. To Sarah Strauss, Valerie Wright, and Melissa Pasanen, I raise my glass and offer heartfelt thanks.

My family, as ever, have been stalwart supporters, offering their palates and ideas without stinting. You'll see recipes from them in this book, and you'll also benefit from their behind-the-scenes comments that helped me create the dishes. Thank you to Abby Krasner Balbale for tasting, thinking, writing, conceptual, and research help; to Musab Balbale for some great recipes; to Lizzie Krasner for her fine illustrations, and commenting, cooking, testing, organizing the kitchen, and editing; and to my husband, Michael Krasner, who greets each meal with anticipation, eats it with joy, and then cleans the kitchen.

Lizzie's friend (and now ours) James Kenji Lopez-Alt has visited and cooked with me on several occasions, each time teaching me how to fearlessly break down large animal parts and cook them with pleasure. Most recently, Kenji helped us process the year's worth of poultry we raised last summer. Thank you, Kenji, for being part of our kitchen life.

For the past two years, my culinary family (known as the Creampuffs) has been a group of food professionals I cook with monthly. We get together to tackle ambitious dishes, to understand unfamiliar techniques, and to enjoy the company of other passionate cooks and eaters. Two of them, in particular, have generously helped me to develop some of the recipes in this book, and their support has kept me going. A big thank-you and hugs to Marshall Brewer and Tuk Long; I hope we'll keep on cooking and learning together for a very long time.

No book is born from the forehead (or palate) of its author, and cookbooks, especially, grow as much from other people and their books as from a sense of place or taste. I've included

a bibliography to acknowledge the books that inspired me and pushed me in the direction of different dishes. When I've found other people's recipes that are un-improvable, I've cited their authors in the headnotes, even as I've adapted their recipes for grass-fed meat. Many of the cookbooks in the bibliography are particular favorites; if nothing else, I hope to introduce you to some wonderful food writers.

Two sets of friends from our extended Danish family-by-choice, Thomas Kruse and Anne Mette-Kruse, and Lone Klok and Anders Pedersen, gave me a refresher course in Danish meat cookery in Århus and Varde as I worked on this book. We also spent time with Lone and Anders in Sicily, testing recipes and cooking with lots of lemons, oranges, and their own extraordinary olive oil.

A number of local purveyors were immensely generous when we cooked through the book for photography. These include Larry Burdick and Walpole Grocery, Walpole, NH; North End Butchers, Brattleboro, VT; and Harlow's Farmstand, Westminster, VT. I am very appreciative of their efforts, and glad to live in a place that has such outstanding resources.

Finally, I am grateful to Luisa Weiss for assembling such an accomplished support team. She brought in Ana Deboo, the finest copyeditor I have ever encountered; found the superb photographer Marcus Nilsson; and brought in talented food stylist Victoria Granof and prop stylist Angharad Bailey. A heartfelt thank you to Natalie Kaire, who took over editing the book mid-stream with much grace and understanding. A very special thanks indeed to Susi Oberhelman, our hardworking designer. Publisher Leslie Stoker has been a strong supporter from the moment she heard about the idea, and I am deeply grateful for her enthusiasm. I have cherished the opportunity to work on this book.

ORGANIC

BEEF
RIB STEAK - $14 #
GROUND 6.00
PORTER HOUSE 15.
CHUCK FOR POT
ROAST $6.
STEW W/BONE - 5.00
KABOB $8.00

(LA BEURRE)

CONTENTS

FOREWORD

A week before writing this I went to an event for young students who came from ten communities across Vermont and celebrated the fact that each would be using solar panels to create sustainable energy projects in their school. The event was held in a center-city school in Burlington, in the school cafeteria, and it included lunch for the students. Everything in their lunch was local—apples, beans, potatoes, meat, fruit cobbler. Much of it was organic; the meat was grass-fed beef that was made into shepherd's pie.

It was not too long ago that the term *organic* was considered weird and used only for a fringe segment of our agriculture system, and the idea of grass-fed meat was almost inconceivable. In fact, it was extremely difficult to find a vegetable or fruit that had not been sprayed with chemicals, or meat that had not been raised on a factory farm. Wow! Has that changed!

From one end of this country to the other, people from all walks of life are demanding good-quality, organic, locally produced food and searching out meat that is not laced with the residue of antibiotics. In fact, one of the great problems that we now face is that large agribusiness corporations are prepared to abuse and dilute the term *organic*—something we can't allow to happen. We must protect strong organic standards—and in the meat we consume, we must make sure that "grass-fed" is differentiated from "organic."

In my view, the challenge that we now face, in terms of food production, is to break up the dangerous concentration of ownership that exists in agriculture and the food industry, and do everything we can to protect and expand family-based organic and local food production.

For a whole lot of very valid reasons, Americans are more and more concerned about the quality and safety of the food that they, and their children, are consuming. They are aware that some 76 million Americans—one in four of us—are sickened by food-borne diseases each year because of lax standards. They are aware that factory farming abuses not only animals, but the workers employed at those factory farms and in the fields. As this book will make you aware, locally raised, grass-fed animals are healthier, the farmers who raise them are happier with what they do, and the meat that results is better for

us than is the case with the plastic-wrapped meat that is for sale in our supermarkets.

Americans are concerned that much of the food that we import from foreign countries is produced under far lower standards than Americans, or anyone, have a right to expect. Local food is food we know about: As Deborah Krasner tells us in these pages, when we buy meat locally we get to know the farmer who raised it, we can ask questions about what the animals were fed, and we can even, when ordering, determine what cuts of meat we want.

Americans are concerned that when we import food from halfway around the world we waste an enormous amount of energy and create greenhouse gas emissions that worsen global warming. Local meat, grass-fed, is much more beneficial to our planet because it doesn't have to be transported long distances, because it doesn't depend on petroleum-based chemical fertilizers, because it uses far fewer mechanized and energy-dependent processe s: It helps us reduce many of the greenhouse gas emissions that are driving climate change. And while it makes our diet healthier, it also improves the quality of our soils.

Americans are concerned that the high levels of sugar, salt, and trans-fats in processed foods are causing a nationwide obesity epidemic which is creating health problems for millions of people, including more and more children—and for our entire health care system. You will learn from reading this book that meat from animals raised on grass—not corn, meat byproducts, antibiotics, and even plastic pellets, as is the case with factory-farm meat—is actually far more healthy than the conventional meat we buy in stores. Grass-fed beef is much lower in saturated fats than supermarket beef, and higher in vital omega-3 fatty acids and conjugated linoleic acid (CLA).

The bottom line is—and we're seeing this every day—that more and more Americans want a food production system that protects their health and their environment, and treats the people who work the land with respect and dignity. They also understand how important local food production is for our economy. Buying direct from a farmer plows 90 cents of each dollar back into the farm and protects our local communities. That is why, in Vermont and throughout this country, we are seeing an explosion in farmers' markets and community supported agriculture (CSAs). That is why more and more farmers are selling their locally raised meat directly to consumers.

This book addresses the new American interest in, and need for, sustainable agriculture and the healthy products that sustainable farms produce. Although it has one chapter on side dishes and another on eggs, it is mostly about meat. For while the meat we should be eating—meat from animals fed on grass, not fed some premixed diet in crowded pens where the only aim is to fatten animals as quickly and cheaply as possible—is healthy for us and for the land, it is also *different* from the meat we are used to.

Pasture-fed meat requires different cooking methods. Some of the recipes in this book preserve the wonderful rich flavor of good meat, the kind of meat our great-grandparents took for granted, but which years of factory farming have displaced. Some of the recipes address the fact that good beef is leaner than what we are accustomed to—and, interestingly, good pork is fattier. Some of the recipes teach us to use cuts of meat we don't encounter at the supermarket: Yes, there are wonderful recipes for chuck steak and leg of lamb, but there are also recipes for the parts of the animal that get made into bologna and hot dogs in conventional meat processing.

This is a wonderful book, from its gracious and generous writing to its lovely and useful photographs to its diagrams of cuts of meat. At its center are two things: an introduction to a new way of eating and why we should embrace that way—the way of sustainable, grass-fed meat—and a wonderfully rich array of recipes, so that we can make this sustainable food a part of our everyday lives.

Deborah Krasner is part of a revolution in food, in agriculture, in nutrition, that is taking place in our nation. Her book is a fine contribution to that revolution, teaching us how to eat more healthfully, how to buy from local farmers, how to cook what they raise. *Good Meat* draws on a wide array of cooking traditions—French, Indian, North African, Italian, Chinese, German, Korean, Cuban, and many others—to show us how, as we eat more healthily and sustainably, we can also cook, and eat, with great delight.

Senator Bernie Sanders, I-VT

INTRODUCTION

Over the years, many small incidents and experiences inspired this book.

One such moment came when I read a *New York Times* article in which the author wrote about not knowing how to cook lamb shoulder from the Union Square Greenmarket. I was struck by how quickly we've lost our ability to cook anything more than steaks, burgers, and chops.

A second was the recognition that, years before anyone was talking about locavores or one-hundred-mile diets, nearly all the meat, fruit, and vegetables my family ate came from within a twenty-mile radius of our home. I thought this was interesting but not terribly useful for other people, until I began to notice that it was increasingly possible to eat this way nearly everywhere in America, thanks to CSA (community supported agriculture) shares, farmers' markets, Web sites that lead consumers to local farmers, and other direct farm-to-market schemes.

A third incident made an even bigger impression—my husband, who has high cholesterol, happened to have his blood tested after our first year of eating from a freezer full of local, entirely grass-fed and pastured meat of various kinds. Although he had eliminated butter and desserts from his diet, he *had* also eaten a prodigious amount of meat. Without further effort on his part, though, his LDL count had gone down a whopping forty points! That astonishing fact made me start researching the health benefits of such meat.

The reason our freezer was so full was that I had ordered meat from various farmers over the course of several months . . . and had failed to keep track of my orders. Suddenly in September, I got calls from the beef farmer, the pork farmer, and the sheep farmer, who all wanted to make arrangements for pickup. This was the year my youngest child went off to college, which I think had something to do with my absent-mindedness.

As I cooked my way through a quarter of beef, a half pig, and a whole lamb, I discovered cuts and tastes I hadn't experienced in years. Here in Vermont, grocery stores and even our local co-ops often don't stock briskets, short ribs, lamb breasts, pig's trotters, or pork shanks. It was a treat to cook them and a delight to share their flavors with friends and family. Those long-simmering pot roasts and braises and soup bases were, for me, the stuff of memory—some of them were the foods I remember my grandmother and mother cooking, and some were the dishes I cooked in the early days of our marriage.

What is extraordinary is that, once tasted, the lively, honest flavors of pastured meat create instant converts. This was true not just for me, but for my culinary guests as well. People from all over the country who attend my culinary vacations ate these ingredients enthusiastically, saying this was how meat tasted when they were kids! In the past, guests used to have to order meat from my Vermont suppliers, but these days they can often go home and order meats comparable in taste, sustainability, and price from their own local farmers.

This is a sea change, and a promising opportunity both for the continued viability of sustainable farms and for consumers looking for great taste, healthful food, and a chance to support environmental responsibility.

As I began to taste, cook, and source more broadly, I became an increasingly passionate advocate for grass-fed and pastured meat. Although I had been ordering pastured lamb for a very long time, I began, in that meat-filled year, to buy grass-fed beef and local heirloom pork in half and whole animal quantities, going further in subsequent years to include local poultry and rabbits. Recently I've begun raising poultry, eggs, and lamb myself.

Because of my experiences, I wanted to write this book to show everyone how it's possible to eat healthy, fairly priced, and sustainable meat no matter where you live. Today, all over this country, people can buy traditionally raised, pastured meat from farmers in their state (see www.eatwild.com and www.localharvest.org), as well as fresh by mail order in retail portions from such national consortia as Heritage Foods USA. (See Sources, page 371, for more places to start your research.) Consumers can choose meats from heirloom animals or from more familiar breeds, all raised outside and fed a mostly traditional foraged diet. (I say "mostly" because there are some purchased or locally grown feeds and minerals that enhance meat production without adding ingredients that should not be part of a ruminant's diet.)

Our Icelandic lambs Coconut, Meringue, and Caramel

I want to encourage others to cook the whole animal, piece by piece, and nose to tail, in ways that honor both the animal and the farmer who raised it, ways that enhance the vitality of the diners at your table, the environment in general, and your local landscape.

My other hopes are easily listed. I hope you'll

- bypass the industrial food system and support local farmers who raise sustainable food;
- buy local pastured meat from the farmers who raise it and from farm stands or specialty retailers, asking lots of questions in the process;
- buy this meat in quarter, half, or whole animal quantities to reap great savings; and
- become knowledgeable about the choices available to you when buying this way so that you, not the processor or farmer, determine the cuts you get.

Bypassing the industrial food system benefits all of us, allowing transparency along the whole chain, from growers to consumers.

Much like buying vegetables at a farmers' market, buying meat from local farmers enables consumers to understand how the animal was raised, fed, and processed. In turn, they know much more about what goes into their mouths.

This approach, new to many of us, usually sparks a number of questions, which I will attempt to answer in this book.

What is grass-fed and pastured meat, and why is it sustainable?

Beef is called "grass fed," while pork, lamb, and poultry are referred to as "pastured." While these terms are often used interchangeably, the essential point is that animals spend their whole lives eating what they were designed by nature to eat, and getting exercise, fresh air, and sunlight as they forage. They tend to be healthy, with no need for antibiotics and other drugs. Because they range through rotating pastures large enough for their needs, they are not stressed or crowded. And because grass-fed animals grow slowly and naturally to the appropriate weight for processing, they don't need growth hormones.

Consequently, meat and dairy products from grass-fed animals are clean in the sense that they are without drugs and hormones that industrially raised animals are given for weight gain and disease prevention, and in terms of their environmental impact. Such meat is humanely raised, from birth to slaughter, on family farms (not large food factories), usually by one farmer. Pastured animals produce manure that enriches the fields they roam on and nourishes birds and other wildlife, promoting a diverse ecosystem. Their meat and milk are increasingly being recognized as healthier than conventional products. They are consistently lower in fat (grass-fed beef, lamb, and bison have about the same amount of fat as a skinless chicken breast) and may have other benefits as well.

In addition to taking part in a cycle that nourishes pasture rather than depleting the soil, grass-fed and pastured animals are a sustainable choice because the meat can be obtained locally in every state, drastically reducing the distances products must be shipped—and because buying it helps small farmers to make a living caring for their land and animals.

What is "conventional" or "industrial" meat?

Conventional or industrial meat starts out grass fed but is raised or finished in severely cramped quarters, often where animals cannot even turn around; they may never see open land or walk in the sun. By any standard, their treatment is stressful and inhumane. Fed an unnatural diet of animal by-products such as chicken dung, fast-food refuse, and corn, along with plastic pellets for roughage, they need drugs to keep them alive. Their highly concentrated waste products become sources of pollution that blight whole areas of land, rivers, and seas. As Wendell Berry so cogently puts it, this system "takes a solution [the traditional pasturing of animals] and divides it neatly into . . . problems." And, as Michael Pollan points out, the monoculture corn farming that supplies feedlots also consumes vast amounts of fossil fuel and pesticides, thus creating enormous pollution in its own right.

The conditions that industrially raised and finished animals suffer are also difficult for their human caretakers, and are equally inhumane. Those who work on factory-style meat and poultry farms are often unhappy with what they are forced to do to earn a living. Farmers naturally feel affection for their animals, and there are few farmers who actually feel

Slaughtering Practices for Large Animals

It's not easy to write about the slaughter process, but some may want to know how large animals are processed. In just about all commercial slaughterhouses, animals proceed to the killing floor after spending at least a day waiting in pens, fasting and drinking nothing but water to empty their systems of digesting food. The best producers and processors will do all that they can during this period to keep the animals comfortable and relaxed in this new environment; a poor slaughterhouse will keep animals dirty, crowded, starving, and thirsty in this limbo for days or even longer.

Purging should only last twenty-four hours, and afterward, in the best of all possible worlds, the animals will be washed down and herded to the killing floor in small groups, going from one pen to the next until they reach a chute that leads them, one at a time, to the knocking box. There, they are rapidly stunned with a bolt gun (which makes them brain dead) or shot, then hung from one leg while a quick throat cut drains them of blood. (In halal or kosher slaughtering practices, following religious dictates, animals are not stunned prior to draining.)

Temple Grandin, an authority on humane slaughterhouse practice and the author of *Animals in Translation: Using the Mysteries of Autism to Decode Animal Behavior,* has created a series of protocols designed to reduce animal stress, which set a new standard for humane processing. These include pens without sharp corners, silence, privacy for the animals, and more. If you have the opportunity to choose your own processor, look for these signs that they are concerned about animal welfare.

The carcasses are then sent through the processing section, where they are cut in half lengthwise; the head, skin, and organs are removed; and parts are inspected and tested by resident USDA inspectors. The split carcass is chilled (and possibly aged) before it is carved into primals and subprimals.

In general, the smaller the facility, the more likely it is that this process will be clean, relatively quiet, humane, and rapid but not rushed. Those conditions are of great benefit to the animals and to consumers, especially because stress affects the flavor of meat. Your conscience will be the better for it as well.

good about conditions on conventional feedlots, hog farms, or poultry farms. Many of them feel trapped in the system—they owe money to the bank and have contracts they must fulfill. American farm policy underwrites unsustainable industrial agriculture with subsidies, so change is difficult for large-scale farmers who may want to try an alternative.

What is the difference between natural, vegetarian diet, organic, and grass fed?

In this context, it's useful to point out that "natural," at least the USDA's definition, merely means that no artificial flavors, colors, or preservatives have been added. It has nothing to do with how an animal was raised or fed. In this sense, all meat sold in America is "natural" meat, even if it isn't labeled as such. Ranchers I've spoken with define "natural beef" as meaning no hormones, which are administered to make steers gain weight fast.

Meat labeled "vegetarian diet" means only that an animal was not fed meat by-products (which are supposed to be illegal for cattle feed anyway), but was instead fed grasses and grains. This is a designation designed to address fears of bovine spongiform encephalopathy (or BSE, commonly called "mad cow" disease), which can be spread when cattle eat meat by-products. It does not mean the animal was raised outdoors on pasture, or even that it ever saw the outdoors.

"Certified organic" means merely that the animal was given feed certified as 100 percent organic and did not receive any antibiotics unless they were needed to treat an actual illness. Again, it doesn't mean that an animal was raised any differently from those in industrial settings. I know an organic egg farm where the chickens never go outside. Their eggs are indeed organic—the chickens have

eaten only organic chicken feed and garden scraps—yet their only exposure to fresh air and sunlight has been through the small windows of the building they live in from birth to death.

What can you expect from grass-fed and pastured products?

You will discover that the products of sustainable farming methods look and taste different—the yolks of the eggs are deep orange, the pork is firm and flavorful, the beef tastes like that great steak you may have eaten in France years ago, and the lamb reminds you of why it's a sacramental food in so many traditions.

Grass-fed beef and pastured lamb taste meatier, purer, more mineral—with less fat and more flavor. Pastured chicken and pork are not flaccid; they have a distinct taste and texture. There are variations in flavor due to the breed of the animal, its age at processing, the climate, geography, and quality of the pasture it fed on, as well as whether it was well processed, aged, or frozen. For this reason, savvy consumers ask lots of questions of farmers and processors.

You'll find that because these meats are naturally lean, they may improve your health. Consider the astonishing fact that eating red meat, rather than compromising your health, might be an actual benefit. One hundred percent grass-fed beef is much lower in saturated fats than conventional beef. What fat there is, is higher in omega-3 fatty acids (good, heart-healthy fats) and the antioxidant vitamins A and E. Grass-fed beef, in particular, has a high level of CLA (conjugated lino-leic acid), which in laboratory tests shows promise at fighting tumors and breast cancer. Similarly dramatic beneficial nutritional profiles describe grass-fed and pastured lamb, pork, poultry, and eggs in comparison to their conventionally produced counterparts.

The sad thing is that these flavors and health benefits were once the birthright of every meat, egg, dairy, and poultry consumer in this country before the advent of industrial meat production and the loss of so many family farms. The good news is you can once again have these benefits, as long as you are willing to order directly from farmers and to store the meat yourself for the coming season or to buy it in smaller cuts from specialty retailers.

Can you buy 100 percent grass-fed beef and pastured meat at retail?

It is becoming increasingly possible to buy grass-fed meat piece by piece from retailers, specialty butchers, and markets. While this will always be more expensive than buying directly from farmers in quantity, it is a real convenience for those who prefer fresh meat or those with limited freezer space. My only caveat is this: Make sure you are really getting grass-fed or pastured meat. If the beef label doesn't say "100% grass-fed beef"—unambiguously and without room for loopholes in interpretation—assume that it is not.

The latest trend, and one worth both applauding and emulating for those who do not buy meat in large quantities, is meat CSAs. This model is based on the practice of selling shares of a farm's fruit and vegetable harvest. Several families or CSA members split whole pastured animals serially and systematically. The animals are preordered by a group who takes charge of filling out the cut sheets for everyone, then divides the meat equitably among the members. One benefit of this model is that it's possible to order only enough meat to fit in the freezer compartment of a small refrigerator, and more can be ordered as it is used up.

How do you plan ahead for a season's eating?

What does it mean to think about your meat consumption weeks and months in advance? Many of us shop daily or weekly for food, and decide the day of a meal that we feel like eating pasta or chicken or a steak. Buying so much meat so far ahead may seem like a foreign idea.

In fact, though, I found that the plunge into ordering part of an animal and keeping it in my freezer, then getting pieces cooked and on the table, was a surprisingly easy adjustment. When I have a freezer full of meat, my choices are often easier. If I do think of a menu idea ahead of time, I defrost tomorrow's meat the night before, or turn to meat I've been dry-aging in the refrigerator. If I haven't made plans, I can defrost something in a bowl of cold water pretty rapidly, particularly ground meat or a small steak or chops (see page 54). It is often a relief not to have to run out and buy ingredients.

How do you find the time to do all this cooking?

The issue of time is a significant one. Cooking my way through a whole animal, I soon learned why only a few people cook much meat beyond burgers, chops, and steaks. Most of the rest of the animal demands long, slow cooking. This is not at all a technical challenge—making an oven roast, a stew, or a pot roast is as simple as frying a burger—but it does take appreciably more time. Throughout this book, I have offered suggestions for how to integrate cooking into a busy schedule, perhaps by browning tomorrow's meat while cooking tonight's burgers, so that you can either use a delayed oven feature, use a slow cooker (if yours can be set low enough), or put the dish on to cook when you get home, in order to get in an hour or two of slow-cooking before dinner while you relax with your family.

Such timing may still be out of the question for you, but that doesn't mean you have to give up the idea entirely. Just keep your schedule in mind when you fill out your cut sheet. Ask for as much ground meat as possible beyond the usual steaks, chops, and roasts. That way you can always pull a quick meal together, knowing you are feeding your family the healthiest, best, and most sustainable meat you can buy.

There is one way this approach saves you time: Buying a whole animal means you can shop less often and spend less

time doing it, and I find that a great pleasure. I depend on the farmers' market and my garden or CSA to supply me with seasonal vegetables and local fruits, and this means that from spring to late fall I have only to shop for staples such as flour and sugar, occasional cleaning and paper supplies, and milk and dairy products (which I am increasingly able to buy directly from farmers as well). It is an extraordinary experience and a privilege to know the faces of the farmers who provide my food, and to know how that food was raised. What's more, it is of great benefit to the farmers to be able to sell directly to the consumer.

How is this book organized?

My goal is to offer recipes for every part of grass-fed or traditionally raised large animals—cow, pig, lamb—that one would be able to get whole or in part from local farmers or specialty retailers, along with recipes for sustainably raised small birds and flesh we eat in whole-animal quantities, such as chicken, turkey, duck, goose, guinea fowl, and rabbit, as well as pastured eggs. The recipes are designed for the unique characteristics of leaner grass-fed meats.

Some of the recipes I've written are for the familiar "center of the plate" model of eating, in which meat serves as the main focus of the meal. But many recipes use meat as a flavoring for dishes that may be primarily pasta or beans or rice or salad. All of us make choices daily about how we want to eat, how we want to live, and how we can do so more sustainably. Many choose to include meat in their diet only in moderation.

Further, because I believe that if we choose to eat meat, we are obliged to honor the animal's sacrifice by cherishing every edible part, I have offered recipes in support of that goal. To those used to the Styrofoam-encased ground beef of the supermarket meat aisle, these items will be unfamiliar. Nearly all of the meat used in these recipes came from local farmers or processors, although I had to search out some of the less conventional meat cuts especially for this book.

I hope these recipes will help you to cook less-familiar parts with confidence and eat them with delight and pride.

I have devoted each chapter to one animal, starting with descriptions of their largest parts (called primals and subprimals in the meat trade) from a cook's perspective, and then offering detailed cut sheet information that lays out all the choices for each primal part for those who order meat in larger quantities, either by the quarter, half, or whole. Recipes in sequence, going part by part, offer ideas for cooking every cut of naturally lean grass-fed and pastured animals. At the end of the book, the sources section will provide you with the contact information for various organizations that aim to make sustainable meat available around the country.

Thus, if you decide to order beef in large quantity from a farmer, and are filling out a cut sheet, you can look at the section called "round" to see the choices you have for this primal. Then, when you've got your meat in the freezer, you can pull out a package labeled "top of the round roast" and know where to go for recipes. Similarly, if you buy your meat piece by piece from retailers, farm stores, or farmers' markets, you'll have a guide to what to do with that package mysteriously marked "beef round, sirloin end."

In addition to recipes for meat by each cut of a primal part, you will find recipes for preparing offal, bones, and fat (including how to render that fat and use it in other dishes or make pastry with it).

I also share my experiences in the kitchen, in the meadow with the lambs, turkeys, geese, ducks, and guinea fowl, and in the chicken coop with the laying hens. I will tell you stories about my animals and how I've learned to eat meat from animals I've known and cared for.

We are now in the midst of a great change in thinking about how we want to live and go forward. Individuals can make a difference every day. We can choose to repair and nurture our environment by supporting humane and responsible farmers, and by eating foods that enrich rather than pollute our bodies and the land. I hope this book will be one more link in the chain, helping you to make informed choices about how and what you eat.

EQUIPMENT

The pots and pans and tools you use make a big difference in cooking—while they don't always have to be expensive, they do have to work reliably. A cast-iron frying pan, for example, allows you to cook meat over high heat to produce a seared crust and a tender, rare interior. This is much harder to do in a lightweight pan or one made from another material. Here is a detailed list of the equipment I find most useful, and therefore mention in recipes.

> Unless you use nonstick pots, always heat the pan before adding oil—it keeps food from sticking and helps minimize the fat in your finished dish. Heat the pan until it feels very warm when you hold your hand close to the bottom or quickly touch the rim. Add the oil and let it thin and become fragrant. Then add the food. You'll know the food is ready to turn when it no longer sticks! (This is also true of meat on a preheated grill—when it does not stick, it's ready to turn.)

Pots and Pans

Enameled cast-iron Dutch oven: These heavy braising pots (such as those made by LeCreuset) come in a variety of sizes. I find the round five-quart to be most useful, but I also use the smaller three-quart size a lot. A three-quart oval is also very useful for braising a chicken, as the chicken fits inside closely. Always use a wooden utensil to avoid scratching the interior finish.

Nine- or ten-inch cast-iron frying pan: You can buy one new (Lodge makes them)—but you'll also find them used at tag sales. Rub the pan lightly with cooking oil, then bake it in a slow (250-degree) oven for a couple of hours to season it before using it the first time. When you cook with the pan, wipe it out and dry it right after washing. Even though it goes against conventional wisdom, I wash my well-seasoned, older cast-iron pans with soap when necessary, and they still keep their finish. You can always re-season a pan if the iron looks dry or if food begins to stick. I also find that **smaller cast-iron frying pans** are useful for pieces of meat such as a strip steak or a loin chop, so snap those pans up when you see them reasonably priced.

Huge thirteen-inch sauté pan: This is more expensive than cast-iron, but I cherish having such a big pan for browning a good quantity of meat, such as a batch of meatballs, in one go, and I particularly like having a pan with a cover. I like the relative lightness of Calphalon's anodized aluminum, and I avoid nonstick versions.

Chinese sand pot: These very reasonably priced ceramic stovetop pots are glazed in the interiors and over a portion of the lid, but are unglazed on the outside. They are wrapped in a grid of metal wire and are surprisingly durable. I've had my five-quart one for more than twenty years, and I just bought a new three-quart one for less than ten dollars. They are wonderful for long, slow braises and can be found in most Asian grocery stores and hardware stores. Sand pots work best on gas stoves, but can be used with a flame tamer on electric cooktops.

It's important to know that you should never put your sand pot on a hot burner empty. In recipes that call for sautéing in oil, you should always pour the oil into the pot and heat both pot and oil together.

Römertopf: This unglazed clay pot is a specialty item, so although you could easily live without it, it's a pleasure to use. It's made for roasting and oven-braising without added fat, and produces succulent results. These pots can easily be found online and in specialty stores. The three-quart size holds a whole chicken.

Soufflé dishes: Traditionally made of porcelain, these fluted, deep, straight-sided pots make for impressive and foolproof soufflés. I use both the standard size and mini soufflé dishes.

Ceramic gratin and shallow baking dishes are inexpensive and hold heat. I use them often for both cooking and serving.

Assorted Kitchen Tools

Bulb baster: Often called turkey basters, these familiar bulb and tube arrangements draw up pan juices and allow you to drizzle them back onto roasting meat.

Colanders and strainers: A big one for draining pasta and smaller strainers for soups and sauces make kitchen life easier. A package of cheesecloth or butter muslin can convert a large-holed colander or strainer into one that can be used to trap tiny particulates. **A fine-mesh soup skimmer** is the perfect tool for removing meat scum, and a **Chinese brass wire spider** is great for plucking dumplings from water. **Paper coffee filters and a coffee filter holder** are useful for straining the dirt out of dried mushroom water and for clearing rendered fat of particles of meat or skin.

Cutting boards: I use big, thick plastic boards for meat, sanitizing them in the dishwasher. Smaller plastic boards work well for onions and garlic, as well as other vegetables. I prefer wooden boards for carving cooked meats, especially boards with a depression in the center or a groove along the border to collect juices. I also use wooden boards for cutting greens, breads, and cheeses. It is a little-known fact that bacteria thrive on plastic boards and yet don't thrive on wooden ones. I hand-scrub wooden boards with hot water and soap before drying them immediately, and I wash them with a dilute bleach solution every once in a while before oiling them with mineral oil.

Fat-separating pitcher: Made with a spout at the lowest part of the pitcher, so that juices can be poured out without including the fat that has risen to the top, these come in both "gravy" sizes and a larger "soup" size.

Kitchen scale: A good scale is essential, especially for baking and sausage making. I use a small digital model by Escali that fits in a drawer.

Kitchen twine: Either cotton or linen in spool form is essential for tying rolled pieces of meat. You can find it in kitchen stores or restaurant supply houses.

Knife sharpener: There are lots of different styles and brands, but find one that is easy to use and idiotproof so that you don't damage the edge you are trying to hone. For a manual sharpener, I like Furi's Diamond Fingers.

Knives: The knife I reach for most these days is an inexpensive white-handled chef knife made by Dexter that I bought at a restaurant supply house for about seven dollars. Tough and versatile, it slices without strain. If I had only this knife, a paring knife, and a serrated knife for bread and tomatoes, I could be quite happy, although I love my Furi knives, as well as the old stained carbon-steel Sabatiers I received as wedding presents.

Mandoline or Benriner slicer: These hand tools allow you to control the depth of a slice as you pull vegetables or semi-frozen meat across the blade. Mandolines are all metal

Oven Temperatures and Masonry Mass

There are two kinds of problems with ovens. First, the heating mechanisms vary widely, so always use an oven thermometer to check the accuracy of your oven and adjust accordingly. Second, ovens can take very different amounts of time to actually come to temperature. If you depend on your oven's bell to tell you when it is hot, you will not always get the best results because the oven's internal thermometer measures the air temperature near the probe, not the temperature of the walls, floor, ceiling, and shelf, which will leach heat from the air until they, too, reach temperature. I find that keeping a heavy ceramic pizza stone on the bottom shelf of my oven at all times means that heat is absorbed by the stone and released back into the atmosphere of the oven, creating a much more even and long-lasting bake. I allow a good 15 or 20 minutes for preheating (rather than the 5 to 10 minutes it takes my buzzer to let me know it thinks the oven is hot). I find baking results are much more consistent, and baked goods and roasts are well-cooked in the times indicated on a recipe.

TYING A ROAST USING KITCHEN TWINE

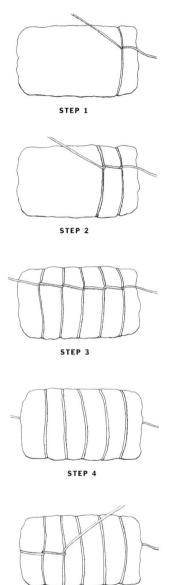

STEP 1

STEP 2

STEP 3

STEP 4

STEP 5

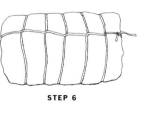

STEP 6

1. Tie one end of a yard-long piece of twine around the circumference of the rolled roast, seam side down. Be sure to leave a 4" tail.

2. Move down the roast by 2", use your thumb to hold the string in place, and make another loop around the meat. Thread the end of the string back through the loop in the opposite direction (toward the knot). Pull down (toward the untied end) to tighten.

3. Continue in the same manner, making loops, threading the end of the string under each loop toward the knot at one end, and pulling it in the opposite direction, toward the untied end of the roast.

4. Turn the meat over to expose the loops along the back and pull the string around the base of the roast to the underside.

5. Thread the remaining string through each of the back loops, again pulling the string through each loop in the opposite direction of the one you are traveling in to form a net that holds tight.

6. Tie the loose original tail (from the first knot) to the string that now meets it. After cooking, cut to release and discard.

and more expensive; Benriners are mostly plastic and are much more affordable. Both come with a variety of blades for straight or waffle-shaped cuts, and adjust for thick or thin slices.

Mesh tea ball: These inexpensive metal tea infusers come in a variety of sizes, and are useful for holding a mixture of herbs in soups or braises, obviating the need to fish them out after cooking.

Microplane zester and cheese grater: Based on wood rasps, these tools are easy to use, making a fine shower of citrus zest or hard cheese.

Mortar and pestle: I use a palm-sized marble set from Lee Valley Tools (where it is called the "low-profile mortar and pestle") almost every day for smashing cloves of garlic before peeling them; it's also great for grinding small amounts of spice. You can even run it through the dishwasher without damage.

My big stone mortar and pestle is from Thailand and is available at many Asian groceries. It cost about the same as the tiny one, above, but it holds much more and works for larger amounts of spices and for pastes.

Parchment paper: Available both in rolls and flat sheets sized to fit sheet pans, parchment paper's silicone coating creates a nonstick surface for baking and also serves well to create an inner cover when braising meats.

Pie crust bag: This may look like a plastic shower cap with a zipper, but it makes rolling pie crust easy and fail-safe. (See box, page 252.)

Sausage-making equipment: Meat grinders and sausage-stuffing horns can be manual or electric, free-standing machines or attachments for stand mixers. (See the pork section, page 178, for more information.)

Steamers: These come in a variety of styles—the most familiar may be a perforated pot that fits on top of another pot that holds water. There are a number of very useful and inexpensive Chinese versions, including a series of bamboo baskets that stack, a flat disk steamer that comes in a large variety of sizes to fit inside nearly any pot, and a grid steamer that is designed to hold a plate above water.

Thermometers: Perhaps the most important tools when cooking grass-fed and pastured meats, thermometers offer precise information about where you are in the cooking process. Both instant-read versions and probe thermometers with monitors that report the temperature from outside the oven are extremely useful.

Wooden toothpicks are also very useful for closing up stuffed meat rolls and poultry cavities.

Small Electrical Appliances

Aside from the usual food processor, blender, and stand mixer, there are a number of other countertop appliances I would be sad to live without.

Electric knife: I find an electric knife invaluable for cutting meat. Like a miniature chain saw, this tool makes quick work of carving poultry into professional-looking slices, separating bones from flesh in cuts like standing rib roast, and carving neat, thin slices or portions from just about any cooked meat. The one I use is made by Black & Decker.

Electric spice grinder: I dedicate a small blade coffee grinder to spices, cleaning it with a paper towel or a slice of bread between uses. Of course, a mortar and pestle does the same job; it's just slower and more effortful.

Immersion blender: These stick blenders go right into a soup pot to purée the contents. I find it much easier to use than a stand blender, and a little safer too, since I don't have to worry about holding down the lid.

Outdoor Cooking Equipment

Outdoor grills: There are a number of grilled dishes in this book, and they taste best prepared outdoors on a charcoal or gas grill. Such a grill can be small and inexpensive, such as a hibachi, or all decked out with bells and whistles, such as high-end gas grills. The most important thing, besides cleanliness (always hard to maintain with a grill), is to heat the grill well before putting the meat on it. You should always hear the meat searing and sizzling as soon as it touches the grill.

My personal favorite charcoal grill, called the Big Green Egg, is a ceramic, heavily insulated smoker/grill that uses charcoal extremely efficiently. I love the smoky succulent flavor of food cooked in it.

If you don't have access to an outdoor grill, indoor alternatives are a

- broiler (put the meat as close to the broiler element as is safe, and always preheat the broiler for at least 15 minutes before adding the meat) or a
- cast-iron grill pan (iron holds the heat and can sear meat better than other materials on the stovetop, provided it is well heated before the meat goes on the pan—a good exhaust fan is useful when grilling indoors in a pan).

Low Heat on the Gas Range or Cooktop

An appliance repairman told me that most gas stoves are not properly calibrated when installed, and so the lowest setting is rarely as low as it can be. He demonstrated this with my five-year-old gas cooktop, which was connected for me by the local gas company, as mandated by law. After he recalibrated the flame (it was a simple matter of adjusting a screw!), I no longer had to use a flame tamer to achieve low-simmering heat. If you can't get recalibrated, here are some tricks to get the flame low enough:

- Take the grid off an unused burner and put it on top of the burner you plan to use, making a double-height grid that keeps the pot farther from the flame.
- Put your pot in a cast-iron frying pan with water halfway up the pot to create a moderating heat. Make sure the pan doesn't cook dry.
- Use a flame tamer or heat diffuser such as an iron plate made to top a burner to moderate heat.

INGREDIENTS

I live twelve miles round trip from the nearest small village market and thirty-five miles round trip from the nearest big supermarket. That means that nearly everything in this book was built on the staples from my pantry and the local pastured meat in the freezer. My assumption is that if I can cook something in rural Vermont, it's likely you can find it and cook it wherever you are. But, of course, setting up a well-stocked pantry is the first step. To that end, I tend to buy ingredients whenever I travel, whether it's to a city nearby or one on the other side of the world. When I see a great spice, dried wild mushrooms, barrels of culinary flower petals, or tins of salted anchovies, I'm happy to pack them and bring them home.

No matter where you shop, however, being discerning about the food you buy is perhaps the best assurance that a meal will be good eating—no matter how well you cook, a dish is only as good as its parts. In fact, I believe that the more you leave great ingredients alone, the better your meal will likely be.

Salts of the Earth (and Sea)

There are lots of wonderful salts, and while they are not a very expensive indulgence, they do make a huge difference in the taste of food. There are salts from different parts of the world, such as Hawaiian pink salt, France's fleur de sel, and Britain's Maldon salt, to give only a few choice examples (try them all!). These same salts all provide great textural variations as well, and you can buy ordinary sea salt in fine and coarse textures. Also worth exploring are seasoned salts and smoked salts, which open up a whole other world of flavor and can be used as condiments. I often do a salt tasting with culinary guests and routinely keep three salts on my table at any time so that diners can choose their table salt to match the dish. Because you can put a few tablespoons of a great salt in a small bowl and leave it on the table, it's a very easy way to add variety to your food.

Crème fraîche: While this can be purchased ready-made, it's easy to make at home and far less expensive. Blend 1 cup heavy or whipping cream that is not ultrapasteurized (look for an organic brand) with 2 tablespoons buttermilk in a clean glass jar. Shake well, and leave the mixture at room temperature for a day or until it is visibly thick—much like sour cream. Refrigerate the crème fraîche and use it within a week or so.

The great thing about crème fraîche is that it doesn't break easily when stirred into a hot sauce, and it adds an incredible unctuous quality that is most welcome with grass-fed meat. It is also wonderful with fresh berries as a dessert.

Greek yogurt: Greek yogurt is much thicker than American yogurt—about the consistency of sour cream—and is creamy and sweet. My favorite is a brand called FAGE, available nationally in many supermarkets, and at Trader Joe's. For cooking, I use the full-fat version, because it stands up best to heat.

If you are making your own yogurt at home and want a similar taste, buy a container of Greek yogurt to use as a culture and strain your yogurt through damp butter muslin when it's finished, so that it is thick.

Olive oil: In my kitchen, olive oil is *always* extra virgin. I taste my oils and try to match the intensity of an oil with the food I cook. My book *The Flavors of Olive Oil* explains this in detail, but know that the most important thing you can do with olive oil is protect it from heat, light, and air and use it with pleasure and alacrity. Don't save good oil for a special occasion—use it now. I reserve the greatest oils for drizzling over cooked dishes and for salads, and the more ordinary oils for cooking.

Pomegranate molasses: I use this over and over to add a tart/sweet note to meats. Remarkably inexpensive, it can be found in Middle Eastern stores and online.

Rose water and **orange blossom water** are both Middle Eastern ingredients with a potent fragrance and a delicate taste. They are wonderful in desserts.

Mise en Place

The most efficient way to cook is to lay out all the ingredients, in order, before attempting a recipe—this is called *mise en place*. Ideally, you even measure everything into little dishes, so that putting the meal together is a breeze. In truth, I rarely measure ahead, but I do lay out the ingredients in order, and I put them all on one side of my work area. Then, as I use each one, I move it to the other side of the work space. That way, if the phone rings or if I am otherwise interrupted, I can immediately see where I left off.

Salt: In this book when I specify coarse salt, I usually mean that I used coarse gray Celtic or gray Atlantic sea salt. In addition I always have (noniodized) pure kosher salt next to my stove. While I think kosher salt is less salty than fine sea salt, any of these can be used interchangeably in recipes. I also enjoy smoked salt, and use it occasionally as a condiment.

Salt-packed anchovies and **salt-packed capers:** These are both preferable in their salt-packed form, rather than brined, because they are more flavorful and have a better texture. With both, rinse the salt off very well, in several changes of water. With capers, that's all you need to do. With anchovies, you'll need to use your thumb to open the belly and pull out the spine, twisting off the extremities at the same time. You won't believe how robust they taste in contrast to canned or brined versions. These both last for months in the refrigerator, although I repackage anything that starts off in a can by layering the contents with salt in a glass jar.

Virgin coconut oil: I use a very pure fair trade coconut oil offered by Tropical Traditions (www.tropicaltraditions .com), which also sells high-quality shredded dried coconut. The oil has great flavor and is high in antioxidants. I use it in dishes that contain coconut, in popcorn, and occasionally with scrambled eggs.

Asian Ingredients

There are a number of recipes in this book that require a trip to an Asian grocery for certain ingredients. These are all long lasting and inexpensive and having them in your pantry will make it easy to cook Asian recipes anytime. Here's a quick rundown of the ones I use most often so that you'll have a list to start with. They are all quite stable in pantry or refrigerator storage.

Bean thread or cellophane noodles come in packages of a dozen or so in a pink net bag. They last for years.

Dried mushrooms will keep forever sealed in a glass jar.

Ground bean sauce is made from soybeans, sugar, sesame oil, and spices. It tastes like a strong soy sauce paste. Koon Chun brand is widely available.

Kecap manis is an Indonesian sweet soy sauce and can be used like hoisin.

Mirin is sweetened sake with a syrupy consistency, so it thickens a marinade and aids in browning.

Nam prik pao is a spicy hot Thai chile sauce that can be substituted for Chinese chile paste.

Oyster sauce and **hoisin sauce** are both condiments as well as flavorings. Oyster sauce is salty and deepens flavor in the same way anchovies do—that is, you can't taste the sauce, but it adds complexity. Hoisin sauce is sweet and thick; it sticks to food and aids caramelization.

Rice wine (Shaoxing wine) and **rice wine vinegar** add subtle flavor, and their alcohol content enhances the taste of a dish. A substitute for Shaoxing wine is sherry, and the substitute for rice wine vinegar is a sherry vinegar. **Black vinegar** is a very strong, dark vinegar, for which there are no substitutes.

Soy sauces: Thin soy sauce is less strong and less salty than regular soy sauce; it's sometimes called light soy sauce. **Black soy sauce** is the opposite—very strong and potent in flavor, much more so than regular soy sauce.

Toasted sesame oil is a flavoring condiment, not a cooking oil. It has a distinctive fragrance and taste.

Spices

When culinary guests come and cook with me, often the thing they most remark on is the potency and liveliness of the spices in my spice drawer, and how vividly they contribute to our finished dishes.

When spices are old or dead, they don't add anything to a dish. Smell the spices in your cupboard, and if they don't smell strong and clean, replace them—the rule of thumb is to replace your old spices every year.

I get my spices from several different sources (and none of them are a supermarket). Either I buy them in the bulk section of my local food co-op or from specialty vendors such as Vanns, Penzeys, and Kalustyan's (see Sources, page 371). These spices are considerably higher in quality and more flavorful than grocery-store spices—and they're often less expensive. I repackage bulk items in reusable tins from Specialty Bottle (see Sources, page 371), and I keep them protected from heat, light, and air in a dedicated spice drawer sized to fit the tins.

Some of my favorite spices may not be familiar, so I'm listing them below. They are all available online as well as from specialty spice shops.

Korintje cassia has a mild sweetness and fragrant flavor that makes it very different from more ordinary cassias or cinnamons.

Spanish **pimentón de la Vera** is a smoky, deeply red dried ground pepper, available in sweet (*dulce*) or hot (*picante*) versions.

Wild fennel pollen is made from the tiny golden pollen removed from wild fennel flowers. It is intensely flavorful, and although it is expensive, it lasts a long time when kept from air, heat, and light.

Homemade Spice Blends

I have to confess that in the past, when I read recipes for spice blends in cookbooks, I used to turn the page. It seemed like too much work. I hope you will be more tolerant than I was, because once I started blending spices, I began to understand their magic. Try one of these blends and see if you agree—it can make cooking easier, because you don't have to measure out many spices each time.

Each of the following recipes produces enough for use in a couple of different recipes. Make the blends ahead of time and you'll have them ready whenever you need them. Or make a blend when a recipe calls for it and you'll have some left over for a future use.

If you don't have an electric spice mill, you can grind spices in a mortar and pestle or stir together the already ground versions of these spices in a bowl, using the same amount as specified for seeds. Blends made with already-ground spices will be less intense, and their shelf life will be shorter, but they are still worth using.

SALT AND SPICE CURE

Perhaps one of the most versatile rubs I've ever used, this spice blend improves every meat I rub it on. I've taken some liberties with Dan Barber's original recipe from Epicurious.com, greatly reducing the amounts and changing the proportions somewhat to make it more domestic in scale and ingredients.

1 tablespoon fennel pollen or fennel seeds
    (or ground fennel seeds)
1 tablespoon cumin seeds (or ground cumin)
1 teaspoon coriander seeds (or ground coriander)
½ teaspoon whole black Tellicherry peppercorns
    (or ground pepper)
1 star anise (or ¼ teaspoon ground star anise)
½ cinnamon stick (or 1 tablespoon ground cinnamon)
1 whole clove (or ¼ teaspoon ground cloves)
1 tablespoon coarse sea salt, such as gray Atlantic or Celtic
2 tablespoons sugar

Combine all the ingredients in an electric spice grinder and whirl into a powder. Store in an airtight tin or jar, away from heat and light, and use as a rub or cure for pork, beef, chicken, or lamb. *Yield: about 7 tablespoons*

ADVIEH

This Iranian spice blend is used with rinsed and soaked basmati rice and comes from one of my favorite cookbooks, *A Taste of Persia*, by Najmieh Batmanglij. Dried rose petals can be found in Middle Eastern food stores and online, and can be pulverized in a blender or food processor or a mortar and pestle, if you don't have a spice grinder. Use about 1 teaspoon of the blend per 3 cups raw rice, and be sure to butter and salt the rice as well. Any of the lamb dishes in this book taste wonderful with Advieh-flavored rice pilaf.

2 tablespoons dried rose petals
2 tablespoons ground cinnamon
2 tablespoons ground cardamom
1 tablespoon ground cumin

Pulverize the rose petals and combine them with the remaining ingredients. Store in an airtight tin or jar, away from heat and light, and use when cooking rice for dishes containing Persian or Middle Eastern spices, particularly lamb. *Yield: 7 tablespoons*

YEMENI SPICE BLEND

Used to spice a beef shank braise, this salt-free blend of pepper and Middle Eastern aromatics is a winner. Try it with other grass-fed beef braises such as pot roast or stew, or combine it with a little salt and a pinch of sugar to use it as a rub for meats you plan to grill.

1 tablespoon whole black peppercorns such as Tellicherry (or ground pepper)
1½ teaspoons caraway seeds (or ground caraway)
Good pinch of saffron threads (about ½ teaspoon)
½ teaspoon cardamom seeds (or ground cardamom)
1 teaspoon ground turmeric

Combine all the ingredients but the turmeric in an electric spice grinder and pulverize to a powder. Pour the spice mixture into a small bowl, and stir in the turmeric. Store in a small airtight tin or glass jar, away from heat and light. *Yield: about 2½ tablespoons*

MOROCCAN SPICE BLEND

This combination of spices offers the taste and smell of Morocco and is easy to use as a rub on meats destined for the grill.

2 tablespoons cumin seeds (or ground cumin)
1 teaspoon sweet paprika
½ teaspoon hot paprika or crushed red pepper flakes
1 tablespoon kosher salt

Combine all the ingredients in an electric spice grinder and whirl into a powder. Store in an airtight tin or jar, away from heat and light, and use as a rub with lamb or beef. *Yield: 3½ tablespoons*

QUATRE ÉPICES BLEND

Essential for many French pâtés and potted meats, *quatre épices* is hauntingly aromatic While many versions of this blend have only pepper, cloves, cinnamon, and nutmeg, this version is adapted from one in Madeleine Kamman's *When French Women Cook*.

2 teaspoons ground cinnamon
1 tablespoon plus 1 teaspoon whole allspice (or ground allspice)
1 teaspoon whole cloves (or ground cloves)
2 teaspoons freshly grated nutmeg
4 teaspoons coriander seeds (or ground coriander)

Whirl all the ingredients together in an electric spice grinder to form a powder. Store in an airtight tin or jar, away from heat and light. *Yield: about ¼ cup*

JANE LAWSON'S MADRAS CURRY POWDER

I love Jane Lawson's book *The Spice Bible* since it always makes me want to cook something new. This is her Madras curry blend recipe.

¼ cup coriander seeds (or ground coriander)
2 tablespoons cumin seeds (or ground cumin)
1 tablespoon plus 1 teaspoon black mustard seeds
1 teaspoon whole black peppercorns (or ground pepper)
1 tablespoon plus 1 teaspoon ground turmeric
½ teaspoon ground red pepper
½ teaspoon ground ginger

Heat a dry, seasoned cast-iron frying pan over medium heat, then toast the coriander, cumin, black mustard, and black peppercorns for 1 minute, or until they are fragrant.

Using an electric spice mill or a mortar and pestle, grind these spices, along with the turmeric, hot pepper, and ginger, until they are ground into a powder. Store in an airtight tin or jar, away from heat and light. *Yield: about 9 tablespoons*

RED BARN SPICE RUB

Named after the converted barn I live in, this is a versatile rub for beef and lamb.

1 tablespoon kosher salt

2 tablespoons sugar

2 teaspoons sweet (*dulce*) pimentón de la Vera
  (smoked Spanish paprika)

1 tablespoon ground coriander

1 tablespoon ground ancho chile

1 tablespoon ground ginger

Stir all the ingredients together and store in an airtight tin or jar, away from heat and light. *Yield: about 7 tablespoons*

RAS EL HANOUT

This means "top of the shop" in Arabic, and each shop sells a slightly different blend, often with as many as twenty-four ingredients. You can buy this online from any number of spice merchants, but here is a recipe to make your own. It is my adaptation and a simplification of a recipe by Paula Wolfert in *Couscous and Other Good Food from Morocco*. It contains half as many spices as a *ras el hanout* you would buy in the Middle East, so it is not as complex. Nevertheless, it works—it's full of flavor and smells wonderful.

1 whole nutmeg, grated (about 2 tablespoons)

5 dried rosebuds

1 tablespoon ground cinnamon (or 1 small cinnamon stick)

1 teaspoon ground mace

½ teaspoon ground aniseed

2 tablespoons ground turmeric

1 teaspoon cayenne or Aleppo pepper

½ teaspoon dried lavender buds

1 tablespoon ground ginger

¼ teaspoon ground cloves (or whole cloves)

½ teaspoon ground allspice

1 tablespoon white cardamom seeds

Use an electric spice grinder or mortar and pestle to process or grind all the ingredients into a uniform powder, and store in an airtight tin or jar, away from heat and light. *Yield: ½ cup*

HERBES DE PROVENCE BLEND

As with any traditional spice blend, there are lots of variations of this French mixture—some have a dried bay leaf, some have more or less lavender or rosemary. This particular version works well for me.

2 tablespoons dried thyme leaves (or ground thyme)

2 tablespoons dried marjoram or oregano
  (or ground marjoram or oregano)

2 tablespoons dried summer savory
  (or ground savory)

1 tablespoon dried rosemary needles
  (or ground rosemary)

2 tablespoons dried lavender, rubbed between fingers
  to break it down

1 teaspoon dried sage (or ground sage)

Whirl all the ingredients together very briefly in a spice grinder in pulses, stopping when the texture is well short of powder. Store in an airtight tin or jar, away from heat and light. *Yield: about 9 tablespoons*

CHINESE FIVE-SPICE BLEND

There are probably as many versions of this blend as there are provinces in China, but this is a good one to start with. You can also purchase five-spice powder at any store that sells Chinese ingredients or at a good spice purveyor.

2 teaspoons Szechuan peppercorns (or ground Szechuan pepper)

2 teaspoons ground cassia, preferably Korintje cassia

12 whole star anise (or 2 tablespoons ground star anise)

2 tablespoons fennel seeds (or ground fennel)

6 whole cloves (or ½ teaspoon ground cloves)

Toast the Szechuan peppercorns, using a cast-iron pan and a wooden spoon to stir them. You'll know you are done when they smell aromatic and start to pop. Transfer these immediately to a plate to cool.

Combine the peppercorns, cassia, anise, fennel, and cloves in an electric spice mill and grind until you have an even powder. Store in an airtight tin or jar, away from heat and light. *Yield: 5 ½ tablespoons*

BEEF

American Beef

While *all* beef can be described as having been grass fed (or pastured), even when grain finished, this chapter is devoted to animals raised all their lives on pasture, with the option of some additional feed in the form of haylage (fermented hay) and supplements. Grass-fed beef should be labeled "100 percent grass fed." If it isn't, be suspicious.

Commercial beef in America is feedlot beef, which is the reverse of slowly raised, entirely pastured beef. Instead of growing slowly on grass, young cattle are sold to commodity beef companies to be fattened as rapidly and cheaply as possible. They are herded into cramped corrals and fed a diet of corn blended with refuse and growth hormones. This fattens them quickly, even though corn is indigestible for ruminants when it's their primary food—it's acidic and makes them sick. To compensate for that, the animals are dosed with sodium bicarbonate. In fact, feedlots are the largest users of sodium bicarbonate in this country; it arrives by the tanker load. The cattle are also routinely given antibiotics to prevent the diseases that arise in the concentrated, ever-changing feedlot population. Altogether, this produces meat that looks, feels, and tastes very different from grass-fed meat, along with producing drug-resistant strains of *E. coli* that make our meat supply less safe.

So-called natural beef is much like commercial beef, except that the animals are not fed hormones, and there is no added coloring. If beef is labeled "organic," it is hormone- and color-free, and the animals were fed certified organic feed, typically a mixture of corn, barley, and forage. Organic beef cannot be genetically modified. None of these things mean that the animals lived in conditions any better than those of commercial beef.

Incidentally, those who choose kosher or halal meat may be dismayed to learn that it is usually essentially commercial commodity beef. The animals are frequently raised and fed exactly the same way, but are sold at auction to kosher and halal meat dealers, who operate according to religious rules. Indeed, much halal meat is processed by the same companies who do conventional meat, the difference being that the actual slaughter is performed by approved religious butchers. In any case, the cattle are not necessarily better fed or treated more humanely than any other commercial beef in America. There are exceptions—farmers who raise 100 percent grass-fed beef and process it according to halal or kosher rules—but finding them requires some investigation.

By contrast, all grass-fed or traditionally raised beef is hormone- and antibiotic-free. The cattle move around, often changing pasture daily or two or three times a day, fertilizing the landscape (instead of producing toxic runoff as feedlot cows do). This natural diet keeps the cows healthy, promotes an ecosystem that supports birds, other wildlife, and grasses, and protects rural landscapes. Perhaps not surprisingly, 100 percent grass-fed beef is less likely to be contaminated by harmful *E. coli* O157:H7 bacteria.

Beef that is produced locally and fed only grass or forage earns the designation "sustainable grass-fed beef." Because many grass-fed beef producers typically raise their animals from birth to processing, raising such beef provides a way for small family farms to survive, because they can produce a niche product to sell directly to consumers at a premium.

As of this writing, although the USDA published (in November 2007) a regulation devoted to labeling and marketing of grass-fed beef, there are still lots of misleading and false marketing claims around. Be suspicious of terms like "pasture-raised" or "grass-fed, grain-finished." Support producers whose meat is labeled "100 percent grass-fed beef." This matters because such beef comes from animals that have been carefully raised on rotational pastures, moving sometimes more than once a day. This method, sometimes called "mob grazing," forces them to eat down a small area before being moved to a new pasture, where they repeat the process. This ensures that the grass eaten is optimal in nutrients and that the manure from the animals is limited in amount and deposited evenly. The soil improves with each rotation, so farms gain productivity and steers gain weight appropriately on grasses alone.

Beef producers in short-season climates have to work much harder to raise their animals entirely on grass, sustaining them over at least one winter on stored hay or haylage and mineral supplements. They can also supplement hay and pasture with kelp, alfalfa pellets, and beet pellets and still call their meat "grass fed."

It's not easy raising good grass-fed beef. Beef cattle need to gain a certain amount of weight every day, and if they are not thriving, they won't make good eating or reach market weight. It takes time, education, sensible breeding, and lots of practical experience to learn how to achieve all this, which is why it's important to either talk with farmers to assess the depth of their experience or buy beef raised according to a proven published protocol. When I talk to farmers who can say exactly how much weight their steers have to gain in a

day and what they intend to do to make that possible, I feel more confident that their meat will be worth eating.

Purely grass-fed beef has a very different nutritional profile than conventional beef (or "natural beef," which is conventional beef minus hormones). One grass-fed-beef farmer of my acquaintance likes to say that his beef has "the same amount of omega-3s as salmon, but without the mercury!" It's a great line, but actual studies show that while grass-fed beef is indeed higher in omega-3s and has a better omega-6 to omega-3 ratio than conventional beef, it still contains only about half as much omega-3s as wild Alaskan salmon.

Compared to conventional beef, grass-fed beef is lower in both calories and cholesterol; it's high in CLA (conjugated linoleic acid), vitamins A and E, beta-carotene, and omega-3s, and because these are antioxidants, grass-fed beef may well offer health benefits not found in industrial beef. CLA is found in all grass-fed food (including dairy products) and may be a cancer-fighting agent. Grass-fed animals are less likely to be infected with harmful *E.coli* bacteria because eating grass keeps their internal bacteria count low. Beef from grass-fed cows is four times higher in vitamin E than grain-finished beef, and it contains more omega-3 fatty acids. People who have high levels of omega-3s in their blood appear less likely to suffer from certain heart problems. And because grass-fed beef is leaner and lower in cholesterol than grain-finished beef, eating it regularly in place of grain-finished beef may help to lower bad cholesterol—it certainly seems to have done this for my husband. It is important to note that many of the benefits of the grass diet immediately diminish when a steer begins to be fed grain. Purely grass-fed beef has a good ratio of omega-6s to omega-3s, while beef that is only partially grass fed is less balanced. The animal loses valuable antioxidants every day it is off grass.

The Flavor of Grass-Fed Beef

Recently, I've been hearing from chefs who say they sometimes get complaints from customers who have been served grass-fed beef. To their palates, used to the marbled and deliciously fatty and mild flavor of corn-fed beef, grass-fed beef tastes strange. It is certainly true that such meat is leaner, less marbled, more flavorful. To those who grew up before the industrialization of meat in this country, grass-fed beef tastes like the meat of childhood. To those who

have traveled and eaten their way around the world, grass-fed beef can taste like a bistro dinner in France, a meal in Argentina, or a family lunch in Italy. If grass-fed beef is new to you, try meat in single cuts from several different farmers. There will be variations in the flavors, and some will please you more than others. It may be an Irish Dexter rather than a Belted Galloway cow, it may be a young animal rather than an older one, or you may prefer meat that is more or less dry-aged after processing. In any case, the variables are so numerous that only your palate can be the final arbiter.

Finding Sustainable Beef

You can find grass-fed beef at farm stands, farmers' markets, and increasingly at retail, either fresh or frozen. You can also order grass-fed beef directly from farmers in varying quantities that range from individual cuts and sampler boxes, to the quarter, half, and whole animal. When buying in bulk, you'll have the opportunity to fill out a cut sheet, which offers a chance to customize your order to deliver the cuts you prefer. Buying meat in larger quantities and storing it in a home freezer is always considerably less expensive than buying individual cuts of meat at retail, but it does mean that you have to be committed to storing the meat and cooking it within a year.

Until very recently, the only 100 percent grass-fed beef you could consistently buy at stores like Whole Foods was from New Zealand. (But do note that even when it is transported frozen from the Southern Hemisphere, New Zealand meat is *still* more sustainable than American industrial or "natural" beef because it is grass raised.) Frozen grass-fed beef from Uruguay is also widely available.

Since 2009, Whole Foods stores in the Northeast have been selling Hardwick beef, the only regional supplier of fresh, local, sustainable 100 percent grass-fed beef. Hardwick is an exciting model, because they have created and trained a network of small New England family farms to produce completely grass-fed beef that conforms to a sustainable protocol, they pay a premium to grass-fed beef producers who raise meat well, and they offer consumers protection, in that all their beef can be traced back to the farm it was raised on. Hardwick beef can be found in specialty stores from New York City to Burlington, and from Portsmouth to Boston, perfectly illustrating the range of a sustainable "food shed" (an idea based on watersheds that illustrates the distance food travels from farm to fork). Similar sources across the country include American Grassland Beef, who sells at selected Whole Foods mostly in the Midwest and East; Schnucks stores in Missouri and Tennessee; and Thousand Hills Cattle Company, whose grass-fed beef is available through retailers in Minnesota, Iowa, Illinois, and Wisconsin. In the West, La Cense raises grass-fed beef in Montana and sells it directly to consumers, as do all of these other producers.

When buying meat, be diligent in your research. Some beef producers, distributors, and retailers have come together to label and market their products, offering Web sites that detail their feeding protocol. One example of this is the Northeast Family Farms label, which offers, at least at this writing, "natural" beef that's finished for three hundred days on a diet that is 49 percent (local whenever possible) *grain*. This information is available on the Web site, but not on the beef label, and at least when I've seen this meat in retail cases (under a big sign that reads PASTURED), it is easy to mistake it for grass-fed beef.

In response to USDA regulations, it's hoped that clear and truthful labels will become more visible at the

Models for a New Kind of Meat Production

Some farmers are working hard to create new models of farming that provide an alternative to larger factory farms. Joel Salatin, a well-known and innovative farmer and author in Virginia, is one of those who use the phrase "grass farmer" to describe an alternative small-scale model for raising meat and fowl on rotating pasture. While Salatin sells chickens, eggs, pork, and beef, his primary concern is for the pasture that sustains all these animals. Such pasturing encourages biodiversity, improves the soil, and reduces greenhouse gases because the thriving grasses and legumes draw carbon dioxide from the air and return it to the soil as carbon. Like Salatin and other sustainable farmers, most grass farmers use a minimum of fossil-fuel-burning equipment and work hard to improve the environment. Supporting such farms not only supports good health and enriches your environment, it also saves the landscape from being turned into housing developments or industrial factory farms. There are grass farmer associations in most states, and a newspaper, *The Stockman's Grass Farmer,* that addresses these issues.

Grass farmers use portable housing pens and rotating pasture schedules to feed livestock and enrich pasture. Salatin's model has chickens follow his ruminants, while hogs aerate the bovine winter barn waste to aid in composting before Salatin spreads this waste on the pastures as fertilizer. His articulation of these methods—using catchy phrases like pigolators and eggmobiles—has attracted other farmers, particularly since he is successfully rebuilding and reenergizing the tired land he inherited. The books he has written are influential among sustainable farmers because they are so practical and intelligent, and his methods are replicable.

Even for someone like me, who has what's called a hobby farm, putting the chickens in a movable pen and (in the words of another farmer and author, Andy Lee) "day-ranging" them by setting their movable coop within pasture eaten down by the lambs makes good sense because it enriches the pasture and starts the manure composting. These portable models also eliminate the need for traditional barns, as the animals can be housed in smaller shelters such as A-frame arks, wire pens, or tents. This makes the start-up costs for small-scale sustainable farming much lower.

Around the country, as you talk with traditional and grass-fed meat producers, you'll find they all know of this model (and many follow it). When grass is the focus, there is no toxic waste problem; the number of animals on the ground is in balance with the ground's ability to use waste profitably. If you travel to these farms, you'll see that the pastures actually look different—green and vital—they smell sweet most of the time. There are no foul waste "lakes," no tightly penned and dirty animals.

One caveat, however: I recently attended a presentation by a huge commercial beef rancher in Colorado who described himself as a grass farmer. While I am sure he is deeply concerned with the quality of forage in his industrial cow/calf operation, his is hardly a small-family grass farm. This farmer supplies steer for feedlot beef, and while his cattle feed on grass in their youth (as do all young cattle), they (like all commercial beef cattle) are moved to a feedlot for at least 180 days (or even as much as almost twice that) to gain weight in confinement on commercial feed.

retail level, particularly as consumers ask more questions and demand more choice. Keep in mind, though, that buying fresh meat in small amounts at retail will always be significantly more expensive than buying frozen meat by the quarter, whole, or half animal. It may also benefit the farmer less, as he has to sell his meat at a wholesale price to the distributor.

If your local farmers' market does not have a grass-fed beef stand, look in the sources section of this book to find other leads and seek out grass-fed beef producers in your area. You will find a whole world of farmers eager to introduce you to their products. When you follow up with them, ask lots of questions. Buy samples and taste for yourself. If you can, visit the farm and see their practices in person.

Custom Dry-Aging

One great advantage of buying a whole cow and having it custom slaughtered is that you can ask for the maximum dry-aging time your processor is comfortable with. (Longer aging means more flavorful meat, but as the meat ages, it shrinks, so it's not a viable commercial practice, except for high-end steak houses.) This might require some negotiation, because it means additional trimming on his part before freezing, so it's more work, and he will need to have the available chill space. It will also affect your per-pound price, which is calculated by the original hanging weight of the animal. As the meat shrinks and becomes more flavorful, you end up paying more per pound. On the other hand, if your meat has a good fat cover and can be aged for longer, it will be incomparably more flavorful and tender.

Other factors to consider in dry-aging include the breed of the cow, its age, and its fat distribution. All are taken into account in determining the optimum aging time for flavor, but most producers set eight to fourteen days as a goal. Chef and author Hugh Fearnley-Whittingstall, among others, urges us to try meat that has been aged twice as long—as I've not had the opportunity to taste grass-fed meat that's been aged so thoroughly, I can only report this information, not attest to its truth.

Here are the questions you might want to start with:

- Is the animal entirely grass fed?
- Do your cattle also eat other foods?
- If so, what else do you feed, and when do you supplement?
- Are these supplements commercially produced, or are they made by you?
- If commercial, what does the supplement contain?
- Is it organic?
- How much grain or what other supplements are available to the cow (and when)?

If you are buying in quantity—a quarter, half, or whole animal—ask:

- How long is your beef dry-aged?
- Can I fill out a detailed cut sheet, or are the cuts determined by you or the processor?

Cut Sheets

When you have decided to order a large portion of an animal, it's usually time to fill out a cut sheet. Broadly speaking, a cut sheet directs the butchers at the processor, letting them know if you would rather have steaks or roasts, chops or burgers, from different primal parts of the cow. They'll want to know how thick you like your steaks, and whether you would rather braise a pot roast or have more packages of hamburgers.

I have yet to see a really good cut sheet, and they are such a trial that many producers and processors actually don't offer consumers the chance to fill one out. Every cut sheet I have encountered has been geared to the most conventional cuts and assumes that you will want to grind up many of the great slow-cooked cuts rather than use them whole. (Often as much as half the weight of the steer is in hamburger.) One of my goals here is to offer some help in filling out and greatly amending a cut sheet so that it is customized for the way you cook and eat.

Another great difficulty with cut sheets is understanding what cuts you are sacrificing each time you make a choice. For example, if you choose a roast, you may have lost the chance to have steaks or chops (which potentially provide many more nights' worth of dinners), because they come from the same part of the animal. It's helpful to analyze

The Skinny on Red-Meat-Processing Choices

With thanks to the Niche Meat Processor Assistance Network, here are the details of different processing options:

- Federal inspection, which is done by USDA inspectors at fixed sites, such as an approved slaughterhouse, or at mobile processing units based in trailers. Such inspected meat can be shipped over state lines and internationally. It will have a USDA stamp.

- State-approved facilities, offered by twenty-seven states, are supposed to be equal to or better than federal standards, but the meat inspected there cannot be sold across state lines. In some states, however, a plant can offer both federal and state inspection.

- Custom-exempt slaughter and processing of a particular animal provides meat for the use of a single owner; it cannot be sold to anyone else. A regular state or USDA plant can do custom-exempt processing, so the distinction is not necessarily about place—it's about the type of inspection.

- Retail-exempt processing is another distinction, this time for those who want to sell meat at their own retail storefront; the livestock must be inspected, and the meat is subject to spot inspection. A limited quantity of retail-exempt products can be sold wholesale to restaurants and institutions.

- On-farm processing is done without inspection, and is for the farmer's private use only, not for sale. There are exemptions in some states to allow producers to sell a limited number of on-farm-processed poultry and rabbits to customers at farm stores and at farmers' markets, provided the meat is labeled as such.

Choosing a Producer and a Processor

Because beef from different breeds of cow, different producers, and different processors can vary enormously, it makes sense to sample several small pieces from a couple of farmers ahead of time to find the meat, breed, or producer and processor you like best. (The producer and processor tend to come as a pair.) You may prefer meat from one source over another either because they age longer (or for less time) or package more consistently or are reputed to provide bigger yields.

how you cook, so that you can order accordingly. If you often entertain on weekends, or work at home, then slow-cooking meat for roasts, braises, and soups can be a good choice. If you rarely entertain but come home to cook fast weekday dinners for your family, it makes sense to favor quick-cooking (and quick-thawing) cuts such as steaks, chops, and ground meat. Many of us fall in the middle, and order a variety of cuts for lots of different needs.

When you buy a quarter, rather than a half or whole, custom-slaughtered animal, your choices will be more limited, and butchers tend to make everyone's order essentially the same when dividing up the cow. You can expect an expert but conventional assortment of chops, roasts, pot roasts, steaks, stew meat, kebobs, and burgers—although you may be able to customize the order a little by specifying the thickness of the steaks or the size of the packages, and you can request some of the less well known cuts in hopes that none of the other owners of your steer will want them. These might include offal (tongue, liver, and the like), soup bones, hanger steak, and brisket.

If you contract for a half or whole cow and divide it yourself among friends or family, you can customize the cut sheet considerably. You can ask for packages of different sizes, so that your ground meat is always in 1-pound packages while your roasts run to 3 pounds. You can ask for scraps from the shoulder to be packaged separately for you to grind at home if you wish, so that your Bolognese sauce (see page 75) is made from only the most flavorful parts of the cow. Custom cutting also means you can ask for parts that others may shun, such as tongue, liver, shanks, oxtail, and cheeks. Don't be afraid to annotate the printed cut sheet considerably—I find that letting my processor know that I am interested in exploring all possible cuts means that he is more adventurous in his meat-cutting.

Filling out a cut sheet well means that you will have several seasons of good eating with plenty of variety in your meat choices. When you fill out a cut sheet poorly, you simply get a whole lot of ground meat. That's because grinding is the default treatment for cuts that may require braising or stewing, or that may be smaller than the roast size you requested. And, frankly, it is easier to throw smaller bits of meat into the grinding bin than to trim them into recognizable but perhaps less familiar cuts. Unless you have a family of burger or meat loaf addicts, it can be discouraging to come up with new recipes for ground beef night after night. Rest assured that you will still probably have more ground beef than you planned for in any case.

Beef, like other meats, is measured by what is known as hot carcass weight (HCW)—the weight of the unchilled animal just after it has been killed and the hide and other parts have been removed—and yield. It is the yield that usually serves as the basis for the actual per-pound cost (although one usually pays for an animal by HCW plus processing fees). Industrial grain-finished animals yield about 70 percent from carcass to meat, while grass-fed cattle average 55 to 65 percent yield.

More on Yield

It is rather an open secret in meat circles that there is some amount of theft in many processing facilities and that when the processing is done by an honest processor, yields can increase dramatically. It is in our interest as consumers to support those processors who have proved their honesty by providing yields farmers can brag about. If you order beef by the quarter, half, or whole, ask your producer what yields he usually gets. He should be able to tell you this easily.

In contrast, my beef last year came from a breed that is small compared to most, the Dexter. It was raised in southern Vermont and processed in northern Vermont. I filled out a very detailed cut sheet and talked with the processor before he custom-slaughtered the whole steer for me. We divided it among four families. It yielded a little more than 78 percent from carcass to meat, or just under 303 pounds of meat from a hanging weight of 385 pounds. The farmer I bought the steer from was amazed by the yield and so we felt the need to account for it.

We came up with three reasons: The first was that we used a new processor who is famous for his honesty. The second was that I asked for all possible bones for culinary use, so that I got soup bones, shank bones, and so on. The third was that I asked for all the offal possible. It's important to note as well that our steer was over thirty months in age, which meant that all the meat near the spinal cord had to be delivered off the bone, in accordance with USDA regulations for avoiding BSE, so those bones did not enter into the calculation of yield.

Packaging Meat

The common choices for packaging bulk purchases are butcher paper lined with plastic wrap or vacuum-sealed Cryovac, and most processors only do one of these (although some will offer you a choice). Cryovac packaging is more expensive; it's airtight, so the meat lasts longer in the freezer and can be "wet-aged" in the refrigerator. I have come to accept it, as it's also easier to thaw a Cryovac package in a bowl of cold water. Paper wrapping with a plastic liner is less expensive, and some feel meat tastes better if it's not vacuum sealed. A third option is one farmers who sell at markets often prefer—Styrofoam trays and plastic wrap, which make it easy for consumers to see the product.

Frozen meat, Cryovac sealed or wrapped on Styrofoam trays

Understanding Cow Anatomy

The Primals

In the United States, there are eight primal cuts—the **chuck**, **brisket**, **rib**, **plate**, **short loin**, **flank**, **sirloin**, and **round**. (Other parts of the world do it differently.) Each primal is then further divided, mostly along the lines of muscles and other natural barriers, to create cuts we know by names such as top round and sirloin steak.

When beef is processed, it is split top to bottom to form two identical halves. Each half is called a side and can be divided into the eight primals. Half a side is called a quarter cow—the part from the front is the forequarter, while the part from the rear is the hindquarter. A "mixed quarter" (confusingly sometimes called a "mixed half" or a "split half") blends cuts from the fore- and hindquarters to make a more diversified assortment.

Each of the primals can be broken down into a number of retail cuts, some of which are the same in every part of the United States, while others are more regional (such as tri-tip steak or roast).

When you actually look at a primal cut of meat, you begin to recognize familiar cuts. Many primals have lines of fat or gristle or bone that define how to cut them into smaller portions. Let's start by looking at approximately how much of each primal there is per cow, because that clarifies why we get the proportions of cuts we do when we order beef from a farmer. (These percentages are gross calculations that include some fat and bones.)

The chuck and the round offer the most meat, with 26 percent coming from the chuck, and nearly 24 percent from the round. In contrast, we get the smallest percentages from the flank (almost 6 percent) and the sirloin (6.4 percent). Similarly low percentages of meat come from the plate and brisket at 8.8 percent, the rib at 10 percent, and the short loin at nearly 12 percent.

Some primals come from highly worked muscle areas (like the chuck or shoulder) and others from more protected and less-hardworking areas (such as the short loin). This means that, in general, the meat from the shoulder will be

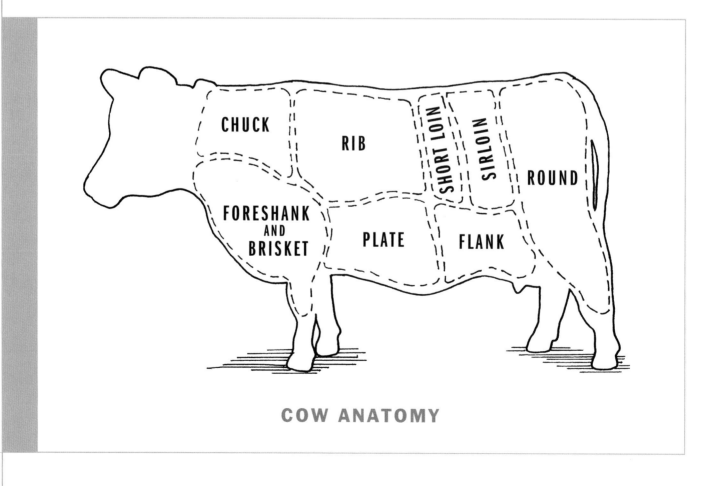

COW ANATOMY

both more flavorful and tough and will tend to taste best when cooked slowly in a moist atmosphere, such as braising, or ground into hamburger, which tenderizes the meat. But even within such guidelines, there are exceptions—chuck steak, for example, is deliciously flavorful, even if chewy when rapidly grilled or pan-seared instead of braised. Furthermore, there are lots of other ways to make a tough cut tasty besides grinding it into hamburger or braising it—meat destined for roasting or grilling can be marinated overnight in red wine and spices, or yogurt and garlic, before cooking, or it can be roasted for a long time at an extremely low temperature, or pounded before cooking, or sliced thinly against the grain to make a more tender mouthfeel.

In contrast, tender meats, such as those from the loin, can be cooked at high heat with speed. Such steaks go on the grill with ease, just as a beef tenderloin roast cooks swiftly in a hot oven.

Of course, every food culture has found different ways of dealing with both kinds of cuts. Many of the dishes are the classics we crave and order in restaurants or cook at home, such as *osso bucco* or *involtini*. Others are cornerstones of culture and memory, such as pot-roasted Passover brisket, or Southern barbecue, for which the same brisket is smoke-cooked low and slow, or corned beef, which is yet another way to cure and cook brisket.

One of the most interesting things about studying beef charts is that different countries divide their meat differently. France, for example, has thirty-three primals, each dedicated to particular cooking methods. (The Centre d'Information des Viandes has a wonderful Web site that offers recipes as you click on each primal—see Sources, page 372, for the URL.) Similarly, Britain, the source of so many of our culinary traditions, divides a steer into twelve primals linked to cooking style, and they routinely use more of the neck and shank than we do.

Beef Primals Explained

Starting at the neck of the cow, the **chuck** is the arm/shoulder section, incorporating ribs 1 through 5. Chuck cuts are often cooked with slow, moist heat (that is, braised) or ground into hamburger. This is because these are well-exercised parts of the animal and so contain more connective tissue. Conventionally, processors will make most of the chuck into hamburger and stew beef, but there are many more exciting and delicious options. Possible chuck cuts include chuck steak, bone-in cross rib roast, and boneless shoulder pot roast, shoulder roast, chuck roast, chuck eye roast,

A Side of Beef, Fore and Hind

This list of meat cuts from the front and back ends of a cow, along with offal and fat, is here to start the process of explaining where cuts come from, and to show what variety there is in a side of beef.

From the forequarter and shanks:

- Chuck or shoulder choices: steaks, roasts, stew, or ground
- Rib: rib steak, rib roast
- Plate: short ribs, flanken, ground meat, rolled roast, outside skirt, lifter meat
- Brisket: pot roast, braise, stew
- Shanks: braise

From the hindquarter:

- Top round steak or roast
- Bottom round roast
- Eye round
- Sirloin tip: steak, oven roast
- Sirloin steak
- Culotte steak
- Flap meat
- Tri-tip
- Inside skirt
- Hanging tender
- Porterhouse steak
- T-bone steak
- Flank: steak
- Minute steaks
- Shanks
- Stew meat

Offal from the innards:

- Liver
- Heart
- Sweetbreads

From the head:

- Tongue
- Cheek

In addition:

- Kidney fat
- Other fat or suet

flatiron roast, shoulder tender. Cuts from the chuck tender include medallions and mock tender. Chuck steaks include flatiron steak (from the tender top blade). I ask for my shoulder scraps to be left unground, packaged in 1-pound packs, and labeled as shoulder. Then I grind them at home to make Bolognese sauce, or use them for rich curries.

Next up is the **brisket**: This is a fine example of the kind of cut that is hard to find at retail, but one that repays long, slow cooking with lots of flavor. Brisket is wonderful as a pot roast and is equally wonderful as barbecue. A big steer has 20 to 25 pounds of brisket in all; a small cow's brisket will be correspondingly diminutive. That means that you'll probably get only a couple of brisket portions at best with a whole or partial animal order—treasure this cut, because it's wonderful.

Going down the spine toward the tail, the next primal cut is the **rib**, which ranges from ribs 6 through 12. It is particularly tender and flavorful, and offers some of our most festive and cherished beef cuts, including the standing rib roast, prime rib, and rib-eye roasts, as well as Delmonico steak (rib-eye steak). Because it's made up of one large muscle (the "eye") and several smaller muscles, cuts can vary in the size and direction of the grain and in the relative fattiness.

The **plate** is the center of the underside of a steer. It is very flavorful and also relatively tough because it's muscle layered with connective tissue. This is the source of the inside and outside skirt steaks and short ribs. Because the grain is open on skirt steaks, they are great for marinating before cooking; they absorb flavor well and gain tenderness both from an acid marinade and from carving against the grain. Short ribs, of course, are wonderful for long, slow cooking or for marinating and grilling as the Koreans do.

Next up, the **short loin** is the center cut of the cow. Again, it's full of flavor. It includes the tenderloin (located next to the backbone), a source of steaks and roasts. Although you could have a whole tenderloin, when cut it includes the pieces we know as fillet steaks (from the butt tender) and chateaubriand (large center section). The tenderloin is, as you might expect from the name, extremely tender, and there are only two per animal. T-bone and porterhouse steaks come from the loin as well, and are justly famous for their flavor. Because they are bone-in steaks that include part of the spinal column, the law currently specifies that they can only come from young cattle. This primal is also the source of hanger steak (which "hangs" from the kidney suet), and there is only one such steak per animal,

so if you are getting a beef half, you'll have to request it—and negotiate with the person buying the other half of the cow.

Heading to the back end of our steer, the next primal is the **flank**. Aside from flank steaks and inside skirt steaks, scraps from the flank portion tend to be ground up for hamburger.

Proceeding onward, the next primal is the **sirloin**, which starts at the upper hip of the animal, and is located between the short loin and the round. The sirloin offers both full flavor and a satisfying texture—one that is a good mouthful without too much toughness or tenderness. (You will have noticed by now that there is a trade-off: Tender meat has less flavor; flavor comes from more-exercised meat). It's divided into two basic parts, the top sirloin and the bottom sirloin. The top of the sirloin also contains the sirloin cap, which is known as the culotte, and the sirloin heart, which is a source of rich steaks or roasts. Bottom sirloin is the source for the tri-tip, a triangular part of the bottom sirloin that is made into a roast or steak better known on the West Coast than in the East. Another part of the sirloin is called the sirloin flap, which can be grilled whole or sliced into steak tips. My most recent beef steer came back with cuts labeled unappetizingly "butt flap steak," but they were in fact from the bottom sirloin near the flank. Such butt flaps are often made into cube steak or are otherwise tenderized or else ground into hamburger. In France this cut is the cherished *bavette* steak.

Next comes the **round**, again one of the largest portions of the cow. It comprises the entire upper leg. This primal ends just above the shin or shank, and it's a lean and slightly tough portion of the cow. There are four subprimals: the sirloin tip, the top round, bottom round, and eye round. The sirloin tip is the source of roasts; for steaks it's known for minute steak and sirloin tip steak. These cuts can further be cut into kebobs, London broil (another name for sirloin tip steak, which like all sirloin tip steaks is cut against the grain; London broils are usually marinated), Stroganoff, or rolled roasts.

Top round can also be a London broil, among other cuts, as well as minute steak. It can be used for roast beef, and braised pot roasts. Either top or bottom round is the source of cuts for the thin rolls of beef, stuffed and braised, known as *involtini* to Italian food lovers (see page 110).

Bottom round is also known as rump roast, and is used for stew beef (from the tougher parts of the round) and kebobs (from the more tender portions). It can also be sliced for London broil.

Beef Forequarter

Whole Primals (right):
1. Chuck and brisket in one piece
2. Chuck (arm)
3. Brisket
4. Rib

Retail Cuts (below):
1. Top blade
2. Shoulder tender
3. Chuck tender
4. Whole brisket
5. Rolled beef navel
6. Shoulder pot roast
7. Short ribs
8. Royal short ribs
9. Chuck roll
10. Rib primal

Beef Hindquarter

Primals and subprimals: 1. Bone-in strip loin **2.** Tenderloin **3.** Sirloin **4.** Culotte **5.** Eye round **6.** Bottom round **7.** Flank **8.** Sirloin tip **9.** Oxtail **10.** Top round

Eye of round can be sliced for minute steaks, braised as a pot roast, or roasted for roast beef.

In addition to the primal cuts, one can ask for **bones** and odd bits from the extremities as well as the internal organs known as **offal**. Bones can be used for marrow (leg bones) and for soup and stock (neck and knuckle). Cheeks are delicious if you can get them—try them slow-cooked in a braise. Oxtail also makes a wonderful braise or stew, as do shanks.

Brains, heart, kidneys, liver, tongue, and **tripe** make up the offal family. I can't get brains (no longer available from USDA-inspected processors due to BSE regulations) or tripe, but I can often get tongue, heart, kidneys, and liver. In fact, the amount of liver that comes with one cow is astonishing—as many as thirty 1-pound packages. It's delicious pan-sautéed with onions and served with a reduced red wine sauce. Green, or raw, tripe cannot be sold, according to USDA

regulations; it must be bleached, and not every processor is willing to do this. It's easy to get suet from local processors, and it's useful for making old-fashioned steamed puddings, and pastries and for frying.

Beef Cut Sheet Choices:
What Substitutes for What

When you fill out a cut sheet, your choices will likely not be indicated in any detail. In fact, farmers I know say that the hardest part of selling directly to consumers is having to explain how a cow is divided. It is difficult for consumers used to shopping at the meat counter to understand that a whole cow only has one hanger steak, for example.

That's where the following list comes in. Prepared with the help of skilled meat cutter Adam Tiberio, it is designed to help you choose the cuts that work best for you. Each

Beef Hindquarter

Retail cuts: 1. Bone-in strip loin **2.** Culotte **3.** Top round **4.** Tenderloin roast **5.** Top sirloin **6.** Sirloin fillet **7.** Eye round **8.** Oxtail **9.** Sirloin flap meat **10.** Flank steak **11.** Tri-tip **12.** Sirloin tip **13.** Bottom round

primal or portion of the animal is identified, and within the primal or subprimal are a series of choices. Sometimes you only get one choice. Often, though, each choice has a variety of alternatives. Once you've looked at the chuck choices, for example, and selected boneless chuck steaks/roasts, you'll also get stew meat and top blade/flatiron steaks. Then the only other question will be what thickness you prefer for those steaks. As scraps from every part of the animal tend to get ground into hamburger, I mention it only when it is a significant choice.

CHUCK
Neck

- Boned and cubed for stews

  OR
- Rolled and tied

Ribs 1 Through 5 (including bottom and top blade)

- Bone-in chuck steaks/roasts ("7-bone")

  OR
- Boneless chuck steaks/roasts from below the blade bone, and boneless top blade steaks/flatiron steaks and stew meat (from the chuck tender) from above the blade bone

  OR
- Square-cut chuck split in half along the spinal groove, producing bone-in chuck eye steaks from one side, and one or two crosscut roasts from the other side

Shoulder (clod only)

Each option also produces shoulder tender.

- Shoulder steaks (cut 1½ inches thick) for London broil

  OR
- Clod heart tied for shoulder pot roast

BRISKET

- Left whole (can be rolled and tied on request)

  OR

- Divided in half into the flat cut (just the deep pectoral) and the point cut (the fattier end)

  OR

- Cubed for stew meat

FORESHANK AND HIND SHANK

- Sliced 1½ to 2 inches thick for braising or stewing

  OR

- Boned and the meat ground (thus producing extra marrow bones)

RIB

Each option comes with "lifter" or rib cap meat, which can usually be requested as stew meat.

- Bone-in rib steaks/roasts

  OR

- Boned and cut into rib eye steaks/tied roasts (which yields beef back ribs from the bones)

  OR

- Boned and ribs inverted and tied back on for a "standing" roast

PLATE (Ribs 6 Through 12)

Each option also produces outside skirt.

- Conventional short ribs

  OR

- Ribs 6–9 cut into flanken-style short ribs, and ribs 10–12 cut into conventional short ribs

  OR

- Plate split in half across the rib bones; upper (meatier) half cut into conventional short ribs, and lower half boned and rolled for braising

FLANK

Each option produces a flank steak that's best cooked whole.

- Sirloin flap meat cut into steak tips

  OR

- Sirloin flap meat left whole for grilling (Argentine "*vacio*")

  OR

- Sirloin flap meat butterflied for stuffing (beef "pinwheel")

SHORT LOIN

- Porterhouse/T-bone steaks and a butt tenderloin sliced into steaks or tied as a roast. (Note: Within this choice you may request a 3-inch cut piece from the center of the short loin—a super-thick T-bone steak, used for a traditional Italian *bistecca fiorentina*).

  OR

- Boneless NY strip steaks and boneless tenderloin steaks (tenderloin can also be left whole and tied)

  OR

- Bone-in NY strip steaks and boneless tenderloin steaks/whole tied butt tenderloin roast

SIRLOIN

Each option produces a tri-tip that can be left whole or sliced, and a ball-tip that is best cut into stew meat.

- Bone-in top sirloin steaks/roasts

  OR

- Boneless top sirloin steaks/roasts (cap, or culotte, left on)

  OR

- Boneless top sirloin steaks/roasts and culotte removed to be sliced or left whole

ROUND

If not broken into subprimals, the round can be sliced into round steaks, or left whole as a "steamship" banquet roast with the shank frenched.

Top Round

- Subprimal left whole, fat removed, cap and veins removed for curing as *bresaola*

  OR

- First-cut steaks from the front (either sliced 1 inch thick for serving medium rare or sliced ⅛ inch thick and pounded for either minute steaks or *braciole*), center-cut steaks from the middle sliced 1½ to 2 inches thick for London broil, and two tied roasts from the back

  OR

- All steaks, or the front half as steaks and the other half as kebobs

  OR

- Quartered and tied into four roasts

  OR

- Sliced into thin strips for further processing into jerky

BREAKING DOWN A SIDE OF BEEF

Whole hindquarter

Removing the flank

Removing the kidney fat

Breaking off the short loin

Taking off the aitchbone

Pulling the sirloin tip

Seaming out the top round

Boning the hind shank

The remaining femur

Removing the flank steak

Trussing the tenderloin

Trussing the top sirloin

Trimming the bottom round

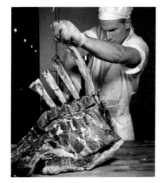
Boning the chuck and brisket

Removing the arm bone

Trussing the chuck roll

Bottom Round

The heel round that adjoins the thin end of the muscle can be cut into stew meat without affecting any of the following options.

- Cut into two or three roasts

  OR

- Point (rump) separated for pot roast, and remainder sliced 1½ inches thick for London broil or left whole for pot roast

  OR

- Point separated and sliced across the grain into sandwich steaks, and remainder sliced for London broil or left whole for pot roast

  OR

- Cut into stew meat

  OR

- Side muscles removed and sliced for jerky

Sirloin Tip

- Sliced for 1½-inch-thick London broil

  OR

- Cap removed and sliced into steaks, sirloin tip center left whole and tied, or sliced into thin steaks for beef cutlets

Eye of Round

- Left whole, or split into two pot roasts (if oven-roasting, best if larded or barded)

  OR

- Sliced into minute steaks (or half reserved for roast)

  OR

- Sliced 1½ inches thick for braising steaks or cut for stew meat

EXTREMITIES, ODD BITS, AND OFFAL

- Beef liver
- Beef cheeks (not always available)
- Brain (currently not available because of concerns about BSE)
- Sweetbreads (hard to get from processors)
- Lights, or lungs (difficult to get—I have never been able to)
- Tripe, or stomach (must be bleached before sale, so most processors don't sell it)
- Heart (sliced into strips, cubed for stew, or left whole for stuffing)
- Kidneys
- Tongue
- Oxtail
- Suet

Cooking Beef

Cooking grass-fed beef is different from cooking corn-finished beef because it has less fat and less marbling (which insulate and help keep the juices in the meat); grass-fed beef toughens much more rapidly and requires more careful cooking. That means it's essential, when roasting, to rely on a thermometer rather than timing to ensure that you don't overcook the meat, and to avoid salty or soy-sauce-based (liquid) marinades when preparing dishes. Instead, choose spice rubs or marinades that are oil and herb based, and plan to serve all fast-cooked cuts medium rare. Watch braises and stews to make sure that they cook at an *extremely low* temperature to break down the meat rather than toughen it. Such careful cooking guarantees complex and satisfying beefy flavors, with good mouthfeel and texture.

Cooking Ground Meat

Ground beef from grass-fed cows must be cooked carefully—either quickly seared on the outside to stay rare within or cooked very slowly to a more advanced state of doneness.

Tips for Cooking Grass-Fed Beef

- Never pierce the meat with a fork—valuable juices will be lost. Use tongs or a spatula to turn the meat. Use the back of a carving fork to hold the meat in place as you slice it.
- Add salt in the form of a rub, or in the pan as the meat cooks, not in a marinade, which tends to draw out the moisture.
- Use a meat thermometer to judge doneness, and stop cooking the meat when it registers 10 or so degrees less than the ideal temperature. This allows for "oven rise"—the continued internal cooking that occurs when the meat is first removed from the heat source and is rested.
- Always let roasted meat rest for at least 15 minutes before carving—this is particularly important with grass-fed beef, as it contains less fat to hold in moisture than industrial meat does.
- Serve grilled, seared, or roasted grass-fed beef rare.

How to Thaw Properly

I find the best way to thaw meat is to let it defrost, still wrapped, on a plate in the refrigerator overnight (or longer, if wet-aging). You can also thaw meat on the counter or on a sheet pan or cast-iron pan (which seems to thaw meat more rapidly) for several hours, taking into account the temperature of the room. Either way, this does mean you have to decide what you are having for dinner in advance, not always an easy task. In practice, last-minute events can overtake a planned meal.

Dry-aging and wet-aging (see page 56) can buy you some time by keeping thawed meat available. But there will be days when it is seven o'clock and you're starving and you've forgotten to thaw *any* meat for dinner. Here are two strategies:

- Best, put your vacuum-packed meat in a large bowl in the sink and run *cold* water over it every few minutes for about 20 minutes. If your meat isn't vacuum packed, put it in a resealable freezer bag. I know cold water is counterintuitive, but it works. This is a particularly good method for steaks, chops, and ground meat.
- Second, you can start cooking the frozen meat over fairly high heat, increasing both the initial temperature and the cooking time. This works best for dishes that you enjoy eating rare, such as steaks or roasts, since they will cook from the outside toward the frozen center.

Don't bother putting the meat in the microwave on the defrost setting—this will take at least the same 20 minutes as the cold water method, *and* it starts cooking the meat, which forces it to lose lots of juices.

Cooking the Chuck

Chuck contains portions that can cook low and slow, such as pot roast and stewing beef, but also offers steaks (chuck steak, for instance) and cuts for the frying pan, grill, or broiler, such as London broil. Conventionally, large amounts of chuck tend to be ground, which tenderizes meat. Alternatively, you can ask that chuck trim be set aside and labeled, so that you can grind it at home for Bolognese sauce, or use it for stew or curry.

Cooking Brisket

Whether left whole, divided into two cuts, or cubed for stew, this cut is best slowly braised in a flavorful liquid blend or slow-smoked. Alternatively, sometimes brisket is ground and mixed with ground beef from other parts of the cow to add fat and flavor.

Cooking Shanks

Another great braising cut, shanks can be more or less meaty, but are always worth cooking slowly, whether on or off the bone. (On the bone offers more flavor.) Shank meat may be ground if not specified as a separate cut. Shank bones (with meat removed) offer marrow, which is delicious when roasted, but be sure to ask that the bones be crosscut for ease of presentation and marrow removal.

Cooking Rib Cuts

Rib steaks are tender, and can be cooked rapidly over high heat on the grill, in a grill pan, or under the broiler. Rib roasts (on or off the bone) are always festive, and are roasted in the oven (or in a covered grill). Both roasts and steaks from grass-fed beef are best served rare or medium rare.

Cooking Plate Cuts

The great cuts from the plate, short ribs and flanken, make for memorable braised dishes. Time and long, slow cooking bring these cuts to melting tenderness.

Cooking the Flank

Flank steak, with its open grain, is usually marinated in a tasty mix of sweet and acid elements before pan-cooking or broiling. It's cut across the grain, on the bias, to create tender slices. Other cuts from the flank include portions of the sirloin (the flap meat), which is cut into steaks, steak tips, and meat suitable for stuffing and rolling.

Cooking Short Loin

Great tender and flavorful steaks and roasts come from this portion of the cow, including porterhouse, T-bone, and tenderloin, as well as strip loin. Cook to rare or medium rare, with or without spice rubs.

Cooking Sirloin

Tri-tip roasts and steaks, stewing beef from the ball tip, plus sirloin steaks and roasts, as well as the culotte (used for stuffing and rolling), make up the offerings from this portion of the cow. Stews should always cook very slowly with the lowest possible heat (in the oven or on the stovetop), while steaks can cook more rapidly over direct heat on the stovetop, grill, or under the broiler.

Cooking the Round

Divided into top, bottom, sirloin tip, and eye of round, this portion of the cow offers a wide mix of steaks and/or oven roasts as well as stew meat and pot roasts. That's because some parts of this primal are more tender than others, and so profit from different cooking methods and cutting patterns. Minute steaks, for example, are cut thinly, pounded, and textured to create tenderness when rapidly cooked,

The Case for Pink Veal

Dairy cows are bred to have calves and produce milk. When the calf is female, it is destined to become another dairy cow. When it's male, it is usually surplus. Here in Vermont, many dairy farmers give away newborn male calves or sell them for a nominal amount to anyone who will raise them. If bottle-fed with a milk substitute and then put on grass until slaughter, these young calves can become "pink veal." Unlike traditional veal, pink veal is neither crated nor force-fed, and buying pink veal provides a market for animals that would otherwise be killed soon after birth. A few farmers are beginning to market pink veal, creating a new market.

Aging Beef at Home

I learned this **dry-aging** technique from my grandmother, who used to trick her second husband into providing a bigger grocery allowance by dry-aging supermarket beef and claiming she bought it at the much more expensive specialty butcher. Marital deception aside, it's a useful way to make meat more flavorful.

Unwrap the meat, blot it well, salt it lightly, and lay it on a wire cake-cooling rack that has been set on a plate lined with folded paper towels. This way, liquids will drip down onto the paper and air can circulate around the meat. Cover the top of the meat loosely with another sheet of paper towel, and put the meat back in the coolest (always the lowest) part of the refrigerator. Cook it in the next two or three days.

If you are concerned about other foods touching meat as it ages, do as Alton Brown suggests in his television show *Good Eats*, and create a meat-aging bin by cutting holes in the sides and top of a plastic refrigerator storage container large enough to hold a roast and a wire rack. Put the meat inside on a rack above paper towels, but put the top on the container as well. Air will circulate through the box, but no other food will be able to touch the meat.

There is lots of controversy about **wet-aging**—that is, storing the vacuum-sealed, defrosted meat under refrigeration for a period of time. Purists say that this is not aging at all—it is simply marinating the meat in blood in an anaerobic atmosphere. This is the way supermarkets age meat, and the meat in grocery stores has likely been wet-aging for *weeks* before you buy it.

There's no question that dry-aging creates the most flavorful meat. However, for cooks, it is comforting to know that meat defrosted several days ago (or even last week) is still edible as long as the Cryovac seal is unbroken (if the meat is not discolored and the package doesn't leak, you can be sure it is still sealed).

Local beef farmers tell me that they often wet-age beef (as long as it is in a sealed Cryovac pouch) for as long as three weeks. They feel this method tenderizes steaks and roasts considerably. If you do choose to wet-age, be sure to rinse the meat well and blot it dry before cooking it.

WHEN YOU'RE IN A HURRY

If you haven't had the time or forethought to dry-age your meat, you can still make do. Try blotting the meat and leaving it on a rack at room temperature for at least 30 minutes (if you have a fan you can aim at it, all the better). Even this small amount of time will dry out the surface and aid in browning.

while London broil's open texture absorbs flavorful marinades to provide a tasty and tender mouthfeel when sliced on the bias. For those who are interested in curing meats, eye of round is the choice for *bresaola*, the great Italian air-cured dried beef.

Cooking with Offal and Odd Bits

Liver, heart, kidneys, sweetbreads, and tongue are generally referred to as offal, even though the USDA does not categorize beef heart as "variety meat." All of these are worth cooking carefully and well, and offer good eating. Odd bits such as oxtail or beef cheeks are equally rewarding when braised, and beef fat (suet) is a valuable ingredient in its own

right for pastries as well as for larding lean roasts. Cuts such as brains, testicles, and tripe can be very difficult to source from local processors, but may be available from on-farm sources, or ethnic markets.

Cooking with Suet

Beef fat, or suet, is the hard white fat that is the analogue of the fine lard that comes from pork. When you buy a whole steer and ask for all the suet, you get an enormous amount. (It's actually called HPK fat at the processors—that stands for "heart, pancreas, and kidney.") Suet is very good for all kinds of baking and frying; it makes the best french fries in the world!

BEEF RECIPES

GROUND BEEF: Even when I specify that only otherwise unusable scraps are the meat I want ground, I still get an astonishing amount of ground beef from every cow—often 30 to 40 percent, or more!—of the cow's weight. Happily, ground beef defrosts easily and makes a great variety of main-course dishes.

Grilled Ground Beef Kebobs with Cinnamon, Allspice, and Cardamom

These Lebanese kebobs are especially delicious when cooked on a real grill, whether charcoal or gas. If you don't have a grill, try cooking them, without skewers, in a ridged cast-iron grill pan over high heat. (Turn your exhaust fan on high when you grill indoors.) I have not had good luck using a broiler with these—domestic broilers just don't get hot enough. Serve the kebobs on the skewers or not, as you choose. The traditional method is to present them with pieces of flatbread to use when pulling the meat off the skewer; the bread is then wrapped around the meat for fork-free eating. You'll need 12 bamboo skewers for this recipe if you are making the kebobs on sticks; be sure to soak them in water for 10 to 15 minutes to make sure they don't catch fire.

SERVES 4 TO 6 AS AN APPETIZER

1 pound ground grass-fed beef

1 small onion

10 fresh mint leaves

½ teaspoon salt

1 teaspoon ground cinnamon

½ teaspoon ground allspice

1 teaspoon bruised black cardamom seeds (or ground cardamom)

½ teaspoon freshly ground black pepper

For serving:

Fresh flatbread such as lavash, Afghan bread, or pita, warmed and covered with cloth to steam, torn or cut into 12 (4-inch) squares

Optional garnishes:

Olive oil, for drizzling

Fresh cilantro leaves

Lime wedges

Using a food processor fitted with the steel blade, process the meat, onion, mint, salt, and spices until the mixture forms a paste and rides the blade. Scrape the meat mixture into a bowl or onto plastic wrap and chill for at least 15 minutes. Meanwhile, soak 12 bamboo skewers, if using, in water. Lightly grease the grill rack and heat the grill to high.

Form the chilled meat paste into twelve 3-inch-long cigar-shaped pieces. Push a skewer through each cigar, and flatten the meat with your fingers so that the kebobs have a front and back but no real sides, since they taper toward the edges.

Grill the kebobs until dark brown on both sides, about 10 minutes total. Serve at once with the flatbread. If using the garnishes, sprinkle each piece of flatbread with a drizzle of olive oil and some cilantro leaves, wrap it around the meat, and pull away the skewer. Squeeze a little lime juice on top of the meat before wrapping it entirely with the bread.

Glazed All-Beef Meat Loaf

Created for those who don't mix meat and milk, who don't eat pork, or who have nothing but grass-fed ground beef in the freezer, this all-beef meat loaf does not compromise on flavor. The secret, as in so many American meat loaves, is rolled oats. If you like a loaf-shaped entrée, mold the meat by packing it tightly into a greased loaf pan and then turn it out onto a baking sheet or an ovenproof skillet before baking. It needs to brown on all sides. For a free-form loaf, shape it into a round or oval and bake it in a cast-iron skillet for lots of bottom heat and crust. The glaze adds a layer of sweet mysterious flavor, but it is optional. Like all great meat loaves, this makes for good sandwiches later in the week.

SERVES 4 TO 6, WITH LEFTOVERS

½ cup rolled oats

½ teaspoon freshly ground black pepper

½ teaspoon cayenne pepper

1 teaspoon fresh or dried marjoram

1 teaspoon dried thyme

Leaves from 4 to 5 sprigs fresh flat-leaf parsley

Freshly grated zest of 1 lemon

1 small onion, chopped

1 carrot, chopped

3 cloves garlic, smashed

2 pounds ground grass-fed beef

2 tablespoons extra-virgin olive oil

½ teaspoon kosher or sea salt

1 egg, beaten

For the glaze (optional):

1 tablespoon grainy mustard

1 teaspoon honey

1 teaspoon soy sauce

1 teaspoon tomato-based sauce such as ketchup or barbecue sauce

Heat the oven to 425 degrees and position the rack in the middle of the oven.

In the bowl of a food processor, combine the oats, peppers, herbs, lemon zest, onion, carrot, and garlic. Pulse until these are all a uniform size, taking care not to overprocess into a liquid or mush.

Transfer the mixture to a bowl and combine it with the meat and olive oil, season with the salt, and (using your hands or a spatula) mix in the egg. Do not overwork the mixture—just combine well.

Shape, either in a loaf pan as described above or into an oval or a round in an ungreased but seasoned cast-iron skillet. If you are using the glaze, mix the glaze ingredients together and pour the liquid over the meat loaf. Bake for 30 minutes, then reduce the heat to 325 degrees and bake for another 20 to 30 minutes, until the internal temperature registers 155 degrees on an instant-read thermometer.

Let the meat loaf rest for at least 10 minutes before removing it from the pan, slicing it into ¾-inch slices, and serving.

Beef and Lamb Meat Loaf

There are so many virtues to meat loaf. It turns a couple of pounds of ground meat into luxury eating for a crowd—and there's the sheer deliciousness of meat loaf sandwiches the next day. This version, which features homemade bread crumbs soaked in cream, is rich and deeply flavorful, flecked with carrot, celery, herbs, and onion. Whether or not you top it with pancetta or good bacon, this makes for a memorable loaf.

SERVES 8

2 to 3 broken-up slices of stale artisanal bread

¼ cup cream or whole milk

1 small Vidalia onion, coarsely chopped

1 carrot, coarsely chopped

1 stalk celery, coarsely chopped

¾ cup freshly grated Parmigiano-Reggiano

1 egg, beaten

Tiny leaves from 4 sprigs fresh thyme (about 1 tablespoon)

10 fresh sage leaves, chopped (about 1 tablespoon)

1 teaspoon sea salt

Generous amount of freshly ground black pepper

1 pound ground grass-fed beef

1 pound ground pastured lamb

3 slices of pancetta or bacon (optional)

Heat the oven to 350 degrees.

In a blender or food processor fitted with the steel blade, whirl the bread pieces to fine crumbs. Soak the crumbs in the cream or milk until the cream is absorbed. In the bowl of the same blender or food processor (no need to wash it), pulse together the onion, carrot, and celery until they are a fine mince (be careful not to overprocess into mush).

Mix the cheese with the egg in a large mixing bowl. Add the soaked crumbs, the minced vegetables, and all the remaining ingredients except the meats, and combine. In another mixing bowl, combine the beef and the lamb, using your hands. Add to the crumb mixture and mix only until everything is evenly distributed. Form the mass into an oval, slapping the meat into shape and compacting it. Turn this into a cast-iron pan and slap the meat a little more to eliminate air pockets and refine the shape. If using the pancetta or bacon, arrange the slices on top of the loaf. (If you are not using the pancetta or bacon, baste the loaf with its pan juices every once in a while as it bakes to keep it moist.)

Bake the meat loaf for 50 to 60 minutes, until the internal temperature registers 155 degrees on an instant-read thermometer. Let the meat loaf sit for 10 minutes before serving it, to raise the internal temperature a little and to firm the loaf.

Three-Meat Loaf or Pâté

The richest meat loaves of all feature three kinds of meat—beef or veal, pork, and lamb. This one, especially when packed firmly into shape, makes some of our favorite sandwiches. It can also be served like pâté in small slices, accompanied by capers, gherkins, olives, and toasted brioche or crisp crackers. If you've bought pastured lamb, beef, and pork from farmers, you'll have lots of ground meat in the freezer. This is a fine way to showcase their variety, and you can easily change the proportions, as long as you end up with 2 or 3 pounds in all.

SERVES 6 TO 8 AS A MEAT LOAF ENTRÉE OR 12 AS A PÂTÉ APPETIZER

½ pound ground pastured lamb

¾ pound ground grass-fed beef

1 pound ground pastured pork

1 onion

1 carrot

1 cup loosely packed fresh flat-leaf parsley leaves

½ cup rolled oats, plus more as needed

½ cup whole milk

1 egg, beaten

¾ cup freshly grated Parmigiano-Reggiano

4 slices of bacon (optional)

Bring the meats to room temperature and remove them from their wrappers. Blot if necessary.

Heat the oven to 350 degrees. Choose a cast-iron frying pan if you are preparing the meat loaf or a loaf pan if you want to serve it as pâté.

Using a food processor or a chef's knife, chop the onion, carrot, and parsley together into a fine dice. Take care, if you're using a processor, to avoid creating a mush.

Combine the thawed meats, the vegetable mixtures, and all the remaining ingredients for the meat loaf in a large mixing bowl, and work them together using your hands so that they are well blended. Do not overmix. If the ingredients seem too wet, add more rolled oats as needed. Form the meat into a loaf or an oval, patting it firmly in place in your chosen pan. Layer the slices of bacon on top of the meat.

Bake for 1 hour. Let cool for 10 to 15 minutes before slicing and serving as meat loaf. For pâté, let the loaf cool in the pan, then pour off any juices and cover with foil and a piece of cardboard cut to form a lid that rests just on top of the meat. Weight the lid overnight in the refrigerator with a can or other similar item to compress the meat as it cools. Serve cold, cut into thin slices.

Summer Squash Stuffed with Beef, Toasted Pine Nuts, Chèvre, and Parsley

In late summer, it's always a delight to see round summer squash in yellow and green varieties. The round green ones are usually about the size and shape of tennis balls, while the yellow ones feature pretty scalloping around their bottom halves. When carefully hollowed out, these gems are great for stuffing. Of course, you can also use regular long zucchini, split in half lengthwise and cored out to a canoe shape. Either way, these make a nice, light dinner or a first course for a larger meal.

MAKES ENOUGH TO FILL 10 TO 12 ROUND SQUASH OR 6 LONG ONES

½ cup pine nuts

1 tablespoon extra-virgin olive oil

1 onion, finely chopped

10 to 12 small round summer squash

1 pound ground grass-fed beef

1 teaspoon sea salt

Freshly ground black pepper

1 teaspoon ground allspice

½ cup fresh flat-leaf parsley leaves, finely chopped, or a mixture of parsley and fresh basil

1 egg, beaten

½ cup crumbled chèvre or feta cheese

Choose a baking dish large enough to hold all the squash in one layer, such as a lasagna pan. Heat the oven to 350 degrees.

Using a seasoned dry cast-iron or other heavy-bottomed frying pan over medium heat, toast the nuts until fragrant and golden, stirring and shaking the pan often to prevent burning, about 3 minutes. Pour the nuts onto a plate to cool.

Pour the olive oil into the warm pan and when it has thinned and become fragrant, add the onion and sweat until it is limp, about 5 minutes.

As the onion begins to cook, cut off the stem end of each squash about three-quarters of the way from the bottom. Using a small spoon or scoop, carefully remove and reserve the inner flesh of the squash a little at a time, taking care to tear the shell as little as possible. If the squash does not sit flat, remove a tiny bit from the bottom to make it flat. You are making a hollow shell to fill with stuffing.

Add the beef to the pan, crumbling it so that it mixes with the onion. Add the salt and pepper to taste and stir the mixture around. Add the small pieces of reserved squash flesh, and continue to cook until the meat is no longer raw-looking.

Put the meat mixture in a bowl and add the toasted pine nuts, allspice, parsley, egg, and crumbled cheese. Mix well.

Arrange the hollow squash in the pan and fill each with the meat mixture, spooning it in and tamping it down to fill the cavity. Pour just enough water into the bottom of the pan to come to a depth of ½ inch, and bake for 35 minutes. (If you are using larger squash, begin by covering the pan with foil for the first 15 minutes of baking and then removing it for another 30 minutes of cooking.)

Serve the squash warm or at room temperature.

Cabbage Risotto with Meatballs

round beef and cabbage are a duet that's played in lots of food cultures—see My Grandmother's Stuffed Cabbage (see page 66) for one example, and think of cabbage and meat dumplings and cabbage and beef ravioli for two other ways of hitting the same notes. Here, the meatballs are made separately and are added to the cabbage risotto at the end. It's a wonderful dish for a cold, foggy night.

I've written the recipe in two parts, so that the first time you make it, you can focus on each part alone. However, if you are an experienced risotto maker, feel free to cook the meatballs at the same time as the risotto, in two pans side by side.

SERVES 8 AS A FIRST COURSE
OR 4 AS AN ENTRÉE

For the meatballs:

1 pound ground grass-fed beef

1 cup panko (Japanese bread crumbs)

1 egg, beaten

½ cup freshly grated Parmigiano-Reggiano

1 clove garlic, minced

¼ cup chopped fresh flat-leaf parsley

1 tablespoon rubbed dried sage

Sea salt and freshly ground black pepper

2 tablespoons extra-virgin olive oil

For the cabbage risotto:

5 cups chicken or beef stock, preferably homemade (see page 303 or 124)

1 small onion

1 stalk celery

1 small carrot

1 clove garlic

2 tablespoons unsalted butter

2 tablespoons extra-virgin olive oil

1½ cups arborio rice

½ cup white wine or white vermouth

1 small green cabbage (about ½ pound, cored, thinly sliced, and shredded)

½ cup freshly grated Parmigiano-Reggiano, plus more for serving

1 tablespoon chopped fresh flat-leaf parsley

FOR THE MEATBALLS

Mix together the meat, panko, egg, grated cheese, garlic, parsley, sage, and salt and pepper, using your hands or a spatula to combine everything well without overworking the ingredients.

Using wet hands, pinch off walnut-sized pieces and form them into firm balls. When all the meat is formed, heat a large sauté pan and pour in the olive oil. When the oil has thinned and become fragrant, add the meatballs. Cook over medium-high heat, shaking the pan to turn the meat, until all the meatballs are well browned, 5 to 7 minutes. When done, remove from the pan and set aside. Loosely cover the meatballs with aluminum foil to keep them warm while you cook the risotto.

FOR THE RISOTTO

Bring the stock to a boil in a small saucepan and turn the heat down to maintain a slow simmer.

Using a food processor fitted with the steel blade or a chef's knife, finely mince the onion, celery, carrot, and garlic together.

Heat a large sauté pan or Dutch oven and melt 1 tablespoon of the butter and the olive oil together. Add the minced aromatic vegetables and, using a wooden spoon or heatproof silicone spatula, turn them in the fat to coat, cooking them over medium-low heat until they are soft but not brown. Add the rice and turn it to coat. Add the wine or vermouth and stir well. Wait until the wine is completely absorbed before proceeding.

Stir the shredded cabbage in with the rice and adjust the heat to medium. Begin adding the hot broth by the ½ cup or ladleful, stirring and waiting to add the next ladle until the previous broth has been completely absorbed. The whole process of cooking the rice should take just under 20 minutes, so be prepared to go slowly. If you run out of broth before the rice is done, heat some water and use that instead.

When the rice is slightly resistant to the tooth (al dente) but thoroughly cooked, take it off the heat and quickly stir in the remaining 1 tablespoon butter, the cheese, and the parsley.

Pour the risotto into a warmed large, shallow serving platter and stir in the meatballs. Serve at once, passing additional cheese at the table.

My Grandmother's Stuffed Cabbage

My Hungarian grandmother used to make her version of these adorable packages whenever she came to stay with us. She always used regular green cabbage, but I've made them with curly Savoy, Napa, and even bok choy with its big leaves. Really, any large, fairly tough leaf will do, as long as it can take an hour's worth of cooking and can be stemmed, if necessary. The dish has classic sweet and sour flavors common to traditional Jewish, Arab, Moorish Spanish, and southern Italian cuisines. If you love the sweet elements particularly, you can add a handful of chopped raisins to the meat before stuffing the leaves. In that case, toasted pine nuts sprinkled on top are also a good addition.

SERVES 6

12 to 16 large cabbage leaves	2 cups canned tomatoes, juices included
1 onion	2 tablespoons balsamic vinegar
1 pound ground grass-fed beef	2 tablespoons sugar or honey
Salt and freshly ground black pepper	1 teaspoon ground cinnamon
½ cup uncooked rice such as jasmine or basmati	1 cup water

Have a large bowl of cold water ready with ice in it. Blanch the cabbage leaves by boiling them briefly, in batches if necessary, for about 3 minutes, or until the leaves are limp. Plunge the leaves in the ice-water bath to stop the cooking process and then drain them on clean dish towels.

Using a chef's knife or a food processor fitted with the steel blade, finely mince the onion. Combine the minced onion, beef, salt and pepper, and rice in a medium-sized mixing bowl using your hands or a silicone spatula.

Take about 2 tablespoons of the meat mixture (or as much as will fit in the leaf) and roll it between your palms to form an oval cigar shape. Place the meat horizontally near the stem end of a cabbage leaf, turn the sides in over it, and roll the leaf like a burrito, toward the leaf's tip. Secure the roll with a wooden toothpick (inserting it like a sewing needle— in, out, and in) and place each roll, seam side down, in a large sauté pan with a lid or an enameled cast-iron Dutch oven. The rolls can be layered if your pan will not hold them all in one layer. Pour in the tomatoes with their juices, add the vinegar, sugar, and cinnamon, and then pour the water over all.

Bring the liquid to a boil, and immediately turn the heat to the lowest setting and cover tightly. Cook for 45 minutes, or until the rice and meat are cooked through.

Remove the cabbage rolls with a slotted spoon. Let them cool a little until you can pull out the toothpicks. Arrange the rolls on a platter or on dinner plates. Reduce the pan juices, if desired, by cooking them down further. Serve the stuffed cabbage rolls napped with the pan juices.

Polpettini (Little Meatballs)

When made with grass-fed beef, these are the best meatballs I have ever eaten. They are good on an antipasto platter, or as a first course or lunch. In Italy, the added fat would be lardo (cured pork fat) rather than butter, so if you have access to lardo, do use it.

You'll think of plenty of ways to serve these morsels, but here are two good choices:

For a first course, whirl a couple of very ripe tomatoes in a food processor with a little good salt and olive oil. Add two or three drops of vodka to really bring out the tomato flavor. Put a couple of tablespoons of sauce in the bottom of shallow soup bowls, place three or four meatballs on top, and add a final drizzle of extra-virgin olive oil.

For appetizers, thread the polpettini onto bamboo skewers, along with whole grape tomatoes or halved cherry tomatoes, basil leaves, and tiny mozzarella balls. Place the skewers on a platter or tray and pass.

Polpettini are also very good made with pastured pork.

MAKES 12 TO 14 MEATBALLS

½ pound ground grass-fed beef

1 lemon (preferably organic)

1 to 2 tablespoons unsalted butter, cold or semifrozen

1 to 2 tablespoons panko (Japanese bread crumbs), plus more for coating

1 to 2 tablespoons freshly grated Parmigiano-Reggiano

½ teaspoon ground cinnamon

1 egg

¼ teaspoon kosher salt

2 tablespoons extra-virgin olive oil

Blot the surface of the ground beef. Zest and juice the lemon and reserve both. Line a baking sheet with parchment paper.

Chop 1 tablespoon of the cold butter into small pieces and, using your hands, mix it rapidly (so as not to melt it) into the beef along with 1 tablespoon each of the panko and the cheese.

Add the lemon zest to the mixture. Add 2 teaspoons of the juice, along with the cinnamon and egg. Sprinkle on the kosher salt. Test for texture—you want a juicy, fairly wet mix. But if it seems too wet, add more grated cheese and panko; if it's too dry, add more butter and lemon juice.

Shape the meat mixture into balls about the size of cherry tomatoes. Roll each briefly in panko to coat them and then set them aside on the baking sheet to dry for 10 minutes.

Heat a large pan over medium-high heat, then add the olive oil. When it has thinned and become fragrant, sauté all the meatballs at once until golden but still rare in the center, about 5 minutes, shaking the pan to turn them as they cook.

Braised Lion's Head

Lion's head is a classic Chinese dish that's usually made with ground pork because ground beef is relatively rare in China. Essentially a meatball made with dried black mushrooms, scallions, and ginger, it can be braised (as it is here) or deep-fried. It is always served with hearty greens, usually mustard greens. If you go to an Asian market for ingredients, pick up some broad chow fun noodles—this is a great dish to serve them with. Just mix the cooked noodles in with the meat, greens, and sauce at the end.

MAKES 20 MEATBALLS, ENOUGH FOR 4 TO 6 SERVINGS WITH RICE OR NOODLES

4 dried black Chinese mushrooms

2 scallions (white part only), finely chopped

1 (1-inch) piece fresh ginger, peeled and finely diced

1 teaspoon cornstarch

1 egg, beaten

1 teaspoon sugar

1 pound ground grass-fed beef

2 tablespoons canola or peanut oil

2 tablespoons soy sauce

1 tablespoon sherry or Shaoxing wine

1 bunch mustard greens (12 to 15 ounces)

Soak the dried mushrooms in about 1¼ cups hot water until softened, about 30 minutes. Remove the mushrooms and save the soaking water. Pour the soaking water through a coffee filter or a paper-towel-lined strainer to remove any grit. Reserve 1 cup of the strained liquid. Remove and discard the hard stem of each mushroom and finely chop the mushroom caps.

Put the scallions, ginger, and mushrooms in a bowl, sprinkle in the cornstarch, and mix well. Add the egg, sugar, and beef to the bowl. Mix the ingredients using your hands or a rubber spatula; avoid overworking the meat.

Wet your hands with cold water and make 20 golf-ball-sized meatballs, packing them into shape vigorously. In a wok or a large frying pan big enough to hold all the meatballs in one layer, heat the oil and brown the meat on all sides, shaking the pan or stirring as needed over high heat. Reduce the heat to low. Add the soy sauce, sherry, and reserved mushroom water, and simmer, covered, for 15 minutes.

While the meatballs simmer, separate the leaves of the mustard greens. Lay each one flat and cut out the stem. Chop the stems into 1-inch-long pieces. Cut the leaves into 4-inch sections. After the meatballs have cooked for 15 minutes, add the stems and leaves to the pot and simmer for 20 minutes more.

Serve with rice or Chinese wheat noodles.

Because some people like their hamburgers soft on the outside, while others prefer a seared crust, here are four recipes that cover both ends of the preference scale: the Bistro Burger (below) is French-inspired, and is made on the crisp side but rare within, as is the Salt-Seared Burger (see page 72). On the soft side of the line, both the Gorgonzola Burger (see page 72) and the Composed Butter Burger (see page 73) cook at lower heat to protect their delicate ingredients.

Bistro Burger Topped with a Poached Egg

nspired by a story I read by Jane Sigal in the New York Times *on Paris burgers, this is based on a recipe from Café Salle Pleyel, which uses classic beef tartare ingredients in a slightly cooked burger. I like to serve it on split half baguettes or on a bed of tiny salad greens that include peppery arugula or watercress, both of which go wonderfully with the egg.*

SERVES 4

1 teaspoon red wine vinegar

4 pastured free-range eggs

¼ cup sun-dried tomatoes

¼ cup capers, drained and rinsed

¼ cup fresh tarragon leaves

½ cup fresh flat-leaf parsley leaves

½ teaspoon kosher salt

Freshly ground black pepper

1 pound ground grass-fed beef

1 tablespoon plus 1 teaspoon extra-virgin olive oil

2 ounces Parmigiano-Reggiano, thinly sliced into curls with a vegetable peeler

Bring a frying pan half-filled with salted water to a simmer, then add the vinegar. Break each egg into a ramekin and then slip the egg into the simmering water. Using a slotted spoon, gently lift each egg out of the water when it is cooked to your liking (a slightly runny center is good—that takes about 3 minutes). Shake the spoon to drain as much liquid as possible, and gently put each poached egg in a separate small bowl until needed.

Chop the sun-dried tomatoes with the capers, tarragon, parsley, salt, and pepper to taste, pulsing in a food processor or by hand.

Using your hands, and working the meat as lightly as possible, combine the meat with the tomato-and-herb mixture and the 1 teaspoon olive oil. Shape the meat firmly into 4 patties, each about ½ inch thick.

Heat a cast-iron skillet, add the tablespoon olive oil, and wait until it thins and becomes fragrant. Add the burgers to the pan. Cook over high heat for about 2 minutes per side for very rare. Set on a platter of split baguettes or salad greens; top each burger with a poached egg and then a couple of cheese curls. Serve at once.

Salt-Seared Burger with Red Wine Reduction Sauce

Heating a well-seasoned cast-iron frying pan until hot and then shaking coarse sea salt on the surface is a fun thing to do because the salt starts to pop like popcorn as it heats. Put the meat in the pan as soon as you hear or see the first pop, and you'll be guaranteed a great burger that's seared crisp on the outside and is pink and juicy within. Just be sure to flip it as soon as it does not stick anymore—you don't want to overcook the meat. It is easier to scrape up the browned bits and make the wine reduction sauce in a flat-bottomed pan than a ridged one.

SERVES 4

1 pound ground grass-fed beef

1 teaspoon coarse sea salt such as gray Atlantic or Celtic (for pan-searing only)

Freshly ground black pepper

½ cup red wine

1 tablespoon unsalted butter

Bring the meat to room temperature for about 30 minutes. Blot the surface of the meat dry when you take it out of its package. Form the meat into 4 burgers, slap-patting them firmly into shape. Use your thumb to make an indentation on the top center of each one.

Heat a dry, seasoned cast-iron frying pan or grill pan to hot over high heat. (For safety's sake, have a big lid ready to smother flames in case of flare-ups.) Pour the salt into the pan, scattering it so that it loosely covers the surface. As soon as the salt begins to pop, turn on the exhaust fan and add the burgers. Cook for about 3 minutes per side over highest heat, flipping the burgers as soon as they do not stick and are browned. When the patties are done, put them on a plate to rest and shower them with black pepper to taste.

Keeping the pot lid within reach in case the wine flames, pour the wine into the hot burger pan over medium heat. Using a wooden spatula, scrape the browned bits from the surface of the pan into the wine as it bubbles. Reduce the wine by half, to about ¼ cup, 3 to 5 minutes. Turn the heat to low and swirl in the butter to blend. Pour this sauce over the burgers. Serve at once, either on a plate or on a bun or split hard roll.

Gorgonzola Burger

Made with real Italian Gorgonzola cheese, this is a standout. Even if all you can find is a domestic Gorgonzola, this is still worthwhile. Try it with other great blue cheeses, too, such as Stilton or Maytag blue, and see what you like best.

SERVES 4

1 pound ground grass-fed beef

Salt and freshly ground black pepper

4 ounces Gorgonzola cheese, cut into 4 small rough cubes

Combine the meat with salt and pepper to taste and gently form it into 4 balls, taking care not to overwork it. Poke holes in the meat and insert the cubes of cheese, sealing the cheese inside the burgers by pinching the meat over it.

Heat a dry, seasoned cast-iron skillet over medium heat until the edges of the pan are hot to a glancing touch. Immediately turn the heat to low. Put the patties in the pan, and cook them slowly and gently. The meat will brown but not sear. Turn the meat at the 4-minute mark and repeat on the other side.

Serve at once with rolls, sesame buns, or on a bed of cooked or raw greens.

Composed Butter Burger

Composed butter is made by chopping fresh herbs and combining them with soft butter. The herb butter is then scraped into plastic wrap and formed into a roll to chill in the freezer. Finally, the butter is sliced into portions to be buried in each hamburger patty, releasing its flavor as the burger cooks over low heat to rare. This is a highbrow French-chef way to make a lowbrow dish, but it creates a burger you'll never forget. If you make a number of composed butter logs at one time and keep them tightly sealed in the refrigerator, you'll always have the fixings ready to go.

SERVES 8

4 tablespoons (½ stick) unsalted butter, softened	2 pounds ground grass-fed beef
1 tablespoon chopped fresh basil leaves	Freshly ground black pepper
1 teaspoon chopped fresh thyme leaves	1 teaspoon coarse sea salt such as gray Atlantic or Celtic (for pan-searing only)
1 teaspoon fresh flat-leaf parsley leaves	

Using a food processor fitted with the steel blade, mix and chop the softened butter with the herbs to make a smooth, greenish paste. Scrape it out onto a sheet of plastic wrap and roll it into a cylinder about 4 inches long and 1 inch in diameter. Wrap it completely, twist the ends of the plastic closed, and freeze for a few hours, overnight, or longer. (If you plan to freeze the butter for a long time, put the roll into a resealable freezer bag to protect it.)

When you are ready to cook, bring the ground meat to room temperature for 30 minutes. Remove the butter from the freezer, unwrap it, and cut it into 8 slices. Divide the meat into 8 equal portions, and form each into a ball. Make an indentation in the center of each ball of meat and insert a slice of herb butter. Close the meat over the butter and form each portion into a thick patty about ½ inch deep, making a dimple on the top with your thumb. Sprinkle black pepper over the top.

Heat a dry, seasoned cast-iron pan, griddle, or grill pan over high heat until hot. Sprinkle it with the coarse sea salt, and when the salt starts to pop, immediately reduce the heat to low. Wait for 1 minute, then add the burgers, cooking them for 4 to 5 minutes per side for medium rare.

Serve plain or with toasted buns, grilled bread, or salad.

Ground Meat

Since so much of a whole animal is ground meat, it is important to consider the meat-to-fat ratio. Conventional processing converts a whopping 40 percent of the usable meat from an animal into ground meat, as they assume that no one wants all the slow-cooking and unusual cuts. While this may change as more people cook nose to tail, it's still important to consider the quality of all the ground meat you will inevitably get when you purchase a portion of a whole animal.

Especially with grass-fed beef, the ideal meat-to-fat ratio in ground meat is 80 to 85 percent (that is, about 80 or 85 percent meat and 20 or 15 percent fat). If you are buying a portion of an animal, you can ask for this ratio. You can also ask for the trim and fat and grind it yourself at home in a food processor or meat grinder. A 90 percent mix is wonderful for steak tartar but little else, and would require lots of butter or oil to make it palatable for cooking.

Fat from grass-fed beef is good fat, filled with the antioxidants and the CLA you buy the meat for. It acts as an insulator and helps keep hamburgers, for instance, juicy and richly flavored.

CHUCK: Chuck can be tender or tough, depending on how it's cut and how it's cooked. Braising cuts of grass-fed beef have such flavor (especially when cooked rare and sliced thinly), they can even be marinated and grilled. Know too that stewing grass-fed beef also produces excellent results, whether braised with aromatic spices or wine or cooked in coconut milk.

Madras Coconut Cream Beef Curry

Even though this dish is loosely based on one of Jane Lawson's recipes in The Spice Bible, I know she would not approve of my using a commercial Madras curry blend. However, the blend I buy from Penzeys is very fresh, fragrant, and delicious, so I offer only minor apologies. If you can't buy a good blend, I highly recommend Lawson's blend on page 31. Any curry is, of course, a wonderful way to make memorable use of great stewing beef.

This curry cooks for 2 hours on the stove. I think it's worth every minute, and it's wonderful reheated or even frozen and thawed, so don't worry about having leftovers. I serve this with basmati or jasmine rice.

SERVES 4 TO 6

2 tablespoons virgin coconut oil or other cooking oil

1 large onion, chopped

1 (13.5-ounce) can coconut milk

1½ tablespoons prepared Madras curry blend (or make your own; see page 31)

3 cloves garlic, chopped

2 pounds grass-fed stew beef (or boneless shoulder), cut into cubes, drained, and blotted dry

Salt

½ cup water

For the garnish:

Chopped fresh cilantro

Melt the oil in a large stewpan (such as a 5- or 7-quart Dutch oven or a Chinese sand pot), and fry the onion to a golden brown, stirring as necessary.

While the onion browns, open the can of coconut milk and spoon out the thick "cream" that usually rises to the top. Set aside the remaining thinner milk to use later. (Some brands of coconut milk are homogenized, and if this is the case, use all but ½ cup, which will be added later.)

Mix the curry powder and thick coconut cream (or the unreserved homogenized coconut milk) to form a paste. Stir this, along with the garlic, into the browned onion, and cook until the mixture is gently fragrant, 2 to 3 minutes. Add the meat and stir to coat it with the curry mixture. Add salt to taste.

Mix the reserved coconut milk and ½ cup water (or just ½ cup water and ½ cup coconut milk if your coconut milk was homogenized) into the pan and bring it all to a boil. Immediately lower the heat and reduce to a simmer. Cover and cook over the lowest possible heat for 2 hours, stirring every once in a while to make sure nothing is sticking. The curry is done when the meat is fork-tender. Taste for salt or other seasonings. Serve over rice, garnished with chopped cilantro.

Bolognese, My Way

Bolognese sauce is both so delicious and time-consuming, it's worth doubling or tripling this recipe and making some for the future. The sauce will keep for up to 2 months in the freezer and can be stored as long as 3 days in the refrigerator. Note that while it cooks for a long time, it doesn't take a lot of attention. It's traditionally served with spaghetti or fettuccini, but I also love it with risotto or polenta. The pancetta contributes salt to the recipe, so if you leave it out, add salt early in the process and taste at the end to see if more is needed.

I value Bolognese sauce so much that when I fill out my beef cut sheet, I ask for the flavorful shoulder trim to be packaged separately in 1-pound packages, which I grind at home (by pulsing the semifrozen meat in a food processor fitted with the steel blade) just for this sauce. My processor labels this meat "boneless beef." Although it's irregular in size and shape, you can also use it for stews or kebobs.

SERVES 6

¼ cup extra-virgin olive oil	1 bay leaf
2½ ounces pancetta, finely chopped	1 tablespoon fresh thyme leaves
1¼ pounds ground grass-fed beef, preferably from shoulder trim	½ teaspoon dried marjoram
¾ cup red wine	½ teaspoon rubbed dried sage
2 cloves garlic	Sea salt and freshly ground black pepper
1 onion	1 pound dried pasta (spaghetti is traditional, but fettuccini and even penne are also very good)
2 carrots	
½ small can tomato paste (about ⅓ cup)	½ cup sour cream
2 cups beef stock, preferably homemade (beef is best, but chicken or turkey will do; see page 124, 303, or 318)	¼ cup freshly grated Parmigiano-Reggiano, plus more for serving
¼ teaspoon freshly grated nutmeg	

Heat a large frying pan. Pour in 2 tablespoons of the olive oil, and when it thins and becomes fragrant, add the pancetta and turn the heat to low. Render the pancetta until the meat begins to color (about 10 minutes), turning it occasionally to brown all sides. Choose a 5-quart Dutch oven or Chinese sand pot to make the rest of the sauce in, and put the cooked pancetta in it.

Brown the beef in the fat left in the frying pan, stirring to make sure it is evenly browned. Add the browned meat to the Dutch oven. Pour off the fat in the frying pan, leaving any browned bits, and deglaze the pan with the red wine, scraping up all the browned bits and cooking off the alcohol for a few minutes. Pour the cooked wine into the Dutch oven.

Using a chef's knife or a food processor, finely chop the garlic, onion, and carrots, and set them aside.

Wipe out the frying pan with a paper towel, add the remaining 2 tablespoons olive oil, and when the oil is warm, lower the heat. Add the vegetables, and slowly sweat them until they are soft. Deglaze the pan with a mixture of the tomato paste and about ½ cup of the stock, scraping up any browned bits and incorporating them into the liquid. Pour this mixture into the Dutch oven.

Add the remaining stock along with the nutmeg and all the herbs to the Dutch oven. Taste the sauce and add salt and pepper. Simmer slowly, partially uncovered, over the lowest possible heat for about 3 hours, or until the sauce is thick and fragrant. (If you find that it is cooking too vigorously even on low heat without a cover, put the Dutch oven in a large frying pan half-filled with water and continue to cook, adjusting the heat below this arrangement to make the sauce slowly bubble and replenishing the water as necessary, or transfer the Dutch oven to a preheated 275-degree oven and make sure the sauce is cooking slowly, adjusting the temperature as needed.)

Just before serving, make the pasta according to the package directions. When the pasta is nearly ready to drain, scoop out ¼ cup of the cooking water. Remove the sauce from the heat and stir in the sour cream and the ¼ cup of Parmigiano-Reggiano. Add the pasta water if needed to thin the sauce. Drain the pasta.

Put the sauce in a large, shallow serving bowl, top it with the drained pasta, and toss to coat all the strands. Sprinkle additional Parmigiano on top, and pass more cheese at the table.

Beef Tagine with Prunes, Almonds, Sesame Seeds, and Cilantro

Tagine is the name of both a cone-topped cooking pot and any stewed meat dish. Tagines are a mainstay of Moroccan cooking. This combination of beef and prunes is traditional (as is an almost identical recipe that uses prunes and cut-up chicken instead). Perfumed with ginger, cassia, and saffron, it fills the kitchen with fragrance while it cooks and then offers delight on the plate. Don't omit the garnish of panfried almonds and sesame seeds, and the shower of fresh cilantro—they make the dish! Serve with a flatbread such as naan, or rice, to sop up the sweet gravy.

SERVES 4 TO 6

1 to 2 pounds grass-fed stew beef, cut into 1-inch cubes

Generous pinch of good saffron (about ¼ teaspoon)

20 pitted prunes

1 tablespoon unsalted butter

1 tablespoon extra-virgin olive oil

1 teaspoon ground ginger

2 teaspoons ground cassia (preferably Korintje cassia), or ground cinnamon

¼ onion, finely chopped

Freshly ground black pepper

¼ cup fresh cilantro leaves, coarsely chopped or cut with scissors

2 tablespoons honey

Sea salt

For the garnish:

½ cup whole almonds

1 tablespoon white sesame seeds

Handful of fresh cilantro leaves, coarsely chopped

Rinse the meat in a strainer under cold water, drain well, and blot dry. Infuse the saffron threads by putting them in a small bowl and pouring 2 tablespoons boiling water over them. Put the prunes in another bowl and cover them with cold water to hydrate.

In a Dutch oven, tagine pot, braising pot, covered skillet, or Chinese sand pot (or any heavy pot with a tight-fitting lid and a heavy bottom), melt the butter and olive oil over medium heat. When the fat has liquefied and is fragrant and bubbling, add the ginger, cassia, and onion. Add a generous amount of black pepper, along with the chopped cilantro. Stir-fry this for about half a minute to just get it past raw. Now add the blotted meat and stir to coat with the spice mixture.

Add just enough cold water to cover the meat, and bring the water to a boil. Add the saffron water and half of the prunes, leaving the prune liquid behind. Immediately lower the heat to the lowest possible setting, cover the pot tightly (if your pot does not have a tight-fitting lid, add a sheet of parchment paper under the lid, overlapping the pot, to compensate). Simmer very slowly for 1½ hours.

Uncover the pot and use a fork or paring knife to see how tender the meat has become—it should be tender but not all the way yet. Add the remaining prunes and the honey, along with salt and pepper to taste (and do taste!). Cover the pot again closely and simmer at the lowest setting for another 30 minutes to finish cooking the dish.

During this last phase of cooking, prepare the garnish. Heat a small cast-iron frying pan and add the olive oil. When it is thinned and fragrant, add the almonds and sesame seeds, and cook them over medium heat, stirring, until they are toasted, taking care not to let them burn. Remove them from the pan onto a plate as soon as they are done, and set them aside.

Serve the meat and the gravy in a large, shallow bowl or deep serving platter, garnished with the toasted almonds and sesame seeds and chopped fresh cilantro leaves. Surround the platter with warmed pieces of naan or other flatbread. Alternatively, serve the garnished meat and gravy on top of rice or couscous.

London Broil
(from Beef Chuck Shoulder Steak)

London broil is as much a way of cutting and preparing beef as it is a particular cut of meat. Essentially, it means marinating meat and then slicing it thinly across the grain, much like flank steak. Marinate for as little as 2 hours or as long as overnight, but do bring the meat to room temperature before cooking it. Leftover London broil makes outstanding sandwiches and is also a great addition to salads when thinly sliced.

SERVES 4

2 cloves garlic, finely chopped

2 tablespoons fresh rosemary needles, chopped

Freshly grated zest of 1 lemon

¼ cup extra-virgin olive oil

2 tablespoons red wine or sherry vinegar

1 teaspoon Dijon mustard

1⅓ pounds London broil from grass-fed beef chuck (about 2 inches thick)

2 teaspoons coarse sea salt such as gray Atlantic or Celtic (for pan-searing only)

Blend the garlic, rosemary, lemon zest, oil, wine, and mustard and turn the meat in the mixture so that the marinade coats both sides. Leave at room temperature for 2 hours or refrigerate overnight, taking care to bring the meat to room temperature before cooking.

Heat a dry, seasoned cast-iron frying pan, grill pan, or outdoor grill to high heat. If using a pan, sprinkle the coarse salt over its surface and heat to popping. Remove the meat from the marinade, shaking and blotting to remove any excess, and lay it in the hot pan—it should sizzle. Cook the meat over high heat for about 5 minutes, or until it is browned on one side and does not stick. Turn the meat over and cook on the other side for about the same period of time. Remove from the pan and let the meat rest for 10 to 15 minutes before slicing thinly against the grain.

Beef Chuck Underblade Steak with Ancho Rub and Coffee Sauce

This sauce has become one of my favorites. Try it on any steak and any other chile-pepper-rubbed beef cut, and you'll see what I mean. Think the combination is strange? It's based on chili, which is often spiked with a little coffee (you can use decaf). Start marinating the meat early in the day, and by evening it will be ready to cook. To make your own ancho chile powder, whirl whole dried anchos in a spice grinder. If you don't want too much heat, remove the seeds and inner ribs first.

SERVES 4

4 boneless chuck underblade steaks from grass-fed beef (8 to 12 ounces each)

2 tablespoons ancho chile powder

1 teaspoon paprika

1 teaspoon ground cumin

½ teaspoon kosher salt

1 tablespoon extra-virgin olive oil

¼ teaspoon ground cloves

3 tablespoons light brown sugar

3 tablespoons honey

¼ cup strong black coffee

1 teaspoon Worcestershire sauce

Coarse sea salt such as gray Atlantic or Celtic (for pan-searing only)

2 tablespoons unsalted butter, cut into pieces

Bring the meat to room temperature and blot it dry. Mix 1 tablespoon of the ancho powder, the other spices, and the kosher salt together and rub over the meat. Drizzle the meat with the oil and rub it in. Put the meat in a container and refrigerate for 1 hour.

Start the sauce by combining the cloves, brown sugar, honey, the remaining 1 tablespoon ancho powder, the coffee, and Worcestershire sauce in a small saucepan. Bring this to a boil and immediately lower the heat to the lowest setting. Simmer until reduced by half. Cover and keep warm.

Bring the steaks to room temperature and salt lightly. Grill the steaks over a hot grill outside, or on an indoor grill pan or a dry, seasoned cast-iron frying pan sprinkled with coarse sea salt. Grill to medium rare, 4 to 5 minutes per side. When done, set aside to rest while you finish the sauce.

Bring the sauce back to a simmer. Whisk in the butter until it is thoroughly incorporated. Drizzle the sauce over each steak and serve at once.

Spice-Rubbed Chuck Roast
with Whiskey

Chuck roast, because it's a hardworking muscle (the shoulder), is generally cooked as a braise or otherwise tenderized. Sometimes, though, you just want roast beef. Here's an unusual way to cook a chuck roast, from Chris Schlesinger and John Willoughby. Room-temperature beef is rubbed with spices and left to sit for an hour—then it's cooked first at very high temperature for 20 minutes, and then at low temperature for another hour or so. Including resting, the whole process takes nearly 2 hours. Sliced paper-thin, the roast is rosy and tasty, with an edge from the spices and a shot of single-malt whiskey at the end.

SERVES 10 TO 12

1 (4½-pound) grass-fed beef chuck roast

1 teaspoon coriander seeds

½ teaspoon whole black peppercorns

2 tablespoons Moroccan Spice Blend (see page 31)

¼ cup single-malt whiskey, other whiskey, or amber spirits such as bourbon

Bring the meat to room temperature and blot it dry. Using an electric spice grinder or a mortar and pestle, grind the coriander seeds and peppercorns. Blend them with the 2 tablespoons Moroccan Spice Blend. Rub this mixture all over the meat's surface to form a thick coat. Set aside for 1 hour at room temperature.

Heat the oven to 500 degrees. Using a cast-iron frying pan that's close in size to the roast, roast the meat in the center of the oven for 20 minutes.

Turn the oven's setting to 300 degrees and continue to roast for 1 hour, or until a thermometer probe in the center of the roast reads 122 degrees. Remove the meat from the oven, pour the whiskey over the meat, and let rest for 20 minutes. Remove the meat from the pan and cook the pan juices mixed with the whiskey over medium heat, stirring and scraping up the browned bits to incorporate them into the sauce, until thickened and reduced by a third.

Use an electric knife or a very sharp carving knife to cut the meat into thin slices, drizzle with the sauce, and serve.

Why Does Meat Have to Come to Room Temperature Before You Cook It?

This is a question recipe testers asked over and over. If meat is chilled, it won't cook as evenly, and the timing may be off. When meat is at room temperature, the heat of the pan or oven can immediately begin the cooking process (while the meat remains cold, it is insulated from the heat). Thoroughly blotting away the moisture is also important. That way the meat will begin to sear in a hot pan or oven—if it is wet, it will steam.

Chuck Steak Marinated in Sherry and Toasted Sesame Oil

Marinating Meat

Marinades are wet mixtures, while rubs are dry. Both are effective ways to add flavors to meat. But, while the many spice rubs in this book will certainly add lots of flavor, wet marinades especially enhance steaks with a pronounced grain such as chuck, London broil, and flank steak. If you bear in mind that all marinades are a mixture of oil, acid, aromatics, and (sometimes) sweeteners, you'll be able to devise your own marinades as the spirit and the contents of your pantry move you. Just remember to be cautious with marinades containing soy sauce or other salt-heavy ingredients, because they leach the juices right out of lean grass-fed meat. An hour—no longer—should be allowed for salty marinades.

Here are a few ideas to get started on creating your own marinades:

FISH SAUCE MARINADE

2 tablespoons fish sauce
Juice of 1 lime
¼ cup peanut oil
2 tablespoons Shaoxing wine or sherry
1 tablespoon palm sugar or light brown sugar
½ teaspoon Worcestershire sauce
Finely chopped hot pepper to taste (optional)

RED WINE AND ROSEMARY MARINADE

¼ cup red wine
2 tablespoons soy sauce
½ cup extra-virgin olive oil
2 to 3 cloves garlic, smashed
Leaves from 4 sprigs fresh rosemary, chopped

ORANGE-CHILE MARINADE

Zest and juice of 1 orange
1 tablespoon vodka
⅓ cup coconut oil
1 to 3 teaspoons (depending on taste and tolerance) nam prik pao or other hot sauce
3 cloves garlic, smashed

Briefly marinated in a soy-based mixture, naturally lean grass-fed beef chuck steak lends a weekend festivity to weeknight dining. Use the marinating time to make a big salad or cooked vegetables and a side starch. Then get your grill pan hot, open all the windows or turn on the exhaust fan, and get ready for dinner!

SERVES 2 TO 4

1 boneless grass-fed beef chuck steak (about 1 pound and 1¼ inches thick)

½ cup sherry or Shaoxing rice wine

¼ cup soy sauce

1 tablespoon dark sesame oil

2 cloves garlic, finely chopped

1 tablespoon rice wine vinegar or white vinegar

1 teaspoon light brown sugar

1 teaspoon coarse sea salt, such as gray Atlantic or Celtic (for pan-searing only)

Bring the meat to room temperature and blot it dry. Mix together the sherry, soy sauce, sesame oil, garlic, vinegar, and brown sugar, and pour half into a shallow nonreactive dish, pan, or bowl that will hold the meat. Reserve the remainder of the mixture for making the sauce. Allow the meat to marinate at room temperature for up to 1 hour.

Remove the meat from the marinade and blot it very dry. Discard the used marinade. Set the meat on a pad of paper towels as you heat a dry, seasoned cast-iron grill pan or frying pan over high heat to hot. Sprinkle the sea salt on the surface of the pan, and when it starts to jump or pop, slap on the meat.

Sear for 4 to 5 minutes per side for medium rare. The meat is ready to turn when it no longer sticks to the pan.

Remove the meat to a plate to rest. Turn off the heat under the grill pan and add the reserved marinade mixture. Deglaze the pan in the accumulated heat from cooking, scraping and stirring to incorporate all the caramelized bits of meat. Turn the heat on low and reduce the liquid slowly until it is half its previous volume.

Pour this over the steak, either whole or in slices, and serve.

Mirin-Marinated Chuck Tender "Steak"

Shoulder tender is a braising cut, but because a braise takes a good 5 hours, I wanted to see if there were any alternatives for faster cooking. After reading that in Argentina this cut is grilled fast on high heat, I decided to try it using the stovetop and a cast-iron pan. The key, I discovered, is in cutting the meat two different ways: First, the solid muscle has to be split down the middle horizontally (butterflied) and pounded mercilessly to break the fibers; second, the cooked steak, after a good rest, needs to be sliced extremely thinly (only an electric knife does this to my satisfaction) across the grain and on the bias. If these requirements are satisfied, you've got a fabulous meal in little time.

SERVES 4

1½ pounds grass-fed beef chuck tender

1 tablespoon sesame oil

¼ cup organic shoyu (natural soy sauce) or other soy sauce

¼ cup mirin (sweetened sake) or sherry

Bring the meat to room temperature and blot it dry. Remove any silverskin or membrane that may still be attached. With a sharp boning knife, cut and divide the meat, slicing partway through horizontally, along its long side. Your goal is to open it like a book (if you cut through and make two steaks, that's not a problem either). Using a heavy meat pounder or the bottom of a cast-iron pan, beat the meat flat, working from the center to the edges and trying to make the meat as flat and even as possible. Aim for a ¾-inch-wide steak, if possible.

Mix together the sesame oil, shoyu, and mirin and lay the meat in the marinade, turning it to coat both sides. Leave at room temperature for 30 minutes to 1 hour.

Heat a dry cast-iron pan large enough for the steak on high heat for at least 5 minutes. When the pan is very hot and smoking, remove the meat from the marinade, blot it dry, and put it in the pan. It should sizzle loudly. Reserve the marinade.

Cook the steak for 5 minutes per side, turning it only once and using tongs to avoid piercing the meat. It should develop a good crust on each side, and the pan should continue smoking. After 10 minutes, remove the meat to a board and let it rest for 15 minutes. It will have shrunk dramatically.

Put the reserved marinade in a small saucepan and cook it for precisely 5 minutes at a rolling boil—watch the clock. Remove it from the heat and set it aside.

Slice the meat *very* thinly against the grain, cutting at an angle. Drizzle the cooked marinade over the meat and serve.

Pot-Roasted Chuck Tender with Tomatoes, Cinnamon, and Allspice

Pot roast is mom food of the highest order. This one can be made with any braising cut of beef, but it is rich and satisfying when made with the misleadingly named chuck tender, which requires long, slow cooking to live up to its last name. Make any whole grain to serve alongside, as the sauce is not to be wasted, or shred the meat into the sauce and use it for pasta such as pappardelle, or polenta (this recipe makes enough pasta sauce for 2 nights' worth of dinners). Note that while this cooks for 4 or 5 hours, it can be done in a slow oven, which requires no attention.

SERVES 6 AS A POT ROAST, 10 TO 12 SERVINGS SHREDDED FOR A PASTA SAUCE

2 pounds grass-fed beef chuck tender

Kosher salt

¼ cup extra-virgin olive oil, plus more as needed

½ cup pine nuts

3 onions, roughly chopped into small pieces

1 teaspoon ground allspice

1 teaspoon ground cinnamon

Generous amount of freshly ground black pepper

1 (28-ounce) can chopped tomatoes

1 tablespoon white wine or vermouth or vodka

1 teaspoon pomegranate molasses

For the garnish:

Freshly grated zest of 1 orange

Bring the meat to room temperature and blot it dry. Trim any silverskin and discard. Sprinkle about 1 teaspoon salt over both sides and let sit for 30 minutes.

Heat a braising pot and add the olive oil. When it shimmers, fry the pine nuts until crisp and golden, watching closely and stirring nearly constantly to make sure they don't burn—the process only takes about 45 seconds. Remove with a slotted spoon and set on a plate. Reserve for garnish.

Using the remaining oil in the pot, sear the meat until browned. Remove with tongs and let rest on a plate.

Using the same oil (adding more if necessary), sweat the onions over medium-low heat until they are soft and translucent. Stir in the allspice, cinnamon, and pepper. Make a space in the bottom of the pot and return the meat along with any juices it has released. Add the tomatoes and their juices, along with the wine and the pomegranate molasses. This liquid should reach about three-quarters of the way up the meat; if it doesn't, add a little water or use a smaller pot. Bring to a simmer, reduce the heat to the lowest setting, and simmer until the meat is tender and shredding, 4 to 5 hours. (Alternatively, cook it in a 275-degree oven for the same period of time or more, making it a good candidate for leaving all day.)

Remove the meat with tongs and let rest for 15 minutes. Cook the sauce down over medium-low heat to concentrate its flavors. Taste for seasonings, and add more salt and pepper if necessary.

If serving as a pot roast, slice the meat across the grain and return it to the pot, along with the pine nuts. Serve at once with rice or couscous, garnished with the orange zest.

If serving as a pasta sauce, slice and shred the meat and return it to the gravy, stirring it in. Cook the pasta and drain it and dress it with half the sauce. Reserve the rest for another night (it freezes well, without the pine nuts or orange zest).

Spice and Olive Oil Rubbed Shoulder Tender Steak

The shoulder tender I got weighed half a pound and was round and shaped like the letter J. I straightened it and pounded it flat with a smooth meat mallet, then decided on a spice mix to rub on it with olive oil. I left it for 10 minutes to let some of those flavors ripen. Seared in a hot cast-iron pan, rested, and then cut across the grain, it was delectable and as tender as could be. This is dinner in less than a half hour.

SERVES 1 OR 2

½ pound grass-fed beef shoulder tender

1 teaspoon Salt and Spice Cure (see page 30)

1 teaspoon kosher salt

1 tablespoon extra-virgin olive oil

Bring the meat to room temperature and straighten it out if curled. Using the flat side of a meat pounder or the underside of a small cast-iron skillet, pound the meat from the center to the edges to make it uniformly flat. It should look like a slightly triangular steak with a prominent grain that runs slightly diagonally along its length, and be about ½ inch thick.

Rub each side of the steak with ½ teaspoon of the cure and sprinkle on a like amount of kosher salt. Pour the olive oil into a shallow bowl and dredge the rubbed steak in the oil. Let the steak sit for 10 minutes while you heat a small, dry cast-iron frying pan (about the size of the steak) over high heat. Let it become very hot but not smoking. When the pan is hot, slap down the steak and let it sear (put on the fan or open all the windows!).

Sear for 3 to 4 minutes per side, until the outside is browned and the inside still pink. Remove from the heat and rest on a board for 10 minutes. Slice thinly, on the bias, cutting across the grain.

Serve on a bed of baby spinach or mesclun or on mashed potatoes, polenta, or any starch that will sop up the juices.

Don't Be Afraid to Experiment

Recently, confronted with a chuck tender (a misleadingly named thick, tough pot-roasting cut) when I had planned to grill, I took my sharpest, thinnest blade in hand and butterflied the meat laterally into thinner portions. Once cut, a line of gristle up the center of each side was revealed, and I noticed that the grain of the meat changed direction on either side of this line. I painstakingly cut the gristle out, and divided each piece into two parts, using the gristle as the dividing line. At this point I had four pieces of meat, roughly the same size and close to triangular in shape. I decided to make them into minute steaks, so I butterflied each again, cutting not quite all the way through so that they could open like a book into pieces half as thick but with about twice the surface area. Then I took a meat pounder to them to flatten them further. I bathed them in a soy sauce, mirin, and toasted sesame oil marinade while the grill heated up, and then cooked them rapidly on high heat. They were tasty and tender, proving that cutting tough meat thin enough can yield a delicious, quick-cooking meal. A number of the recipes in this section illustrate ways of cutting and marinating tough portions of the chuck to achieve this effect.

BRISKET: As each animal offers only two brisket portions, this is a cut to treasure. One of the greatest braising cuts of all time, brisket makes for extraordinary pot roast that can be oven-braised or cooked on the stovetop. Alternatively, try cubing brisket to make an unforgettable stew, or smoke it for real barbecue. The key to cooking this cut is to take your time and always use the lowest possible heat.

Brisket of Beef with Red Wine, Prunes, and Spices

Brisket was the first piece of grass-fed beef I ever cooked, and it remains one of my favorite cuts. Slow-cooked to deep tenderness and flavor, this recipe offers a little heat from the ground peppers and a little sweetness from the fruit. It's a recipe I use over and over again with almost every brisket, except for the ones I smoke for real slow-cooked barbecue. If you prefer, you could substitute dried apricots for the prunes or make a half-and-half mix of dried fruit.

SERVES 8

4 to 5 pounds grass-fed beef brisket

1 teaspoon sea salt

1 tablespoon sugar

2 teaspoons ground cumin

1 teaspoon freshly ground black pepper

1 teaspoon potent ground red pepper or hot (picante) pimentón de la Vera (smoked Spanish paprika)

1 teaspoon sweet paprika

2 tablespoons extra-virgin olive oil

1 cup red wine (I use Merlot)

6 onions, sliced

1 cup chicken, turkey, or beef stock, preferably homemade (see page 303, 318, or 124)

4 carrots, thickly sliced

1 (14½-ounce) can whole or diced tomatoes

1 whole head garlic, cut in half, outer papery cover removed

½ pound dried prunes (about 1½ loosely packed cups)

6 sprigs fresh thyme

For the garnish:

Minced fresh flat-leaf parsley

Blot the meat dry. Blend together the salt, sugar, cumin, ground black and red peppers, and paprika and rub the mixture over the dried meat. Let the brisket rest on a rack to bring it to room temperature, about 1 hour. (You could apply the rub a day ahead: Refrigerate the meat until about 1 hour before you intend to cook it, then allow it to return to room temperature.)

Heat the oven to 325 degrees. Heat a large Dutch oven and add 1 tablespoon of the olive oil. When the oil has thinned and become fragrant, brown the meat well on both sides, fat side first, 7 to 10 minutes per side. It is ready to turn when it stops sticking to the pot. Transfer the browned meat to a deep platter and deglaze the pot with the red wine, scraping up any browned bits. Cook the wine down by half and pour it over the meat on the platter.

Wipe out the pot, add the remaining 1 tablespoon olive oil, and sweat the onions until they are soft, translucent, and just beginning to brown. Deglaze the pot with ½ cup of the stock, scraping with a wooden spatula.

Return the meat and reduced wine to the pot, along with the remaining ½ cup stock, carrots, tomatoes, garlic, prunes, and thyme. Cover the pot and set it in the oven for 3 hours, turning the meat every half hour or so. The meat is done when it is meltingly soft and you feel no resistance if you pierce it with a skewer.

Remove the meat to a platter, and cook down the sauce if necessary. One great advantage of grass-fed beef is that the sauce will have very little fat—you can strain and skim it, but you will not collect much at all.

Cut the meat against the grain into thin slices. Top the slices with the sauce and garnish with a shower of parsley.

Brisket, Moroccan Style, with Green Olives and Preserved Lemons

urmeric, ginger, and cinnamon lend this brisket the aroma of a Moroccan medina, while preserved lemons (see page 174), green olives, and masses of fresh parsley and cilantro increase the depth of flavor and add freshness. Do try and make this a day before serving, as an overnight rest deepens the taste. This recipe is adapted from Joan Nathan's Foods of Israel Today, *and it's just wonderful served with large Israeli couscous.*

SERVES 8 OR MORE

6 pounds grass-fed beef brisket

4 cloves garlic

Kosher salt

5 tablespoons extra-virgin olive oil

½ cup sweet red vermouth

4 large onions, diced (about 8 cups)

½ teaspoon ground turmeric

½ teaspoon ground cinnamon

1 teaspoon ground ginger or grated peeled fresh ginger

Generous amount of freshly ground black pepper

Sugar

3 bay leaves

1 stalk celery, finely diced

1 carrot, thinly sliced

1 (28-ounce) can diced tomatoes

1 cup water

½ pound Moroccan green olives, pitted

⅓ cup roughly chopped fresh flat-leaf parsley

⅓ cup roughly chopped fresh cilantro

3 preserved lemons, rinsed, flesh discarded, and peel finely chopped

Rinse the meat, blot it dry, and leave it on a wire cake rack (so air can circulate around the meat) for 30 minutes. Heat the oven to 350 degrees, and set a rack in the center.

Rub the whole brisket with the cut side of 1 clove of garlic. Lightly dust the meat with ½ teaspoon salt. Cut the garlic into slivers and use a small pointed knife to make shallow slits in the meat, especially where it is fatty. Push slivers of garlic into the slits.

Heat a large casserole or Dutch oven (one big enough to hold the brisket flat) over medium-high heat and add 2 tablespoons of the olive oil. When the oil is thinned and fragrant but not smoking, sear the meat on both sides until browned, about 30 minutes. Transfer to a deep platter using tongs (to avoid piercing the meat).

Add the ½ cup vermouth to deglaze the pan, scraping and cooking for 2 minutes. Pour over the meat and wipe out the pan.

Add another 2 tablespoons of oil to the pan and sauté half of the onions until they are translucent. Add the turmeric, cinnamon, ginger, pepper, sugar (reserving 1 pinch), bay leaves, celery, carrot, and half the tomatoes with their juices. Reduce the heat to low, to incorporate everything, and cook for a minute or two.

Push the onion mixture to one side, return the brisket to the pan, then rearrange the onion mixture around it. Add the water, pouring down the side of the pan.

Use a piece of parchment paper to make a tight inner seal by pushing it down close to the meat and onions. Cover and roast for 3 hours, or until the meat is completely tender.

While the brisket roasts, blanch the olives by boiling them in a pan of water for 1 minute, then drain them. Taste them, and if they are still very salty, blanch them again with fresh water. Set aside.

Heat the remaining 1 tablespoon olive oil and sauté the remaining onions until they are limp and translucent. Add a pinch of sugar and a pinch of salt, along with the remaining diced tomatoes, and simmer for 3 to 4 minutes, covered, until the onions lose their raw taste. Set aside.

When the meat is done, allow it to cool completely (never slice brisket while it is hot if you can help it). Refrigerate the meat in its liquid overnight, if possible. This will make it easier for you to remove the fat. Cut the meat against the grain and on the diagonal into ¼-inch slices, then return the sliced meat to the pan along with the juices and the vegetables it cooked with.

Before serving, heat the oven to 350 degrees. Bake the sliced brisket in its juices for 30 minutes, or until heated through. Gently heat the tomato-onion sauce in a saucepan over medium-low heat, along with half of the parsley and cilantro, the olives, and the preserved lemon peel.

Arrange the brisket and vegetables on a serving platter. Cover with the warmed sauce and a shower of the remaining parsley and cilantro. Serve at once.

> **BEEF SHANKS:** Beef shanks, usually crosscut (and sometimes labeled "shin bones"), are the basis for a number of memorable dishes. Even when the meat is cut off and used for stew or ground beef, naked shank bones hold *gold*! That's because they are filled with the most delicious marrow.

Braised Crosscut Beef Shanks, Yemeni Style

What makes this slightly spicy dish special is the homemade Yemeni Spice Blend. The flavor mellows and deepens as it cooks because, like most braises, this one cooks slowly for a long time, rewarding the cook with melting texture. I've written this recipe for one or two crosscut shanks weighing about a pound and a half, which is how they are often packaged, but it can also be made with smaller pieces.

SERVES 2 OR 3

1½ pounds crosscut grass-fed beef shanks

1 teaspoon extra-virgin olive oil

2 onions, cut into wedges

1 or 2 fresh tomatoes, chopped or grated

4 cloves garlic

1 teaspoon Yemeni Spice Blend (see page 31)

1 small chile such as jalapeño, halved and seeded

Sea salt and freshly ground black pepper

3 or 4 pieces of flatbread, torn into smaller pieces

Bring the shanks to room temperature and blot them with a paper towel.

Heat the oven to 275 degrees and position a rack in the center. Using a large enameled cast-iron Dutch oven or other braising pot on the cooktop, heat the olive oil over low heat until it is thinned and fragrant. Brown the shanks on all sides, move them to a plate, pour off the fat, and wipe out the pot.

Put the shanks back into the pot and fill it with cold water to cover the meat. Bring the water slowly to a boil, and skim off any residue that forms in the first 15 minutes of slow-boiling. When the liquid is clear, add the onions, tomato, garlic, the spice blend, jalapeño, and salt and pepper to taste. Transfer the pot to the oven to simmer for 4 hours, or until the meat is completely tender. Remove the meat from the pot, and if the sauce is thin, reduce it on top of the stove, uncovered, until it thickens.

Serve on top of flatbread to sop up the gravy.

Tomatoes on the Box Grater

Paula Wolfert showed me this great trick: When you grate a whole ripe tomato on the largest holes of a box grater, the pulp comes out finely chopped and the skin remains in your hands (and out of the dish you are cooking). It's an easy way to add fresh tomatoes without having to blanch, shock, and peel them.

Crosscut Beef Shank Osso Bucco

This variation on the classic Italian dish does not use the traditional, more thinly cut veal shank, but instead calls for a large crosscut grass-fed beef shank, whole or in pieces. It cooks up into a wonderful braise studded with shreds of beef. The traditional dish is served with risotto, but I usually pair it with plain rice, pasta, or polenta.

CUT SHEET ALERT: Ask your processor to slice the shank into ½-inch slices, bone and all.

SERVES 2 OR 3

1 large crosscut grass-fed beef shank (about 1½ pounds and 3½ inches thick)	2 fresh large ripe tomatoes, grated (see box, opposite) or 2 to 3 drained canned tomatoes
¼ cup unbleached all-purpose flour	2 bay leaves
	4 sprigs fresh thyme
Salt and freshly ground black pepper	1 cup dry white wine
3 tablespoons extra-virgin olive oil	1 cup chicken stock, preferably homemade (see page 303) or water
2 large yellow onions, finely chopped	Freshly grated zest of 1 lemon
2 cloves garlic, finely chopped	½ cup chopped fresh flat-leaf parsley

Bring the shank to room temperature and blot it dry. Dredge it through the flour, coating on all sides. Salt and pepper it thoroughly.

Heat an enameled cast-iron Dutch oven over medium heat and add 2 tablespoons of the olive oil. When the oil has thinned and become fragrant, brown the meat on all sides (about 10 minutes), taking care not to burn it and lowering the heat if necessary. Transfer the meat to a plate, pour off the oil, and wipe out the pot.

Return the pot to the stove over medium-low heat and add the last tablespoon of olive oil. When it is hot, add the onions and garlic and cook gently until wilted but not browned.

Add only the pulp of the tomatoes (not the skin, if you are using fresh ones). Use a box grater to grate the tomato flesh (see page 86), or squeeze them by hand over the pot to break up the pulp while dropping it into the pot. Add the bay leaves and thyme sprigs, along with the meat. Pour the wine and stock over all. Bring the contents of the pot to a slow simmer, cover, and cook for about 1 hour over the lowest possible heat that maintains the slow simmer.

After 1 hour, add half the lemon zest and cook for another 30 minutes or so, until the meat is falling off the bone. Remove the lid and reduce the liquid by about half, stirring often to make sure that nothing burns or sticks. The sauce should become visibly thicker and silky, studded with shreds of beef. The bone is filled with delicious marrow that can either be reserved and eaten separately (perhaps for tomorrow's lunch?) with salt and parsley (see page 88) or be pushed out and added to the braise.

Serve the osso bucco over rice, pasta, or polenta. Mix the remaining lemon zest with the parsley and garnish the finished dish with it.

Roasted Shank Bones or Marrow with Parsley Salad

Although roasted marrow bones are a staple of traditional French bistro menus, Fergus Henderson offers a version at his London restaurant St. John that is paired with a salty parsley salad, and it's unforgettably good. It is extremely easy (and fast) to make at home, even if you don't have any experience with marrow bones. Since my meatless shank bones came 5 inches long and two to a package (the ideal length would have been 2 to 3 inches), I've written the recipe to reflect that. On next year's cut sheet, I hope to remember to ask for shorter pieces. You can get long, fancy marrow spoons to help with the task of getting the marrow out of longer bones, or you can just use a chopstick to push it out onto the plate instead.

CUT SHEET ALERT: Ask the processor to crosscut all shank bones, with or without meat on them.

SERVES 4 AS A FIRST COURSE OR
2 AS A LIGHT DINNER

1½ pounds grass-fed beef shank bones without meat

½ cup fresh flat-leaf parsley, stems removed

1 shallot

1 teaspoon salt-packed capers, well rinsed

1 tablespoon extra-virgin olive oil

1 teaspoon fresh lemon juice

4 to 8 slices of great bread such as diagonally cut French baguette

Coarse sea salt such as gray Atlantic or Celtic or other good crunchy salt

Heat the oven to 450 degrees. Bring the bones to room temperature, rinse them, and blot them dry. Spread foil on a sheet pan and stand the bones upright in the pan. Roast the bones for about 15 minutes.

Meanwhile, make the parsley salad by roughly chopping the parsley, shallot, and capers using a chef's knife or by pulsing in a food processor.

Put these ingredients in a bowl and pour the oil and lemon juice over them, tossing to coat. Toast or grill the slices of bread until golden. Have the crunchy salt ready, along with 4 serving plates plus a kitchen plate to work on.

When the bones are leaking very, very slightly onto the foil, they are done. Remove them from the oven with tongs, then use a sharp steak knife or long paring knife to cut deeply around the edges of the marrow within each bone. Invert the bone onto the kitchen plate to remove the marrow, doing this at each end if it doesn't all fall out in one go.

To assemble the dish, spread each piece of toast with the marrow, sprinkle generously with salt, and top with the parsley salad. Serve immediately.

RIBS: Tender and luscious, steaks and roasts from the rib are always celebratory. These are the kinds of steak made famous by steakhouses, often paired with a baked potato and creamed spinach. Even more festive, standing rib roast is a dish best saved for a holiday or special occasion. Because grass-fed beef is naturally lean, cook these cuts to medium rare (or rare) to showcase their flavor and texture, and always rest the meat well before slicing.

Flatiron (Top Blade) Steak

his tender and flavorful cut is best rubbed with a salt-and-spice mix and cooked only to medium rare. Like all juicy sliced steaks, this is wonderful served on a bed of raw or cooked greens, or with polenta.

SERVES 2

¾ to 1 pound grass-fed
flatiron steak

1 tablespoon Salt and
Spice Cure (see page 30)

½ cup red wine (optional)

Bring the steak to room temperature, rinse it, and blot it dry. Rub it with the spice mix and let it sit for 30 minutes.

Heat a grill pan or grill to high heat, and when it is hot, slap the steak onto the grill. Cook for about 2 minutes, then reposition the steak so that the grill marks will cross the grill marks you just made, for a total of 4 minutes for the first side, and about 3 minutes for the second side. Let the steak rest for 10 minutes before slicing thinly on the diagonal, much like a flank steak.

If you wish, deglaze the pan with the wine, cooking the sauce down by half and drizzling it onto the sliced steak.

Delmonico Steak with Faux Bordelaise Sauce

here's some controversy about what cut of meat a Delmonico steak really is—a top sirloin, bone-in top loin (from the short loin), or rib eye. Although some say it can only be rib eye, in my experience, steaks labeled "Delmonico" can be boneless or bone-in and come from different parts of the cow. Wherever the steak comes from, it is always tender and rich, and it's made even more so by its nearly traditional accompaniment—my version of Bordelaise sauce. (If you want to go all out, add mashed potatoes topped with grated cheese and bread crumbs.)

I call my sauce faux because classic Bordelaise uses bone marrow and demi-glace, which are not always found in the average home pantry. I substitute butter for the marrow (although if you have marrow, do use it!). If you don't have homemade beef stock, be wary of using beef bouillon for two reasons: First, it's not from grass-fed beef, and second, it tends to be salty. If you save the drippings from roasting beef, you may have a supply of the dark jelly that separates from the fat—if so, use this culinary gold here instead of stock.

SERVES 2

For the steak:

1½ pounds grass-fed Delmonico steak

2 tablespoons coarse sea salt such as gray Atlantic or Celtic (for pan-searing only)

For the sauce:

¼ teaspoon black peppercorns

4 tablespoons (½ stick) unsalted butter or bone marrow (see page 88), diced

¼ cup finely chopped shallots

½ cup red wine

Leaves from 1 small sprig fresh thyme

1 cup beef stock, preferably homemade (see page 124), greatly reduced, or ½ cup of the jelly layer formed by saved beef drippings

Bring the meat to room temperature, rinse it, and blot it well.

Heat a dry, seasoned cast-iron frying pan large enough to hold the steak flat. When the pan is hot, add the salt so that it is scattered all over the pan. When the salt begins to pop, add the steak.

Cook until the meat no longer sticks to the pan, about 3 minutes. Turn it and cook the other side the same way, removing the meat promptly to rest on a plate while making the sauce.

Coarsely crack the peppercorns in a mortar and pestle or in a plastic bag using the underside of a cast-iron frying pan. Set aside.

Heat a shallow pan such as a frying pan over medium-low heat, and then add half the butter (or marrow) until gently melted.

Over medium heat, cook the shallots in the fat until translucent and wilted, about 2 minutes. Add the wine and cook until it has reduced by half, 3 minutes or so.

Lower the heat and add the thyme and peppercorns and cook until there is very little liquid left, being careful not to burn the contents of the pan.

Add the reduced beef stock or beef jelly and the remaining half of the butter, and cook, whisking as needed, for about 5 minutes or until further reduced and silky.

Pour the sauce over the steak and serve.

Salt and Spice Beer-Braised Whole Beef Back Ribs

Beef back ribs are the beefy equivalent of pork spare ribs—full of great flavor and made for finger-licking barbecue. They're what's cut off of a boneless rib roast (they're left on for a standing rib roast), so be sure to ask for all the bones if ordering a rib roast off the bone.

Here, the meaty bones are rubbed with a salt and spice rub and oven-braised in beer for 2 hours or more at moderate heat. When they come out of the oven, they can either be slathered with barbecue sauce and quick-roasted in a covered grill over medium-low heat (or under the broiler) until sticky and heated through, or served straight from the braise with a honey-basil dipping sauce.

NOTE: The recipe also works well with pork ribs.

SERVES 2 TO 4

2¾ pounds grass-fed beef back ribs (about 7 ribs)

4 to 5 tablespoons Salt and Spice Cure (see page 30)

1 (12-ounce) bottle good dark beer

For barbecue sauce:

Blend ½ cup ketchup, 2 tablespoons tomato paste, ¼ cup cider vinegar, ¼ cup honey, and a dash of Tabasco.

For honey-basil sauce:

Purée the leaves from 1 bunch fresh basil with ½ cup honey.

Heat the oven to 325 degrees. Choose a low-sided pan such as a broiler pan or sheet pan that will hold the meat in one layer, flat, with room for some liquid.

Rinse off the ribs and blot the meat. Rub the ribs on all sides with the Salt and Spice Cure, put them in the pan, bone side down (meaty side up), and pour the beer down the side of the pan to avoid washing the spice cure off the meat. Using heavy-duty aluminum foil, seal the pan well to keep all the steam inside.

Braise, covered tightly with foil, for 2 hours or more, until the meat starts to shrink away from the bones and is very tender.

If grilling and using barbecue sauce, heat a covered grill to medium-low or use an indoor broiler, and while it is heating up, brush the ribs generously with barbecue sauce on both sides. Place them on the hot grill or under the broiler, and heat through until a sticky glaze forms, about 10 minutes.

Alternatively, serve the ribs as they emerge from the braise, using honey-basil sauce as a dipping sauce.

Resting Meat Before Carving

Resting meat before carving allows the juices to settle and redistribute throughout the muscle. If you carved it straight out of the oven, it would release all its juices onto the carving board and leave you with dry slices of meat. Bringing meat to room temperature before cooking it, using a thermometer to confirm the internal temperature, allowing time for the cooking to finish after you remove the meat from the oven, thus resting it before you carve, may be the most important factors in cooking any meat—but they are especially important for grass-fed meat, which is naturally leaner. When resting meat, cover it loosely with just a drape of foil (you don't want to steam it), or nothing at all if your kitchen is warm. That 10- to 20-minute rest will make an extraordinary difference in the way it tastes.

Standing Rib Roast Rubbed with Pimentón de la Vera and Salt, Served with Red Wine Sauce

Pimentón de la Vera is Spanish smoked paprika, and it's a genuine "secret ingredient" that makes food taste wonderful. This recipe is adapted from Chef Ashley Christensen's recipe in Bill Niman and Janet Fletcher's Niman Ranch Cookbook, *and it is both easy and stunningly good. I serve the meat with corn grits and garlicky greens. I've written this recipe for a 3½-pound rib roast from a small cow. If you are cooking a larger roast, scale the rest of the recipe accordingly by doubling the rub ingredients and adding a little time to the cooking (use a meat thermometer to be sure you are not over- or undercooking), but no matter what size your roast is, start the meat at the higher cooking temperature for only 15 minutes before reducing it for the balance of the cooking.*

SERVES 4

1 grass-fed beef rib roast (4 ribs, about 3½ pounds)

3 cloves garlic

Kosher salt

1 teaspoon freshly ground black pepper

1 tablespoon sweet (*dulce*) pimentón de la Vera (smoked Spanish paprika)

¾ cup red wine

2 tablespoons heavy cream (optional, but helps to smooth out the sauce)

Remove the meat from the refrigerator and blot it dry on all sides. Cut each garlic clove into slivers. Using a sharp paring knife, make cuts into the fat parallel to the meat but not piercing it. As you make each cut, insert a garlic sliver into it.

Blend 1 teaspoon salt, the pepper, and the pimentón in a small bowl. Sprinkle this onto every side of the meat and rub it in. Let the meat rest at room temperature for 45 minutes to 1 hour.

Meanwhile, heat the oven to 450 degrees. Select a roasting pan that just holds the meat, as one that is too large will evaporate all the pan juices before you can recover them. A cast-iron frying pan will also do, as will a clay cazuela (if you have a gas stove—clay can't take direct electric heat without a flame tamer and you'll be deglazing this pan on the stove eventually). Set the meat in the pan, fat side up.

Roast for 15 minutes at 450 degrees, then lower the heat to 350 degrees and roast for another 45 minutes, or until the internal temperature is between 125 and 130 degrees. (Larger roasts can take as much as an additional 40 minutes to get to temperature.) Remove the meat from the oven to a platter and let it rest for a good 15 minutes, during which time the internal temperature of the meat will increase to rare.

While the meat is resting, put the roasting pan over medium-low heat and deglaze the pan with the red wine, scraping with a wooden spatula to loosen any browned bits and incorporate them into the sauce. Allow the wine to bubble slowly and reduce by about half, keeping an eye on it and stirring as necessary. Remove the sauce from the heat and add the cream (if using), swirling it in to enrich the sauce. Taste the sauce for salt and correct, if necessary. Pour the sauce into a gravy boat or pitcher.

Carve the meat in one fell swoop off the bones, reserving them. (These bones make excellent eating for those who like to gnaw, so save them for tomorrow's lunch, if you wish. They are the same ribs you cook for beef ribs on the grill.) Slice the now boneless roast into thin slices and drizzle them with sauce or pass the sauce separately at the table.

PLATE: Slowly braising short ribs with aromatics over the lowest possible heat produces outstanding dishes. Such long, slow cooking allows flavors to blend and intensify to produce comforting, deeply layered tastes and melting textures. These patiently prepared dishes are the kind of home food that makes memories.

Short Ribs Braised with Juniper Berries, Red Wine, and Prunes

When you've got good, meaty short ribs, this is the dish to cook. And if you should happen to have the gelatinous stock left from cooking oxtail (see page 123), this is the time to pull it out of the freezer. If not, any good beef or chicken stock will do as the braising medium, along with red wine. This dish tastes best when made over 2 or 3 days to allow the flavors to meld and to make time to chill the sauce and defat it, but it can also be made in 1 day if you use a defatting pitcher.

SERVES 4

2 pounds grass-fed beef short ribs (flanken), cut into serving portions

Kosher salt and freshly ground black pepper

2 tablespoons extra-virgin olive oil

2 tablespoons unsalted butter

1 tablespoon unbleached all-purpose flour

1 cup red wine

4 cups beef or chicken stock, preferably homemade (see page 124 or 303)

1 cup prunes, pitted and cut into pieces

2 carrots, cut into 1-inch chunks

1 onion, cut into wedges or thick slices

2 bay leaves

1 tablespoon juniper berries, smashed or bruised

5 whole cloves

3 tablespoons honey

Bring the meat to room temperature and blot it dry. Salt and pepper it on both sides, put it on a plate (uncovered), and leave it for several hours or overnight in the refrigerator. This preliminary salting tenderizes the meat and promotes flavor, and unlike a soy marinade, doesn't seem to dry out the meat.

Bring the meat back to room temperature. Heat the oven to 325 degrees and position an oven rack in the center of the oven. Using an enameled cast-iron 3- or 5-quart Dutch oven, heat the olive oil. Brown the meat well on all sides over medium-high heat, in batches if necessary, at least 8 minutes in all. Remove the meat to a plate, and pour off the oil in the pot, leaving any browned bits stuck to the bottom.

Using the same pot, melt the 2 tablespoons butter over medium heat and sprinkle the flour over it. Cook, stirring, for 2 or 3 minutes, until this paste has a pale golden color. Add the wine, stirring and scraping up any browned bits, and then add the stock. Bring to a boil, reduce the heat, and add the prunes, carrots, onion, bay leaves, juniper berries, cloves, and honey. Return the meat and any juices it has released to the pot, cover, and put the pot in the oven to cook for 2 hours, or until the meat is very tender and about to fall off the bone.

Use a slotted spoon to remove the meat from the liquid, setting it aside to rest. Strain the liquid through a sieve to remove all the aromatic solids, pressing them with a wooden spoon to add their last bit of flavor to the liquid before discarding them.

At this point, you have two choices: Either pour the liquid through a fat-separating pitcher before serving (or before reducing it further, if it is too watery) or chill the liquid overnight to make removing the congealed fat easier. In either case, after removing the fat and carefully reducing the sauce, if desired, reheat the meat in the sauce before serving each portion on top of your starch of choice, whether mashed potatoes, noodles, rice, or other grain.

Red Wine–Braised Short Rib Sauce with Pappardelle or Polenta

This recipe makes enough rich sauce for 2 nights' worth of dinners, so I always freeze a quart of it to serve to company at a later date. I pair it with pappardelle, or with polenta (see page 366). Here, short ribs are first browned on top of the stove, and then oven-braised for 2 hours in a 300-degree oven. They're delicious just for eating off the bone at that point, too.

If you make this sauce a day ahead, the flavors will deepen and mellow; it's also much easier to remove the fat from the chilled sauce. Skim the chilled fat with a spoon, then remove the meat from the bones, shred it, and return it to the sauce. Put away half in an airtight, close-fitting freezer container and reheat the rest gently while you prepare the pasta.

NOTE: The recipe also works well with crosscut beef shanks.

MAKES ABOUT 2 QUARTS SAUCE, ENOUGH TO SERVE 4 AS A MAIN COURSE

¼ cup extra-virgin olive oil

1 stalk celery, roughly chopped

1 leek (white part only), cleaned and thinly sliced

1 onion, roughly chopped

2 cloves garlic, roughly chopped

1 large carrot, roughly chopped

4 cups chicken stock, preferably homemade (see page 303)

Salt and freshly ground black pepper

2 pounds grass-fed beef short ribs

¼ cup unbleached all-purpose flour, for dredging

1 cup red wine (whatever you have opened, or a good drinkable red)

1 cup tomato purée (canned is fine)

4 sprigs fresh thyme

2 cinnamon sticks

1 bay leaf

1 package dried pappardelle (I like Bionature brand, which comes in an 8.8-ounce package and cooks in 4 minutes)

Garnishes:

2 tablespoons chopped fresh flat-leaf parsley

Freshly grated zest of 1 orange

Heat the oven to 300 degrees.

Using a 5-quart braising pot such as an enameled cast-iron Dutch oven with a tight-fitting lid, heat 2 tablespoons of the olive oil over medium-low heat. When the oil is fragrant and has thinned, add the celery, leek, onion, garlic, and carrot, and stir them to coat. Cook these vegetables for about 10 minutes over medium-high heat, or until they begin to caramelize and brown but not burn. When they are lightly browned, remove them to a bowl and deglaze the pan with ½ cup of the chicken stock, scraping up any browned bits with a wooden spoon. Add this stock to the bowl of vegetables and wipe out the cooking pot with a paper towel.

Put the remaining 2 tablespoons olive oil in the pan and set it to heat slowly. Salt and pepper the short ribs and dredge them in flour. Shake off any excess. When the oil is hot but not smoking, brown the short ribs until darkly golden. Transfer these to the bowl and pour off any accumulated fat. Deglaze the pan with the red wine, scraping up any browned bits with a wooden spoon, and cook down the wine by one-third.

Add the tomato purée, the balance of the chicken stock, the thyme sprigs, cinnamon sticks, and bay leaf. Return the meat and vegetables to the pot, bring it to a slow simmer, cover the pot, and transfer it to the oven.

(If you feel your cover is not a tight fit, take a sheet of parchment paper cut to a size slightly larger than your lid and push it down to nearly touch the meat, then place the lid over that to help prevent steam from escaping.)

Braise for 2 hours, or until the meat shrinks from the bones and shreds easily with a fork. If serving at once, remove the meat and skim the fat from the sauce using a spoon or by pouring the sauce through a fat-separating pitcher. When the meat has cooled sufficiently, cut it from the bones and shred it into thin pieces. Return the meat to the sauce.

If you are freezing a portion, pour it into a freezer container. Let cool to room temperature, cover tightly, and freeze.

Taste the remaining sauce and add salt to taste. Reheat the sauce gently (you don't want to boil away all that carefully created water-soluble slow-cooked flavor, so use the lowest possible heat and keep an eye on the sauce) while boiling the water for preparing the pappardelle according to the package directions.

Drain the pasta and serve it at once, transferring it to a prewarmed shallow platter and tossing it well with the meat sauce. Garnish with the chopped parsley and orange zest, and serve.

FLANK: Marinated flank steaks make great family meals, as long as they are carefully cooked only to medium rare. Be sure to slice the meat on the bias, holding the knife at an angle, cutting across the grain, thinly.

Flank Steak with Maple and Soy Glaze

Because flank steak has an open grain, it absorbs flavor beautifully. Use half this glaze as a marinade, then save the rest to use as sauce at the table.

SERVES 4

2 pounds grass-fed
flank steak

⅔ cup rice wine vinegar

½ cup soy sauce

½ cup mirin (sweetened
sake) or sherry

½ cup maple syrup

1 teaspoon coarse sea salt
such as gray Atlantic or
Celtic (for pan-searing only)

Bring the meat to room temperature and blot it dry.

In a small, heavy saucepan, simmer the rice wine vinegar, soy sauce, mirin, and maple syrup over low to medium heat until the mixture is reduced by a third and thickened considerably. This will take about 20 minutes.

Pour half of the mixture into a container large enough to use for marinating; reserve the rest to reheat for serving.

Marinate the meat in the refrigerator for several hours or overnight. When ready to cook, bring the meat to room temperature and blot it dry.

Heat a charcoal or gas grill, or heat the broiler or a dry, seasoned cast-iron pan on the stove (if using a pan, put the coarse sea salt in the pan and wait until it pops before proceeding). Sear the meat for about 6 minutes, then turn and cook on the other side for another 5 minutes, or until the meat is pink in the center and crusty brown on the surface.

Remove the meat from the heat and let it rest for 15 minutes. Meanwhile, reheat the reserved glaze over low heat.

Slice the meat on the bias, angling the knife on the diagonal and cutting across the grain. Aim for thin slices, using an electric knife if you have one, or a very sharp, thin-bladed carving knife. Drizzle the warm sauce over the sliced meat, and serve.

FLANK

BEEF

95

SHORT LOIN: Steaks and roasts from this primal are enticingly tender, and should be cooked no more than medium rare. Strip loin steaks cook best on the grill or in a cast-iron pan. Serve them with a reduced wine glaze, or rub the meat with spices before searing. Slice the precious tenderloin into medallions to make a dish that's perfect for the most special of occasions, served with a rich sauce.

Tenderloin Medallions, Tournedos Style

Tournedos, an elegant and classic quick-cooking French restaurant dish, are always made from tenderloin. Here, I've paired them with a red wine reduction enriched with butter, shallot, and mustard. This is my idea of a romantic dinner for two, but you can cook as many medallions as you have guests.

SERVES 2

2 grass-fed beef tenderloin medallions (about ¼ pound each and 1 inch thick)

1 tablespoon coarse sea salt such as gray Atlantic or Celtic (for pan-searing only)

Generous amount of freshly ground black pepper

1 tablespoon unsalted butter

1 small shallot, diced

½ cup red wine

1 tablespoon Dijon mustard

Bring the meat to room temperature, rinse it, and blot it dry on both sides.

Heat a dry, seasoned cast-iron pan just large enough to hold the medallions over high heat, and sprinkle the salt across the surface of the pan. When the salt starts to pop, slap the meat down, and pan-sear it for 3 to 4 minutes per side. Transfer the cooked meat to a serving platter, using tongs or a spatula so as not to pierce the meat. Pepper each medallion generously.

Immediately reduce the heat under the pan to low and add the butter. When it has melted, add the shallot and stir-fry until it is limp. Deglaze the pan with the red wine, scraping up any browned bits and reducing the volume by half.

Remove the sauce from the heat and stir in the mustard.

Strip Loin Steak with Garlic and Red Wine Sauce

imple, fast, and delicious—what more could you want? This is a master recipe for any steak with a red-wine reduction sauce.

SERVES 2

¾ to 1 pound grass-fed strip loin steak

1 clove garlic, cut in half

1 to 2 tablespoons coarse sea salt such as gray Atlantic or Celtic (for pan-searing only)

Freshly ground black pepper

½ cup robust red wine such as Montepulciano d'Abruzzo

1 teaspoon unsalted butter

Bring the meat to room temperature, rinse it, and blot it dry. Dry-age it on a cake-cooling rack set over a bed of paper towels overnight in the refrigerator, or on the counter for about 30 minutes.

Rub the meat all over with the cut side of the clove of garlic. Heat a dry, seasoned cast-iron frying pan over high heat, and scatter the sea salt over the surface. When the salt begins to pop, slap down the steak and turn on the kitchen fan. Sear the meat on both sides until brown, about 8 minutes in all.

Transfer the steak to a plate to rest for at least 10 minutes, and grind pepper over the surface. Pour the red wine into the frying pan and scrape the pan to incorporate anything sticking to the pan. Reduce the liquid by half over medium-high heat. Remove from the heat and swirl in the butter.

Slice the steak and plate it, pouring sauce over the slices.

Spice-Seared Strip Loin Steak with Indian Flavors

dapted from a recipe by The Healthy Butcher, Toronto's grass-fed meat retailer, this spice blend lends loin steak South Asian flavors. Try serving it with Coconut Rice (see page 365) and cooked spinach topped with toasted sesame seeds and dried shaved coconut flakes.

SERVES 2 TO 4

¾ to 1½ pounds grass-fed strip loin steak

1 teaspoon ground coriander

1 teaspoon sugar

1 teaspoon ground cumin

1 teaspoon freshly ground black pepper

½ teaspoon curry powder

½ teaspoon kosher salt or fine sea salt

1 teaspoon coarse sea salt such as gray Atlantic or Celtic (for pan-searing only)

Bring the meat to room temperature, rinse it, and blot it dry.

Combine the coriander, sugar, cumin, pepper, curry, and kosher or fine sea salt and rub this on the steak. Let sit for 30 minutes at room temperature or in the refrigerator, depending on how warm the kitchen is.

When ready to cook, choose a dry, seasoned cast-iron frying pan that fits the meat, and heat it to a high temperature. Toss on the coarse sea salt, and when it begins to pop, slap on the spice-rubbed steak.

Sear for about 4 minutes per side, or until the steak is dark on the outside and rosy within. Set the meat aside to rest for 10 minutes before slicing it thinly across the short side and serving.

Top Sirloin Steak with Baby Spinach and Home Fries

Sirloin steak has real tenderness and consequently cooks best when rapidly pan-seared or grilled over high heat until the outside is crusty and the interior is rare. This is a very fast and easy dinner.

SERVES 2 TO 4

2 to 4 cups raw baby spinach, washed and spun dry

¼ cup extra-virgin olive oil, plus more for drizzling

1 or 2 large waxy potatoes, very thinly sliced

Salt and freshly ground black pepper

1 pound grass-fed sirloin (top loin) steak

¼ cup red wine

Arrange the spinach across the surface of a serving platter and set it aside.

Heat the olive oil in a cast-iron skillet over medium-high heat and fry the potato slices until crisp on both sides. Remove them from the hot pan and arrange them in a single layer on top of the raw spinach.

Salt and pepper the steak, and wipe out the pan. Return it to the stovetop over high heat, and pan-sear the steak until browned on the outside and medium rare within, 3 to 4 minutes per side. Remove the steak from the pan and lay it over the potatoes and spinach to rest and to further wilt the spinach.

Turn off the heat. Immediately pour the red wine into the hot pan and scrape up any particles sticking to the pan to incorporate them. Pour this sauce over the meat along with a drizzle of olive oil. Serve at once, dividing the steak at the table.

Sirloin Steak with Red Wine

ecause the beef I buy is from smaller-sized Dexter or Lowline cows, the steaks are somewhat miniature. I find that a half-pound piece of meat can easily feed two if served on a bed of good mesclun salad, accompanied by a loaf of great artisanal bread. If your steaks are larger, plan accordingly.

SERVES 2

½ pound grass-fed sirloin steak

1 tablespoon coarse sea salt such as gray Atlantic or Celtic (for pan-searing only)

2 cloves garlic

½ cup red wine

Small knob of unsalted butter

2 cups mesclun mix, washed and spun dry

Kosher salt

1 tablespoon good red wine vinegar

1 teaspoon grainy mustard

3 tablespoons extra-virgin olive oil

Freshly ground black pepper

Blot the meat, rinse it, and let it sit, exposed to air on a wire-grid cooling rack, for at least 30 minutes before cooking.

Heat a dry, seasoned cast-iron frying pan or grill pan, and sprinkle it with the coarse sea salt. Turn on the exhaust fan.

Cut 1 clove of the garlic in half, and rub the cut side over the surface of the meat (discard the garlic once used). When the pan is hot, slap the steak down on the salt—you should hear a sizzle. Turn the meat after 3 minutes (if it sticks, give it a little more time and heat the pan longer next time). Cook on the other side for another 3 to 4 minutes. Using tongs, transfer the meat from the hot pan and set it on a plate to rest for 10 to 15 minutes. Turn off the heat.

Pour the red wine into the same pan and stir up the browned bits on the bottom to incorporate them into the sauce. Reduce the mixture to about 2 tablespoons, melt in the butter, and set aside.

Put the mesclun mix in a shallow serving bowl or deep platter. Lightly salt it and toss. Finely mince the remaining clove of garlic.

Mix the salad dressing by combining the vinegar, mustard, and garlic in a small jar or drinking glass. Slowly pour in the olive oil while mixing with a fork or tiny whisk so that the mixture emulsifies. Toss the mesclun with this dressing and divide it between 2 plates.

Slice the steak with the grain, at an angle. Place the slices on top of the dressed mesclun, and drizzle the red wine reduction on top. Grind black pepper over all and serve.

ROUND : A large hardworking primal with a wide array of offerings, the round yields cuts made for braising, as well as oven roasts and steaks. When cut thinly, almost any part of a grass-fed beef round can be pounded, marinated, and cooked like a steak, or rolled and stuffed before braising. When thickly cut, these pieces are usually pot-roasted, or further cubed for stew. Eye of round makes a great roast beef.

Minute Steaks, Cuban Style

Thinly sliced minute steaks are another cut from the round. Because minute steaks cook so quickly, they do not get too chewy. Here they are briefly marinated in a Cuban-inspired citrus blend and then served with white rice and an onion salsa. If you can get sour oranges, use them here in place of the orange-and-lime blend. But, whatever you do, don't be tempted to use bottled orange juice or lime juice—take the trouble to squeeze it yourself. If you prepare the rice and the marinade at the start of cooking, everything will be ready at the same time. This is a very speedy weeknight meal.

SERVES 4

For the rice:

3 cups water

1 teaspoon kosher salt

1½ cups medium-grain white rice

For the marinade, meat, and salsa:

Freshly grated zest and freshly squeezed juice of 1 orange

Freshly grated zest and freshly squeezed juice of 2 limes

1 clove garlic, very finely chopped

1 pound (4 to 6) grass-fed minute steaks

1 large onion

½ cup fresh flat-leaf parsley leaves

Salt and freshly ground black pepper

1 tablespoon extra-virgin olive oil

Bring the water to a boil, add the kosher salt and rice, and lower the heat to the lowest possible setting. Simmer, covered, for 20 minutes, or until the rice is cooked through and little holes mark the surface.

While the rice is cooking, make a marinade using all of the orange zest and half of the orange juice and the zest and juice of 1 of the limes. Add the garlic. Rinse and blot the minute steaks and put them in the marinade for 15 minutes.

While the meat marinates and the rice cooks, make the salsa in the small bowl of a mini food processor by puréeing the onion, parsley leaves, zest and juice of the remaining lime, and the remaining juice from the orange. Scrape the sides of the bowl down as necessary to make a slightly chunky purée. Taste it and add salt and pepper, then set it aside to mellow while you cook the meat.

Heat a cast-iron or other large frying pan, add 1½ teaspoons of the olive oil, and wait until it is thinner and liquid. Add as many minute steaks as can fit without crowding, and cook these over high heat for 1 or 2 minutes per side, until slightly browned. Be careful not to overcook them. Remove the steaks to a platter and repeat for the remaining steaks, using the remaining 1½ teaspoons oil.

Serve at once, putting a generous amount of rice in the center of each plate, topping this with a minute steak, and topping the steak with a big spoonful of salsa.

ROUND

BEEF

Red Barn Spiced Eye of Round Roast with Beer Sauce

ubbing this no-grind spice blend (named for my barn home) onto the surface of an eye of round an hour before roasting provides an intense spicy edge on each slice. Because you'll want to slice this very thinly when it's rested, use an electric knife if you can, or a very sharp thin slicing blade if you prefer hand-slicing.

SERVES 4 TO 6

4½ to 5 pounds grass-fed eye of round roast

5 tablespoons Red Barn Spice Rub (see page 32)

For the sauce:

1 (12-ounce) bottle dark beer such as Negra Modelo

2 tablespoons heavy cream

Rub the spice mix all over the beef. Let the meat sit at room temperature for about 1 hour.

Heat the oven to 350 degrees. Using a pan that fits the long, thin roast as closely as possible, such as an oval oven-proof frying pan or gratin pan, or a small sheet pan (with sides) that can hold the roast on a diagonal, roast the meat, fat side up, for 20 minutes, then raise the oven temperature to 425 degrees for 15 minutes, or until the internal temperature reaches 130 degrees. Transfer the meat to a platter and let it rest for 15 minutes while you make the sauce.

Deglaze the roasting pan with the beer, scraping to incorporate any caramelized bits of meat. If necessary (if your pan is not stovetop heatproof), pour the contents into a saucepan. Add any juices that have accumulated under the resting roast, along with another tablespoon of Red Barn Spice Rub, and boil this mixture down until it is reduced by almost half (it should be 1 to 1¼ cups in all), about 15 minutes over high heat. Off the heat, whisk in the cream to incorporate.

Slice the meat very thinly across the grain, arranging the slices on individual plates or a serving platter. Nap each slice with a little sauce.

On Surface-Salting Raw Grass-Fed Meat

When meat is lightly salted before cooking, it seems to incorporate the salt flavor into the meat, rather than leaving it on the surface. I try to layer flavors as I cook, so salting a little on the surface of the meat before cooking gives me room to add more salt later if necessary. (Note that this is different from soaking meat in a liquid marinade with salt, which drains the meat of juice.) Salt added to a spice rub promotes flavor and brings out the inherent sweetness in a dish—it is always a good addition to grass-fed beef.

Marinated Bottom Round Roast

When you marinate with oil, vinegar, and spices, while the flavors penetrate only the top layer of the meat, they do add a flavored edge to each slice. The longer the meat marinates, the stronger the flavor, so marinate this overnight if possible, or all day if not. Because the spices here sing with an Indian accent, I like to serve this with saffron rice sprinkled with shredded coconut and offer a little chopped fresh cilantro on the side. It's essential to slice the meat extremely thinly, since it's not a naturally tender cut.

SERVES 4 TO 6

2 to 4 pounds grass-fed bottom round roast

For the marinade:

½ cup extra-virgin olive oil

2 tablespoons sherry vinegar

1 teaspoon ground coriander

1 teaspoon sugar

1 teaspoon ground cumin

1 teaspoon freshly ground black pepper

½ teaspoon curry powder

½ teaspoon kosher salt or fine sea salt

2 to 4 pounds grass-fed bottom round roast

Salt and freshly ground black pepper

Rinse the meat and blot it dry. Mix the marinade ingredients together in a bowl big enough to hold the roast, and roll the roast in the marinade. (You can do this in a resealable freezer bag if you prefer.) Marinate the meat in the refrigerator for as long as possible (either overnight or all day).

Half an hour before cooking, heat the oven to 325 degrees and remove the meat from the refrigerator.

Put the roast in a roasting pan or ovenproof frying pan that is not much bigger than the piece of meat, and salt and pepper it lightly. Pour the marinade over the meat and roast the meat for 20 minutes a pound, or until an internal meat thermometer reads between 140 and 145 degrees.

Discard the marinade, and let the meat rest for 15 minutes to continue to cook and allow the juices to settle before carving very thinly.

Beef Round Sirloin Tip Steak

This cut is a slice of the bottom round roast, and as it is thicker in some areas and thinner in others, it offers several cooking choices. You could braise it as a pot roast, or pound, roll, and stuff it as Involtini (see page 110). Alternatively, this cut can be butterflied (cut horizontally almost enitrely to make an evenly thick piece of meat), marinated, and cooked like a flavorful (but not so tender) steak. Finally, still-partially-frozen sliced round can be made into homemade beef jerky (see page 108).

Beef Round Sirloin Tip Roast

*D*on't be fooled by the sirloin reference in the name of this cut; this is a part of the round, a working muscle that generally offers more flavor than tenderness. Nevertheless, this end of the round (also known as the knuckle) makes an outstanding roast beef, especially when rubbed with Salt and Spice Cure (see page 30), cooked in this high-low fashion, and then sliced thinly. The probe style of meat thermometer, a model that can be read outside the oven, is especially helpful here. Any leftovers make memorable sandwiches.

SERVES 4 TO 6

2½ pounds grass-fed beef round sirloin tip roast

1 onion, finely chopped (mashed in a mortar and pestle, if desired)

2 cloves garlic, finely chopped or mashed

¼ cup Salt and Spice Cure (see page 30)

1 tablespoon extra-virgin olive oil, plus a little to grease the pan

½ cup red wine

1 tablespoon unsalted butter or cream or crème fraîche (see page 28)

Salt and freshly ground black pepper, as needed

Bring the meat to room temperature and blot it dry. Using a mini food processor or a larger food processor fitted with the steel blade, process the onion and garlic with the cure seasonings and the olive oil, scraping down the sides of the bowl as necessary, until the mixture forms a paste. Rub the meat well with this paste on all sides and let it rest for about 1 hour before you roll it up and tie it with kitchen twine.

Heat the oven to 425 degrees, using convection if possible. Choose and lightly grease a pan that will fit the rolled-up meat closely, such as an oval iron gratin pan or a small cast-iron frying pan. Cut 4 or 5 lengths of kitchen twine, each about a foot long. Lay these in a row across a cutting board.

This roast is thicker at one end than the other, so you will roll from the thin end to create a roast that will cook evenly. Put the meat crosswise on top of the strings with that thinner part facing you and roll it into a neat package of equal thickness throughout. Use the twine to make a series of loops or knots around the meat along its length (see page 24).

Place the roast in the pan, seam side down. When the oven has come to temperature (at least 20 minutes after turning it on), put the meat in the oven. Roast without disturbing for 30 minutes—*do not open the door!* Then reduce the heat to 375 degrees for another 12 to 15 minutes, until an internal thermometer stuck in the middle of the roast reads 120 degrees.

Let the roast sit on the counter on a platter for at least 15 minutes before carving, to allow the juices to settle.

While the meat is resting, make a pan sauce by placing the roasting pan over medium heat and adding the red wine, scraping the pan to dislodge any caramelized bits, and incorporating them into the sauce. Working quickly, before the wine has reduced completely, add the butter or cream and immediately remove the pan from the heat. Taste for seasoning, adding salt and pepper as necessary.

Slice the meat thinly, drizzle the sauce over it, and serve.

Marinated Beef on a Stick

Skewered chunks of meat seem to be perfect summer food— easy to make and even easier to eat. Serve this with mounds of rice pilaf or couscous, along with a big salad, yogurt and cucumber sauce, and the all-important flatbread such as tandoor naan or pita or lavash. Here, portions of round or chuck are made into kebobs (this is another good alternative to grinding such scraps into hamburger; you can ask for kebob meat when you fill out a cut sheet). The meat is marinated in Middle Eastern spices and citrus for a couple of hours before grilling. This recipe also works for lamb kebobs, with about the same timing. Choose Nishat's Chutney (see page 160) or Musab's Cilantro, Mint, and Yogurt Chutney (see page 165) to make as a condiment, alongside purchased pickles and chutney.

SERVES 4

For the marinade:

4 cloves garlic, chopped or put through a garlic press

¼ cup extra-virgin olive oil

2 tablespoons red wine vinegar

2 tablespoons freshly squeezed lemon juice

1 teaspoon tomato paste

¼ teaspoon ground allspice

¼ teaspoon ground cardamom

¼ teaspoon ground cassia (preferably Korintje cassia) or ground cinnamon

¼ teaspoon freshly ground black pepper

¼ teaspoon crushed red pepper flakes

For the kebobs:

1 pound grass-fed stew beef, cut for kebobs, or meat from the round or shoulder, cut into 1-inch cubes

4 onions, cut into wedges from stem end to bottom to preserve the core

1 green bell pepper, cored and cut into 1-inch pieces

Cherry or grape tomatoes, or larger tomatoes cut into wedges like the onions

Combine all the marinade ingredients in a nonreactive bowl or refrigerator container and add the meat. Stir it to coat with the marinade, and leave to soak for 2 to 3 hours, but no longer. (If you soak the meat longer, it will begin to "cook" in the citrus—like ceviche—and discolor.)

Heat an outdoor grill to very hot. (If using a gas grill, add some soaked wood chips to provide a smoky flavor.) Soak 4 wooden skewers in cold water for 15 minutes, or use 4 metal skewers.

Remove the beef from the marinade and blot it dry. Thread each skewer with an alternating assortment of meat, onion wedges, pepper pieces, and tomatoes (or tomato wedges). Thread the wedge-cut vegetables through the wedge from wide arc to wedge core to help prevent food from falling off the skewer.

Grill, turning as appropriate, until the meat does not stick and is seared on the outside and rare within, about 6 minutes in all.

Present the skewers on a platter, with large pieces of flatbread and condiments of chutney and yogurt-and-cucumber sauce placed in bowls all around, so that each person can pull the food off the sticks with the bread to make a wrap, drizzling on condiments as desired.

Beef Stew with Vermouth, Yam, and Mint

*A*ny stew is a slow braise in which time and moisture combine to bring meat to fork-tenderness. This one sings with some Middle Eastern flavors, although I like to serve it with wild rice, a distinctly American grain. It's also perfect with couscous. Note that you'll need a big sauté pan with a cover for browning the meat and a Dutch oven to cook the stew in. The whole process will take about an hour and a half. Prepare your favorite starch as the stew simmers, so that they'll be ready together. Use stew beef or meat labeled "boneless beef pieces," or cut up a larger piece of round yourself.

SERVES 4

1 to 1½ pounds grass-fed stew beef or boneless beef pieces, cut into evenly sized chunks

½ teaspoon kosher or sea salt, plus more to taste

3 tablespoons extra-virgin olive oil

½ teaspoon freshly ground black pepper, plus more as needed

½ teaspoon ground allspice

½ cup white vermouth or white wine

1 onion, thinly sliced

1 garnet yam, peeled and cut into 1- to 2-inch cubes

1 eggplant, peeled and cut into 1- to 2-inch cubes

1 tablespoon pomegranate molasses

½ teaspoon ground ginger

4 to 8 fresh mint leaves, cut into slivers

Blot the meat and bring to room temperature on a rack over paper towels or in a colander so that it drains. When you are ready to prepare the meat, blot it again and sprinkle it with the salt.

Heat 1 tablespoon of the extra-virgin olive oil in a hot sauté pan big enough to hold the meat in one layer if possible (if not, plan on browning it in two batches). The meat should sizzle as it hits the hot pan. Brown it well on all sides (this will take 10 to 15 minutes). Add ¼ teaspoon each of the black pepper and allspice, and stir the meat to distribute the spices. Pour the Vermouth over, and use a wooden spatula to scrape up any bits that have stuck to the pan and incorporate them into the sauce. Cover the pan, reduce the heat to very low, and slow-simmer the stew for 30 minutes.

Meanwhile, in a large Dutch oven, heat the remaining 2 tablespoons olive oil over medium heat. Sweat the onion until it is soft and translucent but not browned. Add the yam and eggplant cubes and cook, stirring occasionally, to allow the vegetables to soften, about 10 minutes. Add the remaining ¼ teaspoon black pepper and allspice, along with the meat and its liquid. Add boiling water to cover the whole mass by a scant inch, and cover the pot. When the stew returns to a boil, reduce the heat to medium-low and simmer slowly until the meat is fork-tender, about 1 hour.

Stir in the pomegranate molasses, ginger, and mint. Taste for salt and pepper and serve.

Beef and Olive Stew with Scented Red Wine

Make the marinade and soak the meat the day or night before serving and then cook it down with the meat the next day. Even an everyday red wine cooked down with orange rind, cinnamon, whole cloves, and peppercorns gains lots of character. I make this winter stew in an enameled cast-iron #22 Dutch oven, and it perfumes the whole house as it cooks. The topping is optional, but highly recommended; it does really add a nice bright finish.

SERVES 4

For the marinade:

⅔ cup red wine

Zest of 1 orange removed with a vegetable peeler in big strips

1 stick cinnamon

3 whole cloves

½ teaspoon whole black peppercorns

1 bay leaf

4 or 5 sprigs fresh thyme

1 to 1½ pounds grass-fed stew beef

1 teaspoon extra-virgin olive oil

¼ cup chopped bacon or pancetta (or all olive oil, if preferred)

1 onion, finely chopped

1 carrot, finely chopped

1 stalk celery, finely chopped

1 cup water or beef stock, preferably homemade (see page 124)

1 cup olives, mixed green and black or all one type

Kosher salt

For the optional topping:

1 clove garlic, finely chopped

½ cup finely chopped fresh flat-leaf parsley

Finely grated zest of 1 lemon

Mix the marinade ingredients together and add the beef. Refrigerate all day or overnight.

Heat the oven to 325 degrees.

Remove the meat from the marinade, reserving the marinade. Bring the beef to room temperature and blot it dry. Heat the pot you will cook the stew in, and add the olive oil. Brown the meat on all sides and remove it to a plate.

Add the bacon or pancetta to the pot and cook it over medium-low heat to render the fat (or use ¼ cup olive oil); add the onion, carrot, and celery. Cook, stirring occasionally, until the vegetables have softened, 5 to 7 minutes. Return the meat to the pot, along with the marinade. Add as much water or stock as necessary to just cover the meat. Add the olives and salt to taste. Bring just to a boil and immediately remove from the heat.

Put the pot in the middle of the oven and slow-bake for about 2 hours, or until the meat is soft and fragrant. If you plan to use the topping, mix all the chopped ingredients together.

To serve, discard the stems left from the thyme, as well as the orange peel. Ladle the stew into shallow bowls on top of noodles, polenta, rice, or mashed potatoes. Sprinkle with a little of the topping.

Red Wine–Braised Beef Pot Roast with Porcini, Rosemary, and Cloves

This is the essence of good home cooking, the food your children will remember you for, and any friend lucky enough to eat at your table will reminisce about this meal for years! Have a coffee filter ready to strain the mushroom water, and plan to make polenta (see page 366) while the stew cooks. Use a good red wine here—it doesn't need to be great—the flavors do come through.

SERVES 6 TO 8

½ ounce dried porcini mushrooms

½ cup extra-virgin olive oil

1½ cups minced onions

2 tablespoons pancetta or bacon

Salt and freshly ground black pepper

1 cup shredded carrots

6 bay leaves

6 whole cloves

2 sprigs rosemary

3 to 4 pounds grass-fed beef round or other pot roast cut

1 tablespoon tomato paste

1 (750 ml) bottle good red wine

1 cup coarsely chopped drained canned plum tomatoes

6 cups beef or chicken stock, preferably homemade (see page 124 or 303), low-salt, if purchased

Heat about 1 cup water to hot and soak the porcini in it until soft, about half an hour. Strain the soaking liquid through a paper coffee filter and reserve the clear liquid. Discard the hard stems, dice the mushroom caps, and set them aside.

In a large Dutch oven, heat the oil over low heat, and sweat the onions and pancetta or bacon until golden, about 7 minutes. Season lightly with salt and pepper, add the carrots, bay leaves, cloves, and rosemary, and stir. When the carrots are wilted, remove the contents of the pot using a slotted spoon and set aside.

Blot the meat, season it with salt and pepper, and add it to the fat remaining in the pot. Over medium-high heat, brown the meat on all sides, about 15 minutes in all. Reduce the heat, return the onion mixture to the pot, add the tomato paste, and stir well. Add the wine and simmer over medium-low heat for 30 minutes, turning the beef occasionally.

Add the plum tomatoes, the porcini and their liquid, and about 5 cups of the stock, or just enough to reach close to the top of the meat. Bring to a simmer and cook, covered (setting a piece of parchment paper just above the level of the food), until the meat is tender, about 2½ hours. (Alternatively, you can start the meat on the stove and then place it in the oven at 350 degrees for 2 hours.) The meat should be pretty tender when done.

Remove the meat from the pot and set it aside for the moment. Pour the sauce through a sieve, pressing on the solids to extract all the goodness.

Return the meat and strained sauce to the pot, and simmer slowly, uncovered, until the liquid is reduced by about a third and the meat is extremely tender, another 30 to 60 minutes.

Rest the meat on a cutting board for 15 minutes, then cut it crosswise and on an angle into ¼-inch slices (an electric knife is great for this).

Arrange the meat on a serving platter on top of polenta, and pour the sauce over it.

Beef Jerky

was so excited when I realized I could make my own jerky from grass-fed beef. Note that it's really crucial to have the meat nearly frozen when you try to slice it; otherwise, it just shreds. The degree of thin-slicing you need is nearly impossible to do by hand, even with the sharpest of knives. These days, I use an electric meat slicer, but in the past I have cut the meat to fit the feed tube of a food processor before partially refreezing it. Then it can be easily cut with the thin slicing disk. This jerky is based on a recipe from Lisa Fain's blog, The Homesick Texan. Be careful— it is easy to overdry the meat and end up with pieces of petrified wood (obviously, I did this once), so keep a close eye on the meat while it dries.

MAKES ABOUT 45 PIECES

½ pound boneless grass-fed beef top round or sirloin tip roast, fat trimmed, partially frozen

¼ cup Worcestershire sauce

2 tablespoons water

1 garlic clove, finely chopped

1 teaspoon chili powder

½ teaspoon ground dried chipotle

½ teaspoon freshly ground black pepper

¼ teaspoon salt

¼ teaspoon cayenne

Using a meat slicer or a food processor, cut the partially frozen meat into thin strips about ⅛ inch thick and as long as possible.

Choose a medium bowl and mix the Worcestershire sauce, water, chopped garlic, chili powder, chipotle, black pepper, salt, and cayenne. Put the meat strips into this marinade and turn everything over with your hands. Cover the bowl with plastic wrap and refrigerate overnight to allow the flavors to blend and penetrate the meat.

The next day, heat the oven to 175 degrees. Line 2 sheet pans with foil. Arrange the meat strips side by side on the pans, discarding any bits of garlic and blotting off any liquid clinging to the meat.

Slow-roast the strips for 3 hours, then turn them over and roast for another hour or two more. The goal is a leathery texture that is *still pliable*. The jerky will keep, refrigerated, for 3 weeks. It is stable enough to pack in lunches or for trips as long as a day without refrigeration.

Sauerbraten

This recipe is one of my favorites and is worth every minute of the 4 days of soaking and the 4 hours of cooking it takes to make. It's like beef barbecue without the smoke—not everyone has access to a low-temperature slow-smoker, and this is definitely the next best thing. Traditional sauerbraten uses honey-cake crumbs or gingersnap crumbs at the end to further sweeten or thicken the sauce (some people prefer raisins for this), but I find the sauce to be perfectly sweet, reduced, and not fatty (thanks to the grass-fed beef) just as it comes from the pan. The usual accompaniments are potatoes and red cabbage, but I also like rice with this sauce and shredded meat.

SERVES 4 TO 6

2¾ pounds grass-fed top round roast

1 cup red wine

1 cup water

½ cup vinegar such as red wine, cider, or champagne vinegar

1 small onion or shallot, cut into wedges

6 whole black peppercorns

6 juniper berries

6 whole cloves

2 bay leaves

½ teaspoon kosher salt, plus more as needed

2 tablespoons extra-virgin olive oil

¼ cup sugar

On day one, bring the meat to room temperature and rinse it and blot it dry. In a large pot, bring the wine, water, vinegar, onion, spices, bay leaves, and the ½ teaspoon salt to a boil, covered. Lower the heat and let this mixture simmer for 5 minutes. Turn off the heat and let it cool.

Put the meat in a lidded nonreactive container large enough to hold it flat along with the cooked marinade. A large glass refrigerator dish with a cover is perfect, if you have one; otherwise, a bowl tightly covered with plastic wrap will do. Refrigerate this for 3 or 4 days, turning the meat once or twice a day to make sure that the marinade reaches all the surfaces.

When you are ready to cook, heat the oven to 325 degrees and position the rack in the middle. Remove the meat from the marinade. Strain the marinade through a sieve to remove the solids, and save the liquid. Blot the meat dry. Heat a large Dutch oven and add the olive oil. When the oil is hot and fragrant, brown the meat deeply on both sides, about 15 minutes in all.

Set the browned meat on a dish to rest, and pour off any oil left in the pot. Add the strained marinade to the pot, along with the sugar, and bring this mixture to a boil. Stir to make sure the sugar is dissolved, and remove from the heat. Put the meat and any juices that have accumulated on the plate back into the marinade, and cover the pot. Slow-simmer the meat in the oven for 4 hours, or until it can be cut with a spoon.

Remove the meat from the marinade, and let it rest for at least 30 minutes or until cool enough to handle. Slice it thinly along the grain so that it forms shreds. (If you prefer slices, cut against the grain on the bias.)

If the marinade is not already thick and flavorful, cook it down over low heat on the stovetop (I find it is usually perfect just as it is).

Place the meat on a platter and drizzle it with the sauce, or return it to the pot and mix the shreds with the sauce. Any leftovers will be even better in the days to come.

Involtini

These beef roll-ups are the stuff of memory—they are the kind of food a doting Italian mother makes for her family for a special occasion. Essentially, involtini are pounded thin strips of beef, spread with an herb pesto, then layered with fatty pork such as pancetta or bacon, and then with slices of cheese. They are rolled up, dredged in flour, and browned before being braised in a wine bath. Although they are rather a lot of trouble, they taste wonderful. They also offer another alternative to having tougher cuts made into ground meat. Making culinary gold out of those hard-to-use cuts is very satisfying.

You will need to have your meat semifrozen to slice it well. After that you'll need to defrost the slices completely before proceeding, so allow enough time (a day, for example) for these preliminary steps. These days I use an electric rotary meat slicer, but in the past I've used a sharp knife or cut the meat to fit in the feed tube of a food processor fitted with the thin slicing blade after semifreezing it.

You will also need a way to pound the meat—a meat pounder, or the underside of a cast-iron frying pan—and you'll need to decide whether you want to secure the roll-ups with kitchen twine or wooden toothpicks, or take your chances without securing the rolls at all. I have tried all three methods, and twine offers the most fail-safe method; toothpicks are easier to put in but harder to remove; doing nothing is a bit risky but not impossible if you roll tightly and start the browning process with the seam side down to secure the filling.

SERVES 4 TO 6

1 to 2 pounds semifrozen grass-fed beef top round or bottom round	As many thin slices Parmigiano-Reggiano as there are beef strips
1 cup mixed chopped fresh flat-leaf parsley and basil leaves	As many thin slices pancetta or bacon as there are beef strips
½ onion	½ cup unbleached all-purpose flour
1 clove garlic	1 teaspoon unsalted butter
Salt and freshly ground black pepper	½ cup white wine
2 tablespoons extra-virgin olive oil	

Slice the semifrozen beef as thinly as you can, using a sharp knife, an electric rotary meat slicer, or (if the meat has been cut to fit the feed tube) the thinnest slicing blade of a food processor. Lay out each slice on a sheet of waxed paper and let the meat defrost, either at room temperature for about an hour or overnight, well wrapped, in the refrigerator. (The recipe can be done ahead to this point and the meat refrigerated for as long as a day.)

Sandwich a slice of defrosted meat between two sheets of plastic wrap. Working on a wooden cutting board, so that you don't damage your counter, pound the meat to an even thinness, aiming for about ⅛ inch, pounding from the center to the edges. Set each finished slice on waxed or parchment paper in a sheet pan, placing another sheet of paper on top of the pounded slices to add another layer of meat, if necessary.

Make a paste of the basil and parsley, onion, garlic, salt and pepper, and 1 tablespoon of the olive oil in a food processor or using a mortar and pestle. You want a chunky purée.

Using a cheese shaving knife, cut as many thin slices of cheese as there are slices of meat (these tend to break into shards, but it's not a problem). Use a sharp knife to do the same with the pancetta if it is not already sliced.

To assemble the involtini, lay out a beef slice, spread it evenly with about ¼ inch herb paste, then add a slice of pancetta, followed by the cheese. Roll firmly, starting from the short end. Either tie the bundle like a package using kitchen twine (see page 26), use a toothpick to secure the end of the roll, or do nothing to secure the roll. Repeat the process for all the beef slices.

Pour the flour into a shallow bowl and dredge each roll, shaking off the excess. Heat the butter and the remaining tablespoon olive oil in a large pan with a tight-fitting lid; the pan should be big enough to hold all the rolls in one layer. Brown the rolls on all sides over medium-high heat. This will take 5 to 8 minutes.

Add the wine, reduce the heat to the lowest possible setting, and cover. Cook for 45 minutes, adding water if necessary, until the beef is tender. (This is a good time to make rice or polenta, as well as a salad or side vegetable.)

Remove any strings or toothpicks from the beef rolls and serve with the pan sauce poured over the meat.

OFFAL AND ODD BITS: Unless you have grown up eating offal, or come from an offal-eating ethnic tradition, you will probably feel the *ew* factor when you contemplate cooking tongue, heart, kidneys, or some other lesser-known cut of the animal you've purchased. It's worth persevering, however, because such variety meat offers extraordinary eating.

Grilled Beef Heart on a Bed of Salad Greens with Roasted Beets

This easy-to-like dish is adapted from a recipe by San Francisco chef Chris Cosentino (his restaurant is Incanto), who is a great advocate of nose-to-tail eating. His Web site, offalgood.com, is a wonderful source of information and terrific recipes for lesser-known cuts of meat. For his version of this dish, Chris takes marinated meat and grills it fast to crusty perfection, then serves it on a bed of roasted golden beet salad sparked with a champagne vinegar and horseradish dressing. It's a real winner, but a lengthy process. In the interest of making a recipe for more harried cooks, I have abbreviated it. The heart is briefly brined before marinating and fast-grilling. The thinly sliced meat is served with salad greens and purchased or home-cooked beets.

SERVES 4 TO 8 AS A SALAD COURSE OR LIGHT LUNCH

For the marinade:

3 cloves garlic

Leaves from 12 thyme sprigs

1 cup freshly squeezed orange juice

1 cup white wine

1 tablespoon extra-virgin olive oil

For the meat:

1 half or whole grass-fed beef heart (1 to 2 pounds)

¼ cup kosher salt

For the salad:

3 to 4 beets, roasted or steamed, or 1 (8-ounce) package precooked, vacuum-sealed beets

10 ounces salad greens

¼ cup champagne vinegar or other good white wine vinegar

1 tablespoon prepared horseradish such as Gold's

2 tablespoons freshly squeezed orange juice

1 cup extra-virgin olive oil

Start the marinade by chopping the garlic and thyme together. Put the mixture in a bowl and add the orange juice, white wine, and olive oil. Set aside to let the flavors develop while cleaning and brining the meat.

Clean and trim the heart by removing all the visible fat, sinew, and silverskin using a sharp knife. Using a large bowl, dissolve the salt in a little hot water. Add the heart and cold water to cover, give it a good stir, and soak it for 30 minutes.

Remove the meat from the brine and rinse it well under cold water. Put it on a cutting board and check to see if any silverskin remains. Cut to divide each chamber into a separate piece of meat, slicing sideways so that the meat lies flat (as you do this, you may find spots you missed trimming). Discard the trim and cut the meat into 2-inch strips along the grain. Put it in the marinade to soak for at least 30 minutes, or up to 2 hours.

Meanwhile prepare the salad: Cut the beets into rounds or wedges, or run them through the grating disk of a food processor. Wash and dry the salad greens and chill them. Make the vinaigrette by combining the vinegar, horseradish, and orange juice, then drizzling in the olive oil as you whisk the dressing, until it is slightly emulsified.

Heat the grill or a grill pan or the broiler to high. Blot each piece of meat dry with a paper towel or cloth. Cook the meat by grilling each piece for about 3 minutes per side for medium rare.

To serve, combine salad ingedients and dress the salad with the vinaigrette. Distribute it onto plates. Slice the meat very thinly, and arrange the slices over the dressed salad.

Beef Heart Stew with Tomatoes, Black Olives, and Herbes de Provence

Beef heart can be simply cut up and made into stew after a short soak in a brine to expose the bits that need removing. Try this long, slow braise with Provençal flavors to see the versatility of this often ignored cut.

SERVES 4

1 grass-fed beef heart (about 1½ pounds)

½ cup kosher salt, plus more as needed

Freshly ground black pepper

¼ cup unbleached all-purpose flour

2 tablespoons extra-virgin olive oil

1 salt-packed anchovy fillet, rinsed and cleaned

3 cloves garlic, chopped

2 large onions, roughly chopped

½ cup red wine

1 (14-ounce) can whole tomatoes

1 tablespoon Herbes de Provence Blend (see page 32)

1 cup black olives, pitted

1 bay leaf

1 tablespoon salt-packed capers, drained and rinsed

4 Yukon Gold potatoes, peeled and cut into ½-inch cubes

Wash the heart and trim all visible fat and membranes. Make a brine with 3 quarts water and the kosher salt, and let the heart sit in it for 1 hour or so. Remove and rinse, then cut off any other extraneous bits that show up, such as silverskin. Blot the meat dry and cut it into 1- to 2-inch cubes. Lightly pepper the meat and toss it with the flour to coat.

Using a Dutch oven or a braising pan, heat 1 tablespoon of the olive oil until it thins and becomes fragrant. Cook the anchovy and garlic together over very low heat, stirring as necessary, for about 1 minute. Add the onions and cook them down slowly to limpness. Transfer this mixture to a bowl and reserve.

Wipe out the pot and add the remaining 1 tablespoon olive oil. When it is hot, brown the meat, in batches if needed to prevent crowding, until brown on all sides. Deglaze the pan with the red wine, scraping up any browned bits and reducing the wine to half its original volume.

Return the onion mixture to the pot and add the tomatoes with their juices. Add the herb blend, olives, bay leaf, capers, and potatoes. Simmer very slowly over the lowest possible heat, covered, for 3 to 4 hours, until the meat is tender. Taste and adjust for seasonings and serve in bowls.

Beef Heart

I recently learned from a grass-fed-beef dealer that heart is usually ground into hamburger. It is often mixed into ground meat because the USDA doesn't classify the heart as organ meat or "variety meat." Thus it's not, technically, offal, even though it is an internal organ. In short, you've probably been eating beef heart for years! But treated with respect and cooked by itself, it can offer a dish that is special in its own right.

Beef Liver Mousse

Serve this silky and elegant mousse with toast points or crackers at a party, or use it as a spread for sophisticated sandwiches made with great artisanal bread, a little mustard, and arugula.

MAKES ABOUT 4 CUPS (LEFTOVERS WILL KEEP FOR 3 TO 4 DAYS, REFRIGERATED)

1½ quarts water

12 whole black peppercorns

3 stalks celery, finely chopped

2 bay leaves

1 pound grass-fed beef liver

5 tablespoons unsalted butter

2 cloves garlic, minced

1 onion, diced

1 tablespoon cognac

2 teaspoons kosher salt

1 teaspoon fresh thyme leaves

½ teaspoon ground allspice

3 to 4 tablespoons heavy cream

3 tablespoons whole green peppercorns packed in water, drained

Using a deep pan, heat the water with the black peppercorns, celery, and bay leaves. When it comes to a boil, turn down the heat and cook at a slow simmer for about 10 minutes. Add the liver and gently poach it for 10 minutes more over the lowest possible heat (it should be cooked to pink inside). Drain the liver and discard the poaching liquid and flavorings.

When the liver is cool enough to handle, use your hands to tear it into smaller pieces, pulling off and discarding the rubbery membrane. Put the liver in the bowl of a food processor fitted with the steel blade.

Melt the butter in a skillet and sauté the garlic and onion gently over low heat until the onion is limp.

Using the food processor, purée the liver, onion, garlic, cognac, salt, thyme, allspice, and cream until smooth and silky. Add 2 tablespoons of the green peppercorns and just blend them in.

Pour the purée into a serving dish, cover with plastic wrap, and refrigerate until chilled. Serve the mousse sprinkled with the remaining 1 tablespoon green peppercorns and accompanied by toast points or crackers.

Beef Liver with Onions and Red Wine Glaze

Each whole animal you buy will yield up to thirty 1-pound packages of liver, with several pieces per package. I find grass-fed beef liver to be just as tender as calf liver. The trick is to cook it rapidly in a very hot cast-iron pan so that the outside sears and the interior remains tender and rare. This is my favorite way of cooking beef liver; my family never seems to tire of it.

SERVES 2 TO 4

1 pound grass-fed beef liver (this will probably be in pieces)

2 tablespoons extra-virgin olive oil

3 small onions, thinly sliced

Pinch of sugar

Salt

½ cup red wine

6 fresh sage leaves, finely chopped (optional)

Remove the liver from its package and blot it dry.

Heat a cast-iron pan big enough for the liver to lie flat (or cut the meat into pieces to fit). When the pan is hot but not smoking, add 1 tablespoon of the olive oil and swirl it around to coat the pan. It should immediately thin and become fragrant. Immediately add the onions and turn down the heat, stirring the onion slices to coat them with the oil. Sweat them to softness, adding the sugar and salt to taste as they cook. When they are slightly caramelized, with spots of brown, transfer them to a platter and reserve.

Wipe out the pan, increase the heat to high, and add the remaining 1 tablespoon olive oil. When it is fragrant and thin, add the liver (it should hiss as it hits the hot pan). Keeping the heat high, sear the liver on both sides, about 3 minutes per side, or until cooked to rare in the center. (Timing will depend on the thickness of the liver.) As the pieces are cooked, remove them to the platter with the onions.

When all the liver is cooked, turn off the heat and add the red wine to the pan and deglaze, scraping up the browned bits from the bottom of the pan to incorporate them. Reduce the wine by half, 3 to 4 minutes.

Pour the red wine glaze over the liver and onions and serve, garnished with the slivers of fresh sage, if desired.

Liver with Parsley, Garlic, and Red Wine Vinegar

Cooked for less than a minute per side and sauced with aromatics and reduced vinegar, this dish makes a memorable, fast, and easy work-night dinner. More refined than the preceding recipe by virtue of a flour coating, and enlivened by the acidity of vinegar, it goes especially well with a baguette, a salad, and a good red wine, and cheese and fruit for dessert.

SERVES 2 OR 3

1 pound grass-fed beef liver (this will probably be in pieces)

1 cup unbleached all-purpose flour

2 cloves garlic

¼ cup fresh flat-leaf parsley leaves

½ teaspoon sea salt

2 tablespoons extra-virgin olive oil, plus more as needed

¼ cup red wine vinegar

Bring the meat to room temperature and blot it dry. Put the flour in a shallow bowl such as a soup bowl. Dredge the meat in the flour to coat it lightly on both sides. Set it aside.

Chop the garlic, parsley, and salt together on a cutting board.

Heat a cast-iron frying pan large enough for the liver over medium-high heat. When the pan is hot, add the olive oil and let it thin and become fragrant, about 30 seconds. Add the meat and cook for about 45 seconds per side, or until the meat does not stick and is browning. Transfer it to a serving platter.

Immediately add the garlic mixture to the hot pan and stir it in the remaining fat (add a little more oil if there is no fat left). Add the vinegar—it will bubble furiously—and scrape the pan rapidly to incorporate the browned bits into the sauce, taking care not to let all the sauce boil away. Pour this sauce over the liver and serve immediately.

Readying Testicles for Cooking

Before you can bread and fry testicles, you have to peel the tough membrane off each one, soak them in salted water for an hour, give them a quick parboil, then chill and slice the meat. These steps can all be done a day ahead of cooking, if desired.

By far the hardest part of the process is peeling off the tough skin, so let me encourage you strongly to make sure they are still partially frozen when you attempt it. You will need a very sharp boning knife (I kept my sharpener at my elbow and used it frequently) and a bowl of cold salted water.

I find the best way is to make four vertical cuts lengthwise in each testicle, cutting through the skin but not cutting the flesh. Then it is possible to peel down each skin segment, pulling hard, so that it can be cut off at the bottom and discarded. The larger the testicle, the easier it is, perhaps because the larger pieces are more frozen than the smaller ones (there are enormous variations in size).

In addition to beef testicles, you can use the same methods to cook the testicles of water buffalo, veal, sheep, lamb, venison— even turkeys and ducks, although smaller poultry testicles do not need slicing and can be panfried in butter whole.

There's a proud tradition of eating "Rocky Mountain Oysters" in the American West, and there's an annual testicle-cooking contest in Serbia every August that has gotten considerable press. Naturally, there are all kinds of beliefs about the relationship between eating testicles and virility. Let me be discreet and say that you'll have to judge for yourself to see if they are true.

Monte Verdi Oysters

I was not able to get beef testicles, but thanks to Hardwick Beef, John Wing of Over the Hill processors, and some of the bulls from the herd that produce milk for the only real mozzarella di bufala in Vermont, I was instead able to get the next best thing—2 pounds of water buffalo testicles. For those who want only to read the recipe and not cook it themselves, let me say that these tasted quite good, although I imagine testicles from younger animals would be more tender. Of course, nearly anything deep-fried and doused with hot sauce tastes delicious.

SERVES 4 TO 6

2 pounds grass-fed beef testicles, partially frozen

1 cup red wine

1 cup unbleached all-purpose flour

¼ cup stone-ground yellow cornmeal

Salt and freshly ground black pepper

2 eggs, beaten

Vegtable oil, lard (see page 250), or suet (see page 125) for deep frying

Hot sauce such as Sriracha, for serving

Carefully cut the partially frozen testicles into quarters lengthwise, then peel off and discard the skin. Put the peeled meat in a bowl of salted cold water for 1 hour. Drain and rinse the meat and put it in a large pot filled with enough cold water to float the meat. Fill a large bowl with ice water and have it at hand. Bring the meat to a boil, then transfer it immediately to the ice-water bath to stop the cooking. When the meat is cool, remove it and blot it dry.

Slice each testicle into ¼-inch-thick ovals, cutting at a slight angle to maximize the surface area. Put the slices in a large, shallow bowl with the wine.

Combine the flour, cornmeal, and salt and pepper in a shallow dish. Put the eggs in another shallow dish.

Choose a large pot for frying with sides deep enough that the fat won't splatter when you cook (too deep is much better than too shallow). Heat enough fat (I use vegetable oil) so that the meat can deep-fry in batches; you only need a few inches of hot fat, and the ideal temperature is 375 degrees. Have a pile of paper towels ready for draining the finished slices.

Working quickly, remove a slice of meat from the wine bath and run it through the flour mixture to coat. Shake off any excess, then dip it in the egg bath and the flour mixture again. Repeat with each slice.

Put as many of the slices as can fit without crowding into the hot oil (it should bubble furiously), and fry until they are golden brown on the outside and tender within. Work quickly (about 3 minutes)—the more rapidly the meat cooks, the more tender it will be.

Serve warm, sprinkled with hot sauce.

Pan-Fried Sweetbread in Butter with White Wine Sauce

Sweetbreads are the thymus and pancreatic glands of a young cow (or lamb). I had to special-order them from a distributor to find grass-fed versions for this book, but it was well worth the trouble when it came time to eat. They do require a special handling over a period of days: First soak them overnight in cold water, then blanch them and press them for another night; finally, quickly panfry them to a crisp and serve them with a pan sauce. Classic sauces for sweetbreads were too much trouble, so I made a simple white wine reduction, which tasted perfect to me.

CUT SHEET ALERT: You may not be able to order these from your processor.

SERVES 2

1 grass-fed beef sweetbread (about 8 to 16 ounces)

Kosher salt

Freshly squeezed juice of ½ lemon

Freshly ground black pepper

1 tablespoon unsalted butter

3 tablespoons light white wine such as an unoaked Chardonnay

Lemon wedges

Several sprigs fresh flat-leaf parsley

Soak the sweetbread for up to 24 hours or at least overnight in cold water in the refrigerator; this removes the blood. Fill a large bowl with ice water and have it at the ready.

Drain the sweetbread and put it in a pot, cover it with cold water, and add 1 tablespoon salt and the lemon juice. Bring to a boil and cook for about 3 minutes. Remove with a slotted spoon and plunge it into the ice-water bath to stop further cooking. Look it over closely, trimming off and discarding any veins or membranes. Lightly salt and pepper the meat.

Lay a tea towel on a quarter-sized sheet pan or other small baking pan; lay the sweetbread on one side of the cloth and fold the cloth over it. Place another small sheet pan on top and weigh it down with a bowl of water. Press, refrigerated, overnight.

The next day, slice the sweetbread on the bias into medallions about ¾ inch thick. Heat a cast-iron frying pan and melt the butter in it. Rapidly panfry the medallions, sprinkling them lightly with salt and pepper to taste, aiming for a crisp, browned exterior and a custardy interior (this is only possible when the cast iron is very hot). This will take 4 minutes or so, total. Transfer the medallions from the pan to a plate to rest. Pour the wine into the pan and scrape and deglaze to incorporate the browned bits stuck to the bottom of the pan. When the sauce is reduced by half (about 1 minute), pour it over the medallions and serve with lemon wedges on the side, decorated with a parsley sprig or two.

Beef Tongue with Sweet-and-Sour Sauce

If you've never seen or tasted tongue, the all-too-familiar texture and shape can be off-putting at first, but persevere, because it is absolutely delicious when served with a savory or (as it is here) sweet-and-sour sauce. Try this with mashed potatoes, or any of your favorite side starches.

SERVES 4 TO 6

1 grass-fed beef tongue (2 to 4 pounds)

2 onions

2 carrots, coarsely chopped

1 stalk celery, thickly sliced

1 clove garlic, chopped

2 tablespoons unsalted butter

⅓ cup raisins

¼ cup plus 1 tablespoon finely chopped almonds

⅓ cup white wine vinegar, champagne vinegar, or white balsamic vinegar

1 tablespoon tomato paste

⅓ cup Madeira wine or sweet Marsala

Salt and freshly ground black pepper

Rinse the tongue well. Coarsely chop one of the onions.

Using a large, heavy pot such as a Dutch oven, cover the tongue with water and add the chopped onion and carrots, the celery, and garlic. Bring just to a boil, skim if the water gets cloudy, and then lower the heat to maintain a gentle simmer for 3 hours, covered.

When the tongue is tender and can easily be pierced with the point of a knife, let it cool in the broth until it can be handled. Remove it from the pot (reserving the broth), and use a knife to peel away the membrane that covers the tongue. Discard that skin and thinly slice the meat crosswise, arranging it on a serving platter and putting the platter in a 200-degree oven to keep warm.

Finely chop the remaining onion. Heat a medium frying pan and gently melt the butter. Sauté the onion until it wilts, then add the raisins and almonds and fry until the almonds are toasted, golden, and fragrant.

Stir in the vinegar, tomato paste, and Madeira, along with ⅔ cup of the reserved cooking broth. Simmer, uncovered, for 10 minutes to slightly reduce the sauce and thicken it. Add salt and pepper to taste.

Pour the sauce over the meat and serve at once.

Kidney with Porcini and Onion

*T*his is based on a recipe from Clotilde Dusoulier's blog Chocolate *& Zucchini. (Since she's Parisian, her recipe title is in French—* rognons *sounds so much more appetizing than* kidneys, *doesn't it?) Most kidney recipes direct you to boil the kidneys for an hour to remove any off odors, but I found that such treatment is a sure way to end up with rubbery meat. If your kidney is young and fresh, or freshly frozen and very recently defrosted, Clotilde's method will work, and it makes for a fast meal. I've made this several times, and it is best when cooked in a cast-iron frying pan, both because the pan is shallow and because of the way the metal conducts heat. I serve it with pasta or mashed potatoes.*

SERVES 2

¾ pound grass-fed beef kidney

2 tablespoons red wine vinegar

4 dried porcini mushrooms

3 tablespoons olive oil

1 onion, thinly sliced

1 teaspoon kosher salt, plus more as needed

¼ cup red wine

1 clove garlic, chopped

1 tablespoon sour cream or crème fraîche

1 tablespoon Dijon mustard

Freshly ground black pepper, as needed

For the garnish:

1 tablespoon finely chopped fresh flat-leaf parsley

Rinse the kidney and look it over carefully. Using a very sharp knife, slice it down the center and remove all the bits of fat and any silverskin or membrane. Cut the kidney into thin slices, and put these in a colander to drain.

Boil 2 cups of water and add the vinegar. Pour this slowly over the sliced meat in 3 or 4 batches, shaking the colander well after each pour. This preliminary blanching helps to eliminate off odors. Continue draining the meat until you are ready to cook it, air-drying it as much as possible.

Pour just enough boiling water over the mushrooms to cover them. Allow them to rehydrate for 10 to 15 minutes. When the mushrooms are plump, discard the tough stems and cut the caps into slices, reserving the liquid. Pour enough of the mushroom water through a paper coffee filter to provide ¼ cup strained liquid. Set it aside.

Heat 1½ tablespoons oil in a small frying pan or saucepan over medium heat and sweat the onion, stirring as necessary to prevent browning. When the slices are limp and translucent, remove them to a plate.

Add the remaining 1½ tablespoons oil to the pan and sauté the kidney slices, stirring as needed, for about 5 minutes. Add the salt, mushrooms and reserved mushroom water, the onion, red wine, and garlic. Bring the mixture to a slow simmer and cook for 10 minutes or so, uncovered, until the meat is done and the sauce tastes good.

Off the heat, stir in the sour cream and mustard. Taste for seasonings and add salt and pepper as needed. Serve with pasta or mashed potatoes, garnished with the fresh parsley.

Oxtail Cooked in Sherry

This long-cooking (6 hours) classic Spanish dish is both simple to make and full of complex flavor. The authentic ham to use is Iberico, if you can get your hands on it. Otherwise, bacon or country ham contributes an American stamp to the stew. Serve this with fried potato slices if you want to be traditional. I also like it with bomba rice. If your oxtail comes in one piece (as mine did, because I didn't think to specify slices), try to find the places where the bone is separated by cartilage and cut through each section with a heavy knife or a cleaver. This dish can easily be made over a 2- or 3-day period, which makes it more flavorful, easier to defat, and fit better into a working life. As a bonus, you get the most amazingly rich gelatinous stock, worth saving for making other dishes.

▌ **CUT SHEET ALERT:** Ask the processor to crosscut the oxtail.

SERVES 4

For part 1:

1½ pounds grass-fed beef oxtail, cut into pieces

1 stalk celery, thinly sliced

2 carrots, chopped

Leaves from 5 sprigs fresh thyme (about 1 tablespoon)

1 onion, cut into rough wedges

Salt and freshly ground black pepper

For part 2:

2 tablespoons unbleached all-purpose flour

½ teaspoon sweet (*dulce*) pimentón de la Vera (smoked Spanish paprika)

2 tablespoons extra-virgin olive oil

1 onion, finely chopped

3 ounces Iberico ham, slivered, or finely chopped good bacon or country ham

4 cloves garlic, finely chopped

1 cup Fino or Manzanilla sherry

For the garnish:

2 to 3 tablespoons very finely chopped fresh flat-leaf parsley

PART 1:

Bring the oxtail to room temperature, rinse it, and blot it dry. Put the meat, celery, carrots, thyme, and onion in a 3-quart enameled Dutch oven, season with salt and pepper, and cover the ingredients with enough water to reach the top of the meat. Bring the pot rapidly to a boil, skimming off and discarding the scum as needed. Turn the heat to the very lowest setting, cover the pot tightly, and cook for 3 hours.

Transfer the meat from the stock to a plate. Strain the stock and set aside ¾ cup to use later for this dish. Save the remaining stock (it is lushly gelatinous) for other stews or soups—it freezes well. Clean and dry the pot for the next part of the cooking.

PART 2:

Mix the flour and paprika together and dredge the meat in it, saving any remaining flour mixture. Heat the olive oil in the clean pot, and sweat down the onion to translucency, adding the ham and garlic when the onion is partly cooked. Remove the onion mixture to a plate and brown the oxtail thoroughly on all sides. Return the onion mixture to the pot and sprinkle the remaining flour mixture over all. Stir this in to cook it a little, and then stir in the reserved ¾ cup stock. Add the sherry, cover the pot tightly, and cook for another 3 hours, or until the meat is tender and falling off the bone.

If you have time, chill the dish to remove the fat before reheating it gently and serving it with panfried potatoes or bomba rice to sop up all the good gravy. Garnish with the very finely chopped parsley.

Rich Brown Stock

Roasting bones for stock produces a deep brown color and gives it an especially rich flavor. If you are short on freezer space, you can reduce the finished stock to a concentrate and freeze it in smaller containers or in old-fashioned ice cube trays (you can transfer the cubes, once frozen, to a resealable freezer bag). Making cubes is especially useful for concentrated stock; when you need just a little flavor, it is easy to drop a few cubes into a dish. Remember to leave a little headroom in each covered container when you pour in the stock; it will expand as it freezes.

Made in quantity, this is a frozen asset you'll find lots of uses for, from making soup to gravy. The method is loosely based on the one described by Jennifer McLagan in her wonderful book, Fat.

MAKES 3 TO 4 QUARTS

6½ pounds grass-fed beef bones	1 tablespoon tomato paste
2 carrots, cut into chunks	2 bay leaves
2 stalks celery, cut into thick slices	5 sprigs fresh thyme
6 cloves garlic, peeled	8 sprigs fresh flat-leaf parsley
2 large yellow onions, unpeeled, cut into quarters	15 whole black peppercorns

Heat the oven to 425 degrees and set the rack in the upper center. Rinse the bones under cold running water and blot them dry.

Scatter the carrots, celery, garlic, and onion in the bottom of a roasting pan. Lay the bones on top and roast for 1 hour, turning once, until the bones are deeply browned.

Leaving the fat in the roasting pan, use tongs to transfer the bones and vegetables to a large stockpot, along with cold water to cover by at least 5 inches. Add the tomato paste, bay leaves, thyme, parsley, and peppercorns.

Bring this slowly to a boil over medium heat, and when it boils, immediately lower the heat to maintain a slow simmer. Skim off the scum that accumulates at the top, especially in the first 30 minutes of cooking. Continue to simmer slowly, partially covered, for 5 or more hours, or until the stock is fragrant, flavorful, and dark.

Setting a wire strainer or cheesecloth-lined colander over a large bowl or stockpot, strain the stock to remove all the bones and vegetables, pressing down to extract all the vegetable juices that you can. Put this bowl or stockpot in a sink filled with ice water to chill it fast so that you can refrigerate the stock promptly. (Stock is a perfect medium for bacteria, so rapid chilling and refrigerating is a good practice.) If you live in a suitable climate, put the covered pot in a pile of snow that reaches halfway up the pot or more.

After the stock has chilled completely, remove the layer of white fat that has congealed on top.

At this point, you can

- package the stock for freezing as is, labeling it "salt-free," so that you know to add salt when you use it, OR
- cook the defatted stock down to concentrate it, then add salt at the end to insure that it isn't too salty, and chill it again before pouring it into freezer containers or ice cube trays.

Roasting Bones for Homemade Stock

When I order my grass-fed beef, I always ask for the bones so I can make stock. Having quarts of homemade stock in the freezer is an asset I'm not willing to do without. While it does take time—about 5 hours of simmering—it's mostly spent attending to other things, since the process requires little direct attention. I make stock in large quantities, so it's not an onerous task, and always try to do it in winter so that I can chill the pot of finished stock in the snow or on the floor of my cold mudroom before removing the fat. If I had no alternative but the refrigerator for this step, I'd have to make less stock at a time.

BEEF FAT: Beef fat from grass-fed cows contains 50 grams of saturated fat, 42 grams of monosaturated fat, 4 grams of polyunsaturated fat, 109 mg of cholesterol, and 0.2 mg of selenium per hundred grams. Of the 50 percent of suet that is saturated, more than half of it is stearic acid, which is treated like a monounsaturated fat in our bodies and converted to oleic acid.

Grated Suet

As I'm not from a suet tradition, I learned Jennifer McLagan's method, described in her book Fat. *Although removing the membrane is the hardest part, it's worth doing because (after grating) you'll have enough suet ready to use for the year to come. Suet, unlike fat from other animals, does not need to be heat-rendered. Note this recipe is a 2-day project, as the fat should be refrozen before grating. Frozen grated suet will last 12 months.*

YIELDS FLUFFY GRATED SUET, READY FOR PASTRIES OR FRYING

Any large amount of grass-fed beef fat

Unbleached, all-purpose flour, for dusting

Defrost the frozen suet until it is soft enough to cut, and look it over very closely. Trim off and discard any parts that are meaty or discolored. Cut the fat into pieces that fit the feed tube of your food processor. Look closely at each piece; you will need to remove and peel off the many plastic-wrap-like membranes that separate bits.

Pick up lumps of fat and crumble them between your fingers, saving the fat bits and discarding the membrane. Put the crumbled bits and cut pieces of suet in a resealable freezer bag and freeze them again overnight, along with the shredding disk of your food processor.

The next day, working fairly quickly, dust the cold shredding disk with a little flour and grate the frozen fat, adding more dustings of flour as necessary. Discard any bits that stay on top of the disk, as they are likely to contain shreds of membrane. Put all the finely grated suet in a resealable freezer bag or two, taking care to push out any trapped air.

Rendering Suet

Even though you don't have to render suet to use it for baking, I thought I'd try it to see if it made a difference. Once I had crumbled and picked my way through 3 pounds of solid suet, I had a large bowlful of crumbled white fat ready to cook down.

I put the suet into a Chinese sand pot and added a couple of cups of water (eventually, the water cooks off, but it prevents the fat from browning) and melted the suet slowly in a 250-degree oven. It took about 4 hours until much of it was liquid, but not colored. It still had many visible lumps and bits that didn't melt. I strained it through cheesecloth and then poured it into a clean quart-sized glass jar. (Had there been any water left, this would have separated in the jar and I could have poured it off.) I remelted the leftover solid bits several times, each time adding more water and, later, pouring off the newly rendered fat through a cheesecloth-lined strainer. Finally, when I couldn't stand to work with the bits further, I gave them to the chickens, who could really use it to stay warm in wintertime.

This rendered suet can be used interchangeably with grated suet for baking, but I think it was more trouble to process and probably not worth the bother. On the other hand, the fine texture and purity of the rendered fat proved much better for frying.

Maple Sugar Walnut Pie

In Quebec, pies like this are winter staples, and provide lots of energy to help people get through a cold season. You must use a conventional 9-inch pie pan—the shallow kind, not a deep-dish model—or this recipe won't work. Note, too, that it makes two crusts and you need only one, so freeze one for a later date. This pie, with its wonderful crust, is one you will long remember. It's very rich, so cut thin slivers when you serve; that'll be plenty.

SERVES 10 TO 12

For the suet-and-butter crust:

3 cups unbleached all-purpose flour, plus more for dusting

⅓ cup granulated sugar

¼ teaspoon kosher salt

8 tablespoons (1 stick) cold unsalted butter, cut into tiny pieces

½ cup cold grated suet (see page 125)

1 tablespoon cider vinegar

1 egg, beaten

About 5 tablespoons ice water

For the maple sugar and walnut filling:

4 tablespoons (½ stick) unsalted butter, melted

½ cup packed light brown sugar

¼ teaspoon kosher salt

1 teaspoon pure vanilla extract

1 tablespoon cider vinegar

¾ cup maple syrup

1 egg

1 cup walnut halves

Using a food processor fitted with the steel blade or working by hand, mix the flour, sugar, and salt together. Add the cold butter and pulse it into the flour (or cut it in by hand with a pastry blender). Do the same with the cold suet, so that the mixture looks like coarse bread crumbs. While pulsing or stirring, pour in the vinegar and egg. Gradually drizzle in 1 tablespoon of the ice water, then add the next; drizzle it in gradually—you may not need all 5 tablespoons. When the dough just comes together and looks like it's ready to ride the blade, immediately transfer it to a floured board.

Gently and briefly knead the dough to amalgamate (overworking makes it tough), and divide it into 2 pieces. Form each of these into a disk and wrap it in waxed paper. Slip one into a resealable freezer bag, press out the excess air, and label and freeze it for another time. Put the other in the refrigerator to chill for 1 hour before proceeding.

When you are ready to finish the pie, heat the oven to 350 degrees and put the rack in the center of the oven.

Combine all the filling ingredients *except the walnuts* in the bowl of a food processor or blend vigorously by hand.

Roll out the chilled dough on a floured board (or in a floured plastic pie crust maker; see page 252) to ⅜-inch thickness. Fit it into an ungreased 9-inch pie pan. Cut, roll, or crimp the top edge and scatter the walnuts over the bottom of the crust.

Set the pie pan on a cookie sheet, pour in the filling, and bake for 40 minutes, or until the pie is fragrant and dry on top. Chill overnight (or at least for several hours) to set the filling before serving.

Old-Fashioned Steamed Suet Pudding with Brandy Sauce

'd never made a real steamed pudding before I tried adapting this vintage recipe, but it wasn't difficult. If you don't have a real English ceramic pudding mold (these hold about 4 cups and have a thick rim, which makes it easier to tie a top on), a metal or Pyrex bowl with an outflaring rim or a soufflé dish with a good lip will do. You can also find metal pudding molds with lids at specialty kitchen shops; they are designed for this purpose.

A steamed pudding is made from a thick batter that is covered tightly and steamed inside a larger pot for 2 to 3 hours. It's served warm with a sweet sauce and is a lovely dessert to prepare on a winter day. It made my kitchen warm and steamy and full of scents, and at the end of the meal my family could hardly stop eating it, in spite of its richness.

SERVES 8 TO 12

Unsalted butter

For the pudding:

¼ cup dried cranberries

¼ cup raisins

¼ cup dried currants

¼ cup boiling water

3 cups unbleached all-purpose flour

1 teaspoon freshly grated nutmeg

1 teaspoon ground ginger

½ teaspoon ground cloves

1 teaspoon ground cinnamon

1 teaspoon baking soda

1 teaspoon kosher salt

1 cup cold finely grated suet (see page 125)

1 cup unsulfured blackstrap molasses

¾ cup whole milk

For the sauce:

8 tablespoons (1 stick) unsalted butter

1 cup light brown sugar

¼ cup heavy cream

¼ cup brandy

Plump all the dried fruits together in the boiling water for at least 5 minutes, stirring the fruit and covering the top to keep the steam in. If your fruit is very dry, you may need to add more water—just drain most of it off before proceeding.

Butter a 1-quart bowl with a flared or pronounced lip. Place a trivet, collapsible vegetable steamer, or Chinese disk (plate) steamer in the bottom of a tall pot large enough to hold the pudding bowl. Put the bowl in the pot and add enough water to the pot to go about three-quarters of the way up the bowl. Start the heat under the pot.

Remove the greased bowl and have it at the ready, along with a piece of parchment paper, foil, and kitchen twine.

In a separate bowl, mix together the flour, nutmeg, ginger, cloves, cinnamon, baking soda, salt, and suet. Mix the molasses and milk together and add this to the dry mixture, along with the plumped fruit and its juices.

Turn this batter into the prepared pudding bowl. Wipe the rim with a damp dish towel. Butter a piece of parchment and set it on top of the bowl, pushing down to make contact with the batter.

Fold a generous pleat in the middle of a large piece of heavy-duty foil that will accommodate the pudding's expansion as it cooks. Put this on top of the bowl, overlapping the lip. Using kitchen twine, make a tight loop around the rim of the bowl, knotting it well. Add two loops of string on opposite sides, making them long enough to overlap half the height of the bowl, and knotting them firmly.

Lower the pudding into the pot, leaving the string handles outside the pot. Bring the water to a gentle simmer, cover the pot, and arrange the handles on top of the lid. Simmer, adding more water if necessary to keep the water at least halfway up the sides of the pudding mold.

At the end of 3 hours, turn off the heat, but let the pudding rest in the steamy water while you make the sauce.

In a saucepan, cream the butter and brown sugar together and gradually add the cream, then the brandy. Heat this mixture gently over low heat. Have a lid handy to smother the flames in case the alcohol catches fire on the stove, although many people prefer to burn off the brandy deliberately.

Thread a wooden spoon through the string loops and carefully lift the pudding. Set on a folded dish towel to cool. Remove the foil and paper, invert the warm pudding onto a serving plate to unmold it, and pour the warm sauce over the top. Serve at once.

LAMB

Pastured Lamb

The first year we raised lambs for the freezer was 2006. Shank and Burger, our long-haired chocolate-brown Icelandic sheep, were grass-eating machines, getting fat off a field that always had needed mowing. (Our younger daughter, Lizzie, referred to them collectively as "the Scharffenbergers.")

Raising the lambs for meat was both very easy (they needed only minerals and fresh water daily) and slightly daunting (they got tamer and more charming as time went on, running over eagerly when I delivered their water, and

sniffing my hands with interest). All of us found it very hard to think that we would be eating these sheep, in spite of their telltale names. We talked a lot about the difference between eating sheep you know and sheep you don't know. It seemed clear to us that our sheep would have been someone's dinner if they weren't ours—sheep don't get a chance to die of old age. Many months later, on our plates, our pastured lambs offered great flavor, along with the knowledge that they led a good life. I've raised a couple of freezer lambs every summer since.

All the recipes in this chapter were tested with my own pastured Icelandic lamb and purchased Katahdin hogget (a hogget is a sheep that is more than a year old but younger than mutton). Some recipes were further tested in northern Vermont using pastured East Friesian sheep (a dairy breed), and with pastured Romney crosses in New Zealand.

Sheep are bred for meat, wool, or milk, and on top of that there are many crosses. Historically, the major meat breeds used commercially in the United States, many of which are English in origin, have been Cheviot, Dorset, Hampshire, Montadale, Oxford, Shropshire, Southdown, Suffolk, Texel, and Tunis. Like beef, most of the lambs we eat are male, because females are used for breeding.

While lambs (like calves) all start out on pasture, most commercial lambs are finished on feedlots, eating grain. While these feedlots may be different from beef lots in terms of space, they are designed to create larger, well-marbled, mild-flavored meat by feeding the animals nothing but manufactured feed.

On the other hand, lambs that are not part of industrial production tend to be raised, like grass-fed beef, by one farmer from birth to slaughter. They are raised as naturally as possible; fed mostly forage with some grain and perhaps other supplements such as kelp and minerals. They are likely to be medicated only when sick. They may also weigh significantly less, and provide smaller chops and roasts than commercial meat. A growing number of lamb farmers raise heritage breeds that need minimal care and thrive on pasture. Some of these include Tunis (one of the oldest breeds in the United States, now listed as rare), Katahdin (from Maine), and Cotswold (from England). Different heritage breeds thrive in different climates, and some have been bred for particular environments, such as Navajo-Churro sheep, which are ideally suited to their arid native landscape. Most such breeds thrive on forage and pasture, thus helping to keep diverse ecosystems healthy.

The Economics of Raising Two Backyard Lambs

While perhaps only a limited number of readers will want to emulate my experience, many may be interested in the economic discoveries I made raising our first couple of backyard lambs three summers ago.

We bought Shank and Burger (you need at least two because sheep are social animals) for $60 each in the spring. We enclosed the two male lambs on grass using lightweight portable electric fencing that we moved regularly to provide fresh pasture—an ancillary benefit was that the pasture they left behind was well mown and freshly fertilized. (The fencing and the electric controller were reusable capital expenses, and totaled $140.)

We fed them small portions of sheep minerals and grain pellets daily (about $25 total for the season) both to provide essential minerals and to train the sheep to respond to humans. The sheep loved the grain, and quickly learned to come running to the fence whenever they heard or saw us opening the metal can we stored it in. This proved important when the electric fence shorted out and the sheep escaped. As soon as we picked up their grain dishes and shook them loudly, Shank and Burger docilely followed us right back into the enclosure to get their treat. As they ate less than half a cup of grain daily, they were primarily pastured, grass-fed sheep.

We kept the sheep from May until October, rotating them from one section of ground to another every few days, covering about three-quarters of an acre in all. They went to the processor in a friend's truck before going into rut. The timing is important, as the onset of rut can affect the flavor of the meat. Rut could have been prevented by castration, but that would have been another expense. Most farmers just process male sheep before they hit adolescence. As we didn't have any female sheep nearby, ours were less likely to develop early.

The fee for processing the sheep was another $60 each, bringing our total cost to $132 per head. One sheep came in at 30 pounds of meat, while the other yielded 35 pounds. We asked the processor to save us the hides, which I salted for several weeks on pallets in the garage and then sent to a tannery (another $50 each). The tanned fleeces could sell for the price of raising the sheep ($150 each) if we didn't want to keep them. (We have them draped on chairs.)

Not counting the capital expenses of fence and controller, or the potential profits from selling either meat or fleece, our freezer lamb came out at a cost of $4.08 a pound. (Interestingly, the grass-fed beef we just took delivery of also came in at around $4.00 a pound; it is remarkable how affordable sustainable meat can be.)

I am now starting my third year of raising my own pastured lambs, but I've been buying pastured lambs from friends and neighbors for more than two decades. If you've got any land at all, and your zoning allows it, I highly recommend raising your own—it's easy and satisfying, and the flavor is extraordinary. Last year I also grazed a mixed flock of meat birds—chickens, turkeys, and waterfowl—on the pastures the lambs had just left, which meant that the birds ate the parasites, ticks, and other leavings from the sheep and further fertilized the field. It was very successful, not much more work, and filled our freezer with poultry of incomparable flavor. As a result, I'm planning to repeat the integrated process this summer.

Heritage breeds offer genetic diversity. When a breed becomes part of an industrial monoculture, like the Holstein dairy cows that produce most of the milk in this country, the whole industry is more vulnerable to diseases that target that breed. Heritage breed meat also provides cooks and eaters with a choice of new tastes and textures. Many of the sheep also yield fleece and/or wool, making them dual-purpose breeds that give farmers two income streams.

Buying local pastured and heritage lamb is a win-win for everyone in the supply chain, as well as the environment, because pastured lamb can be both sustainable and profitable—these days heritage lamb commands a premium price over commodity lamb. It's delicious on the plate as well as easy to buy and store in whole-animal quantities (a whole 30- to 40-pound processed and packaged lamb fits in one cardboard box).

Understanding Sheep Anatomy

The Primals

Lambs have five primals: **the shoulder, foreshank/breast, rack, loin**, and **leg**. Most lambs yield between 25 and 40 pounds of meat, depending on their breed and age at slaughter. A lamb is a year or less, a hogget is a sheep aged one to two, and mutton is older than two years. I've cooked mostly lamb, but I've also cooked hogget and found very little difference in the tenderness or taste, at least when all the meat is pastured and local.

In a lamb, the shoulder (the equivalent of the chuck in beef) includes the upper portion of the front leg and the shoulder blade, as well as some of the rib bones. Because it has fat, bones, and muscles, this primal is full of flavor and can be braised. You can also grind the shoulder, but I also like it as a whole roast with the bones or as a boneless roast that's opened up and then rolled around a stuffing made of greens and herbs, or marinated in a vinaigrette and then grilled or roasted. These roasts can also be cut into chops (shoulder blade chops, arm chops). Portions of the shoulder can be cut into kebob or stew meat. This portion includes some neck meat that you'll want to attend to—you can choose neck slices or have it ground. The foreleg is a source of lamb shanks; a wonderful braise, as I said earlier. As with other cuts of lamb, unless you ask for the shanks, their meat and other scraps from this primal tend to be ground or cut into stew meat.

Next comes the foreshank/breast. I remember a time, now long past, when you saw cuts of breast of lamb at every grocery meat counter. These days, if you want a breast of lamb, you need to order it from a specialty butcher or specify that you want your processor to include it when you buy a

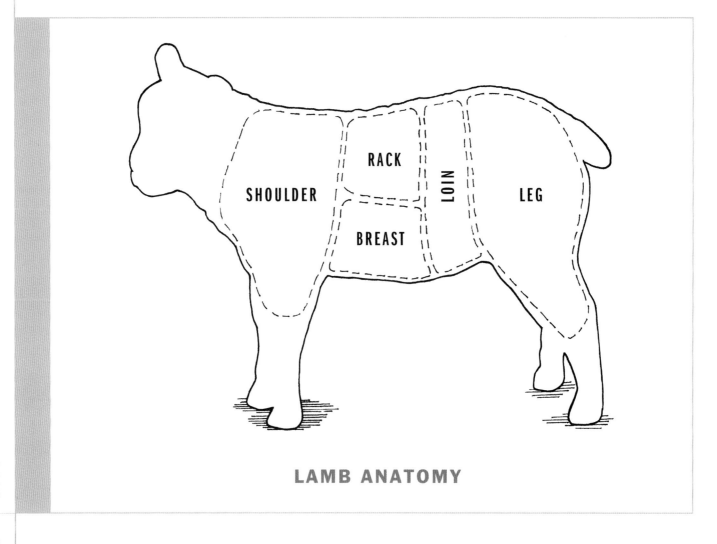

LAMB ANATOMY

From Field to Fork

The emotional challenges of raising our sheep knowing they were destined for the table were balanced by the comfort of knowing we gave them the best life and the easiest death we could. Although it was unfamiliar to feel affection for creatures that we planned to eat, it also felt responsible and right to acknowledge both our nurturing feelings and our appetites.

When I first unpacked the bags of frozen meat and put the packages away, I couldn't help but think of each lamb's character and beguiling traits, and I found myself mourning their absence. I still look out the window every morning to check that the lambs made it through the night without being attacked by predators, only to see the empty field.

My tenderhearted husband, who grew very fond of Shank in particular, asked me not to tell him when we ate our lamb. As we had some lamb in the freezer from another farmer, I was able to keep secret the moment of transition from Judy's lamb to ours. But weeks later, when we delivered the meat from the second lamb to our eldest daughter and her husband, it was obvious from the packaging that we'd been eating our own lambs for a while.

Now I make an effort to celebrate the meat by turning each lamb dinner into a festive occasion, but the experience of knowing firsthand the meat on the plate remains somewhat odd. Farmers do this all the time, but as a child of the suburbs, it does not come naturally. Frankly, though, I thought eating my lambs would be harder—I remember those particular living lambs with fondness, but they are disassociated in my mind from the meat in the freezer.

whole or half animal. Commercially, breast meat is often ground, and yours will be, too, unless you specify otherwise.

Last year, my breast of lamb came back as riblets (only two packages, sadly), which were delicious glazed with a blend of pomegranate molasses, lemon juice, and olive oil. You can also stuff whole breast of lamb, or lamb ribs can be treated like pork ribs and barbecued.

The rack of lamb is the rib portion. Tender and succulent, it can be cut into rib chops or served whole for a stunning presentation. These are the chops with bony ends that are sometimes "frenched" and dressed in frilly white pinafores, but even served straight from the pan they are elegant and delicious.

Lamb loin is also a source for chops and roasts. Most of these roasts are boneless, and provide great dinner party fare because they are flavorful, easy to carve, and lend themselves to being stuffed, tied, and sliced into pretty spirals. If boneless and very lean, they can be coated with strips of bacon or pancetta, or rubbed with olive oil, rosemary, and garlic for added flavor. Alternatively, this primal can be cut into loin chops to provide plenty of quick-cooking weeknight dinners.

Leg of lamb is made from the rear legs and can be bone-in or boneless. It is one of the great roasting cuts of all time.

When boneless, it can be butterflied, stuffed, and rolled, or left flat to marinate and grill. Alternatively, leg portions can be cut into sirloin chops, roasts, or leg steaks; portioned for kebobs or stew meat; or ground. Lamb cutlets can also be made from parts of the leg; they are boned-out single slices of muscle that can be pounded thin.

The lower part of either hind leg, the shank, makes for great eating when braised (again, like its beef equivalent). Such shank portions are usually whole. The shank end is also used for ground lamb. (As usual, because they're tougher and perhaps more time-consuming to cook, the most flavorful and interesting cuts are often ground into anonymity for cooks who either don't ask for them or don't know how to deal with them.)

Lamb offal is also called variety meat. This includes brains, heart, kidneys, liver, sweetbreads, testicles, and tongue. Using local Vermont processors, I have succeeded in getting lamb heart, kidneys, liver, and tongue, but never the brains (perhaps because of the way the lambs are killed), sweetbreads, or testicles. You need a number of little lamb's tongues to make a meal, but as most customers don't want them, your processor may be able to give you some from other lambs. Lamb's liver can be panfried or grilled and has a delicate flavor.

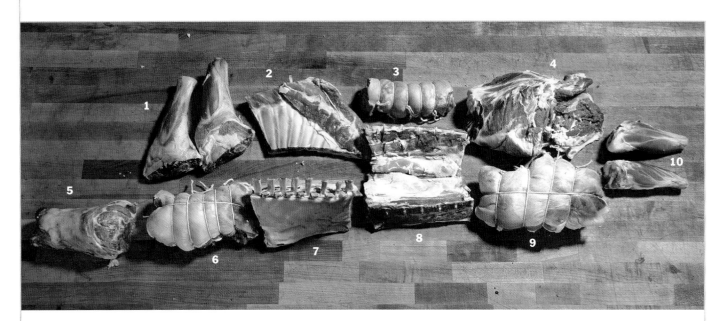

Lamb

Retail cuts: 1. Foreshanks **2.** Lamb riblets/Denver ribs **3.** Rolled lamb belly **4.** Bone-in leg **5.** Lamb neck **6.** Boneless lamb shoulder **7.** Lamb rack **8.** Lamb loins **9.** Boneless leg **10.** Hind shanks

BREAKING DOWN A LAMB

Whole lamb, hanging

Removing the arm

Cutting the flanks

Boning the rib cage

Loin/leg separation

Frenching the lamb rack

Boning the shoulder

Trussing the lamb shoulder

Lamb Cut Sheet Choices: What Substitutes for What

The list that follows goes primal by primal, with attention to the smaller cuts and choices that each may offer. Unlike beef, lamb is not split lengthwise, but is broken down into subprimal cuts—shoulder, foreshank/breast, rack, loin, and leg.

SHOULDER

Choice #1:
- Bone-in or boneless shoulder roast

Choice #2:
- Shoulder blade chops

  AND
- Arm chops

FORESHANK/BREAST

Each option produces a foreshank for braising.
- Bone-in lamb ribs left whole (rack of ribs; aka Denver ribs)

  OR
- Sliced (these are riblets)

  OR
- Boned and rolled lamb breast with the flank on for stuffing

RACK

Choice #1:
- Rib chops

Choice #2:
- Rack of lamb

LOIN

- Whole, bone-in roast

  OR
- Chops

  OR
- Noisettes (boned and rolled lamb chops)

LEG

- Hind shank for braising

  AND

Choice #1:
- Whole, bone-in leg

  OR
- Cut into center leg steaks

  AND

- A little shank roast

  AND
- A little sirloin roast

Choice #2 (good for grilling or roasting):
- Butterflied and boneless

  OR
- Boned and rolled

Choice #3:
- Seamed out into subprimals to be sliced into cutlets, or left whole as mini roasts

Choice #4:
- Cut for kebobs

ODD BITS AND OFFAL

- Sweetbreads
- Testes (hard to get from processors, as this is a kill floor item)
- Tongue

A Further Note on Size and Portions

As noted earlier, most of these recipes were tested on lamb I raised—relatively small Icelandic rams. When I repeated recipe tests and used purchased pastured lamb from local growers who raised different breeds, the relative size of their chops, roasts, and steaks were enormous. I know from my recipe testers in Vermont, Maine, and New Zealand that these recipes will work for any breed of pastured lamb, of any size, but, of course, the timing and the amount of marinade or spices will have to be adjusted somewhat. In terms of portions, I generally figure about ¼ to ½ pound per person (the larger weight is appropriate if the meat is bone-in). Sometimes when I encounter a very large (nearly 1-pound) bone-in shoulder lamb chop, for example, I divide it into two servings.

Cooking Lamb

Pastured lamb is much leaner than grain-fed lamb, and is best cooked with care to medium rare. Because there is less fat, it doesn't get a "mutton-y" flavor, even when more than a year old (although most pastured lamb is sold younger). Because a whole lamb generally weighs less than 50 pounds after processing, it is a very practical animal to buy whole, since cuts will fit in the freezer section of a refrigerator. Like beef, a good portion of a lamb is ground, while the rest is made into roasts and chops.

Cooking Lamb Shoulder

A hardworking part, shoulder offers roasts and chops (blade and arm) that are suitable either for quick-cooking or for braising. These chops are tougher than rib or loin chops, but offer plenty of flavor. They can also be braised. Roasts can be marinated and oven-baked, roasted in a covered grill, or braised like pot roast. When cooked in an oven, they are best thin-sliced after resting. Shoulder can also be cut into quick-cooking kebobs.

Lamb neck is also part of the shoulder, and can be labeled "lamb neck steaks," "cross-cut neck," or "lamb soup neck bones." These can be sliced into rounds, each with a bone at the center, or alternatively packaged as a large, cigar-shaped piece of meat wrapped around a few vertebrae. Whether sliced or not, this cut is made for stews or braises, and you'll get several packages with each lamb. In Ireland, this is the preferred cut for lamb stew, and much of northern Europe uses neck slices in layers with cabbage and rice or barley to make stew or soup.

Cooking the Foreshank/Breast

Lamb ribs and riblets can be cooked like pork ribs, and offer a similar hands-on chewing experience. Alternatively, lamb breast can be boned and stuffed, although you'll need to ask your processor or butcher to do this especially for you, as it's not standard. The foreshank is cooked just like the hind shank, as a wonderful braise that can be eaten like a stew or used as a pasta sauce.

Cooking the Rack

This rib portion of the animal can be cut through the spine to provide tender steak-like rib chops, or left attached to create a rack of lamb. Either way, the rack is rich and delectable.

Cooking the Loin

Loin lamb chops from the saddle are the equivalent of T-bone steak, and are meltingly tender. They need little more than good salt and careful cooking over high heat—either on the grill, in a grill pan, or under a hot broiler. Bone-in loin oven roasts are equally appealing, as they are big roasts for festive occasions. Noisettes, which are boned, rolled, and tied as a fillet, offer cooks the opportunity to add herbs and spices to a pan or oven roast.

Cooking the Leg

Perhaps one of the most well-loved cuts of lamb, leg can be roasted on the bone, or boned, butterflied, stuffed, rolled, and tied (which creates pretty and flavorful spirals of herbs and greens when sliced). Legs can also be cut into kebobs, or even ground, but in my view these both waste a cut that is well worth cherishing. Scraps can certainly be used for these purposes, however. Another option is to cut the leg into steaks, which makes sense for those with small families, or those who need quick-cooking portions. The leg also includes the hind shanks, which are one of the great braising cuts. These can be left on the bone whole or crosscut for braising (be sure to specify when ordering a whole or half animal), or boned for grinding.

Cooking Odd Bits and Offal

Tongue, kidneys, heart, and liver are all available as part of a whole lamb order and worth including in your cooking repertoire, both because they are delicious and because it honors the animal to waste as little as possible. If you are able to get lamb sweetbreads, they can be cooked exactly the same way as beef sweetbreads (see page 118).

Lamb tongue

LAMB RECIPES

Middle Eastern Lamb Meatballs with Cinnamon and Cherries

dapted from Ghillie Basan's The Middle Eastern Kitchen, *this dish is especially easy to make if you have a jar of cherries in syrup handy. If not, soak dried cherries in warm water for a minimum of an hour, or overnight, or use fresh pitted cherries. Sour cherries are best for this recipe, but if you only have sweet ones, add the juice and zest of a lemon to the sauce to make the flavors more complex. I serve this accompanied by saffron-infused rice and wilted spinach (see page 362; I add yogurt and nutmeg for this meal).*

SERVES 4

½ pound ground pastured lamb

1 teaspoon ground cinnamon

½ teaspoon ground cumin

½ teaspoon ground cloves

1 tablespoon extra-virgin olive oil

1 tablespoon unsalted butter

½ cup Morello cherries in syrup, drained, or fresh pitted or dried sour cherries

If using fresh or dried cherries:

¼ cup water

1 to 2 tablespoons sugar

¼ teaspoon ground cinnamon

Using a food processor fitted with the steel blade, grind the meat and 1 teaspoon of the cinnamon with the cumin and cloves to make a paste. Wet your hands and roll the meat paste into balls about 1½ inches in diameter.

Heat a large frying pan over medium-high heat, then lightly coat it with the oil. When the oil is thinned and fragrant, brown the meatballs on all sides, shaking the pan vigorously every so often to prevent sticking and to keep them round, 5 to 7 minutes in all.

At the same time, melt the butter in a saucepan over low heat. Add the cherries and toss. If you are using fresh or dried cherries, add the water to cook them further without burning. Crush the cherries with the back of a spoon or a potato masher, and stir in the sugar and ¼ teaspoon cinnamon if you are using fresh or dried fruit. Bring to a slow boil over medium-low heat.

Using tongs, transfer the meatballs to the cherry sauce and simmer slowly for about 15 minutes, or until both meat and cherries are cooked through. Allow the sauce to caramelize slightly before arranging on a bed of saffron-infused rice.

Lamb Sausage, Eggplant, and Orzo Salad

Roasting eggplant cubes in the oven with garlic and olive oil is a great hands-off cooking method that yields lots of flavor. When this mixture is tossed with cooked sliced lamb sausage or cooked ground lamb, along with orzo (the rice-shaped pasta), and paired with tomatoes, walnuts, olives, and parsley, it's a great summer meal that can easily be made ahead.

SERVES 6 TO 8

½ cup extra-virgin olive oil

1 pound orzo

½ cup freshly grated Parmigiano-Reggiano

5 cloves garlic, smashed

1 large eggplant, peeled or not, and cut into cubes

Salt

1 pound pastured lamb sausage, thinly sliced, or ground pastured lamb

½ small red onion, finely chopped (about 3 tablespoons)

¼ cup white wine

¼ cup walnuts

8 to 12 grape tomatoes, or more if you wish

½ cup black olives, pitted

½ cup chopped fresh flat-leaf parsley

1 tablespoon finely chopped fresh rosemary

Freshly ground black pepper, as needed

Heat the oven to 375 degrees. Lightly grease a rimmed baking sheet with a little of the olive oil and set aside.

Cook the orzo in about 8 quarts of salted boiling water until al dente and drain. Toss with ¼ cup of the olive oil and the cheese.

Chop 2 of the garlic cloves and toss with the eggplant cubes and the remaining olive oil on the baking sheet, along with a little salt (keep in mind that if you are using sausage, it can be quite salty—and take care not to overdo the salt here). Roast for 35 to 40 minutes, turning the pan and tossing the contents halfway through.

While the eggplant roasts, cook the meat in a large skillet over low heat until it just begins to brown and is rendering some fat. Add the remaining 3 garlic cloves and the onion, and sweat it down with the meat until it is limp and translucent. Add the wine and allow it to cook down by about a third.

Toast the walnuts, using a dry, seasoned cast-iron frying pan and medium heat, stirring until they smell fragrant and darken slightly.

Toss together the lamb, eggplant, and orzo with the tomatoes, olives, walnuts, parsley, and rosemary. Taste for salt and pepper. Serve warm or at room temperature.

Lamb Burgers, Turkish Style, with Yogurt-Garlic Sauce

Although these are best cooked on a grill outdoors, they are also well worth making inside on a hot cast-iron frying pan or under the broiler. Serve them on a bed of lettuce or arugula, inside warmed pita, or wrapped in warmed flatbread such as lavash.

SERVES 4

1 pound ground pastured lamb

1 small red onion, minced

¾ cup plain full-fat yogurt (cow or sheep)

2 cloves garlic, minced

1 tablespoon flavorful extra-virgin olive oil

Sea salt or smoked salt

Freshly ground black pepper

Combine the lamb and minced onion and form 4 patties, slapping the meat firmly together without overworking it. Make a dimple in the top center of each patty, using your thumb.

Heat a charcoal or gas grill to high, or heat a cast-iron grill pan (and turn on the kitchen fan). Cook the patties, starting with the dimpled side up.

Meanwhile, blend together the yogurt, garlic, oil, and salt and pepper to taste.

When the burgers are medium rare in the center (this takes 3 to 4 minutes per side), remove them from the heat and ladle the sauce over them. Serve at once over salad or with pita or lavash.

Making Burgers

Don't overmix burgers because ground meat gets tougher when it's handled too much. When forming a burger into a patty, don't be shy—use firm pats, almost slaps, as if you were making a snowball, to shove it into shape fast and cleanly. Then, after you've firmly snowballed the burgers into patties, use your thumb to make an indentation in the center of the top. It helps the meat shrink less.

Chickpea Soup with Lamb, Raisin, and Mint Meatballs

Even though this recipe has three separate elements and many ingredients, it's actually quite simple and makes enough hearty soup to feed a crowd. I specify an alternative to the usual overnight soaking of dried beans. If you are really short of time, use canned chickpeas. The slow method really will turn out best, but the fast method, still delicious, is much faster.

The meatballs in this recipe are also tasty on their own, in a sandwich or served with spaghetti and olive oil.

SERVES 10

For the soup:

2 cups dried chickpeas (or about six 15-ounce cans)

2 large red onions, cut into chunks

3 carrots, cut into chunks or slices

3 cloves garlic

1 tablespoon ground turmeric

2 tablespoons ground cumin

1 teaspoon dried thyme

½ teaspoon freshly grated ginger

¼ cup fresh flat-leaf parsley leaves

2 tablespoons extra-virgin olive oil

10 cups chicken stock, preferably homemade (see page 303), or water

½ teaspoon crushed red pepper flakes

For the topping:

1 cup full-fat Greek-style yogurt

1 tablespoon chopped fresh mint

1 teaspoon Greek honey or other dark honey

Sea salt

For the meatballs:

1 pound ground pastured lamb

1 cup toasted almonds, finely chopped

1 small onion, finely chopped

½ cup raisins, finely chopped

1 egg, beaten

2 cloves garlic, minced

1 tablespoon chopped fresh flat-leaf parsley

2 tablespoons chopped fresh mint

Salt and freshly ground black pepper

3 tablespoons extra-virgin olive oil, plus more for your hands

¼ cup sweet red vermouth

¼ cup water

To finish the dish:

Zest and juice of ½ lemon

Salt (as needed)

Chopped fresh cilantro (optional)

Rinse the dried chickpeas and put them in a large pot. Add enough cold water to cover them by an inch and bring to a boil. Turn off the heat and let the beans soak for 1 hour.

Put the onions, carrots, garlic, turmeric, cumin, thyme, ginger, and parsley into the bowl of a food processor fitted with the steel blade. Pulse 2 or 3 times to chop the ingredients into uniform pieces, taking care not to liquefy them.

Heat the oil in the bottom of a large, heavy soup pot over low heat, and sweat down the aromatic ingredients until the onions are translucent, about 5 minutes. Drain the chickpeas and add. Add the stock, along with the red pepper. Cook for 1 to 2 hours, until the chickpeas are tender. (The time will vary depending on the age of the dried chickpeas. If you are using canned chickpeas, you can heat gently for about 20 minutes to allow the flavors to blend.)

While the soup is cooking, mix the topping ingredients together and let them sit at room temperature to blend their flavors for 10 to 15 minutes.

To make the meatballs, mix together the lamb, almonds, onion, raisins, egg, garlic, and herbs. Season with salt and pepper, add 1½ tablespoons of the olive oil, and gently combine, taking care not to overmix. Lightly oil your hands and form the meat mixture into about 40 Ping-Pong-ball-sized meatballs, patting them firmly into shape as if they were snowballs and laying them out on a tray.

Heat a sauté pan big enough to cook all the meatballs at once, if possible, or cook them in batches. Coat the pan with the remaining 1½ tablespoons olive oil and cook the meatballs over medium-high heat until browned on all sides, shaking the pan and turning the meatballs with tongs as necessary. This will take 8 to 10 minutes. Pour the vermouth and water over the meatballs and cook off the liquid for a minute or two, shaking the pan until it is dry again.

When the bean soup is done, use an immersion blender to purée it into a slightly chunky texture. Add the lemon zest and lemon juice; taste for salt and correct if necessary. Put a couple of meatballs in the bottom of each soup bowl, ladle on the soup, and top with a dollop of yogurt topping. Garnish with a little chopped cilantro, if desired.

Spaghetti with Lamb and Tomato Sauce

Musab, my son-in-law, came up with this dish one evening, and it was an instant winner. Lamb brings out a sweetness in tomato sauce that is entirely different from beef sauces, and his additions of mint, juniper, sage, and fennel rounded out the flavors beautifully. I've added the vodka to emphasize the tomato taste.

SERVES 6

1 tablespoon unsalted butter

1 tablespoon extra-virgin olive oil

1 onion, finely chopped

4 cloves garlic, minced

1 pound ground pastured lamb

1 teaspoon rubbed dried sage, or ground sage, or 2 fresh sage leaves, finely chopped

1 teaspoon Herbes de Provence Blend (see page 32)

1 bay leaf

4 juniper berries, crushed

1 teaspoon ground fennel

1 teaspoon finely chopped fresh mint

1 pound spaghetti

2 tablespoons kosher salt

1 (14.5 ounce) can diced tomatoes (such as Muir Glen fire roasted)

Pinch of sugar

1 teaspoon vodka

Salt and freshly ground black pepper

½ cup mixed freshly grated Parmigiano-Reggiano and Romano cheese, for serving

Heat the butter and olive oil in a frying pan over medium-low heat, then sweat down the onion and garlic until fragrant and translucent. Add the lamb, breaking it up with a wooden spatula into crumbs and lowering the heat after the meat has begun to brown. Stir in the sage, herbes de Provence, bay leaf, juniper berries, fennel, and mint and turn off the heat.

Bring 8 to 10 quarts of water to a boil, and set a colander in the sink to drain the pasta when it is ready. Add the kosher salt to the water, and when the water starts to boil furiously, add the pasta and cook to al dente, about 11 minutes.

Meanwhile, in a saucepan over low heat, cook the tomatoes, sugar, and vodka until gently bubbling. Add the meat and herb mixture and continue to cook the sauce until the pasta is al dente. Stir about ½ cup of the pasta-cooking water into the sauce, then drain the pasta. Remove and discard the bay leaf. Toss the sauce with the spaghetti. Salt and pepper to taste. Serve at once and pass the grated cheese at the table.

Five Magic Ingredients

Five ingredients—sugar, salt, alcohol, liquid, and fat—have a magical effect on any dish because they release hidden flavors in food. Try adding even a tiny amount of each of these to any dish to substantially increase depth of taste. In cakes, for instance, which already contain sugar, liquid, and fat, adding salt and the alcohol in vanilla enhances flavor substantially; while a bit of fat (such as olive oil or duck fat) along with salt, wine vinegar, and a pinch of sugar makes for more flavorful bean dishes. Sauces for meats that include wine and butter or cream do more than enhance mouthfeel—they actually make the meat taste more "meaty."

Merguez Sausages

In North Africa and Paris, these sausages vary by the intensity of the spices used. This version combines attributes of a number of different examples and is easily made at home without casings. Note that the meat benefits from having an overnight rest before cooking. Serve merguez with bean soups, lentils, couscous, or Middle Eastern Fried Eggs (see page 352). I freeze the extra merguez meat, well wrapped, after forming it into cigars but before cooking.

If you prefer more heat, feel free to add more hot red pepper or harissa, the fiery spice paste of Morocco and Tunisia. I buy my harissa ready-made and prefer a brand called A Riche A, found at New York's legendary Fairway Market.

**MAKES 1 POUND LOOSE MEAT,
ENOUGH FOR ABOUT 12 SAUSAGES**

1 pound very cold ground pastured lamb (as fatty as possible)

½ teaspoon ground fennel or wild fennel pollen

¼ teaspoon ground cinnamon

1 teaspoon strong hot Hungarian paprika or cayenne pepper

½ teaspoon ground cumin

2 cloves garlic, finely minced

1 teaspoon harissa paste

Combine all the ingredients with your hands, working the meat lightly to disperse all the spices evenly. Form the mixture into a ball, put it in a small bowl, and cover with plastic wrap. Allow the mixture to age at least overnight or up to 3 days in the refrigerator before cooking.

When ready to cook, form the sausage into fat finger-shaped rolls or cigars. Heat a cast-iron frying pan until it is hot and put as many little merguez cigars as can fit comfortably without crowding in the pan. Immediately turn the heat to medium-low and panfry, shaking the pan, until they are browned on all sides. Remove and repeat if necessary until all are cooked to medium rare.

Fava Bean Soup with Merguez

*L*ook for dried fava beans that are already peeled because it's a tedious process to peel them yourself. Gourmet stores are more likely to offer peeled versions than supermarkets. Paired with spicy merguez sausage and homemade croutons, this soup is a whole meal in a single bowl. Note that you need to plan to soak the beans overnight or parboil them and let them sit for an hour at the start of the cooking process.

SERVES 6 TO 8

3 cups peeled dried fava beans

Salt and freshly ground black pepper

2 tablespoons extra-virgin olive oil

2 cloves garlic, minced

2 onions, chopped

1 teaspoon sugar

1 teaspoon crushed red pepper flakes

1½ recipes merguez sausage meat (see page 148)

4 slices artisanal bread, crusts removed, cut into cubes

To finish the soup:

1 cup chopped fresh flat-leaf parsley

1 cup freshly grated Parmigiano-Reggiano, plus more for the table

Drizzle of great olive oil

Harissa paste (optional)

Prepare the beans by pouring them onto a sheet pan and picking them over to remove any broken or discolored beans. Rinse and drain them. Using a large pot, soak the beans overnight in enough cold water to cover them by 3 inches, or parboil them by bringing the pot to a boil and then allowing them to soak for 1 hour. In either case, when ready to cook, drain the beans and place them in a large pot or enameled cast-iron casserole.

Cover the beans with 3 inches of water. Bring to a boil, lower the heat to a simmer, and cook slowly, partially covered, until the beans are tender and beginning to burst open. (The time on this will vary by the age and dryness of the beans—it should take between 1 and 3 hours.) When done, add salt to taste and a good grinding of black pepper, and set the soup aside.

Meanwhile, heat a cast-iron pan to hot, and then heat 1 tablespoon of the olive oil over medium-low heat. Slowly fry the garlic and onions until soft. Stir in the sugar and red pepper and cook a minute or two longer. Add this mixture to the soup pot, scraping the pan to get all the good flavors into the soup.

Using the same frying pan (without wiping it out), cook the merguez over medium heat until browned and crisp on the outside and medium rare within, shaking the pan as needed. Transfer the merguez to a plate to cool.

Add the remaining 1 tablespoon olive oil to the hot frying pan, and when it has thinned and become fragrant, fry the bread cubes until they are browned and crisp on all sides. Drain these on a paper towel.

Reheat the soup very gently (it burns easily), stirring. Add the merguez to the soup. Taste and correct the seasonings, adding more salt and pepper if required.

When the soup is at serving temperature, arrange the merguez and fried croutons in the bottom of a soup tureen or in individual bowls. Ladle the soup over the meat and bread, then add the chopped parsley and a generous mound of freshly grated Parmigiano-Reggiano, passing more at the table. Pour a drizzle of robust olive oil over each portion, or pass a small flask of good olive oil at the table.

If you wish, a small bowl of harissa can also be passed at the table for those who like more heat and spice.

Little Lamb Patties with Apricot "Mostarda"

These little lamb patties, made with retsina, apricots, and coriander, make a lovely appetizer. They can also be dinner when made burger-sized—served with or without the sauce, on bread or not. However you serve them, they have a haunting flavor. Note that you mix the meat mixture and let it blend overnight or a few days before cooking.

Traditional Italian mostarda di frutta is made with candied fruit and a mustard syrup; the version I've created for this recipe is far simpler to make because it's a mixture of jam and mustard.

MAKES ABOUT 24 FLAT LITTLE PATTIES

For the patties:

5 dried apricots, finely diced

2 tablespoons retsina or other dry white wine

1 pound ground pastured lamb

2 cloves garlic, minced

1 teaspoon kosher salt

1 teaspoon freshly ground black pepper

1 teaspoon ground coriander

Freshly grated zest of 1 orange

For the mostarda:

½ cup apricot preserves

½ cup Dijon mustard

Using a large bowl, mix all the patty ingredients together, working the meat as lightly as possible. Cover the bowl tightly with plastic wrap and chill it in the coldest, lowest part of the refrigerator, overnight or for up to 5 days.

When ready to cook, wet your hands with cold water and form the meat into thin flat patties about 2 inches across. Cook these in a cast-iron frying pan over medium-low heat, first heating the pan and then adding the patties without crowding them. They should sizzle when they hit the hot iron. Brown the patties slowly, 2 or 3 minutes per side.

Arrange the patties on a serving platter, and put a toothpick in each one. Whisk the mostarda ingredients together in a small bowl and present the sauce on the serving platter along with the little lamb patties.

Smashing Garlic

You'll notice that many recipes call for "smashed" garlic, meaning garlic that's been crushed with the flat side of a chef's knife, or (as I do) in a small mortar and pestle. This makes it very easy to remove the papery husk, and releases garlic's volatile oils. Often, the garlic needs nothing further, since smashed cloves are perfect for adding flavor to cooking oil without chopping, and are easy to remove. This useful shortcut is faster and simpler than mincing or using a garlic press.

Lamb Stew with Apricots, Ginger, and Cinnamon

This stew doesn't call for browning the meat before braising it, but does require time to spice-marinate the meat, and to rehydrate the dried apricots. (On a workday, you could do this early in the morning and then cook the stew when you get home, because the spices will not break the meat down.) It's a great dish to serve with rice.

SERVES 4

1½ pounds pastured lamb stew meat, cut into cubes

2 teaspoons ground cinnamon

1 teaspoon ground coriander

1 teaspoon ground cumin

1 teaspoon chili powder

Salt

2 cups boiling water

1½ cups dried apricots

1 (1-inch) piece fresh ginger, peeled and finely chopped or grated

3 cloves garlic, smashed

½ teaspoon saffron threads

2 tablespoons extra-virgin olive oil

2 onions, coarsely chopped

1½ teaspoons unbleached all-purpose flour

Freshly ground black pepper

For the garnish:

Greek yogurt

Chopped fresh cilantro

Pan-toasted almonds, roughly chopped

Rinse the lamb, drain it, and pat it dry. In the bottom of a large bowl, mix the cinnamon, coriander, cumin, and chili powder together, along with a scant ½ teaspoon salt. Toss the lamb cubes in the spice blend to coat, and let them sit at room temperature for 30 minutes (or overnight in the refrigerator). At the same time, pour the boiling water over the apricots in a small bowl to rehydrate them. Let sit.

When ready to cook, drain the apricots, reserving the flavorful water. Purée the apricots in a blender, adding the water gradually through the feed tube on top to make a chunky, watery slurry.

Pound the ginger and garlic into a rough paste using a mortar and pestle, or purée them in a mini processor or blender. Dissolve the saffron in a spoonful of hot water and let sit.

Using a heavy pot with a lid, such as a Dutch oven or flameproof clay casserole, heat the oil over medium-low heat, and when it has thinned and become fragrant, cook down the onions, stirring as needed, until they are soft and limp, about 5 minutes. NOTE: *The level of heat is important here because you can easily cook off too much of the great spice flavors— if you smell them powerfully in the air, it's likely that there is less of their flavor in the dish!*

Add the dissolved saffron, stirring well, and then immediately add the spice-covered meat. Stir to blend, taking care not to burn the spices, and add the ginger-and-garlic paste. Sprinkle with the flour and cover with the apricot slurry.

Stir, bring to a boil, and immediately turn the heat as low as possible to maintain a simmer. Cover the pot and cook gently for about 1½ hours, or until both the meat and the fruit are very tender. Season with salt and pepper to taste.

Serve the stew on top of rice, garnishing each portion with a dollop of yogurt and a sprinkling of cilantro and almonds.

Slow-Cooked Lamb Neck

Making this dish a day ahead and refrigerating it makes the fat easier to remove, and allows the flavors to meld. This dish is also a good candidate for the oven or a slow cooker; you can let it braise all day after browning the meat on the stovetop. Just set the oven at 250 degrees or set the slow cooker to the lowest possible heat. I like to serve this stew with potato gnocchi.

SERVES 4

Fine sea salt

1 to 1½ pounds pastured lamb neck slices

2 tablespoons extra-virgin olive oil

1 onion, roughly chopped

2 tablespoons tomato paste

½ cup red wine

3 cloves garlic

1 teaspoon sea salt

2 carrots, diced

1 stalk celery, diced

¼ cup chopped fresh flat-leaf parsley

2 bay leaves

3 sprigs fresh rosemary

Freshly ground black pepper

Freshly grated Parmigiano-Reggiano

Lightly salt the lamb and bring to room temperature, then blot dry. In a heavy soup pot such as enameled cast iron, heat 1 tablespoon of the olive oil over high heat until thinned and fragrant. Brown the neck slices on both sides, 6 to 8 minutes in all, turning the heat down to medium-high as required. Remove these from the pot and set them on a plate. Wipe down the pot and add 1 teaspoon oil over medium heat.

Sweat down the onion pieces until they are just starting to brown at the edges. Add the tomato paste and work it into the onion. Add the wine and deglaze the pot, scraping with a wooden spoon to incorporate any caramelized bits stuck to the pan. Turn the heat to very low.

Using a mortar and pestle, pound the garlic cloves with the coarse salt to make a paste. Add this to the pot, stirring it in. Add the meat, carrots, and celery. You can put the parsley, bay leaves, rosemary, and pepper in a tea ball (for easy retrieval) and drop them into the pot or just stir them in. Add just enough cold water to cover everything by a scant inch, cover the pot, and bring to a boil. Keeping the heat at the lowest setting, cook for about 3 hours, or until the meat is very tender and falling off the bone. (If you decide to cook for a longer period unattended, add more water—enough to cover by 3 inches.)

Using a slotted spoon, remove the meat from the pot and set it aside until it is cool enough to handle. Use a knife and fork to cut the meat into shreds or small pieces and reserve. Remove any marrow and stir it into the pot, then discard the bones.

Remove, press through a sieve, and then discard all the aromatic vegetables and herbs from the pot. Cook down the sauce over medium heat to reduce it by half, about 30 minutes. Taste the sauce and correct the seasonings, if necessary. Add the meat back into the sauce and reheat it gently, stirring as needed, if serving immediately. Otherwise, refrigerate it overnight so you can defat the sauce before reheating and serving. Plate and shower each serving with freshly grated cheese before taking it to the table.

Another Quick Way to Defrost Smaller Pieces of Meat

James Kenji Lopez-Alt, who works in the test kitchen of *Cook's Illustrated,* taught me this method of quickly defrosting relatively small pieces of meat such as lamb neck slices: Use a cast-iron frying pan (or even a metal sheet pan) to hold the meat, wrapped in plastic or unwrapped, at room temperature. The metal, especially cast iron, contains lots of moving atoms that conduct cold as efficiently as they do heat, and this action, carrying the cold away from the meat, makes the meat thaw more rapidly. Simply turn the meat over every once in a while to expose both sides to the metal and watch to see when it is ready to cook. If you keep the meat unwrapped, air-drying the surface at the same time is perfectly safe (as long as your kitchen isn't tropical) and aids in browning. I find thin pieces of meat such as chops defrost this way in an hour or so. Roasts need to be turned regularly (to expose each side to the metal) and are usually defrosted in about 3 hours.

Grilled Shoulder Lamb Chops
with Moroccan Spice Rub

ecause shoulder lamb chops are large and meaty, they take well to assertive spice rubs. Here I've used my favorite Moroccan spice blend and a little melted butter to enhance their already terrific flavor. If you have an outdoor grill, this is a great time to use it. And if you don't, a grill pan over highest heat will also work.

SERVES 2 TO 4

1 pound pastured lamb shoulder chops (4 chops)

1 tablespoon unsalted butter, melted

3 tablespoons Moroccan Spice Blend (see page 31)

Bring the meat to room temperature, rinse it, and blot it dry. Brush it with the melted butter.

Sprinkle the spice blend onto the surfaces of the butter-brushed meat and let sit as long as possible—at room temperature for 15 minutes to 1 hour, or uncovered in the refrigerator overnight. Return the meat to room temperature before cooking it.

Heat the grill or grill pan, and cook the chops for about 4 minutes per side, or until seared on the outside and slightly pink within. Let rest for at least 5 minutes before serving.

Garlic and Lemon Rubbed Shoulder Lamb
Chops with Lemon Vinaigrette

his deliciously lemony recipe is refreshing in hot weather, but greatly depends on the quality of the ingredients. Getting your pan really hot before you put the meat on is essential to sear the outside without overcooking the interior. An exhaust fan or open window is also a must. Since the sauce for the chops is essentially a vinaigrette, serve the meat on a bed of cooked greens or mixed salad.

SERVES 2 TO 4

4 pastured lamb shoulder chops (½ to 1 pound each)

2 cloves garlic

1 lemon, zested and halved

Sea salt and freshly ground black pepper

3 tablespoons extra-virgin olive oil

1½ tablespoons finely chopped fresh or dried oregano

Bring the meat to room temperature, rinse it, and blot it dry. Cut one of the garlic cloves in half and rub each side of the meat with it. Rub the meat with one of the lemon halves. Lightly salt and pepper the chops and let them sit for 10 to 15 minutes.

Heat a cast-iron frying pan to very hot, open the window or turn on the fan, and slap the chops down onto the pan. Cook them for 4 to 5 minutes per side, until they release from the pan and are seared on the outside and slightly pink within. Remove them to a plate to rest.

Juice the remaining lemon half and mince the remaining garlic clove, then combine them with the olive oil, lemon zest, and oregano. Pour this sauce over the chops and serve.

Braised Shoulder Chops with Provençal Flavors

Shoulder chops can often be tougher than one would like, but braising makes them tender. Here, garlic, fennel, tomatoes, and red wine give the meat lots of flavor, making it sing with southern French notes. For a quick accompaniment, make a white bean purée by whirling a drained can of cannellini beans with olive oil, salt, and fresh parsley in the food processor and then heating it gently. White beans and lamb always go well together.

SERVES 2 TO 4

4 pastured lamb shoulder chops	2 tablespoons Herbes de Provence Blend (see page 32)
Salt and freshly ground black pepper	½ cup red wine
2 tablespoons extra-virgin olive oil	1 (28-ounce) can chopped or crushed tomatoes
2 cloves garlic, minced	¼ teaspoon sugar
1 onion, chopped	1 cup couscous or rice
1 bulb fennel (white part only), thinly sliced	¼ cup chopped fresh flat-leaf parsley

Rinse and blot the meat, salt and pepper it, and bring the lamb chops to room temperature.

Choose a heavy sauté pan or frying pan with a lid, or a Dutch oven, large enough to fit the chops in one layer. Heat the pan to hot and then add 1 tablespoon of the olive oil. When the oil is thinned and fragrant, add the chops and sear them over high heat, 3 to 4 minutes per side, depending on the pan. When they are seared, remove them to a plate, reduce the heat to medium-low, and add the remaining 1 tablespoon oil.

Wilt the garlic, onion, and fennel, stirring as needed, for about 3 minutes. Add the herb blend and cook for another minute. Pour in the wine, stirring to scrape up and incorporate any bits that are stuck to the pan. Add the tomatoes and sugar and return the meat to the pan, along with any juices. Cover the pan tightly, reduce the heat to low, and simmer very slowly for 30 minutes.

Cook the couscous or rice according to the package directions while the meat simmers.

Test the meat's tenderness with a fork and knife, and when it is nearly ready to serve, remove it from the pan, and continue simmering, uncovered, to reduce and thicken the sauce, about 10 minutes. Taste for seasonings and correct, if necessary.

Serve on a platter or individual plates by arranging the chops on top of the couscous or rice, and topping with the sauce and a shower of chopped fresh parsley.

Braising Lamb

If you like to make stews in winter, you'll need to make sure that your processor knows you want meat in this form—but be aware that stew meat is often cut from prime roasting cuts, such as the leg and shoulder, as well as from scraps that will otherwise be ground. I prefer to cut my own meat into cubes for stew, and don't want to sacrifice other good cuts, so when I have an accommodating processor, I ask for the scraps to be left uncut and put into 1- or 2-pound bags labeled "stew meat scraps."

Stews can be made with wine, with juice or cider, stock or water, with aromatics like curry or other spice blends. Dairy additions such as yogurt or crème fraîche can be used to smooth and finish a spicy stew, while chopped fresh parsley or citrus zest (or both) can spark plainer meat-and-potato stews. The number of ways you can vary a stew is impressive. What all stews have in common is an aromatic base, a liquid braising medium, the addition of vegetables or fruits or starch to stretch the dish and add flavor, and the need for enough time to soften the meat to tenderness. Stews should never boil—they should cook, tightly sealed, at a very slow simmer over the lowest possible heat on the stovetop or in the oven at about 300 degrees.

Grilled Lamb Shoulder Roast

Unconventionally, I chose to butterfly a shoulder roast by cutting it horizontally almost all the way through, opening up the meat to make it as flat and even a piece as possible. Then I marinated the meat overnight for more flavor. Sliced thinly across the grain after cooking, it was still chewy but full of the satisfying tastes of rosemary and garlic.

CUT SHEET ALERT: Shoulder is one of the parts of the lamb that is often ground. If you want an alternative, you'll need to order it from the choices on the cut sheet.

SERVES 4

¼ cup extra-virgin olive oil, plus more for the grill

2 tablespoons sherry or wine vinegar

2 cloves garlic, thinly sliced

1 tablespoon fresh rosemary leaves, chopped

½ teaspoon freshly ground black pepper

1 teaspoon kosher salt

2½ to 3 pounds pastured lamb shoulder roast, butterflied into a flat piece

Mix together the oil, vinegar, garlic, rosemary, pepper, and ½ teaspoon of the salt. Place the lamb in a shallow refrigerator container large enough to hold it in one layer and pour the marinade over it, coating all surfaces. Leave the meat for a day or overnight, if possible, in the refrigerator.

Heat a grill or a cast-iron grill pan to high and, if you're cooking indoors, make sure there's plenty of ventilation.

When you are ready to cook, blot the meat and sprinkle with the remaining 1 teaspoon salt. Wipe the grill or grill pan with a little oil. Grill the meat for about 6 minutes per side, or until it is seared on the outside and pink within. Let it rest for 15 minutes, then carve it on an angle in thin slices like a flank steak and serve.

LIZZIE'S MANGO, LIME, AND MINT SALSA

Our younger daughter, Lizzie, makes this salsa in summer, and we always beg for more. It's so refreshing, a visiting friend once ate an entire bowlful. This works well with grilled chicken, lamb, or beef—in fact, it greatly enhances most meats and poultry.

2 ripe mangoes, peeled, cored, and diced

Freshly grated zest of 1 lime

Freshly squeezed juice of ½ lime

1 small red onion, finely chopped

1 tablespoon finely chopped fresh cilantro

2 tablespoons chopped fresh mint

¼ teaspoon coarse sea salt

Stir all the ingredients together. Taste for salt and lime juice, and adjust if needed. **Makes about 1 cup.**

Cider-Braised Lamb Shoulder with Yogurt and Apples or Quinces

This is a great way to braise a lamb shoulder in autumn or winter; the marinade infuses the meat with spices. Be sure to use real apple cider—freshly pressed from apples—and not a pasteurized or sweetened juice. If it's starting to get fizzy, all the better. If you do use quinces, they must be grated on the large holes of a box grater, since they are harder than apples. I like to serve this dish with rice or couscous, but any starch, such as noodles or mashed potatoes, would be good.

SERVES 4

1½ to 2 pounds shoulder of pastured lamb, bone in or out

Salt and freshly ground black pepper

Freshly squeezed juice of ½ lemon

1 teaspoon Dijon mustard

½ cup plain yogurt, preferably full-fat Greek-style

2 tablespoons extra-virgin olive oil

1 onion, roughly chopped

1 whole head garlic, each clove smashed

1 teaspoon ground cinnamon

½ teaspoon ground cardamom

¾ cup raw apple cider

1 bay leaf

1 cup chopped, peeled apples or grated peeled quinces

For serving:

1 cup white or brown basmati rice

Chopped fresh cilantro

Yogurt

Chopped toasted almonds

Rinse the meat, blot it dry, salt and pepper it lightly, and set it aside on a rack. Make the marinade by combining the lemon juice, mustard, and yogurt. Coat the meat in the mixture, place it in a dish, and marinate it for 3 hours at room temperature, if the kitchen is cool, or in the refrigerator.

When you are ready to start cooking, scrape off the marinade and discard it. Blot the meat dry. Heat the olive oil in a Dutch oven or other braising pot over medium heat and brown the meat on both sides, turning it only when it no longer sticks, about 5 minutes per side. Remove it from the pot and set aside.

In the same pot, slowly cook down the onion and garlic, stirring as needed, until they start to color and turn golden, about 10 minutes. Add the spices and cook for a minute or two, taking care not to burn them. Add the apple cider and bay leaf, scrape the pot to incorporate any browned bits, and return the lamb to the pot. Cover the braise with parchment, place the lid on the pot, and simmer very gently for 2 hours.

Add the apples or quinces to the pot and simmer for another 30 minutes, or until the lamb is very tender. Taste the liquid for seasonings and adjust, if necessary.

Rinse the rice in cold water, drain, and cook it, covered, in 2 cups salted boiling water in a heavy pot for 25 to 30 minutes, until tender.

Remove the lamb from the pot and let it cool for 15 minutes. Slice it thinly across the grain, and arrange it on a serving platter on top of the rice. Fish out and discard the bay leaf.

Purée the pan sauce and solids together using a food processor, blender, or rotary food mill. Taste for seasonings and adjust, if necessary. Pour this sauce over the sliced lamb and serve at once, garnished with cilantro, a dollop of yogurt, and a handful of almonds.

RACK: The larger lamb ribs can be cut into rack of lamb or delicious little rib chops, while the smaller ones are cut into riblets. All of these make for good eating—they're tender and rich, although a trifle dainty.

Rack of Lamb with Fennel and Garlic

A lamb has two racks, so a side of lamb has only one set of ribs. These can be cut into rib lamb chops or left whole to form a rack of lamb. Serve this with rice or potatoes and a tart green salad or a gratin of leeks, celery, or cardoons.

SERVES 4 AS PART OF A MULTICOURSE MEAL

1 rack of pastured lamb
(about 1½ pounds)

1 tablespoon ground fennel
or wild fennel pollen

2 teaspoons extra-virgin
olive oil

1 large garlic clove, minced

1 teaspoon kosher salt

Bring the meat to room temperature, rinse it, and blot it dry.

Combine the fennel, oil, garlic, and salt to form a thick paste, and apply it to the lamb. Let the meat sit at room temperature with the paste on it for 1 hour to mellow and absorb the flavors, or (even better) in the refrigerator for a day or two, uncovered. Bring to room temperature before cooking.

Heat the oven to 450 degrees. Set the meat inside a cast-iron frying pan or roasting dish, bone side down. Roast for 15 to 25 minutes, until the internal temperature is between 125 and 130 degrees.

Let the meat rest for 15 minutes to allow the internal temperature to reach 135 to 140 degrees. Serve warm with any pan juices.

Cumin-Rubbed Lamb Rib Chops

Nothing could be simpler or faster than rubbing this tender meat with a little spice and salt—and it adds another whole dimension of flavor. You can cook these chops in a pan on the stove or on the grill outside.

SERVES 4

4 pastured lamb rib chops

1 teaspoon ground cumin

Salt and freshly ground
black pepper

Bring the meat to room temperature and blot dry. If you are grilling outdoors, heat the grill. Mix the cumin with salt and pepper to make a rub, and spread it over both sides of the meat. Let rest for at least 15 minutes (or do this early in the day or the night before, and leave it uncovered in the refrigerator, bringing it to room temperature before cooking).

Cook the meat in a hot grill pan or cast-iron frying pan, or on an outdoor gas or charcoal grill, turning the meat when it no longer sticks to the pan or rack, about 6 minutes per side.

Rack of Lamb or Lamb Rib Roast with Whiskey Sauce

One day I pulled a piece of meat from the freezer that was generically labeled "roast," but none of the bones had been cut or cracked for carving. In short, it was the work of a less-than-stellar processor. A close look revealed that the profile looked just like a lamb chop, which gave me the cues I needed to know how to roast it (quickly, with high heat, because it's a tender part of the lamb). Carving it after cooking was a challenge, and there was no way to make attractive portions—but the meat was absolutely delicious.

SERVES 2 TO 4

1½ pounds pastured lamb rib roast, bone in

2 cloves garlic, smashed

¼ teaspoon salt

Freshly ground black pepper

1 tablespoon fresh rosemary leaves, finely chopped (about 3 sprigs)

1 tablespoon extra-virgin olive oil

2 tablespoons Irish whiskey

2 tablespoons heavy cream or half-and-half

Remove the meat from the refrigerator and blot it dry with paper towels.

In a mortar and pestle or food processor, make a paste of the garlic, salt, pepper, rosemary, and olive oil. Rub this on all sides of the meat. Heat the oven to 450 degrees and set the rack in the center of the oven. Allow at least 20 minutes for the oven to come to full temperature and for the spice-rubbed meat to sit.

Place the meat, fat side up, in a cast-iron frying pan or other roasting pan scaled to the size of the roast, and insert a thermometer in the center at the meatiest point. Roast the meat for 25 to 30 minutes, until the thermometer reads 120 to 130 degrees (according to the degree of rareness you crave) and the fat is crisp on top. Transfer the meat to a platter to rest for 15 minutes before carving and serving.

Meanwhile, put the pan on the stovetop and heat the fat and juices that remain (pour off most of the fat if there is an excessive amount). Turn off the heat and pour in the whiskey (be careful—it will tend to flame if the heat is still on), and stir the browned bits into the liquid as it reduces in the residual heat of the pan. Stir in the cream and serve this warm sauce over the meat.

NISHAT'S CHUTNEY

All three of my son-in-law's siblings make their mother Nishat's chutney. What's interesting is that this recipe uses most of the stems of the cilantro and mint, as well as the leaves, because the stems add moisture and flavor. Just trim off and discard any thick, white bottoms (and woody parts of the mint), and use the rest. This chutney improves if aged overnight, and is a great addition to almost any lamb or grilled beef recipe.

1 cup fresh cilantro leaves and stems

Freshly squeezed juice of 1 lime (¼ cup)

¾ teaspoon kosher salt

1 serrano chile, seeded

5 whole almonds

1 teaspoon extra-virgin olive oil

½ teaspoon freshly ground black pepper

20 sprigs fresh mint (about ½ cup leaves and stems)

¼ teaspoon ground cumin

Put all the ingredients in a blender and process into a paste. Store overnight in a nonreactive container and serve with lamb or other meats. **Makes about 1 cup.**

Salt and Spice Cured Loin Lamb Chops

These addictively tasty chops are for special occasions. Marinate the meat overnight or all day and then cook them on the grill, under the broiler, or in a cast-iron grill pan.

SERVES 4

4 pastured lamb loin chops

3 tablespoons Salt and Spice Cure (see page 30)

½ teaspoon chopped fresh roesemary or dried rosemary

½ teaspoon chopped fresh thyme

2 tablespoons extra-virgin olive oil

Rinse the meat and blot it dry. Mix the spices, herbs, and oil together and rub the paste all over the meat. Cover and refrigerate it for a couple of hours (or as long as overnight or all day), turning the meat once. Return the meat to room temperature before cooking.

Heat the grill, a grill pan, or the broiler to very hot. If you're cooking indoors, turn on your kitchen fan. Cook the meat over high heat for about 4 minutes per side, or until brown and crisp on the exterior, and rosy within.

Lamb Chops with Red Wine Sauce

Like beefsteaks, tender loin chops sear beautifully on a coarse sea salt base, and are perfectly delicious finished with red wine. This is a quick and rather elegant meat course. I like to serve it with a fava bean purée and Lacinato kale (often called dinosaur kale) cooked with garlic and olive oil (see page 362).

SERVES 2 TO 4

4 pastured lamb loin chops

1 tablespoon coarse sea salt, such as grey Atlantic or Celtic (for pan-searing only)

½ cup red wine

1 teaspoon unsalted butter

Bring the chops to room temperature and blot them dry.

Heat a dry, seasoned cast-iron frying pan over high heat and sprinkle the sea salt on the pan when it is hot. When it begins to pop, slap down the lamb chops and sear them for 4 to 5 minutes a side, until crusty on the outside and pink within.

Remove the chops from the pan, lower the heat, and add the red wine, taking care lest the wine ignite (have a pot lid handy just in case you need to smother the flames). Use a wooden spatula to scrape up any caramelized bits and incorporate them. Reduce by half or more to make a thick sauce, stir in the butter, and serve the meat with this sauce drizzled over it.

Lamb Chops with Fresh Mint Pesto

My son-in-law and daughter receive the meat from one of the lambs I raise each year, and they invent wonderful recipes. These quick-broiling loin lamb chops are ready to eat in minutes.

SERVES 2 TO 4

4 pastured lamb loin chops

1 big bunch fresh mint, stems discarded, leaves washed and dried in a salad spinner

¼ cup toasted walnuts

½ cup extra-virgin olive oil

2 cloves garlic

¼ cup freshly grated Parmigiano-Reggiano

Bring the lamb to room temperature and blot it dry. Heat the broiler to hot.

Make the pesto by combining the mint, nuts, oil, garlic, and cheese in the bowl of a mini or regular food processor fitted with the steel blade. Process the paste until fairly smooth.

Using the back of a spoon or a pastry brush, coat each chop on both sides with the pesto. Turn on your kitchen fan, put the chops on a broiling rack, and set them close to the heating element for 2 to 4 minutes per side, depending on the strength of the broiler. Aim for rosy centers, and let the meat sit for about 5 minutes before serving.

Grilled Lamb Chops with Herbs and Moroccan Spices

These chops marinate for a scant half hour (any longer, and they'd begin to cook in the lemon juice), then cook in minutes on the grill. Try them with warmed flatbread such as tandoor naan, or with couscous, along with a shredded carrot, cumin, and raisin salad on the side.

SERVES 2 TO 4

4 pastured lamb loin or shoulder chops

3 tablespoons Moroccan Spice Blend (see page 31)

½ cup chopped fresh cilantro

½ cup chopped fresh flat-leaf parsley

2 cloves garlic, chopped

¼ cup extra-virgin olive oil

Zest and juice of ½ lemon

Rinse the lamb and blot it dry. Mix the spice blend, cilantro, parsley, garlic, olive oil, lemon zest, and lemon juice in the bottom of a refrigerator storage container or other nonreactive flat covered dish large enough to hold the chops in one layer. Coat the chops on both sides with the spice mixture and leave them at room temperature for 30 minutes while an outdoor charcoal or gas grill, or the broiler, heats to high.

Lift the meat from the spice mixture, letting any excess oil drain off. Grill the chops for 4 minutes per side, or until they are seared on the outside and medium rare on the inside.

LEG

LEG : You can ask for the leg to be boned for rolling and stuffing, or leave the bone in for lots of flavor and ease of cooking. I like it both ways. Few dishes are as festive as a roast leg of lamb for company dinners, and I save mine for special occasions. Scraps from trimming the leg can be cut into kebobs.

Grilled Lamb Kebobs

These kebobs marinate for up to 3 hours before cooking. If you use wooden skewers, be sure to soak them in water for about 15 minutes to prevent them from burning on the grill. The flattened style of metal skewers (rather than round ones) are well worth the investment; these hold food best of all.

CUT SHEET ALERT: Do specify where you want your kebob and stew meat to come from (I always ask for scraps only); otherwise, you risk losing a good roast.

SERVES 2 TO 4

7 cloves garlic

¼ cup extra-virgin olive oil

2 teaspoons red wine vinegar

2 teaspoons freshly squeezed lemon juice

½ teaspoon tomato paste

¼ teaspoon ground allspice

¼ teaspoon ground cardamom

Pinch of ground cassia (preferably Korintje cassia) or ground cinnamon

¼ teaspoon freshly ground black pepper

Salt

1 pound pastured lamb kebob meat, or meat you have cut from a leg or shoulder roast into 1½- to 2-inch cubes

4 small onions, cut into 4 wedges each

1 red bell pepper, stemmed, seeded, and cut into 1-inch pieces

Cherry or grape tomatoes, or larger tomatoes cut into wedges

½ cup full-fat Greek-style yogurt

4 pieces of lavash

Chop 4 of the cloves of garlic and make the marinade by combining them with the oil, vinegar, lemon juice, tomato paste, spices, pepper, and salt to taste in a nonreactive bowl or refrigerator container. Add the meat, stir it to coat it with the mixture, and set it aside for 2 to 3 hours (if you soak for longer, the acidic ingredients will discolor the meat).

Heat an outdoor grill (preferably a charcoal one) to hot. If using a gas grill, use soaked wood chips in a perforated foil packet to provide a smoky flavor.

Remove the lamb from the marinade and blot it dry. Discard the marinade. Thread 4 skewers with an alternating assortment of meat, onions, bell pepper, and tomatoes. (Thread the skewers through wedge-shaped pieces of tomato and onion from the wide area to the wedge core to hold them securely.)

Make the sauce by finely chopping the remaining 3 cloves of garlic and stirring them into the yogurt (for a smoother sauce, use a food processor or blender). Set aside.

Grill the meat until it is seared on the outside and rare within, about 4 minutes per side. Warm the flatbread by wrapping it in foil and placing it on the grill for a few minutes.

Serve the kebobs with the flatbread to pull the food off the skewers with, along with the sauce to drizzle onto the meat.

Julia's Great Painted Leg of Lamb

*O*ver the years, I've continued to adapt this simple recipe, one of my favorites, from Julia Child's classic Mastering the Art of French Cooking. *These days I omit the soy sauce and use thyme rather than rosemary for the marinating paste, which I make in a mortar and pestle to grind the garlic into submission. I use a silicone brush to paint the paste onto the meat. You can also use this paste on lamb rump steak, which will cook much faster—in about 10 minutes!*

SERVES 4 TO 6

3½ to 4 pounds bone-in leg of pastured lamb

2 cloves garlic

½ cup grainy mustard

1 tablespoon fresh thyme or rosemary leaves, plus additional sprigs for garnish

1 teaspoon ground ginger, or 1 (1-inch) piece fresh ginger, peeled and chopped

2 tablespoons extra-virgin olive oil

Kosher salt

Bring the meat to room temperature, rinse it, and blot it dry. Heat the oven to 350 degrees and position the oven rack in the center. Prepare a roasting pan with a V-rack.

Using a heavy mortar and pestle, pound the garlic, mustard, thyme, and ginger to a thick paste, or pulse the ingredients in a small food processor. Slowly add the olive oil, drop by drop, whisking, to emulsify the oil into the paste.

Set the meat on a V-rack, bottom (lean side) up, salt it lightly, and paint it with slightly less than half of the paste. Turn the meat over so that the fat side is up, salt it lightly, and paint it, along with the two ends, with the remaining paste.

Insert a meat thermometer into the center of the meat and roast it for about 1½ hours, or just until the internal temperature is 135 degrees for medium rare. Immediately remove the meat from the oven and let it rest for at least 15 minutes before carving.

Arrange the slices on a serving platter and garnish them with a few sprigs of thyme or rosemary.

MUSAB'S CILANTRO, MINT, AND YOGURT CHUTNEY

Musab, my son-in-law, invented this chutney when visiting one day, which goes wonderfully with many of the lamb dishes in this book. An overnight rest improves the flavor, so make it ahead if you can.

1 cup fresh cilantro leaves and stems, any thick white parts removed

½ cup fresh mint leaves

Freshly squeezed juice of ½ lime (about 2 tablespoons)

6 heaping tablespoons full-fat Greek yogurt

1 whole serrano chile, seeded

½ teaspoon ground cumin

¼ teaspoon kosher salt

4 whole almonds

¼ teaspoon freshly ground black pepper

¼ teaspoon ground mustard

Combine all the ingredients in a blender and process them to a paste, scraping down the sides of the container as needed. Store in a nonreactive container in the refrigerator for up to 3 days. **Makes about 1 cup.**

Boneless Leg of Lamb Stuffed with Greens, Herbs, and Mushrooms

This traditional Mediterranean festive dish is simply delicious. I often make it with my guests on culinary vacations. You can use almost any good cooking green in the stuffing—spinach, kale, escarole, chard, or even dandelion greens will all taste wonderful. The key is to use lots and lots of fresh herbs—they really make the dish a stand-out. As in any stuffed roast, the slices reveal a pretty spiral of green herbal stuffing. It's great company food.

SERVES 6 TO 8

2 ounces dried cèpes (also called *porcini* in Italian—both are *Boletus edulis*) or chanterelle mushrooms

1 tablespoon unsalted butter

3 tablespoons extra-virgin olive oil

1 small onion, minced

2 tablespoons minced garlic

½ pound white button mushrooms, minced

½ cup cooked greens, drained and squeezed dry

2 teaspoons salt

2 teaspoons freshly ground black pepper

⅓ cup chopped fresh thyme

⅓ cup chopped fresh rosemary

1 cup freshly made bread crumbs

1 small egg, beaten

4 to 5 pounds boneless leg of pastured lamb, butterflied

Preheat the oven to 400 degrees. Rehydrate the dried mushrooms by soaking them in very hot water for at least 20 minutes. When they feel soft and pliant, strain the mushroom water though a paper coffee filter and reserve it. Squeeze the mushrooms dry, discard the tough stems, and chop the caps into small dice. Set the mushrooms aside.

Melt the butter and 1 tablespoon of the olive oil in a skillet over medium heat. Add the onion and sweat it until translucent, 2 minutes or so, then add 1 tablespoon of the garlic and cook for another minute. Add the fresh mushrooms and cook until they have changed color and released their juices,

2 to 4 minutes more. Add the cooked and squeezed greens, and reconstituted mushrooms, reserving the mushroom liquid for another use such as risotto. Stir gently, and after a minute or two, transfer the contents of the skillet to a large bowl. Add 1 teaspoon of the salt and 1 teaspoon of the pepper, half of the herbs, ¾ cup of the bread crumbs, and the egg. Mix well.

If the stuffing seems loose and wet, add more bread crumbs. It should hold together when you squeeze it between your hands, much like hamburger meat.

Blot the meat, open it out, and look at it. You want as even a slab of meat as possible. If it is too uneven to roll well, slice it horizontally as needed and/or pound it flatter with the flat side of a meat pounder, starting from the center and working outward.

Season both sides of the meat with the remaining 1 teaspoon salt and 1 teaspoon pepper, and rub the remaining tablespoon garlic into the cut side of the meat.

Spoon the stuffing onto the slab of lamb, starting from the shorter side. Roll the lamb with its grain (the long way) to enclose the stuffing and tie it securely, using kitchen twine looped around the rolled meat at intervals of 3 or 4 inches (see page 26). Rub the outside of the lamb with the remaining 2 tablespoons olive oil and then with the rest of the herbs. The herbs should make a solid covering. Any extra stuffing can be baked in a greased ramekin covered with foil; this makes a great entrée for any vegetarians at the table.

Place the roast with its seam side down in a shallow baking dish on a rack, and roast for 60 to 70 minutes, until an instant-read thermometer registers 135 degrees for rare. Tent the roast very loosely with aluminum foil, and let it rest outside the oven for 15 minutes to allow for oven rise and the redistribution of juices.

To serve, remove the kitchen twine and cut the meat into ½-inch-thick slices, using an electric knife or a very sharp knife. Spoon any pan juices over the slices.

Leg of Lamb
with Honey-Mint Pesto

usab, my son-in-law, created this fragrant herb paste, and I use it over and over again. You can play with the amount of rosemary if you wish, but the key to success lies in the massive amounts of fresh mint and garlic. I've added a sauce that further refines this dish.

SERVES 6 TO 8

4 to 6 pounds bone-in leg of pastured lamb

2 teaspoons salt, or to taste

6 cloves garlic, chopped

2 tablespoons honey

½ cup chopped fresh mint leaves

2 tablespoons to ½ cup chopped fresh rosemary

¼ cup grainy mustard

About 2 tablespoons extra-virgin olive oil

Freshly ground black pepper

⅓ cup Marsala or sherry

1 to 2 tablespoons heavy cream

Bring the meat to room temperature, rinse it, and blot it dry.

Working by hand or using a food processor, combine the salt, garlic, honey, mint, rosemary, mustard, olive oil, and 5 good grinds of black pepper to form a paste. Use a spatula or your hands to spread it on the meat, coating all sides. Let the meat sit for 1 to 2 hours at room temperature, or refrigerated for a day or two if desired.

Heat the oven to 375 degrees and place the oven rack in the center. Choose a low-sided pan that is only a little larger than the meat, such as a cast-iron frying pan or an oval gratin dish. Roast the meat in the center of the oven, turning it halfway through the cooking, for 1½ hours, or until the internal temperature registers 130 degrees on an instant-read thermometer. Transfer the meat to a carving board and let it rest for 20 minutes.

While the meat is resting, put the roasting pan on the stovetop over medium heat and deglaze it with the Marsala, stirring and scraping the pan to incorporate the caramelized bits of meat and herb paste into the sauce. Reduce the sauce slightly to cook off the alcohol. Remove the sauce from the heat and stir in the cream. Taste for seasonings and correct, if necessary. Serve the warm sauce in a gravy boat or pitcher alongside thin slices of the lamb.

Grilled Lamb Riblets Glazed with Pomegranate Molasses

adore pomegranate molasses, a fabulous and inexpensive condiment, available at Middle Eastern stores and online. It makes this dish (as well as any other grilled meats) absolutely delicious. Here it is mixed with balsamic vinegar and serves both as a marinade and as a sauce.

I like to serve this, doused with the molasses and vinegar sauce, alongside chewy brown rice and a big salad, all on the same plate. Do note that riblets, like traditional ribs, are finger food and are made for gnawing.

SERVES 2

About 10 ounces pastured lamb riblets

¼ cup pomegranate molasses

2 tablespoons balsamic vinegar

Extra-virgin olive oil, for the grill

2 cups salad greens

Bring a hibachi or standard gas or charcoal grill to high heat. (A hibachi is actually the best choice here, as charcoal provides lots of heat, and the grill is appropriately scaled for these miniature ribs.)

Blot the riblets. Mix the pomegranate molasses and vinegar and divide into two small containers. Use one to brush onto the raw meat as marinade, and reserve the other for sauce. Let the meat marinate for 15 minutes or more, while the grill heats up.

Oil the grill grates or grill rack and cook the marinated meat, turning it once, until the outside is charred and the inside is rare. This will take 5 to 7 minutes per side.

Using a sharp knife, divide the ribs into 2 portions, or cut into separate ribs. Line each plate with 1 cup of the salad greens, top it with cooked rice and then the riblets, and finish with a drizzle of sauce over all.

Take Care When Broiling Sweet Marinades!

One of my testers, Sarah Strauss, wrote me a funny but also terrifying account of her broiler catching fire when she tried to cook a romantic dinner for herself and her husband while her baby slept. (You'll see I've changed the recipe to an outdoor grill only!) Sarah said: "The grilled lamb riblets glazed with pomegranate sauce were exciting—no, really exciting—to make. A few minutes into the second side, I noticed the flames. When they shot out to two feet in the air, I began to worry a little. The first floor smoke alarm went off, then the second floor (astonishingly, our son kept sleeping!). After the flames died down and the oven stopped beeping, Matt and I stood in the kitchen and laughed so hard, I thought we would fall over. The recipe was delicious—charred on the outside but juicy on the inside. Next time we'll do it outside!"

Sugar burns easily, and so it's important to put some water in the bottom of a two-part broiler pan, to keep a close eye on the meat while it cooks, and to be prepared to smother any flames that may occur with a large pot lid.

Grilled Lamb Riblets with Moroccan Spices and Brown Sugar Rub

ixing Moroccan spices with brown sugar makes a rub that enhances the flavor of lamb dramatically. If you don't have an outdoor grill, try this in a broiler with the heat set as high as possible and the meat as close to the heating element as is safe (but keep a close eye on it so that it doesn't catch fire). Let the meat sit with the sugar-and-spice blend on it for as long as possible—an hour or all day. But don't worry—even if it isn't applied until the grill or broiler is heating, it will still add flavor.

SERVES 2

About 1 pound pastured lamb riblets (7 ribs)

2 tablespoons cumin seeds or ground cumin

1 teaspoon sweet paprika

½ teaspoon hot paprika or crushed red pepper flakes

1 tablespoon kosher salt

1 tablespoon light brown sugar

1 tablespoon unsalted butter, melted

Remove the riblets from their package and blot them dry. If you are using cumin seeds, grind them to a powder in an electric spice grinder or a mortar and pestle. Blend this with both paprikas, the salt, and the brown sugar.

Brush the riblets with the melted butter and shake on the spice mixture to coat both sides, pressing the powder into the butter to help it adhere. Cover the meat with a sheet of waxed paper and let it sit at room temperature for 1 hour, or wrap it tightly in plastic wrap and refrigerate overnight.

When you are ready to cook the meat, heat the grill or broiler to high heat. Grill the riblets for about 4 minutes per side, or 7 minutes in a two-part broiler pan, the top lined with silver foil, perforated at the slits, and the bottom pan filled with an inch of water. Broil until the outside is seared and the interior is pink, but not raw.

Choosing a Processor

This past year I made the mistake of letting a fellow sheep farmer make a joint appointment to process our lambs, and we used a facility new to us both. Just days before our October processing appointment (too late to make a new appointment elsewhere), the facility revealed their aversion to cut sheets and to precise labeling. I also realized, belatedly, that they only did custom processing and were without a USDA inspector on-site. Normally, this wouldn't matter, since I don't sell the meat I raise. However, it did mean that they acted without any oversight at all, and could mistreat animals and meat without interference.

These omissions were visible in lots of dimensions—the yield from my lambs was extremely low, which made me suspect that some portion of the meat was diverted. Our pick-up date for frozen meat was changed several times, leading me to worry that the lambs had not been processed in a timely manner, stressing the animals. Finally, the meat from both of my lambs came back to me not in Cryovac, but on Styrofoam trays wrapped in plastic wrap, just like at the supermarket—not the best way to protect meat from freezer burn. The pieces were labeled generically, as in "roast" or "chop." There were no indications of what part of the animal they came from, and they had no weights on them.

I noticed, as I cooked my way through the meat, that the pieces didn't keep well because they were so poorly packaged. I sometimes had to throw meat away—a very hard thing to do when you've raised the animal.

The lesson for consumers buying in bulk: Take a good look at a farmer's meat before ordering an animal in whole or in part, and ask him how he feels about his processor and whether you have any choice about packaging.

The lesson for farmers: Pay attention to the details and ask lots of questions before you commit your animals to a facility.

SHANK: One of the great braising meat cuts, lamb shanks offer falling-off-the-bone melting texture and good meaty flavor that takes well to a great variety of ethnic traditions. Shanks can come from the forelegs or hind legs, and can be boned for ground meat or left on the bone (either whole or crosscut) for braising.

▌ **CUT SHEET ALERT:** Ask for whole bone-in or crosscut lamb shanks if you want to make any of these braising recipes.

Marinated Lamb Shanks with Pomegranate Molasses, Tomatoes, and Fresh Mint

Marinating the meat overnight means that it really gets a chance to absorb the flavors—and for this recipe you don't have to brown the meat before braising. Serve the dish with rice, and provide some chutney on the side (try Musab's Cilantro, Mint, and Yogurt Chutney, page 165).

SERVES 2 TO 4

4 meaty bone-in pastured lamb shanks

Salt

2 tablespoons pomegranate molasses

1 heaping tablespoon very finely chopped fresh mint leaves, plus more for serving

3 cloves garlic, minced

2 tablespoons extra-virgin olive oil

2 tablespoons very hot water

1 onion, chopped

2 carrots, chopped

½ cup red wine

1 (14.5-ounce) can crushed tomatoes

1 lemon wedge, as needed

For serving:

Cooked rice, such as basmati

Plain yogurt

Rinse and blot the meat dry, and salt it very lightly. Mix the pomegranate molasses with the tablespoon of mint, the garlic, and 1 tablespoon of the olive oil, beating in the hot water to make the paste a little more liquid. Put it in a refrigerator container or bowl and turn the meat in it to coat all sides. Cover and refrigerate overnight or for at least several hours.

Return the meat to room temperature. Heat an enameled cast-iron Dutch oven or other braising pot over low heat and add the remaining 1 tablespoon olive oil. When it thins and becomes fragrant, add the onion and carrots, and cook until they are limp. Deglaze the pan with the wine, scraping to loosen any caramelized bits. Add the tomatoes and stir in the meat and marinade.

Cut a piece of parchment paper to fit over the meat in the pot, laying it right on top to help it braise more efficiently. Put the lid on the pot and cook over low heat at a slow simmer for 2 to 2½ hours, until the meat is falling off the bone and tender.

Taste the sauce and add salt and a squeeze of lemon to correct the sweet/sour balance, if needed. Serve over rice, topped with a heaping spoonful of yogurt and showered with mint.

Lamb Tagine with Preserved Lemon and Green Olives

*T*his tagine is adapted from a recipe in Couscous and Other Good Food from Morocco *by Paula Wolfert, who has taught so many of us about Moroccan food. The method here is interesting. Instead of browning the meat at the start of the cooking process, you allow it to brown at the very end—it stays in the oven while you finish the sauce on the stovetop.*

If you don't have preserved lemon, you can make this with fresh. The flavor is a little less complex, but the dish will still be terrific. Be sure to serve this with a starch like rice to soak up the flavorful sauce.

SERVES 4

4 bone-in pastured lamb shanks	½ cup chopped fresh flat-leaf parsley
1 teaspoon ground ginger	½ cup chopped fresh cilantro, plus more for serving
1 teaspoon ground cumin	
¼ teaspoon saffron threads	3 cups water
1 teaspoon ground cinnamon	¾ cup flavorful green olives such as Atlas
1 teaspoon sweet paprika	Freshly squeezed juice from ½ lemon (see page 174)
Freshly ground black pepper	½ preserved lemon (see page 174), or 1 fresh lemon, rinsed and zest cut into thin strips
2 tablespoons extra-virgin olive oil	
1 tablespoon unsalted butter	Salt, as needed
2 large onions, chopped	Plain yogurt mixed with a little harissa
4 cloves garlic, chopped	

Bring the meat to room temperature, rinse it, and blot it dry. Combine the ginger, cumin, saffron, cinnamon, paprika, and a generous amount of black pepper and toss the meat with this spice blend in a medium bowl.

Using a ceramic tagine, Dutch oven, flameproof clay pot with a cover such as a Chinese sand pot, or a heavy, shallow braising pan, slowly heat the olive oil and butter over medium-low heat. Cook the spice-coated meat for 2 to 3 minutes, or until it is warmed on all sides, glistening, and aromatic. Remove the meat from the pan and add the onions and garlic, giving them a stir and cooking for a few minutes to reduce them to limpness. Return the meat to the pan, placing it on top of the onion bed. Add the parsley and cilantro along with the water, and bring this to a quick boil. Immediately reduce the heat to the lowest possible setting and cover the pot with a layer of parchment paper that nearly touches the meat, then put the lid on the pot—this really helps to keep the moisture in. Simmer for 1½ hours, or until the meat is nearly tender, checking occasionally to make sure there is enough liquid and turning the meat now and then. (Alternatively, you can roast the meat at 300 degrees for about the same amount of time.)

Blanch the olives in boiling water for about 1 minute, drain them, reserving the liquid, and add them to the pot, along with the lemon juice. (The blanching can be omitted, but the olives are less flavorful and juicy without it.)

If you are using the preserved lemon, scoop out and discard the pulp from the lemon half. Cut the rind into narrow slices and add them to the meat. For the fresh lemon, use the reserved olive-blanching water to blanch the strips of zest for 1 or 2 minutes, then add them to the pot. Cook the tagine, covered closely with parchment paper, for another 30 minutes, or until the meat is meltingly tender. If you wish, the recipe can be done ahead to this point and refrigerated; this will make it easier for you to remove the fat from the top of the braise. If you do this, gently reheat the defatted braise on the stove before proceeding.

Using tongs, transfer the meat to a sheet pan. Heat the oven to 450 degrees and set a rack just under the broiler. Crisp the meat for about 5 minutes per side.

As the oven heats and the meat crisps, skim the braising pan of any fat. Gently reduce the liquid over medium heat, if necessary, to slightly thicken the sauce. The heat must stay moderate so that you don't cook out all the good flavors. Taste and correct the seasonings as needed (be aware that preserved lemon is quite salty, so if you used it, you will need less salt than if you used fresh).

Combine the now-browned meat and the sauce, and serve, garnished with a dollop of harissa-spiked yogurt and a generous sprinkle of chopped cilantro.

Lamb Shanks à la Tangia

A tangia is a tall ceramic pot used for steaming meat in the heat of a hammam furnace—but every one I found in rural Morocco was already chipped on the rim. Unwilling to carry back a damaged pot, no matter how authentic, I decided to make do with more conventional wares. This stew is adapted from a recipe in Casa Moro, *by Samuel and Samantha Clark. It requires a heavy braising pot, a slow oven, and time.*

SERVES 2 TO 4

4 bone-in pastured lamb shanks (about 1½ pounds)

1 preserved lemon (see box), or 1 fresh lemon, rinsed

1 onion, roughly cut into chunks

1 tablespoon cumin seeds, pounded lightly in a mortar and pestle until fragrant

8 cloves garlic, smashed

½ cup fresh cilantro leaves

2 tablespoons extra-virgin olive oil

½ cup water

Sea salt and freshly ground black pepper

Bring the lamb shanks to room temperature, rinse them, and blot them dry. Heat the oven to its hottest setting, anywhere from 450 to 500 degrees. While the oven is heating, remove and discard the flesh from the preserved lemon (you don't have to do this with a fresh one—just remove the seeds with the point of a knife), and cut the lemon into pieces. Add it, along with the onion, cumin, garlic, and cilantro, to the bowl of a food processor fitted with the steel blade. Pulse to make a rough paste. Scrape down the sides of the bowl and add the oil, water, and salt and pepper to taste and pulse again just to blend.

Put the lamb and paste in a heavy braising pot such as a tall ceramic casserole, a clay bean pot with a tight-fitting lid, an enameled cast-iron casserole, or a braising pot, and toss everything to mix it well. Push down a piece of parchment paper large enough to cover the mixture so that it touches the meat. The paper should overlap the edge of the pot. Add a layer of foil around the rim of the pot to make the seal even more airtight. Put the lid on the pot.

When the oven is hot, immediately turn the temperature down to 275 degrees, and cook the meat for about 5 hours, or until it is completely tender and has separated from the bones. If, after 5 hours, you have a high liquid-to-meat ratio, remove the meat, skim off the fat, and reduce the liquid on the stovetop to make a thicker, more intense sauce.

Serve the meat (on or off the bones) in the sauce, along with potatoes, pasta, rice, quinoa, couscous, or flatbread.

PRESERVED LEMONS

I've been making my own preserved lemons for years, and I find when I can use sweet and mild Meyer lemons, they taste best of all. A sterile, wide-mouthed, quart-sized jar keeps well in the refrigerator for more than a year.

6 lemons, preferably Meyer

About ¾ cup kosher (non-iodized) salt

Rinse the lemons; slice lengthwise into quarters, cutting nearly but not all the way through. Using a sterile, wide-mouthed mason jar, cover the base of the jar with a shallow layer of the salt. Holding a cut lemon over a bowl, open it out and pour a generous amount of salt over all the cut surfaces, coating them. Put the lemon in the jar, sprinkling a little more salt on top. Harvest the salt in the bowl to repeat with the remaining lemons, adding more salt as needed. As each lemon is layered into the jar, push down with a wooden spoon to compact and squeeze out the juice. When all the lemons have been added, if they are not submerged in lemon juice, squeeze in enough to cover. Seal the jar, and shake it daily for a few weeks. Refrigerate after opening. When using, rinse each quarter well, then discard the flesh and chop the peel.

OFFAL AND ODD BITS: Tongue, kidneys, heart, and liver are all available as part of a whole lamb order and are worth including in your cooking repertoire. If you can get lamb sweetbreads, they can be cooked exactly the same way as beef sweetbreads (see page 118) and lamb kidney cooks just like beef kidney (see page 122).

Lenguas de Cordero Salteadas

These extraordinarily rich and crisp little morsels of lamb tongue are so delicious, it's hard to stop eating them. Serve them as an hors d'oeuvre or as a main course with rice and salsa. The secret of their allure is braising for tenderness, then dipping each slice in a flour-and-egg wash and crisping it in hot olive oil. Served alone with a generous squeeze of fresh lemon, they are Basque soul food. They're also terrific with Lizzie's Mango, Lime, and Mint Salsa (see page 158).

CUT SHEET ALERT: Since each lamb comes with only one tongue, obviously, you'll need to ask your farmer or processor for the tongues of other lambs. You'll likely find there is little competition for them.

SERVES 4 TO 6 AS AN APPETIZER
OR 2 OR 3 AS A LIGHT ENTRÉE

8 to 10 pastured lamb tongues (1½ to 2 pounds)

1 lemon, cut into wedges

Kosher salt

½ onion

2 bay leaves

12 juniper berries

½ cup unbleached all-purpose flour

2 large eggs, beaten

2 tablespoons extra-virgin olive oil

Sea salt, for sprinkling

Place the tongues, 2 lemon wedges, 1 teaspoon salt, the onion, bay leaves, and juniper berries in a heavy Dutch oven or other braising pot. Cover everything with cold water and bring it to a slow boil. Lower the heat to maintain a slow simmer, arranging the lid of the pot slightly askew so that steam can escape. Cook for a good 2½ hours, or until the tongues are very tender.

Remove the tongues from the liquid with tongs and discard the liquid. Cool the tongues under cold running water and drain them well. The little tongues are vaguely L-shaped, and look like feet or boots; using a sharp paring knife, make an incision at the middle of the "toe" end of each tongue; pull off and discard the skin on all sides.

Using a larger knife, cut each tongue into quarter-inch slices, cutting crosswise and at a slight diagonal to increase the surface area of each slice.

Put the flour in one shallow bowl and the beaten eggs and ½ teaspoon salt in another. Heat the pan and add the olive oil. When it thins and becomes fragrant, begin cooking the meat. Dip each slice first in egg, shake off the excess, and then dredge it in the flour and shake that excess off. Fry each slice in the hot oil until browned on both sides, 3 to 4 minutes in all. Serve hot with a little sea salt sprinkled over and a good squeeze of lemon from the remaining lemon wedges.

Braising and Frying Offal and Odd Bits

Consider this a master recipe for offal, which works for the sweetbreads, tongue, kidneys, heart, and tail of every animal. Just like the lamb tongues, above, the meat is slowly braised to tenderness, then sliced, run through an egg bath, floured, and then fried for crunch. This series of fail-safe techniques works beautifully for these less familiar cuts.

Lamb Liver with Whiskey and Cream Sauce

've simplified an Irish recipe originally published in Saveur *by eliminating an overnight salt-and-milk soak for the liver. Pastured lamb is tender and mild by nature, and this just isn't necessary. My lamb liver came presliced, but slicing is an easy task. The friend who ate this couldn't stop talking about the taste. This is a very quick dinner to prepare, as liver should be served rare. I like it accompanied by a salad and steamed baby potatoes.*

SERVES 4

1 pound pastured lamb liver, cut into ¼-inch slices

¼ teaspoon kosher salt

3 tablespoons unsalted butter

1 onion, finely chopped

1 tablespoon Irish whiskey such as Jameson's

½ cup heavy cream or half-and-half

1 tablespoon grainy mustard

Freshly ground black pepper

Rinse the liver and dry by putting it on a layer of paper towels and blotting the top with more paper towels. Sprinkle it lightly with the salt. Heat a large, heavy frying pan such as one made from cast iron or anodized aluminum.

Melt 1 tablespoon of the butter over medium heat, then reduce the heat and slowly sweat down the onion pieces to limpness. Just as they start to brown, transfer them to a plate and set aside.

If your pan can hold all the liver in one layer, melt the remaining 2 tablespoons butter (otherwise plan on cooking 2 batches, each using 1 tablespoon of butter), swirling it to cover the bottom of the pan. Using high heat, sear as much of the liver as can fit in the pan without crowding, 1 to 2 minutes per side. Using tongs, transfer the cooked liver to a plate and reserve.

Turn off the flame and add the whiskey and cream to the pan, stirring with a wooden spatula or spoon to dislodge any caramelized bits stuck to the pan and incorporating them into the sauce. Turn the heat on to low, and add the mustard, and pepper to taste. Simmer slowly over low heat for a minute or two, until the sauce thickens slightly.

Return the meat and onion to the pan with the sauce and stir everything together gently while heating through to warm. Serve at once.

Lamb Liver Spread

The milk soak in this recipe transforms lamb liver into a spread perfect for crackers or for spooning on endive leaves as a cocktail accompaniment, or for making sandwiches on split brioche for a weekday lunch. It's the opposite of the previous recipe in that the liver is slowly cooked rather than quickly seared.

SERVES 6 TO 8

1 pound pastured lamb liver

2 cups milk

2 tablespoons pastured chicken fat (see page 284), pastured pork bacon fat (see page 257), or unsalted butter

1 egg

1 teaspoon sugar

½ teaspoon paprika, plus more for garnish

1 teaspoon ground coriander

¼ teaspoon ground allspice

¼ teaspoon ground cardamom

Salt

¼ cup sour cream

Soak the liver in the milk overnight in the refrigerator. Drain the liver, discard the milk, and blot the meat dry.

Melt the fat in a frying pan over low heat, and when it is hot, add the liver. Sauté slowly until it is cooked on the outside and slightly pink within, about 5 minutes. Set aside to cool.

Meanwhile, in a small saucepan, submerge the egg in cold water and bring it to a boil. Cover and let the egg sit in the hot water, off the heat, for 10 minutes. Put the egg into an ice-water bath and then peel it, cut it into quarters, and place it in the bowl of a food processor fitted with the steel blade.

Cut the liver in pieces and add it to the food processor bowl, along with the sugar, spices, salt to taste, and the sour cream. Process until you have a smooth paste.

Garnish with a few more shakes of paprika, if you wish.

Offal

Defrost offal overnight in the refrigerator, and make sure to use it the next day. Even when sealed in Cryovac, offal is delicate and can easily smell off. Plan on cooking it as soon as it is defrosted—well rinsed and blotted dry before proceeding with the chosen recipe.

PORK

The Pig and I

I come from a secular Jewish family, so eating pork has always been part of my culinary experience. Even so, pastured pork has been so entirely different in taste and texture from American industrial pork, they could easily be different species of animal. When we lived in Denmark for two years some twenty years ago, we ate lots of Danish pork (mostly Landrace pigs), which was quite good even though it was raised on an industrial scale. Our years in Vermont buying local pork further broadened our experience. More recently, in the last five or six years, local producers have been offering heritage breeds and heritage crossbreeds, allowing all of us to experience a wealth of new flavors.

Heritage-pastured pork provides a dramatically different taste experience from industrial corn-fed meat in part because much of the fat has been bred out of mass-market pigs. Remarkably, these days industrial pigs have 50 percent less fat than they did in the 1950s, and there is a consequent loss of flavor. In the past, pigs were divided into bacon types and lard types, with the latter used more for fat than for fresh meat because lard was such an important commodity both for cooking and preserving.

Heirloom breeds offer some of the benefits of both types of pig and provide unique flavors. They are increasingly popular with grass farmers both because they are hardy and able to forage well and because raising heritage breeds keeps genetic diversity alive and leads to healthier bloodlines.

Thus, some of the breeds used these days for pastured pork are a mix of commercial breeds and older breeds, including Berkshire (prized in Japan, where it is called Kurobuta, or "black hog"), Hampshire, Tamworth, Yorkshire, Gloucestershire Old Spots, Large Black, Choctaw, Red Wattle, and Duroc, as well as crosses that contain these breeds. Of these, Yorkshire and Tamworth are bacon breeds, while Duroc, Hampshire, and Yorkshire are the breeds often used in a three-way cross for today's commercial production. Other commercially popular breeds include Poland China, American Landrace, and Chester White, which are used as crosses as well as single breeds for large-scale meat production.

Crossbreeding is done in hopes that the best traits of both ancestors will show up in the offspring, so commercial pigs are bred to fatten well on feed, while pasture producers might breed a good foraging pig like a Tamworth with a more conventional breed to create a hardy pig that can be sustained in large part on pasture and forest. It is also possible to find purebred heritage breeds of pork. Many farmers raise and sell pork from Berkshires, Tamworths, and Gloucestershire Old Spots, which are known for the hardiness and foraging ability that make them good candidates for pasture raising. Rarer, but increasingly available, Red Wattle pigs, once known as the "woods hogs" of East Texas, are extremely hardy and graze well, producing high-quality meat.

As in the case of cows, the differences between industrial pork and pastured pork are time, feed, and fresh air—industrial pork is raised in (cramped and stressful) confinement and is bred to gain weight extremely rapidly. It is fed refuse and antibiotics, and slaughtered at an early age. Pastured pork, usually raised by one producer from birth to processing, is allowed to roam out of doors on controlled and often rotating pasture; these animals gain weight at a much slower rate and consequently cannot be processed until later in their lives.

All pastured pork comes from animals that live outside and forage for some part of their food supply. Most pigs cannot live on forage alone, so their diet is also supplemented. You can ask your meat producer what he feeds his pigs other than forage—many raise food crops for their pigs and also use pigs as composters, feeding them the same good ingredients they put in their compost piles (waste dairy products, slightly spoiled vegetables, leftover cereal, old bread, and other kitchen leavings). I once bought a delicious half pig from a New Hampshire grower who fed his pigs the waste products from the Stonyfield Farm yogurt factory, located nearby. Increasingly, pastured pork producers are raising pigs in forest settings, letting them feed freely on acorns and other nuts. Some pigs graze between trees in apple orchards, where they function as organic controls to protect the fruit crop from insect blight. Others are used to manage forests, helping to control the growth of "weed trees" and encourage the growth of hardwoods. (In fact, in the nineteenth and early twentieth centuries, pigs helped to create the park-like savannahs of North Carolina's Piedmont by eating down forest floor vegetation, allowing hardwood trees to flourish without competition. Pigs seem to choose soft woods to eat, and they ignore the hardwoods. They also ate down wild berry bushes and other brushy growth, keeping the land between hardwood trees clear.) All pastured pigs become, by virtue of their activities in the field, part of a complex ecosystem that includes small animals, birds, and other wildlife. Historically (and increasingly in the present), pigs and cows

were pastured consecutively in the same paddocks so that the pigs could clean up after the cows, controlling parasites. The cows contribute vitamin B$_{12}$ to grazing pigs, and as a result, companion grazing enhances the health of both species.

Pastured pigs look and smell pretty clean—since they are not closely confined, they clean themselves and keep their sleeping areas free of manure. (Remarkably, pigs naturally designate a separate area for elimination.) By contrast, factory pigs are deeply stressed by confinement, and live amidst their own waste, smelling horrible.

Recently, there has been something of a backlash against pastured pork by some who warn of increased danger of trichinosis and salmonella. James E. McWilliams, author of *Just Food*, is one of those who has spoken out. I believe one must take precautions in handling any meat, cleaning it before cooking and heating it to the correct internal temperature. There may well be a learning curve for farmers new to pasturing animals that compromises the safety of some meats. However, it seems much more likely to me that on balance high-density industrial food production practices produce far more health risks to diners. Further, the deeply inhumane treatment of industrial pigs throughout their lives and at many slaughterhouses creates serious ethical concerns for many consumers.

It is always important to pay close attention to the quality of the meat you cook. Bring all pork to a safe internal temperature of 160 degrees—this destroys any trichinosis. Since oven rise brings roasted meats up a further 5 to 10 degrees, it is possible to remove pork from the oven at 150 to 155 degrees, then measure the internal temperature of a roast 10 minutes later to ensure that the center is sufficiently cooked. If nothing else, I hope this book will encourage readers to buy and use an instant-read thermometer to check their meat as it cooks and settles.

The Flavor of Pastured Pork

The taste of pastured pork reflects the animal's diet—meat from pigs that graze on fruit tastes different from that of pigs that graze on nuts—and today's sustainable producers are offering pork that reflects *terroir* in much the same way as it has always been offered in Europe. Sustainable pork has luscious fat that is worth rendering for cooking, good marbling in the meat, and a texture visibly different from industrial meat. Best of all, the meat from different breeds eating different diets offers new taste experiences. See Sources (page 371) for the names of producers selling such meat, but do investigate your local resources as well.

Once you've found a breed or pastured pig producer whose pork you like (try to buy a few pounds as samples), you'll be ready to make the plunge into ordering a quarter, half, or whole pig. A whole pig generally comes out to 100 to 180 pounds of meat after processing, depending, of course, on a number of variables. As with other animals, you pay per pound for the weight of the pig before it has been cut up, so your actual price per pound is higher than the price per pound of hanging weight.

Let's assume your pig weighs 150 pounds, dressed. If you order half a pig, your order will total about 75 pounds. Processors often turn more than half the yield into ground meat (this is an even larger percentage than is usual for beef or lamb). As ever, you have a choice in this; ask for more varied cuts, if you prefer them. Here are some examples of what you might order or receive in a conventional mix:

- Pork chops
- Roasts from the loin end and rib end (or rib chops) or crown roast (one per pig!)
- Cracklings (skin)
- Picnic shoulder roasts
- Pork butt roasts
- Stew bones
- Fresh ham
- Slab bacon or pork belly
- Spareribs
- Ground pork
- Pork tenderloin (only one per side of pork (two per pig), but you can ask to have it split into smaller roasts)
- Country-style ribs (which are actually from the shoulder)
- Fatback
- Leaf lard
- Ham hocks
- Pork shank
- Heart
- Liver
- Tongue

If you opt to smoke the bacon, ham, and hocks, you'll pay an additional fee per pound to have the smoking done in a smokehouse. The producer will arrange for the smoking, but do be aware that some smokehouses are better than others. I suggest you buy a small ham steak from a producer or smokehouse you are considering before committing to anything larger, to make sure that they cure meat to your liking.

You can also ask for the whole head, or parts such as ears, tail, snout, and cheeks—each of these can be quite delicious, but their availability varies by processor and consumer demand.

Understanding Pig Anatomy

The Primals

Of the three largest sustainably raised meat animals, pork has the fewest primals—four in all. These are the **shoulder**, **loin**, **belly**, and **leg**. Even so, the possibilities for cutting pork are extremely varied, as pork lends itself to lots of different curing and cooking methods.

The shoulder weighs 25 to 30 pounds, and is often subdivided into the Boston butt, which is the upper part of the shoulder, and the picnic shoulder, which is the arm portion and includes part of the front leg of the pig, known as the hock. Both can be cooked like a fresh ham. Portions of the Boston butt can be cut into blade steaks or roasts, ground with fat and made into sausages, or left as ground pork. The picnic shoulder can provide fresh or smoked hock or picnic steaks/roasts, or the whole shoulder can be left as a whole roast, either fresh or smoked.

The loin (around 15 pounds) is located above the belly and offers some of the tenderest eating on a pig—pork chops from the rib, loin or sirloin, backfat, country-style ribs, center loin roast, rib roast, or boneless pork roast. This portion also provides a pork tenderloin (two per pig) or tenderloin medallions.

Perhaps the greatest of all pork cuts, the belly is the source of spareribs and bacon (or pancetta, if unsmoked but cured). This cut also yields salt pork. A whole belly can weigh 18 pounds.

The leg is the source of great roasts and steaks, and is always from the hind portion. It weighs about 22 pounds. Cured ham, such as prosciutto, is made from this primal. This cut also offers ham steaks, ham roasts, ham hocks, and cutlets.

In addition, you can also ask for the neck and jowls, for soup bones, for jowl bacon, for sausage meat from scraps, and for cheeks to braise. The whole head can be used for headcheese, and the ears, tail, and snout are great for stewing with beans, as in Brazilian *feijoada*. The ear is deliciously chewy and crisp when cooked, and makes a great garnish. Learning to prepare it was one of the unexpected bonuses of researching and writing this book.

Offal includes pig liver, used for Denmark's wonderful *liverpostej*, for French pâtés, and in Asian stir-fries. You can also try to ask for the casings for sausages, which come from the intestines, as well as the jowls and caul fat, but I find it's hard to get those parts from local processors who are unaccustomed to saving them for customers. Perhaps as we create more of a demand for nose-to-tail eating in this country, our processors will be able to develop the skill and expertise to deliver more.

Cut Sheet Choices: What Substitutes for What

SHOULDER

Choice #1:
- Whole primal, used for pulled pork and usually cooked on a spit

Choice #2:
- Picnic roast (skin on, bone in or boneless)

  AND

  Fresh or smoked pork hock (skin on)

  OR
- Ham shank (skinless)

  AND

  Skinless shoulder butt (whole, bone in or boneless)

  OR
- Country-style shoulder butt ribs

  AND

  Trotter (smoked or not, can be boned for stuffing)

LOIN

Choice #1 (all bone-in cuts):
- Pork chops (rib chops, loin chops, sirloin chops)

  AND

  Blade chops

  OR
- Country-style ribs

  OR
- Blade roast (preferably with skin)

Choice #2:
- Pork tenderloin (two per pig)

  AND
- Pork loin roast

  AND
- Pork sirloin

  AND
- Baby back ribs

Pork

Whole Primals: **1.** Trotter **2.** Belly and spareribs **3.** Fresh pork leg **4.** Boston butt **5.** Leaf lard **6.** Pork tenderloin **7.** Rack of pork **8.** Boneless pork loin **9.** Pork sirloin **10.** Pork shank

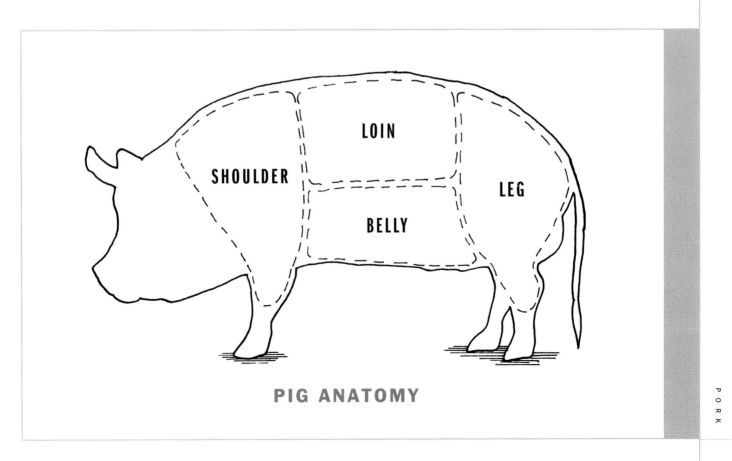

PIG ANATOMY

BREAKING DOWN A SIDE OF PORK

Split whole hog, hanging

Removing shoulder at the fourth rib

Remaining leg after belly is separated

Separating the loin and the belly

Removing the hock from the ham

Splitting the loin

Boning the shoulder

Cutting the shoulder into cubes

Removing spareribs from the belly

Boning the loin

Skinning the ham

The remaining trotter

Lard, Bombs, and the American Diet

Until World War II, lard was the primary cooking fat for most Americans (Jews used chicken fat instead). In addition, it was used as a lubricant for a wide range of industrial applications. Most notably, during both world wars, lard was an essential part of making explosives (it was used as grease). Because it was urgently needed for the war effort, Americans were persuaded to switch to "more healthful" vegetable oils for cooking. Eventually, synthetic and petroleum-based oils were developed and then substituted for lard in military applications, and the market for lard collapsed; lard-type pigs were no longer profitable. Breeders began selecting for animals that would build muscle rapidly for meat, and pork production became centralized and industrial, rather than a by-product of small farming.

Choice #3:

- Pork tenderloin (two per pig)

  AND
- Pork sirloin

  AND
- Bone-in loin chops

  AND
- Bone-in rack of pork

Choice #4:

- Whole loin boned, smoked, and cured for Canadian bacon

  OR
- Whole loin, with bones, for smoked pork loin

Choice #5:

- Whole boneless loin and belly together, to be rolled and stuffed with herbs, salt, and garlic to make a huge *porchetta*

BELLY

- Fresh pork belly

  OR
- Bacon (cured and smoked pork belly)

  OR
- Pancetta (cured and rolled pork belly)

  AND
- Spareribs (whole rack)

  OR
- St. Louis ribs (with the brisket, bone off and cut in half)

LEG

Choice #1:

- Ham (bone in, shank on, skin on, fresh or smoked)

Choice #2:

- 3 to 4 center-cut ham steaks

  AND
- Shank roast

  AND
- Sirloin roast

Choice #3:

- Boneless ham roast (bone out, shank off, with or without skin)

  AND
- Hock (hind shank, skin on)

  OR
- Shank (hind shank, skin off)

Choice #4:

- Seamed into primals, and sliced as pork cutlets (cut ¼ inch or thinner)

  OR
- Pork steaks (cut ½ to 1 inch thick)

  OR
- Pork pot roasts (left whole)

  AND
- Shank (skinless) or hock (skin on)

OFFAL AND ODD BITS

- Jowls
- Snout
- Liver
- Heart
- Kidneys
- Tail
- Cheeks
- Tongue
- Ears
- Fat

Cooking Pastured Pork

Today's heritage and traditional breeds offer real texture and deeper flavors than those of industrial pork, in large part because they are raised outside on a more natural diet. Their meat has a good fat cover, and is generally well marbled, which (because it doesn't dry out) makes it easy to cook. Sustainable pork offers one of the most dramatic flavor and texture contrasts between the products of industrial production and those from farm-based husbandry.

Cooking with Pork Shoulder

The shoulder is a versatile cut from a hardworking part of the pig. It includes the butt, which can be smoked (or not) and cooked like ham, country-style ribs (great for braising), Sunday dinner choices like picnic arm roasts and shoulder blade roasts, and weekday night standbys like picnic and blade steaks.

Cooking with Pork Loin

For pork chops, it's not just the part of the loin that determines their cooking method and timing, cut and thickness also factor in. Thick chops demand more time than thin

On Naming Animals

While many farmers say never to name animals that are destined for the table, others disagree. My own feeling is that one tends to name things involuntarily, even if it's just calling an animal "the big pig" or "the gray sheep," so why not give them a name and respect their identity?

Of course, when you go to eat them, it's not easy knowing you are eating, say, Sally. But on the other hand, it's nearly as hard to eat steer number 34, if you've known him and cared for him all his life. The central question is this: How can you reconcile the affection you inevitably feel for an animal you live with and tenderly care for, knowing at the same time that you are also the agent of its death and destiny as food—especially your own food, and not that of a stranger?

I can only speak from my own rather limited experience here, but to me, giving animals the best life possible and a humane death goes a long way to making the process less hard. I select and commit to my animals knowing that they are destined for meat, and while I certainly feel affection for them, I know that they are not pets. I don't want to minimize the wrench I feel when they are on their way to slaughter—it is hard. But when the meat packages come back, it starts to get less difficult. As time goes on, those packages of meat become disassociated from the animal. I don't think, "Poor Sally," as I defrost or cook, and I don't see her in the meat on my plate. Yes, I know it was Sally, but the "Sally-ness" is gone.

ones, but thin chops dry out faster. Ask for inch-thick cuts, if possible, to ensure succulence, and brine thinner chops if you can. Roasts are more elastic when it comes to timing, and are more flavorful when they have bones. Whether cut into chops or roasts, this primal offers the most tender meat on a pig. Note that the loin is *not* the tenderloin, which is only a small part of this primal.

Cooking with Pork Leg

Whole ham roasts (smoked or fresh) and ham steaks are the stars of this primal, but it also offers shank roasts, sirloin roasts, pork cutlets or steaks or pork roasts. The lower portion gives us shanks and hocks, which are great braising cuts to use in soups, pasta sauces, or stews.

Cooking with Pork Belly

Lush and fatty, this cut is best known for bacon (smoked), but is increasingly valued for fresh belly, which is usually braised or boiled before browning. Spareribs, too, are a well-known and well-appreciated part of this primal.

Cooking with Pork Fat

There are many kinds of useful pork fat, including rendered lard and leaf lard, bacon drippings, fatback, salt pork, and caul fat. Nutritionally, home-rendered pastured pork fat has no trans fat, and has saturated fat that contains stearic acid, which may have a beneficial effect on cholesterol. Lard is also one of the fats high in oleic acid, the mono-unsaturated fatty acid believed to be responsible for so many of olive oil's benefits. It also has anti-microbial qualities, and helps to preserve foods.

PORK RECIPES

GROUND PORK: When you buy a pig in whole or in part, you'll get a great many packages labeled "sausage" (for loose, uncased sausage) or "ground pork," or a mix of the two. The former will likely be seasoned, while the latter will be plain. In either case, the meat will be ground with a good proportion of fat, and offers lots of possibilities for great dinners as well as Sunday breakfast.

Frikadeller, or Danish Meatballs

When we lived in Denmark, every Dane we knew made these often. They were always crowd-pleasers, and every child also seemed to love them. They're traditionally served with lingonberry preserves and thick gravy, but I find they are wonderful with nearly any fruit conserve and Dijon mustard, or with purchased mostarda *(a mustard-and-fruit compote). While many make their* frikadeller *with a mixture of beef or veal and pork, I am crazy about this all-pork version. They make a great appetizer or first course.*

MAKES 20 TO 25 MEATBALLS

1 pound ground pastured pork

1 small onion, grated on the largest holes of a box grater (about 2 tablespoons)

¼ cup unbleached all-purpose flour

About ⅔ cup panko (Japanese bread crumbs) or other bread crumbs

About 3 tablespoons milk

1 egg, beaten

1 teaspoon kosher salt

Freshly ground black pepper

4 tablespoons (½ stick) unsalted butter

About 2 tablespoons Dijon mustard

About 2 tablespoons lingonberry, blueberry, black currant, or red currant preserves

In a large bowl, layer the pork, grated onion, flour, panko, milk, beaten egg, salt, and pepper. Mix this all together, taking care not to overwork the meat but blending it well. If it seems too wet, add more panko by the half spoonful; if it seems dry, add more milk by the spoonful. The mixture should be fairly wet but workable.

I find it is easier to work gloppy mixtures like this with wet hands. Form the meat mixture into loose golf-ball-sized meatballs and set on a plate.

Choose a large, heavy pan such as a cast-iron skillet big enough to hold all the meatballs at the same time (or plan to cook in batches). Melt the butter in the pan over medium heat, and when it is aromatic and sizzling, add the meatballs in one layer. Cook, shaking the pan regularly to maintain their round shape, until browned on all sides, about 8 minutes in all. If they don't roll around, use tongs to turn them.

Serve the meatballs with ¼ teaspoon mustard and ¼ teaspoon preserves dotted on each one.

French Country Pâté

Adapted from Julia Child's recipe in Mastering the Art of French Cooking, *this traditional pâté is very doable for those who buy assorted varieties of sustainable meat in bulk. A visiting friend and I made it one day when we were snowed in, by home-grinding pieces of pork, boning out three frozen chicken thighs, and using a gift of liver from a friend's pig. When you can make a fancy French pâté in the middle of a snowstorm without leaving home, it's a victory for the home cook and local farmers. Use a scale for accuracy, as proportions of meat do matter.*

NOTE: If you don't have the ground meat on hand, you can grind it yourself, as I did during the snowstorm. For the pork, use a 2 to 1 ratio of stew meat or meat scraps and chilled pork fat. For the chicken, use boneless, skinless thigh or breast meat, cut into cubes. Partially freeze all the meat, and place the grinder attachments in the freezer for about an hour before grinding.

MAKES 1 LARGE LOAF OF PÂTÉ, ENOUGH FOR A CROWD

1 tablespoon unsalted butter

1 yellow onion, minced

1¼ pounds unseasoned ground pastured pork or sausage meat

¾ pound ground pastured chicken or turkey

½ pound pastured pork liver

1 cup panko (Japanese bread crumbs) or homemade bread crumbs

1 large egg

½ cup cream cheese

1 clove garlic, minced

1 tablespoon brandy

¾ tablespoon kosher salt

¼ teaspoon ground allspice

¼ teaspoon ground thyme

Freshly ground black pepper

For serving:

Gherkins

Diced hard-boiled eggs

Olives

Grainy mustard or Burgundian Mustard (see page 233)

Artisanal bread

Unsalted butter

Fine sea salt such as Maldon

Heat the oven to 350 degrees, and position the rack in the center. Butter a 4 x 8-inch standard loaf pan and a sheet of waxed paper or parchment cut an inch larger than the top of the pan. Boil enough water to half-fill a bain-marie or roasting pan that easily holds the loaf pan.

Melt the butter in a frying pan and gently sauté the onion until it is translucent. Put it in the bowl of a food processor fitted with the steel blade, along with the ground meats, pork liver, panko, egg, cream cheese, garlic, brandy, salt, and spices. Pulse until the mixture is well blended but still has real texture.

Pour the pâté into the loaf pan, place the waxed paper on top, butter side down, and put a piece of silver foil over the top. Set the pan in the water bath and bake for 1¼ to 1½ hours, until an instant-read thermometer registers an internal temperature of 162 degrees.

Let the pâté cool for 1 hour in the pan, then set a cutting board or a pan of the same size on top of the meat and weight it down with cans to compact the pâté. When the meat is completely cool and sunken in the pan, remove the weight and cover the meat with plastic wrap, still in the loaf pan. Age the pâté in the refrigerator for at least 1 day before serving (2 days is even better).

To serve, lower the pan into a hot water bath, working fairly rapidly and holding on to the rim to keep water away from the meat. Immediately invert the pâté onto a wooden serving board or long platter and unmold it, rapping the underside of the pan with the handle of a knife, if necessary, to encourage release.

Provide a sharp knife so your guests can slice the pâté and serve it accompanied by gherkins, diced hard-boiled eggs, olives, mustard, or just a great bread and a crock of butter and salt.

Soup Dumplings with Pork and Chicken Aspic Filling

These dumplings are filled with a mixture of ground pork, finely chopped shrimp, and chilled chicken soup aspic. When the dumplings are steamed, the aspic melts—as my friend Val says, the soup is in the dumpling, not the other way around! Note that the stock has to be reduced and then chilled overnight to become gelatinous before you make the dumplings. When you are ready to fill them, you'll find that they're the kind of project you want to take on with the help of friends or family, preferably with good music in the background. All the work is more than repaid by the great meal that results. These don't freeze well, so invite lots of friends to feast with you.

MAKES 75 TO 100 DUMPLINGS

1 recipe Chinese Chicken Super Stock (see page 308)

16 peeled pastured chicken feet or 2 envelopes gelatin

¼ pound peeled raw shrimp, very finely chopped

1 pound ground pastured pork

1 bunch scallions (white part only) finely chopped

2 tablespoons sugar

2 tablespoons soy sauce

1 clove garlic, finely chopped

½ teaspoon kosher salt

Freshly ground black pepper

½ teaspoon grated peeled fresh ginger

½ teaspoon Chinese rice wine (Shaoxing wine)

¼ teaspoon dark sesame oil

2 packages dumpling or Gyoza skins (not wonton skins)

6 whole Napa cabbage leaves, plus more as needed

For the dipping sauce:

½ cup Chinese black vinegar

1 tablespoon finely grated peeled fresh ginger

In a pot over medium heat, cook the chicken stock down. If you have chicken feet, first cook them with the stock over low heat for several hours, then proceed to reduce the stock by half. If you are using gelatin, cook until the stock has been reduced to 2 cups, then sprinkle the surface of the hot stock with the gelatin and stir to dissolve. Pour the stock into a 5- to 6-cup shallow refrigerator storage container (removing the chicken feet if you used them) and refrigerate overnight. The next day, invert the gelatin over a cutting board and slice it into ¼-inch squares. Set these aside.

Combine the shrimp, pork, scallions, sugar, soy sauce, garlic, salt, pepper, ginger, rice wine, and sesame oil in a large bowl; mix well. Fold in the aspic cubes, taking care not to break them.

Take out a dumpling skin and drape the rest of the package with a damp tea towel. Line 2 sheet pans with parchment paper, and set out a small bowl of water and a little paintbrush or pastry brush.

Place a dumpling skin in the palm of your hand and paint the edges with water. Put about 1 teaspoon filling in the center of the dough and make sure the dumpling contains 3 or 4 cubes of aspic. Draw the edges of the dough up around the filling, and roughly pleat them to form a package, leaving a tiny hole where the dough edges come together (this is supposed to prevent the dumpling from exploding while it cooks—I have never had that happen, so the ventilation hole must work). The dumpling should look like a squat little drawstring purse. Set it on the parchment, pleated side up, and repeat until you have used up all the filling.

Line a steamer with 3 of the Napa cabbage leaves and bring to a boil. Put in as many dumplings as can fit without touching, and steam for 10 minutes per batch, starting the timing when the water boils. Add new cabbage if necessary for later batches.

Combine the vinegar with the ginger to make the dipping sauce, and pass this alongside the platter of hot soup dumplings.

Ants Climbing Trees

I found this dish in the early 1990s in Leslie Newman's cookbook Feasts, *and I've been making it regularly ever since. If you look at menus in authentic Chinese restaurants, you will see that this is a traditional Szechuan dish. Of course, there are no real ants in it—or trees, either, for that matter—but the crumbs of ground pork standing out against the white bean threads might remind you a little of ants. Cellophane noodles come in small packages, often in pink nylon netting bags; they are inexpensive and are easy to rehydrate under hot tap water.*

Look for Chinese chili sauce (or Thai chili sauce, which is called nam prik pao*), as well as ground bean sauce, which is made from soybeans (Koon Chun brand is easiest to find). Once you get the meat marinating, the bean threads soaking, and the other ingredients prepped, dinner comes together very quickly. Our children always loved it!*

SERVES 4

½ pound ground pastured pork

1 tablespoon cornstarch

1 tablespoon Shaoxing wine or sherry

2 tablespoons plus 1 teaspoon thin soy sauce

4 ounces (2 packets) cellophane (bean thread) noodles

4 scallions, root ends trimmed

1 clove garlic, finely chopped

1 teaspoon grated peeled ginger

1 to 2 teaspoons Chinese chili sauce, plus more for serving

1½ tablespoons Chinese ground bean sauce

½ teaspoon sugar

1 cup chicken stock, preferably homemade (see page 303)

1 teaspoon sesame oil

3 tablespoons extra-virgin olive oil or peanut oil or vegetable oil

Blot the surface of the ground pork. In a large bowl, combine the cornstarch, the Shaoxing wine, and 1 tablespoon of the soy sauce until the cornstarch dissolves, then stir in the pork. Cover and set aside.

Put the noodles in a bowl and cover them in a few inches of very hot tap water. When they become pliant and slippery, after about 5 minutes, use a pair of scissors to cut the strands into 6-inch lengths. Put these in a colander to drain.

Cut off the green tops of the scallions, chop them, and set aside. Chop the white parts and mix them in with the garlic, ginger, chili sauce, and bean sauce. Set aside.

Combine the remaining 1 tablespoon plus 1 teaspoon soy sauce with the sugar, chicken stock, and sesame oil to make a sauce.

When you are ready to cook, line up each of your prepared mixtures in the order to be used: first the flavoring ingredients (the white scallion mix), then the marinated pork, then the cellophane noodles, the sauce, and the tender green scallion parts (the garnish).

Heat a wok or other large stir-fry pan over high heat and add the oil when the pan is hot. Swirl it around and immediately add the scallion mixture. Stir-fry for about 10 seconds, or until the white scallions become fragrant. Immediately add the pork and combine it with the flavorings, breaking the meat into small bits with a wooden spatula. It will take about half a minute until the meat is cooked. Immediately add the noodles and mix for another few seconds.

Add the sauce, mixing it in well to expose it to the hottest part of the pan. Reduce the heat to medium-low and simmer very gently, uncovered, until you can hardly see any sauce, 3 to 5 minutes.

Remove the noodles from the heat and toss in the green scallion parts. Serve at once. Pass more chili sauce, if desired, at the table.

Hmong Watercress Salad with Ground Pork and Asian Pear

Adapted from Sami Scripter and Sheng Yang's Cooking from the Heart, *this salad is both refreshing and unusual. It makes a perfect summer first course or light lunch. I've added slices of Asian pears, which are not traditional, to enliven the dish. If you can't find Asian pears (which are very firm), you could use slices of apples or other pears. Fish sauce is widely available in the ethnic aisle of grocery stores (look for Taste of Thai brand) and at Asian markets.*

SERVES 4

2 tablespoons virgin coconut oil

¼ pound ground pastured pork

1 tablespoon fish sauce

Salt and freshly ground black pepper

2 large bunches fresh watercress, washed and spun dry

2 Asian pears, peeled and thinly sliced into batons

Over medium heat, heat the oil in a cast-iron frying pan until melted and hot. Add the pork and panfry until completely cooked, stirring to break it up into crumbs. Remove from the heat and stir in the fish sauce, and salt and pepper to taste.

When you are ready to serve, pour the meat mixture, including any oil, over the watercress, and toss well; add the sliced pear batons and toss again. Serve at once.

.

Loose Pork and Fennel Sausage

This loose sausage mix, based on traditional Tuscan seasonings, is as simple as can be. Just be careful not to overwork the meat. In addition to serving the patties with pasta and tomato sauce (see page 200), try them with eggs and maple syrup, or with lentils or other beans. Or shape the meat into meatballs instead to serve as an appetizer on a platter with panfried apple or peach wedges.

MAKES 2 POUNDS LOOSE SAUSAGE MEAT OR 20 PATTIES

2 pounds ground pastured pork

2 teaspoons sea salt

1 tablespoon crushed fennel seeds or wild fennel pollen

1 teaspoon crushed red pepper flakes

4 cloves garlic, minced

Coarse sea salt such as gray Atlantic or Celtic (for the frying pan only)

Combine all the ingredients except the coarse sea salt, working them as little as possible.

Form the mixture into golf-ball-sized rounds, then flatten so that each patty is about 2 inches across.

Heat a dry, seasoned cast-iron frying pan, sprinkle it with coarse salt, and when the salt pops, fry the patties until lightly browned on both sides and just cooked through, 8 to 10 minutes in all. Serve warm.

Homemade Mexican Chorizo Loose Sausage

took some liberties adapting this recipe from Lisa Fain's blog, *The Homesick Texan. I used smoky chipotle chiles because I love their taste. These chorizo patties make up loose and wet; cooking them fresh yields lacy, flat lozenges with lots of quiet heat and spice. Serve them for breakfast, lunch, or dinner, accompanied by anything from eggs and maple syrup, to tortillas and tomatoes and lettuce, to hot grated potato cakes or polenta squares.*

The uncooked meat keeps in the fridge for about 5 days, but it will keep for up to 2 months if frozen. To do so, form the freshly made sausage into a rough log and refrigerate overnight. The next day, tightly roll it in plastic wrap and freeze it in a resealable bag taking care to push as much air out as possible. Frozen meat can be sliced into patties with a sharp serrated knife; they hold their shape better than fresh.

MAKES 1 POUND LOOSE SAUSAGE MEAT

1 pound ground pastured pork

2 dried chipotle chiles

¼ cup cider vinegar

¼ onion, diced

3 cloves garlic, chopped

¼ teaspoon ground cinnamon

½ teaspoon ground cumin

½ teaspoon ground paprika

½ teaspoon dried oregano

2 teaspoons kosher salt

Blot the surface of the ground pork dry. Let it sit on a plate while you proceed with the recipe.

Rinse the chipotles, cut off and discard the ends, and slice them lengthwise to remove the seeds. Soak the peppers in the cider vinegar for 30 minutes.

Using a blender or a mortar and pestle, combine the soaked peppers and the vinegar with the onion and garlic. Blend this at high speed, or mix and pound, until you have a smooth paste. Add the spices, the oregano, and the salt and blend again.

Using your hands, a silicone spatula, or a wooden spoon, thoroughly blend the paste with the ground pork. It should be gloppy.

When you are ready to cook, heat a cast-iron frying pan to hot. Spoon out a generous tablespoon of the loose sausage into the pan (it should sizzle); use the back of the spoon to flatten it evenly into a thin patty. Cook until the meat releases from the pan, then flip the patty and repeat. It should take about 8 to 10 minutes in all.

Smoky White Bean Chili with Ground Pork

This refined, mild, and (thanks to the Spanish pimentón) smoky version of chili is made with fast-cooking ground pork and canned beans. It is perfect for a weeknight dinner. Feel free to add an additional canned chipotle chili or two if you like more heat.

SERVES 4

1 pound ground pastured pork

1 onion, diced

3 cloves garlic, finely chopped

2 teaspoons sweet (*dulce*) pimentón de la Vera (smoked Spanish paprika)

½ teaspoon chili powder

1 tablespoon ground cumin

Salt

¼ cup red wine

1 (14-ounce) can diced tomatoes

2 (14-ounce) cans cannellini beans, drained and rinsed

Freshly ground black pepper

For serving:

½ cup chopped fresh cilantro

Sour cream

4 lime wedges

Heat an enameled cast-iron Dutch oven over medium heat and brown the meat, breaking it up into crumbles, until it is rendered of fat, is no longer pink, and begins to crisp. Remove the meat with a slotted spoon, leaving the fat behind. Reduce the heat to low, and gently cook the onion and garlic until the onion is wilted, 3 to 5 minutes. Add the pimentón, chili powder, and cumin, along with a little salt, and cook for about 1 minute.

Deglaze the pan with the red wine and cook off the alcohol for 2 to 3 minutes, scraping the pan with a wooden spatula to incorporate the browned bits into the liquid. Stir in the tomatoes. Return the meat to the pan and mix it in along with the drained and rinsed beans. Cover and cook gently over medium-low heat, stirring occasionally, until heated through, about 15 minutes. Taste and season with salt and pepper.

Serve each portion topped with the cilantro and a small scoop of sour cream, with a wedge of lime on the side.

Fresh Fettuccini with Chunky Tomato Sauce and Sweet Italian Sausage

Ready-made sweet Italian sausages can be found at almost every grocery, but if you make your own from pastured pork, you'll taste quite a difference. Alternatively, you can often find great sausage at farmers' markets, available from the same farmers who sell pork by the piece. The sausage can be in casings or loose for this recipe.

This dish is a great reason to go all-out and make fresh pasta. Of course, you can use dried fettuccini or buy fresh from the supermarket or a specialty store. But if you like to knead and roll things out by hand or with a pasta machine, there's nothing like homemade.

No matter what the source of your pasta, though, do try this chunky tomato sauce, because it is satisfyingly rich. You can make the sauce ahead and let it sit at room temperature while you make the pasta, then just reheat it gently for serving.

SERVES 4

½ pound cased (2 links) or uncased sweet Italian pork sausage, or ½ pound Loose Pork and Fennel Sausage meat (see page 197)

3 tablespoons extra-virgin olive oil

1 large onion, coarsely chopped

2 big cloves garlic, chopped

½ teaspoon ground cinnamon

½ teaspoon freshly grated nutmeg

½ teaspoon dried orange peel

1 teaspoon ground fennel or wild fennel pollen

1 teaspoon dried oregano

1 teaspoon sea salt

Freshly ground black pepper

1 (14.5-ounce) can crushed tomatoes

Pinch of sugar

1 tablespoon gin or vodka

¼ cup water

1 pound fresh fettuccini (see page 201) or dried fettuccini

½ cup freshly grated Parmigiano-Reggiano, plus more to pass at the table

If you are using cased sausages, cut each one in half lengthwise, then slice each half to make chunks of meat. If using uncased, just brown crumbles of meat. Heat a sauté pan over medium-low heat and cook the sausage until it starts to brown and becomes fragrant; it should be about halfway cooked through. Add the olive oil to the pan. When the oil is warm and thinning, stir in the onion pieces and cook them to wilted, about 10 minutes. Add the garlic, along with the spices, orange peel, herbs, salt, and pepper to taste, and cook gently, stirring, for another 3 to 4 minutes. Add the tomatoes, sugar, gin, and water, give the sauce a good stir, and simmer for another few minutes to blend the flavors and cook off some of the alcohol. Set the sauce off the heat while you cook the pasta. Reserve about ¼ cup of the cooking water when you drain the pasta.

When you are ready to serve, toss in the cheese and, if needed, a little pasta-cooking water to thin the sauce to the consistency you like. Toss the sauce with the cooked and drained pasta. Serve at once, offering more cheese at the table.

FRESH FETTUCCINI

This is my gold standard, fail-safe, error-proof egg pasta recipe. While Italians always make this by hand, I'm American enough to want to mix it faster in the food processor even though I finish the kneading by hand. Fresh pastured eggs produce a noticeably better color and texture than industrial eggs.

1½ cups unbleached all-purpose flour, plus more for dusting

½ teaspoon sea salt

2 large eggs, beaten

1 to 2 tablespoons water

Combine the flour and salt in the bowl of a food processor fitted with the steel blade, a stand mixer fitted with the flat blade, or a mixing bowl. Blend the dry ingredients together, make a well in the center if you are using a stand mixer or bowl, and add the beaten eggs and the first spoonful of water. Process or beat to form a fairly stiff dough. Very gradually, add only as much water as necessary to hold the dough so that it can be kneaded (if you are using a food processor, it should start to form a single mass and ride the blade).

The longer you hand-knead the dough, the silkier the finished pasta will be. The ideal is 20 minutes of vigorous kneading, but even if you do it for less, the fresh pasta will taste terrific. Knead for 5 to 10 minutes in the food processor or stand mixer, then transfer the dough to a floured board or counter and knead for another 15 minutes. The texture should be very smooth and silky. Form into a fat snake.

Let the dough rest for 20 minutes under an inverted bowl or wrapped in waxed paper in the refrigerator. This allows the gluten to relax, so the dough will stretch more easily when you roll it out.

If you are using a pasta machine or the pasta attachment on a stand mixer, set the opening for the widest width—number 1. Cut off about one-sixth of the dough. Dust it with flour and run it through the rollers. Fold it in half and run it through again, repeating the folds and the flattening for 4 turns. When the dough rolls out with a smooth texture, it's ready to go to the next setting. If it looks like it has cellulite, it needs more folding. If it tears, it is too wet and needs to be dusted with flour. Continue folding, turning, dusting, and so on, until the dough rolls through the widest setting like silk.

Move the setting to the next smaller opening (number 2) and roll it through *once* without folding. Repeat the process at narrower and narrower settings, with one roll on each setting until you get to number 6 or 7, depending on how thin you like your pasta.

Hang the long piece of pasta dough over a cloth-draped broom handle wedged between two chairs, or hang it over a cloth-draped drying rack, and proceed to the next piece of dough. Do this until all the dough is used up and is drying. Turn the pasta as it begins to dry but while it is still flexible, so that both sides dry evenly.

When the pasta begins to feel a little stiff and leathery, it is ready to cut. If you are cutting by hand, use a floured board, a ruler, and a rolling pizza cutter to cut the dough crosswise into 12-inch lengths, then cut out even ⅜-inch-wide ribbons and loosely gather them into nests. Dust the nests with a little flour and fluff them to prevent the dough from sticking to itself.

If you are using a pasta machine, change to the cutting rollers and cut the lengths into fettuccini. Let each form a nest on a flour-dusted cloth placed below the cutters, allowing the pasta to dry further without clumping. Dust with flour and fluff if necessary.

When you are ready to cook, bring at least 8 quarts of water to a boil, add 2 tablespoons of salt, and put the pasta in the pot. Cook for about 2 minutes, or until the pasta is floating on the top and is al dente. **Serves 6 to 8**

Steamed Tofu with Ground Pork and Shrimp

Based on elements from a Malaysian pork dish and the classic Chinese mo po dofu, this dish is a satisfying and quick weekday dinner. It's especially good made with baby bok choy, but if you can't find that, frozen peas, snow peas, or broccoli will also do, as will fresh Napa cabbage or other greens. Start the rice (I like jasmine rice with this) long before you begin cooking this dish, as it will take at least 10 minutes longer to cook than this speedy entrée.

SERVES 4

1 pound firm silken tofu, cut into ½-inch cubes

1 tablespoon canola oil

2 cloves garlic, finely chopped

1 pound ground pastured pork

3 baby bok choy, chopped (about 1½ cups)

1 tablespoon finely chopped peeled fresh ginger

½ pound peeled cooked shrimp

½ teaspoon crushed red pepper flakes

2 tablespoons soy sauce

½ teaspoon dark sesame oil

1 teaspoon sugar

Jasmine rice, for serving

⅔ cup chopped fresh cilantro, for garnish

Using a steamer, steam the tofu cubes for 5 minutes over boiling water. Set aside.

In a wok or large frying pan over medium-low heat, heat the oil and gently cook the garlic until it is fragrant but not browning. Increase the heat to medium, and add the pork, bok choy, and ginger, and cook, stirring to break up the meat and integrate it with the garlic, until the pork is cooked and the greens are wilted. This will take about 5 minutes.

Stir in the shrimp, red pepper, and soy sauce, and heat gently. Sprinkle on the sesame oil and sugar and turn off the heat. Stir in the steamed tofu cubes, working carefully to avoid breaking them up.

Serve the pork, shrimp, and tofu mixture over rice, topped with a shower of cilantro.

SHOULDER: A hardworking muscle that's full of flavor, this large primal offers roasts, chops, and braising cuts that may require long, slow cooking. Scraps from trimming the shoulder meat are valuable in their own right, and can be used to make classic dishes such as rillettes.

CUT SHEET ALERT: Ask your processor to save and label pork shoulder scraps separately, if possible.

Rillettes of Pork

A *frugal way French farmwives used all the scraps from butchering a pig was to make rillettes—tender shreds of potted, spiced meat and fat used as a spread on bread. If you wish to emulate their careful parsimony, save and freeze all the fat scraps you trim from roasts and chops, as well as any lean you cut off larger pieces to make medallions or noisettes (keep the fat and the lean separately). You can also freeze meaty bones, which will add gelatin to the mix. The key to successful rillettes is to have a ratio of two parts lean meat to one part fat, and it's an essential ratio, so use a scale. Of course, you can also make rillettes using purchased elements, or from parts of the pig you may have in your freezer, as the recipe indicates. Note that the meat needs to age for 3 days in the refrigerator before you cook it—and the dish tastes best when it has aged at least a day longer, once you have cooked it. Rillettes are traditionally used as a spread—serve them with crackers or toast points, along with great salt, cornichons, and perhaps a fruity chutney. They can also be crisped and added to salads, much like other meat confits.*

MAKES 5 TO 6 CUPS

1½ pounds pastured pork back fat (or fat scraps), cut into ¼-inch dice

1 pound pastured pork shoulder (or other lean pork), cut into 1-inch dice

1 pound pastured pork belly, cut into 1-inch dice

1 teaspoon kosher salt

½ teaspoon freshly ground black pepper

1 teaspoon chopped fresh thyme

1 bay leaf, torn or crumbled into large pieces

1½ teaspoons Quatre Épices Blend (see page 31)

1 cup diced onion

⅔ cup dry white wine

Weigh the meat and fat to make certain that you have a 2 to 1 ratio of lean to fat. Arrange each of the diced meats in separate glass bowls or stainless-steel refrigerator dishes.

Stir together the salt, pepper, thyme, bay leaf, and spice blend. Divide this into three parts, and use your hands to vigorously work an equal amount of the mixture into each of the pork ingredients. Cover each container tightly and refrigerate for 3 days.

When you are ready to cook, render the fat in a heavy 3- to 5-quart casserole over low heat. This will take about 45 minutes. When it has all melted, add the rest of the pork, along with the onion and wine, and continue to cook over the lowest heat, partially covered, for about 4 hours, or until the meat is tender and beginning to shred. Do not hesitate to cook for as long as it takes to reach this stage.

Strain the pork, saving both the meat and the rendered fat. Using your hands, pull the meat into tiny shreds, discarding any gristle or fat that hasn't melted. Put the meat shreds into glass or ceramic containers.

Heat the strained fat so that it becomes liquid again. Pour it into the containers so that it covers the shredded meat. Tightly cover the rillettes and store them in the refrigerator or freezer. Allow them to age for at least a day before using.

Rillettes will keep for about 3 weeks in the refrigerator and for months in the freezer, and this recipe makes quite a lot. I suggest you put some in ramekins for serving right away and freeze others in small wide-mouthed canning jars or other tightly wrapped containers to use for gifts.

Slow-Cooked Pork Shoulder in Milk, White Wine, and Spices

Pork cooked in milk is an Italian classic, and once you taste it, you can immediately see why everyone loves it. While many cooks may know Marcella Hazan's wonderful version for pork loin, this iteration, based on one by Skye Gyngell in the book A Year in My Kitchen, *adds spices, vinegar, and wine, and uses pork shoulder instead.*

SERVES 4 TO 6

1¾ pounds pastured pork shoulder

2 tablespoons unsalted butter

2 tablespoons extra-virgin olive oil

Kosher salt and freshly ground black pepper

4 cloves garlic, chopped

1 tablespoon ground fennel

1 tablespoon ground sage

½ teaspoon ground Aleppo pepper or other ground hot pepper

1 tablespoon white wine vinegar or verjuice

1¼ cups white wine

1½ cups whole milk

Rinse and blot the meat.

Choose a braising pot or casserole that closely fits the size of the pork shoulder, and heat the butter and olive oil in it over medium heat. Generously salt and pepper the meat and brown it on all sides, holding it with tongs, if necessary, to press the smaller sides against the hot pan. This will take about 10 minutes. Remove the meat from the pot and discard the excess fat.

Return the pot to the stove, add the garlic, and cook down for a minute. Stir in the fennel, sage, and hot pepper. Add the vinegar and white wine, stirring and scraping the bottom of the pot to incorporate the browned bits, then add the milk. Return the meat to the pan and bring the liquid to a boil. Immediately lower the heat to the lowest possible temperature that will maintain a very slow simmer.

Cook gently, with the lid slightly ajar, for 3 hours, or until the meat is very tender. Remove the meat from the pot to rest for at least 15 minutes, and raise the flame under the pan gravy. Reduce the liquid by about half, or until it tastes pleasantly intense and rich. Adjust the seasonings, if necessary.

Slice the meat thinly, drizzling each slice with some of the pan gravy, and serve.

Shoulder Roast with Banh Mi Brine and Dipping Sauce

love Vietnamese flavors—that variety of hot, sweet, salty, and bitter tastes—and just as a banh mi baguette sandwich served with pickled vegetables is one of the world's great lunches, the roasted meat works well for dinner. You will need a boneless shoulder roast, a cut from the Boston butt that's sometimes called a boneless blade roast. You'll brine it overnight in a banh mi bath and then roast it.

Try serving it with the sort of accompaniments that go on the sandwich: hot sauce for those who like spicy hot flavors, and a platter of pickled vegetables.

SERVES 4 TO 6

2½ to 3 pounds pastured pork shoulder

⅔ cup kosher salt

⅓ cup light brown sugar

2 cups very hot water

2 cloves garlic, chopped

2 jalapeños, seeded and thinly sliced

For serving:

3 tablespoons thin soy sauce

3 tablespoons mayonnaise

1 tablespoon light brown sugar

¾ cup chopped fresh cilantro

Rinse the meat, blot it dry, and bring it to room temperature. If it is not already compact, use kitchen twine to tie it into a tight package (see page 26). Set aside. Choose a lidded container just large enough to hold the pork along with the brine.

Dissolve the salt and brown sugar in the hot tap water in the container, then stir in the garlic and jalapeños. Place the pork in next, and add enough cold water to completely cover the meat. Shake or swirl to blend. Cover the container and refrigerate the pork overnight or for as long as 2 days.

When you are ready to cook the meat, heat the oven to 400 degrees and set a rack in the upper center of the oven. Remove the meat from the marinade, rinse it well in cool water, and blot it very dry. Put it on a rack in a roasting pan or cast-iron frying pan (put a little water in the bottom of the pan to ease cleanup) and roast it for 1½ to 2 hours, until an instant-read thermometer registers 150 degrees when inserted in the center. Let the meat cool for at least 20 minutes before slicing it thinly.

Serve the meat with a dipping sauce made by mixing together the soy sauce, mayonnaise, and brown sugar, and offer a bowl of chopped cilantro on the side.

Pork Shoulder Stew with Cranberry Beans, Chorizo, and Rice

*A*dapted from a dish made by New Orleans chef Susan Spicer *of Bayona, Herbsaint, and Cobalt, this home-style stew makes a hearty meal. Factor the timing for the beans into your plans; you'll either need to start soaking them the night before, or need to parboil and cool them for an hour before cooking the stew. Like all stews, this tastes better the next day, so if you have time, cook it ahead.*

SERVES 6 TO 8

1 pound Vermont cranberry beans or other dried red beans

1 pound pastured pork shoulder, cut into 2-inch cubes

1 onion, chopped

1 red bell pepper, chopped

2 stalks celery, chopped

3 cloves garlic, finely chopped

2 bay leaves

1 tablespoon chopped fresh thyme

Approximately 4 cups water

1 pound chorizo sausage, split lengthwise, or your own uncased pastured pork chorizo (see page 198)

¼ cup chopped fresh flat-leaf parsley

Salt and freshly ground black pepper

2 cups medium-grain white rice

For serving:

½ cup chopped fresh cilantro

Hot sauce such as Melinda's Original Habanero Sauce

Soak the beans overnight in cold water. Alternatively, put them in a saucepan with water to cover and bring them to a boil. Then turn off the heat, put the lid on the pan, and let them sit for 1 hour. In either case, drain the beans.

Heat an enameled cast-iron Dutch oven over medium-high heat and when it's hot, brown the pork cubes on all sides, stirring occasionally when they no longer stick. There will be very little fat rendered, but it will be enough to cook the meat.

When the meat is browned, reduce the heat to medium and add the onion, pepper, celery, and garlic. Sweat them down to limpness, stirring as needed. Add the beans, bay leaves, thyme, and just enough cold water to cover all the ingredients. Increase the heat, cover, bring the stew to a boil, and then reduce the heat to maintain a very slow simmer. Cook, covered, for 2 to 3 hours, or until the beans are tender and the meat is succulent.

Meanwhile, heat a frying pan over medium heat and cook the split chorizo sausage links or crumbles until they are well browned. If you used split links, let them cool and cut them into pieces. Reserve the rendered fat in the pan.

Once the beans have been cooked to tenderness, add the parsley and the chorizo and its rendered fat, along with salt, pepper, and hot sauce to taste, and simmer, uncovered, for an additional 15 to 30 minutes, until the sauce has thickened and the flavors have merged. Taste the gravy and correct the seasonings, if necessary.

While the stew simmers, cook the rice according to the package directions or your favorite method. Remove from the heat and keep covered.

To serve, put a portion of the cooked rice in the bottom of a shallow bowl; top with a ladleful of stew, a shower of cilantro, and a few drops of hot sauce.

New England–Style Slow Pork Butt Roast

ere butt is cooked at a very low temperature for 5 hours to yield a meltingly tender oven-braised roast. I like this flavor base—it is an old-fashioned "shrub," a name for a type of refreshingly sweet and sour summer drink popular in the eighteenth century. Although most shrubs were fruit-based and sometimes had alcohol, this one is made of maple syrup and vinegar. The recipe will work for any kind of pork pot roast, and I think it's outstanding!

SERVES 6 TO 8

1 boneless pastured pork butt roast, rolled and tied (about 3 pounds), or a bone-in pastured butt roast (about 4½ pounds)

½ cup maple syrup

¼ cup cider vinegar

¼ cup dark brown sugar

½ teaspoon salt

1 cup apple cider

Heat the oven to 400 degrees and set a rack slightly below the center position.

Bring the meat to room temperature, rinse it, and blot it dry. Select an ovenproof casserole with a tightly fitting lid that closely fits the shape of the meat. (If the most suitable pan you have is without a lid, you can seal it with foil instead.)

Place the pork in a bowl. Stir the maple syrup and vinegar together and pour this mixture over the meat. Crumble the brown sugar, pressing it onto the meat. Sprinkle with salt, and place the meat in the pan, fat side up. (Discard the remaining shrub.) Pour the cider down the side of the pan, trying to avoid the meat and crust. Place a piece of parchment paper over the meat to create a second close-fitting cover to aid in controlling condensation. Put the lid on the pan (or cover it with foil).

Set the roast in the oven and reduce the heat to 200 degrees. Set the timer for 5 hours, and walk away. Don't open the oven while the meat is cooking! When the time is up, check the meat—if it is not yet as tender as you would like, turn it over in the liquid and roast it for another 30 minutes.

Check with an instant-read thermometer to make sure that the meat has an internal temperature of at least 150 to 155 degrees, then remove and cover it loosely with foil to keep warm. Pour the liquid into a fat-separating pitcher and put the defatted liquid in a saucepan. Reduce this by half its volume, cooking over medium-low heat for about 15 minutes.

Serve the meat warm, sliced and coated with its reduced juices.

Boston Butt Cooked Like Ham

The butt end of the shoulder is analogous to the ham end of the hind leg, and can be cooked similarly. Most Boston butts weigh about 5 pounds, so I often cut them into two parts for 2 nights' worth of dinners (I make, for example, this recipe and the banh mi, on page 205). I find that brining shoulder meat makes it juicy and succulent, even with pastured pork. Try serving this with your favorite potato dish and a generous helping of applesauce or fruit chutney.

SERVES 8

2 ½ pounds pastured pork shoulder (Boston butt)

½ cup kosher salt

½ cup dark brown sugar

12 whole cloves

Salt and freshly ground black pepper

3 tablespoons unsalted butter

2 cloves garlic, chopped

½ cup sweet red vermouth

Rinse the meat, blot it dry, and bring it to room temperature. Take a good look at the meat, and if it is not compact and even, tie it into a neat bundle using kitchen twine (see page 26). Set it aside. Choose a lidded container large enough to hold the pork and the brine inside.

Mix together the kosher salt, brown sugar, cloves, and just enough hot tapwater to dissolve the salt and sugar. Pour that liquid over the meat in the container, and add cold water to cover. Let the meat sit, refrigerated, all day or overnight. When you are ready to cook, remove the meat from the brine, rinse it well, and blot it dry. Lightly salt and pepper the meat and place it on a rack in a roasting pan, fat side up.

Melt the butter over low heat and gently cook the garlic until fragrant, but not colored. Pour this over the meat and let it sit at room temperature for 1 hour.

Heat the oven to 350 degrees. Roast the meat for 30 minutes. Reduce the heat to 300 degrees and begin basting the meat with the vermouth every 20 minutes or so. The meat should cook for at least 20 minutes per pound, about 1 additional hour, or until it registers an internal temperature of 150 degrees on an instant-read thermometer.

Let the meat rest for at least 15 minutes before slicing it and serving it with the pan juices.

Country-Style Ribs
Braised with Pomegranate Molasses, Ginger, and Garlic

*I*t takes 2 hours to oven-braise these ribs to falling-off-the-bone succulence, and it's worth every minute. My ribs came packaged two to a bag, so I've written this for two servings. If you've got a bigger crowd or more ribs in your packages, the timing won't change very much, but you will need to double or triple the ingredients and increase the amount of braising liquid so that it comes up to three-quarters of the height of the meat when it's in the pan.

If you don't have pomegranate molasses, you can use a cup of pomegranate juice mixed with a little honey and lemon juice; omit the boiling water and instead bring the juice mixture to a boil. This dish is very good served with saffron rice or Coconut Rice (see page 365).

NOTE: The recipe also works well with pork shank (roast for 3 hours instead of 2).

SERVES 2

2 country-style ribs from pastured pork (about 1½ pounds)

¼ cup pomegranate molasses

¾ cup boiling water

2 tablespoons finely chopped peeled fresh ginger

2 cloves garlic, chopped

Blot the meat dry and set it aside. Heat the oven to 325 degrees and set an oven rack in the center.

Combine the pomegranate molasses and boiling water. Stir in the ginger and garlic.

Put the meat in an enameled cast-iron Dutch oven, or another high-sided pot not much larger than the meat, and pour the pomegranate mixture over the meat. Cover the pot with the lid or with parchment paper and tightly crimped foil.

Roast until the meat is very tender, about 2 hours in all. Remove the meat from the pot and defat the braising liquid by pouring it through a fat-separating pitcher or skimming it with a spoon.

If you like, cook down the remaining liquid to a thicker glaze or simply use it as is, brushed or poured onto the ribs before serving.

Sicilian Country-Style Ribs Agrodolce

When I host culinary vacations in Sicily, we always cook traditional dishes, such as rabbit (or chicken) in sweet-and-sour sauce. I thought those flavors would complement pork too. See page 271 for the rabbit version, and serve either one with a side starch, such as mashed potatoes, polenta, or rice, to sop up the gravy.

SERVES 4

2 to 3 pounds pastured pork country-style ribs

2 tablespoons extra-virgin olive oil

1 onion, finely chopped

Salt and freshly ground black pepper

1 cup white wine

4 whole cloves

2 bay leaves

About ½ cup chicken stock, preferably homemade (see page 303)

2 tablespoons sugar

½ cup cider vinegar

¼ cup raisins

¼ cup pine nuts

½ cup finely chopped fresh flat-leaf parsley

Rinse the meat and pat it dry. Heat the oil in a large skillet or Dutch oven over medium heat. Add the meat and brown each piece on all sides, scattering the onion pieces in the frying pan, along with salt and pepper to taste, as the meat cooks on the last side.

Add the wine, cloves, and bay leaves, and bring the mixture to a boil. Immediately lower the heat to a slow simmer and cook until most of the alcohol has evaporated and the wine has reduced by about a third, 3 to 5 minutes. Add enough stock for the liquid to come halfway up the meat, and cover the pan. Slowly simmer until tender, 30 to 40 minutes.

Transfer the meat to a plate. If there is a lot of liquid left in the pan, boil it down to reduce. Remove the bay leaves and discard them. Taste for salt and correct with a light hand, as the sauce will reduce further. Stir in the sugar, vinegar, raisins, and pine nuts.

Return the meat to the pan and gently simmer over very low heat, partially covered, until the sauce is reduced and the meat is heated through. (This can take up to 20 minutes.) Stir in the parsley and serve hot, with the pan sauce.

Green Mountain Green Chile Country-Style Ribs Stew

One member of the group I cook with regularly is Marshall Brewer, who is by day a college administrator and by night a custom wedding cake maker. This is Marshall's take on his favorite food memories from the Sonora Desert, using Vermont ingredients. We even used a new non-GMO canola oil from Maine Natural Oils to help keep things in New England. Serve this in bowls along with warm corn or flour tortillas to sop up the juices.

SERVES 6 TO 8

1 to 2 pounds pastured pork country-style ribs, boned and cut into 2-inch lengths

Salt and freshly ground black pepper

2 to 3 tablespoons canola oil

2 onions, finely chopped (about 1 cup)

1 or 2 large cloves garlic, chopped (1 tablespoon)

½ cup white wine

4 cups boiling water

1 (4-ounce) can Hatch diced peeled green chiles, drained and rinsed

1 tablespoon cider vinegar

1 tablespoon maple syrup

2 pounds red potatoes, peeled and diced

For serving:

1 bunch fresh cilantro leaves, finely chopped

Corn or flour tortillas, warmed in the oven in a damp cloth

1 lime, sliced and cut into wedges

Rinse and blot the meat and salt and pepper it lightly.

Heat the oven to 325 degrees and set a rack in the center. Put a braising pot on the stove, over medium heat, and heat 2 tablespoons of the oil until it shimmers. Brown the meat without crowding, in batches if necessary, until it has a deep auburn color on all sides. Set the meat aside.

Add another tablespoon of canola oil if the pot is dry. Sweat down the onions slowly over medium heat until they are lightly colored, but not brown. Add the garlic and cook for another minute, or until it is fragrant. Add the wine to deglaze the pot, scraping up the browned bits with a wooden spoon to incorporate them into the liquid. Add the boiling water, and return the meat to the pot, along with any juices. Roast for 2 hours, covered.

Stir in the chiles, vinegar, maple syrup, and potato cubes. Roast for 1 hour longer.

Serve the stew in bowls with lots of cilantro showered over the top, accompanied by warm tortillas and the lime wedges.

LOIN: Tender pork loin cuts include some of the most delicious chops a pig can offer, along with festive roasts that can be had on or off the bone. The loin is divided into three parts that offer more fat (shoulder end) to lean meat (center cut) to the sirloin end, which has the most bones. The loin is also where the leanest and most tender cut, pork tenderloin, is found.

When filling out a cut sheet, keep in mind that chops offer more weeknight dinners than roasts, which are generally larger and more celebratory.

Honey-Glazed Baby Back Ribs

Adapted from a recipe by the chef Andy Ricker published in Food & Wine *magazine, these Asian-inspired ribs marinate for a day in a blend spiked with bourbon, then slow-cook until the surface is delectably glazed. You can finish them on the grill for a real char or run them under the broiler for a quick fix. This recipe can be doubled or tripled for a crowd. Take note of the dipping sauce, a real winner that is good on lots of different meats. Fish sauce can be found in the ethnic ingredient section of grocery stores and in Asian markets.*

SERVES 3 OR 4

1 rack of pastured baby back ribs (about 1¾ pounds)

For the marinade:

⅓ cup soy sauce

⅓ cup bourbon

3 tablespoons honey

1 tablespoon grated peeled fresh ginger

Freshly ground black pepper

½ teaspoon sesame oil

¼ teaspoon ground cinnamon

⅛ teaspoon freshly grated nutmeg

For the glaze/dipping sauce:

3 tablespoons honey

1 tablespoon hot water

1 tablespoon dark brown sugar

Freshly squeezed juice of 1 lime

2 tablespoons fish sauce

2 tablespoons soy sauce

1 teaspoon crushed red pepper flakes

¼ cup chopped fresh cilantro

Choose a large nonreactive dish with a cover, such as a glass baking dish, that will hold the ribs. (If you don't have a dish big enough, cut the rack into large subsections and overlap them slightly to fit.) Combine all the marinade ingredients and pour the mixture over the meat, turning it to coat completely. Cover the dish and refrigerate the meat and marinade for a full day or at least overnight.

The next day, heat the oven to 300 degrees. Line a large sheet pan with heavy-duty foil and place a wire rack on top. Put the ribs on the rack, meat side up, shaking off the marinade. Roast the ribs for 2 hours, or until tender.

Meanwhile, make the glaze. Combine the honey and hot water, then add the brown sugar, stirring until it is dissolved. Then add the lime juice, fish sauce, soy sauce, red pepper, and cilantro. Reserve half the glaze to use for dipping at the table.

Baste the nearly cooked ribs with the glaze and roast for another 15 minutes, or until the surface is browned and glossy. While they glaze, heat your outdoor grill to high, if you plan to use it.

Turn the ribs, bone side up, and glaze them again, then put them under the broiler or on the hot grill until they are lightly charred.

Cut the ribs into individual pieces, if desired, and serve them warm, with dipping sauce on the side.

Pork Loin (Rib End) Roast with Cider, Apples, and Thyme

I f you have the time, dry the meat overnight on a rack in the refrigerator; this really helps the fat to crisp in the oven. I wrote this recipe for a bone-in roast, but it also works well for a boneless one. If you have fresh cider that has turned a bit alcoholic in the refrigerator, cooking with it is a good way to use it up. Look for juniper berries in the bulk spice section of better grocery stores, at health food stores, or at specialty spice purveyors. This is particularly good when served with Wilted Greens with Garlic and Olive Oil (see page 362). Choose any bitter green such as kale or chard—the bitterness complements the sweetness of the sauce.

NOTE: This recipe also works well for a rack of pork.

SERVES 4

1 bone-in pastured pork loin (rib end) roast (about 4 pounds)

1 tablespoon extra-virgin olive oil

1 teaspoon sea salt

1 teaspoon whole black peppercorns

1 tablespoon whole juniper berries

8 cloves garlic, smashed

4 firm, tart apples, peeled, cored, and cut into wedges

3 bay leaves

3 cups apple cider, fresh or hard

3 sprigs fresh thyme

Rinse and dry the roast, then set it on a baking rack on a paper-towel-lined plate and rest it, uncovered, in the refrigerator overnight. Bring it to room temperature before proceeding.

Heat the oven to 425 degrees, and set a rack in the bottom third.

Rub the meat with the olive oil. Using a spice grinder or a mortar and pestle, coarsely grind (in bursts) or crush the salt, pepper, and juniper until they form a chunky blend. Put the meat, fat side up, in a heatproof pan that is not much larger than the meat, such as a cast-iron frying pan or a small roasting pan. Using your hands, press the spice blend all over the meat, especially on the fat layer. Arrange the garlic around the meat and add the apple wedges and bay leaves. Pour the apple cider around the roast.

Roast the meat for 10 minutes, then reduce the heat to 400 degrees and cook for 1 hour longer, or until an instant-read thermometer registers an internal temperature of 150 to 155 degrees. Remove the meat from the pan and let it rest for 15 minutes.

Meanwhile, remove and discard the bay leaves, then put the roasting pan on the stove and use a potato masher or the back of a spoon to mash the garlic, apples, and cooking juices into a paste. Add the leaves from the fresh thyme sprigs. Cook this mixture down over low heat.

Serve the meat sliced and napped with sauce.

Pork Loin Stuffed with Armagnac and Prunes

This classic French combination of pork stuffed with Armagnac and prunes is especially wonderful with pastured heritage pork breeds. Perfect dinner-party fare, each slice is a work of art. An herb-crusted ring of meat surrounds a dark and luscious core of fruit; each slice is then drizzled with a rich pan sauce. My particular pork loin roast was on the small side and came both boned and tied, but tied is not essential. If your roast is larger, just adjust the cooking time accordingly by leaving the high temperature portion at 35 minutes, but cooking longer at the lower temperature—as ever, your primary decision-making tool should be the thermometer. See page 26 for tying instructions.

SERVES 4 TO 6

3 pounds boneless pastured pork loin roast	2 tablespoons Herbes de Provence Blend (see page 32)
15 dried prunes	Salt and freshly ground black pepper
½ cup plus 2 tablespoons Armagnac	2 tablespoons water
1 tablespoon extra-virgin olive oil	3 tablespoons heavy cream

Bring the meat to room temperature, rinse it, and blot it dry. Heat the oven to 450 degrees, and set a rack in the center. Choose a roasting pan or cast-iron frying pan that is about the size of your piece of meat (if it is too big, the juices will all evaporate or burn). Soak the prunes in the ½ cup Armagnac for about 15 minutes, or until they are fairly soft.

Using a long, sharp-pointed knife, make a cut down the center of the meat, from one end to the other, pushing straight down. Repeat, making a second cut at right angles to the first, so that the two cuts form a cross in the center of the pork cylinder.

Using a wooden spoon with a thick handle, insert the handle into the center of the crosscuts, pushing downward from one end to the other, to create a hollow opening the length of the meat. Enlarge the opening by moving the handle in a small circle to make an even cavity up the center of the roast.

Remove the prunes from the Armagnac (reserving the liquid) and stuff them into the cavity, using the spoon handle to poke them down. When the meat is filled with prunes, lay it in the pan.

Pour the olive oil onto the pork and rub it in on all sides. Sprinkle the herbes de Provence and then salt and pepper all over the meat. Pour the reserved Armagnac around the roast, taking care not to wash off the herb coating.

Roast the meat for 35 minutes, or until the meat starts to brown and crisp, then reduce the heat to 375 degrees. Continue to roast until the internal temperature of the meat is 145 to 150 degrees, about 15 minutes longer for a 3-pound boneless roast. Add a little water to the pan if the Armagnac begins to evaporate.

When the meat is cooked, transfer it to a board to rest for at least 15 minutes.

Meanwhile, deglaze the roasting pan over medium heat with the remaining 2 tablespoons Armagnac mixed with the water, scraping the pan to incorporate the juices and browned bits. When this has reduced by half, turn off the heat and briefly stir in the cream. Serve the warm slices of meat, with the sauce spooned artfully over each.

Pork Loin (Sirloin End) Chops with Bitter Marmalade

Look for marmalade made from Seville oranges, which will say "bitter" in the title. If all you've got is the sweet stuff, increase the vinegar slightly (or add lemon juice) to compensate.

SERVES 4

4 pastured pork loin (sirloin end) chops

Salt and freshly ground black pepper

1 tablespoon extra-virgin olive oil

½ cup white wine

⅓ cup bitter marmalade

2 teaspoons Dijon mustard

1 to 2 tablespoons balsamic vinegar

Bring the meat to room temperature, rinse it, and blot it dry. Salt and pepper it lightly. Heat a cast-iron frying pan over medium heat and add the olive oil. When the oil has thinned and become fragrant, add the chops in one layer; they should sizzle as they hit the pan.

Sear the meat on both sides, 6 to 8 minutes in all, until the meat is cooked in the center. Transfer the meat to a plate to rest and deglaze the pan with the wine, scraping to incorporate any browned bits stuck to the pan, and reduce the wine by half, about 3 minutes.

Mix the marmalade, mustard, and vinegar together. If the marmalade is very chunky, you may wish to chop it finer, using a food processor or a chef's knife.

Turn the heat under the pan to low and stir in the marmalade blend to form a sauce.

Return the meat and any accumulated juices to the pan and heat through. Cook for 1 minute, and serve with the sauce spooned over the meat.

Pork Loin Chops with Red Barn Spice Rub

Rubbed with the spice blend I named for our barn home, these meaty little boneless loin chops take on color and heat, especially when given the spice treatment an hour before cooking. While I like to sear these on top of the stove, you could broil them or grill them outdoors if you prefer, omitting the pomegranate bath at the end.

SERVES 2 TO 4

2 to 4 loin chops from pastured pork, each 1 inch thick (about ⅓ pound)

1 to 2 tablespoons Red Barn Spice Rub (see page 32)

½ cup pomegranate juice, such as Pom brand, or cranberry juice

Rinse the meat and blot it dry. Sprinkle each chop with 1½ teaspoons of the rub, coating all sides, especially the fat. Pat the spices into the surface of the meat and let rest at room temperature for 30 minutes to 1 hour.

Choose a well-seasoned cast-iron frying pan just big enough to hold the chops and heat it over high heat. When the pan is hot, put the chops in the pan, drier side down (the spiced meat will exude liquid while sitting, so put the top side down in the pan). Sear them until they release from the pan, about 4 minutes. Turn the chops, lower the heat to medium, and cook until the meat releases again, about another 4 minutes, checking with the point of a knife to make sure that they are cooked through.

Add the pomegranate juice with care (it will instantly begin to form steam) and immediately cover the pan and cook over low heat for about 3 minutes longer. Remove the chops from the pan, spoon the pan juices over them, and serve immediately.

Pork Loin Chops with Ruby Port, Prunes, Cinnamon, Turmeric, and Ginger

Rub the chops with spices and let the prunes cook at least an hour ahead—better yet, do it the night before. I like to serve this with basmati rice finished with a pat of butter and the floral Persian spice blend, Advieh (see page 30). The reason I use both port and red wine is that the acid of the wine balances the sweetness of the port and prunes.

SERVES 4

4 pastured pork loin chops (about 2 pounds)

Salt and freshly ground black pepper

1 teaspoon ground cinnamon

1 teaspoon ground turmeric

1 teaspoon ground ginger

½ pound pitted prunes

½ teaspoon crushed red pepper flakes

½ cup ruby port

½ cup red wine

Blot the chops dry and set them on a rack. Blend the salt, pepper, cinnamon, turmeric, and ginger, and rub the mixture onto all sides of the meat. Let this rest for up to 1 hour at room temperature or, ideally, in the refrigerator overnight.

In a saucepan on the stove, or in the microwave in a covered dish, cook the prunes with the red pepper and port until they come to a boil (2 to 3 minutes at high power in the microwave). Let them stand for as long as you rest the meat.

When you are ready to cook, heat a cast-iron frying pan over medium heat (add a little oil if you think your pan is not well seasoned) and fry the chops until golden on both sides and cooked through. Timing will depend on the thickness of the chops and the intensity of your stove burners, but about 6 minutes per side is a rough guide. When the chops are no longer pink in the center, transfer them to a platter and deglaze the pan with the red wine, scraping to incorporate any cooked bits into the sauce. Reduce the liquid by about half.

Return the chops and any liquid they have given off to the pan and turn them in the sauce to coat. Add the prunes and port and warm everything through. Serve at once.

Center-Cut Pork Chops with Salt and Spice Cure

IC (Pig Improvement Company) pigs were unknown to me when I bought center-cut pork chops from On the Edge Farm in Woodstock, Vermont. A biotechnology group dedicated to genetic improvement, PIC works to produce healthy lines of non-GMO hybrid pigs worldwide.

SERVES 2

2 center-cut pastured pork chops (about 1½ pounds)

2 tablespoons Salt and Spice Cure (see page 30)

1 teaspoon coarse sea salt, such as gray Atlantic or Celtic (for pan-searing only)

½ cup dry or fruity white wine

Blot the chops dry, rub them with the cure, and let them rest for 1 hour.

Heat a dry, seasoned cast-iron pan or a grill pan to hot and turn on the exhaust fan. Sprinkle the pan with the sea salt. When the salt starts to pop, slap on the meat and cook the chops for 4 minutes per side, or until they are cooked through—charred and crisp on the outside and tender within.

Remove the chops from the pan and pour in the wine. Deglaze the pan, scraping up any browned bits that are stuck to the bottom. Let the wine cook down to half its volume, and pour it over the chops just before serving.

Pork Tenderloin Medallions with Vermouth Sauce made with Orange Zest, Mustard, and Cream

The tenderloin that came with my Berkshire half pig totaled ¾ pound, and when cut yielded nine medallions, enough for three people as part of a larger meal. I like to serve it with rice or mashed potatoes—either starch is delicious with the sauce, and both take longer than the 5 quick minutes you'll need to prepare this main course.

SERVES 3 OR 4

1 pastured pork tenderloin (about ¾ pound)

Salt

2 tablespoons unsalted butter

2 tablespoons extra-virgin olive oil

½ cup white vermouth

Freshly grated zest of 1 orange or 1 teaspoon dried orange peel

1 tablespoon Dijon mustard

¼ cup heavy cream

⅓ cup fresh finely chopped flat-leaf parsley

Blot the tenderloin and put it on a cutting board, straightening it as much as possible. Using a very sharp knife with a long, thin blade, carefully cut the tenderloin crosswise into 1-inch slices. Shape each round to be as even as possible before placing it on a rack to dry. Because tenderloin tapers at both ends, the last two pieces will not be round. Combine them into one piece, using a piece of kitchen twine or toothpicks to hold them together in a yin and yang pattern. Salt the medallions lightly on top and air-dry them at room temperature for about 1 hour.

Choose a heavy sauté pan or cast-iron griddle large enough to hold all the medallions in one layer. Melt the butter and oil in the pan over medium heat until the mixture is fragrant and liquid. Place the medallions in the hot fat (they should sizzle), and fry for about 3 minutes on the first side and 2 minutes on the second side, or until cooked in the center and browned and crisp on the outside. Using tongs, transfer the meat to a platter to rest.

Make the sauce by deglazing the pan with the vermouth, scraping up any browned bits and boiling off the alcohol to reduce the volume by half. Turn off the heat and stir in the orange zest, mustard, and cream. Spoon this over the medallions and serve at once, showered with a little parsley.

A Kitchen Ruler

It is for just such projects as cutting medallions from the tenderloin that I keep a ruler in my kitchen drawer—plastic, so it can go in the dishwasher. If you don't have a ruler handy, the length of your thumb from tip to knuckle is almost always a true inch, remarkably.

PORK BELLY: While everyone loves the spareribs that come as part of this primal, most people who buy a whole or half pig opt to smoke all of the belly for bacon. That is certainly a fine way to use this part, especially if you need 12 pounds of bacon. But pork belly, uncured and unsmoked, is a delicacy; it's worth reserving some of this part to make the dishes that follow.

Hoisin Spareribs

oisin sauce is often called the ketchup of Chinese food, so it stands to reason that it makes an excellent base for Chinese-style spareribs. While this is hardly barbecue, it does offer some of those meaty sweet and sour flavors that make pit-smoked meat so alluring. Leave time to marinate the ribs overnight or all day to let the flavors sink in.

SERVES 2 OR 3

2 pounds rack of pastured pork spareribs

3 tablespoons thin soy sauce

3 tablespoons hoisin sauce

2 tablespoons tomato paste or ketchup

2 tablespoons oyster sauce

2 tablespoons dry sherry

2 tablespoons dark brown sugar

3 cloves garlic, smashed

2 tablespoons honey

¼ cup boiling water

Bring the meat to room temperature, rinse it, and blot it dry. Mix together the soy sauce, hoisin, tomato paste, oyster sauce, sherry, brown sugar, and garlic, and put the marinade in a refrigerator container that can hold the meat in one layer. Coat the meat with the marinade on both sides, cover, and refrigerate all day or overnight.

When you are ready to cook, heat the oven to 350 degrees and set a rack in the upper third of the oven. Line a baking sheet with foil, and set a rack on top. Stir the honey and boiling water together to make a basting mixture.

Roast the spareribs on the rack for about 30 minutes, brushing with the honey mixture every once in a while. Turn the meat and repeat the process on the other side. After about 1 hour total, the ribs should be shrinking away from the bone, and an instant-read thermometer inserted into the meat should read 150 degrees. If the meat is not as charred as you like, set the oven to broil, raise the oven rack, and broil the ribs for 2 to 3 minutes per side, taking care not to let the sugar smoke or catch fire.

Kimchi Soup with Fried Pork Belly

uk Long belongs to a group of food professionals that I cook with monthly, and as she is a skilled Thai chef who also knows lots about Japanese, Chinese, Korean, and Vietnamese cuisines, I always learn new things. This recipe and the Stir-Fried Pork Liver with Asparagus, Mushrooms, and Fried Garlic Chips (see page 242) are two of her contributions to this collection, and each offers tastes and flavor combinations that reward careful attention.

This soup, while lengthy in terms of steps, is uncomplicated when you look at it as a whole: First you marinate the pork belly, then boil it to render much of the fat, then fry it into crisp bacony morsels that will float on the easy-to-make kimchi soup. Save the stock left over from boiling the pork belly; only a little is used in this dish. The remainder can become the basis for a delicious soup another time (see, for example, Rice Noodle and Bok Choy Soup in Pork Belly Broth with Bean Sprouts, page 222).

Kimchi is Korean fermented cabbage. Tuk says you can recognize good-quality kimchi by looking for a mix of white and green cabbage parts in the jar. She uses kimchi labeled "mild" for this recipe—the hot can be absolutely fiery.

SERVES 8

For the marinated pork belly:

1 to 2 pounds pastured pork belly

4 cloves garlic, chopped

1 teaspoon kosher salt

¼ teaspoon freshly ground black pepper

2 tablespoons thin or light soy sauce

5 cups water

For the soup:

8 cups water

2 tablespoons thin or light soy sauce

Kosher salt

Freshly ground black pepper

1 (15-ounce) jar mild kimchi

4 scallions, roots and very top removed

Freshly squeezed juice of ½ lime

If the pork belly has skin, remove it by partially freezing the meat and cutting the skin off with a sharp knife. Reserve the skin for cracklings (see page 237). Cut the pork belly into 1-inch-wide strips, and pierce them all over with the point of a sharp knife to help the marinade to penetrate.

Using a flat refrigerator dish or shallow bowl, lay out the belly strips and massage them with the garlic, salt, pepper, and soy sauce, using your hands to combine everything well. Leave the meat at room temperature for 1 hour to allow the marinade to penetrate.

Using a deep sauté pan or other deep pan, bring the water to a boil. Remove the meat from the marinade, scrape it clean, and lay the meat on a cutting board to drain. Again, pierce the meat all over with the point of a sharp knife (this prevents explosions when boiling!). Cut the meat crosswise into cubes.

Put the meat cubes in the boiling water and reduce the heat to low, stirring as needed, until most of the fat is rendered into the water. Remove the meat with a slotted spoon. Measure out ½ cup stock to use for the soup and save the rest for another use.

Choose a cast-iron frying pan that can hold all the cubes of meat in one layer and place it over medium-high heat. Start to brown the cubes of meat. As the remaining fat renders out, lower the heat so that the meat cooks more slowly and the fat renders at a slower pace without risk of burning. You will end up with browned, crisp cubes of meat and a frying pan filled with rendered pork fat, which you should save for other dishes. Drain the crisp crouton-like meat cubes on paper towels, and reserve them.

To make the soup, bring the 8 cups water and the ½ cup reserved pork stock to a boil in a large pot. Add the soy sauce, 1 teaspoon salt, pepper to taste, and the kimchi. Lower the heat and simmer the soup for about 10 minutes, or until it is heated through.

Meanwhile, split the scallions lengthwise into quarters, and slice them into 4-inch pieces, using all the white part and most of the green. Add the scallions to the soup and simmer gently for another 5 minutes. Add the lime juice, taste for balance, and correct the salt, if necessary.

Serve hot with the cubes of crisp pork belly floating on top.

Rice Noodle and Bok Choy Soup in Pork Belly Broth with Bean Sprouts

*I*f you saved the extra stock from the Kimchi Soup with Fried Pork Belly (see page 221), this fast and easy soup is a great use for it. If not, make a pork stock from a fresh ham bone or substitute homemade chicken stock (see page 303).

SERVES 4

4 cups pork stock or chicken stock, preferably homemade (see page 221 or 303)

1 cup water

1 (2-ounce) package rice or cellophane noodles, soaked in hot water for 15 minutes

3 scallions (white part only), peeled and finely chopped

2 baby bok choy, thinly sliced

1 cup bean sprouts

½ cup finely chopped fresh cilantro

1 juicy fresh lime, cut into 4 wedges

Bring the stock and water to a boil in a soup pot and lower the heat. Add the soaked rice noodles, scallions, and bok choy, and simmer for about 5 minutes, or until the vegetables are cooked but still retain their bright color. Turn off the heat and stir in the bean sprouts. Shower the soup with fresh cilantro and serve with a wedge of fresh lime alongside each bowl.

Pork Belly Dan Barber's Way

*D*an Barber, chef of Stone Barns, cures his pork belly for 3 days before oven-braising it at low heat overnight, then cutting and searing it. This is a lengthy process but worth the trouble. I use his wonderful Salt and Spice Cure (see page 30) to flavor lots of different cuts of meat, in addition to this one. I've adapted his recipe here for a smaller belly portion. Mashed potatoes, mashed Jerusalem artichokes, and sweet potatoes all make fine accompaniments to this dish.

SERVES 4

1½ pounds pastured pork belly

4 to 5 tablespoons Salt and Spice Cure (see page 30)

2 cups chicken stock, preferably homemade (see page 303)

Blot the meat dry. Rub it on all sides with the spice mixture and put it in an airtight refrigerator container that will hold it flat. Refrigerate the spiced meat for 3 days.

On the third day, many hours before (if not the day before) you need to serve the dish, heat the oven to 200 degrees. Place the pork belly in a Dutch oven or gratin dish as close as possible in size to the meat.

Pour the chicken stock over the meat (it should cover it—if it does not, add water to cover). Place a tight-fitting lid on the pan. If the pan doesn't have a lid, or the lid is loose, make an airtight cover using foil. Braise the pork belly for 6 to 8 hours, or overnight, until the meat is completely tender and has a texture similar to pot roast.

Remove the meat from the pan and drain it of braising liquid. Heat a cast-iron frying pan over medium heat. Cut the pork belly into serving pieces 3 or 4 inches in size and sear each piece, fat side down, until it is crisp and browned. Gently sear all the other sides of the meat as well, so that it is warmed through. Serve immediately.

Sean's Braised Pork Belly Glazed with Basil Honey

Chef Sean Buchanan of Stowe Mountain Lodge served this unforgettable appetizer at a buffet for Vermont Fresh Network, an organization that pairs local farmers and restaurants. Here's my version of his great dish: pork belly that is slow-braised, then seared before being tossed with basil honey, a magic ingredient that Sean calls "green gold." I use it to dress pastured chicken, and serve it on the side with lots of cooked meats.

SERVES 12 AS AN APPETIZER

Sea salt and freshly ground black pepper

1½ pounds pastured pork belly

1 (12-ounce) bottle wheat beer

1 (1-inch-long) knob fresh ginger

3 large cloves garlic, roughly chopped

1 lemon, quartered

½ cup strong dark honey

1 cup white wine

For the basil honey glaze:

1 cup fresh basil leaves

⅓ cup honey

To finish the appetizers:

12 slices French baguette loaf, toasted

Fresh cilantro leaves

Heat the oven to 350 degrees.

Heat a cast-iron frying pan over high heat. Salt and pepper the pork belly generously and sear it in the hot pan until it is browned on both sides. At the same time, put the beer, ginger, garlic, lemon, honey, and white wine in an enameled cast-iron Dutch oven or other lidded braising pot that is close to the size of the meat. Bring the braising liquid to a slow simmer on top of the stove.

Add the meat to the hot braising liquid (the liquid should just cover the meat—add water if it does not). Cover the pot and cook it in the oven for 1½ hours, or until the meat is tender. Using tongs, transfer the belly to a sheet pan and cover the meat with a cutting board. Put an empty heavy pot or cans on top to weight down the meat and keep it flat. Let the meat cool with the weight on it.

Make the glaze by blending the basil with the honey in a food processor.

Cut the cooled meat into ¼-inch strips. Heat a cast-iron frying pan over high heat and sear each strip rapidly to brown, 2 to 3 minutes. Toss the hot strips with the basil honey sauce and arrange them on the pieces of toasted baguette; garnish each serving with a cilantro leaf or two.

BACON: Getting bacon may be one of the most exciting parts of buying pastured pig meat—it's full of flavor and unlikely to be overly nitrated, oversalted, or oversmoked like commercial products. Bacon from different heritage breeds tastes appreciably different. I like it best when it comes from Tamworths, Red Wattles, and Berkshires.

Sweet and Salty Bacon Corn Bread

This rich and moist corn bread is wonderful for breakfast or brunch, spread with butter and strong honey. A terrific accompaniment for bean soups, it's especially good when made with high-quality cornmeal. Recently, at my co-op, I found vivid yellow cornmeal from Butterworks Farm here in Vermont that smells so fresh that it makes other cornmeal seem dull. Using a cast-iron skillet as the baking pan makes the corn bread nice and crispy on both the top and the bottom. If you like things on the sweet side, feel free to increase the sugar content.

Cob-smoking is a traditional style of smoking in New England, using corn cobs as the fuel to make smoke. It produces bacon that is stronger, smokier, and less sweet than bacon smoked over fruitwood such as apple.

MAKES ONE 9½-INCH ROUND, ABOUT 8 GENEROUS SERVINGS

3 pieces of thick-sliced cob-smoked or other flavorful pastured pork bacon

4 tablespoons (½ stick) unsalted butter

1½ cups organic yellow cornmeal

1 tablespoon dark brown sugar

1 tablespoon granulated sugar

1 scant teaspoon baking soda

½ teaspoon kosher salt

2 eggs, beaten

1¾ cups buttermilk

Place a 9½-inch cast-iron skillet in the oven and heat both oven and pan to 425 degrees. When the oven has come to temperature, slice the bacon crosswise into batons about ¼ inch in width. Put them in the hot skillet and return the pan to the oven for 10 minutes.

Melt the butter in the pan, either in the oven or on the stovetop. Tilt the pan to coat the inside with butter. Set it aside.

In a mixing bowl, whisk the cornmeal, sugars, baking soda, and salt together. Make a well in the bottom of the dry ingredients and pour the eggs into it. Shake the buttermilk and pour it over the eggs, then pour the melted butter and bacon in, too. Use a rubber spatula to blend all the ingredients, working swiftly.

Pour the batter into the hot pan and bake for 25 minutes, or until the corn bread is nicely golden and fragrant. Let it cool briefly on a rack before inverting it onto a board. Serve it warm (but not piping hot), cut into wedges.

Fettuccini with Bacon, Chèvre, Dandelion Greens, and Toasted Walnuts

Dandelion greens are a sign of spring in the Northeast, and in the old days were widely regarded as a spring tonic for those who had just endured a long winter without fresh greens. Those who choose to eat locally still consider them both a tonic and a treat, tender and filled with the fresh taste of a new season. If your lawn or market doesn't sprout dandelion greens naturally, spinach or chard will work just as well. This is a one-pan meal: You use the same big sauté pan both to make the sauce in and to toss the pasta with the sauce before serving.

SERVES 4 AS A MAIN COURSE, 8 AS A FIRST COURSE

¾ cup walnuts

2 tablespoons kosher salt

1 pound fresh fettuccini (see page 201) or other fresh long pasta or dried pasta

6 slices of smoked pastured pork bacon, sliced crosswise into ¼-inch matchsticks

1 sweet, mild onion (preferably Vidalia), finely chopped

2 cloves garlic, chopped

1 bunch dandelion greens, washed and drained, but not dried, stems removed

½ teaspoon sea salt

4 ounces fresh chèvre, crumbled

½ cup freshly grated Parmigiano-Reggiano

¼ cup heavy cream or crème fraîche

Heat a cast-iron frying pan over medium heat and toast the walnuts in it, watching them closely and shaking and stirring the nuts as necessary to prevent burning. When they smell fragrant and look darker, pour the hot nuts onto a plate to cool. Chop them with a knife or pulse them in a food processor into a coarse texture about the size of grains of bulgur wheat. Set them aside.

Fill a large pot with water and bring it to a boil. Add the 2 tablespoons kosher salt, then the pasta, and cook it to al dente, following the package directions for timing. Drain the pasta, reserving ½ cup of the starchy cooking water.

Meanwhile, heat a lidded sauté pan and arrange the bacon in it (the bacon should sizzle when it hits the pan). Lower the heat and add the onion, cooking and stirring occasionally until the pieces are soft, about 3 minutes. Add the garlic and cook for another 2 minutes, then add the greens, along with the sea salt. Give everything a good stir, then clap on the lid and turn down the heat, cooking until the greens are wilted, 3 to 4 minutes longer. When the greens have wilted completely, stir in the cheeses and remove the pan from the heat. Let the cheeses melt and soften in the pan. Add the cream and the reserved pasta water.

Transfer the pasta to the sauté pan. Toss the pasta with the sauce, pour it into a shallow bowl, and serve at once, topped with the walnuts.

Green Split Pea Soup with Berkshire Bacon Batons

Split peas are among the fastest-cooking dried legumes, and because they are split, they don't need soaking. This is a soup that can be made in an hour or a little longer, depending on the age and dryness of the beans. Drizzling on spirals of olive oil and sherry vinegar at serving time really enhances this (and all) bean soups.

SERVES 4

3 thick slices of pastured pork bacon (about 3 ounces)

1 tablespoon extra-virgin olive oil

1 small onion

2 stalks celery

1 teaspoon fresh thyme

2 tablespoons minced fresh flat-leaf parsley

Salt

½ cup white wine

1 cup green split peas, rinsed and drained

Freshly ground black pepper

For serving:

Fragrant extra-virgin olive oil

Sherry vinegar

½ cup Greek-style yogurt, sour cream, or crème fraîche

Pile the bacon slices on top of each other and cut them crosswise into ¼-inch batons. Heat a 3-quart Dutch oven or saucepan over low heat, and when the rim feels hot to the touch, add the bacon. Cook slowly over low heat to partially render the bacon fat. Add the olive oil.

While the bacon renders, chop the onion and celery and add them to the pot along with the thyme and parsley. Stir in a little salt. Continue to cook over low heat until the vegetables are soft, about 10 minutes. Add the wine, turn the heat to medium-high, and stir with a wooden spatula to incorporate any browned bits into the liquid.

Add the drained split peas and enough cold water to cover the peas by 2 inches. Keeping the heat at medium-high, occasionally skim and discard the foam that floats to the top for the first 10 to 15 minutes. Cover the pot, lower the heat to maintain a slow simmer, and cook for 1 to 1½ hours, until the split peas are very soft.

Taste the soup and add salt and pepper as needed. Ladle the soup into bowls, top each serving with a drizzle of great olive oil, good sherry vinegar, and a dollop of yogurt and serve.

Bacon-Wrapped Apricots
with Goat Cheese

Made in batches in the microwave, these are easy appetizers. If you prefer, they can be made on a sheet pan under the broiler: Cook for about 5 minutes, or until the bacon is browned.

SERVES 4

20 pitted dried apricots

About 3 cups freshly brewed Darjeeling tea

4 ounces goat cheese

Grated zest of 1 lemon

Salt and freshly ground black pepper

10 slices of pastured pork bacon, cut crosswise to form 2 halves

Soak the apricots in enough hot brewed tea to cover for 15 minutes. Remove the apricots and use your thumb to open each one where the pit was removed when they are cool enough to handle to form a pocket. Set aside.

Mix together the goat cheese, lemon zest, and salt and pepper to taste. Fill each apricot with about ½ teaspoon filling. Wrap the apricot with a half slice of bacon, securing the bottom with a toothpick rolling tightly and placing, seam side down, on a china plate.

Cook them in batches of 5 in a microwave set to full power for 3 minutes. Set each apricot on a plate lined with paper towels to drain. Serve warm on toothpicks.

10 More Dishes to Make with Bacon

- Warm Potato Salad with Bacon Crumbles and Red Wine Vinegar Dressing
- Savory Dinner Custard with Bacon and Parsley
- Braised Cabbage with Bacon Batons and Thyme
- Watercress Salad with Shrimp and Bacon Bits
- Hot Tomato Soup with a Bacon Garnish
- Boiled, Mashed, and Buttered Turnips or Rutabaga with Fried Bacon Cubes
- Pasta Carbonara with Bacon, Onion, and Pastured Egg
- Grilled Bacon Panini with Red Pepper Jelly and Muenster Cheese
- Bacon and Avocado Sandwich on Dark Bread with Sprouts
- Honey-Glazed Carrots with Bacon Bits

Pig Candy

*P*eanut brittle made with crisp pastured bacon and a little red pepper—what could be bad about that? Try this with a glass of Bourbon or cocktails, or serve it at a Super Bowl party—either way, it's memorable.

MAKES ABOUT 1 POUND BRITTLE

2 tablespoons unsalted butter, softened, plus more for greasing the baking sheet and spatula

1 cup sugar

½ cup light corn syrup

½ teaspoon sea salt or smoked salt flakes

¼ cup water

1 cup roasted unsalted peanuts

¼ teaspoon crushed red pepper flakes, or more to taste

½ cup crumbled crisp-cooked pastured pork bacon (about 6 slices)

1 teaspoon baking soda

Butter a silicone baking liner or cookie sheet, as well as an offset spatula or icing knife, and set aside.

Using a 1-quart saucepan, heat the sugar, corn syrup, salt, and water over medium heat and cook until the sugar dissolves, stirring with a silicone spatula. Stir in the nuts, red pepper, and bacon pieces. Cook the mixture until it registers 300 to 310 degrees on a candy thermometer—it will form a long thread when you pull the spatula out. Depending on the pan and the efficiency of the burner, this can take up to 20 minutes.

Remove the pan from the heat and carefully but thoroughly stir in the 2 tablespoons butter and the baking soda (take care—the mixture will foam). Immediately pour the mixture onto the prepared pan and, using the offset spatula or an icing knife, spread it into an even layer as thinly as possible. When the brittle is cool enough to handle (but still warm and pliant), use your hands (gloves can help) to stretch and pull it even thinner.

When the brittle is cool, break it into pieces and serve, or store in an airtight tin.

The Versatility of Bacon

Bacon is a terrifically valuable ingredient and can be used as far more than a breakfast side. Be sure to save the rendered fat, which is wonderful to cook with (see pages 254 to 258 for recipes that use bacon fat). It also seems to have become the new little black dress of the food world, appearing in cupcakes and confections as well as savory dishes.

HERITAGE HAM: Cooking carefully smoked hams from heritage breed pastured pork has been revelatory—such meat is filled with flavor beyond just a smoke taste, and is not overly salty. When you can get your hands on ham like this, you'll want to celebrate it in lots of dishes, from center of the platter holiday meals to soups that wring every last drop of goodness from the bones.

Smoked and Glazed Berkshire Ham with Caramelized Pineapple

Taste a sliver of your ham well before cooking it—if it's especially salty, you can remove some of the salt (see box on page 231). I have never had that problem with the ham I get from Green Mountain Smoke House, so I dive straight into glazing. Since the ham is already smoked and therefore essentially cooked, it needs little more than an hour and a half's worth of glazing to achieve perfection. (The general rule I learned from New Hampshire's Fox Country Smoke House is to cook a smoked ham for 15 minutes per pound at 325 degrees.) And after the ham is gone, there is still the bone—be sure to save it for soup!

SERVES 8 TO 12

7 pounds bone-in smoked pastured ham

2 packed cups dark brown sugar

2 tablespoons dry mustard

1 tablespoon ground cloves

1 tablespoon unsalted butter

1 fresh pineapple, peeled, cored, and sliced

Heat the oven to 350 degrees and line a roasting pan that fits your roast size with foil.

Rinse the ham in cold water and blot it dry. Mix together the brown sugar, mustard, and cloves, and add just enough water to make a thick paste. Using your hands or a rubber spatula, spread this paste all over the ham.

Place the ham on a roasting rack in the prepared pan and add about an inch of water to prevent burning (use more or less water as your pan and rack require, but the goal is to prevent the paste and any juices from burning). Roast for 1½ hours, or until the glaze is dark and bubbling, then let the ham rest for about 10 minutes before slicing.

While the meat roasts, melt the butter over medium-high heat in a nonstick sauté pan or frying pan and brown the pineapple until each slice has caramelized spots. Serve the pineapple with the sliced ham, which needs no other accompaniment.

Localvore Glazed Smoked Ham

ere in southern Vermont, "localvore" is universally spelled and pronounced "localvore." The "Localvore Challenge" is a local contest created by Post Oil Solutions designed to encourage seasonal eating within our statewide or hundred-mile food shed; for it, you have to pledge to cook only local foods for either a week or a month. This glaze offers many of the flavors of a traditional brown sugar and mustard coating, but it is made entirely from ingredients grown in Vermont—maple syrup, cider vinegar, and horseradish. Our answer to the pineapple often served with ham is local orchard fruit—apples and pears. Again, be sure to taste a sliver of your ham for saltiness well ahead of the time you need to glaze it.

SERVES 6 TO 8

5 pounds bone-in smoked pastured ham

1 tablespoon very finely grated fresh horseradish

¼ cup cider vinegar

1½ cups dark maple syrup

1 tablespoon unsalted butter

1 baking apple and 1 pear, peeled, cored, and sliced

Heat the oven to 350 degrees, line a roasting pan with aluminum foil, and grease the rack for the pan with oil such as olive oil or canola oil. Rinse the ham in cold water and blot it dry.

Mix the horseradish and vinegar together and let steep for 1 hour. Strain the horseradish out of the vinegar, pressing it in a small sieve to impart as much of its flavor as possible to the vinegar. Discard the horseradish.

Combine the vinegar and the maple syrup, and brush the mixture onto all surfaces of the ham. Bake the ham for 1 hour, or until it is heated through and the glaze is slightly burned and fragrant. Let the ham rest for 10 minutes before slicing it thinly.

While the ham rests, melt the butter in a sauté pan or frying pan over medium-low heat and gently cook the sliced fruit until it begins to caramelize and is fragrant, 10 to 12 minutes. Serve the hot fruit with the sliced ham.

If Your Ham Is Too Salty

It's always a good idea to test the saltiness of a ham by cutting off a little piece and frying it up. You can soak a salty ham in cold water for as much as 24 hours, changing the water frequently, to draw the salt out of the ham. If it is really hopeless and still salty, try simmering it in copious amounts of water to leach the remaining excess salt from the ham. Put the ham in cold water to cover by several inches and bring it to a boil. Lower the heat to maintain a slow and steady simmer. Taste the water once or twice at 20-minute intervals. If it is very salty, pour it out and use fresh water. The goal is to gently cook the ham for a total of 45 minutes. When done, remove the ham, let cool, and blot it dry. It is now ready to bake and/or glaze.

Baked Cured Ham Steak with Honey, Onion Confit, and Bourbon

ather than choosing a whole ham, you can elect to have your ham cut into steaks, smoked or not. This option offers more variety in preparation and is a good choice for small households. Ham steaks are usually a good inch thick, so they offer satisfying eating. Leftovers, cut into thin strips or batons, make great additions to salads and to bean soups.

SERVES 4

1¾ to 2 pounds cured
pastured ham steak

1 tablespoon honey

2 tablespoons onion confit,
preferably homemade (see
box below)

3 tablespoons bourbon

¼ cup water

Blot the ham and bring it to room temperature on a wire rack with paper towels underneath. Heat the oven to 350 degrees and put the rack in the center.

Mix together the honey, onion confit, and bourbon. Place the ham in an ovenproof covered pan such as a sauté pan or braising pan large enough to hold it, and pour the honey mixture over the ham. Pour the ¼ cup water down the side of the pan, avoiding washing off the ham. Cover the pot tightly by first pressing a piece of parchment paper down just over the meat. Put the lid on over this inner cover and oven braise for 1½ hours.

Transfer the ham to a platter. Put the roasting pan on the stovetop, and cook down the braising liquid, stirring, until it is reduced to about ¼ cup of intensely flavored juice. Be careful not to let the liquid burn.

Serve the ham steak whole with the sauce drizzled on top.

ONION CONFIT

Thinly sliced onion cooked slowly down with sugar caramelizes into a savory jam. Try it as a condiment with almost any roast, or use it as an ingredient in recipes that call for it.

1 tablespoon unsalted butter
1 large onion, thinly sliced

1 tablespoon sugar
Salt

Melt the butter in a heavy skillet such as a cast-iron frying pan. When it has foamed, add the onion slices and sprinkle them with the sugar and salt to taste. Cook over the lowest possible heat, stirring as needed, until the onion is completely limp and golden, with a jam-like consistency, about 30 minutes. If not using immediately, store in a sterile glass jar in the refrigerator for up to 1 week.
Makes about ½ cup

Slow-Cooked Spice-Rubbed Fresh Ham Roast

Fresh ham is uncured, unsmoked, and delicious in its own right. Rubbed with a spice blend, cooked slowly, and basted with white wine, this is a great meal for a special occasion. It is superb with Burgundian Mustard—a blend of sour and sweet pickles, mustard, and cognac (see box below). My ham, from a Berkshire pig, was terrific, but unfortunately, it had the skin removed. If yours comes with the skin, treasure it, because it will add crisp cracklings to the edges of each slice.

SERVES 8

4¾ pounds bone-in fresh pastured ham

1 clove garlic, cut in half

1 tablespoon ground sage

1 tablespoon ground cumin

1 tablespoon sugar

1 tablespoon ground ginger

1 tablespoon kosher salt

½ teaspoon ground mustard seed

¼ teaspoon ground cloves

Freshly ground black pepper

½ cup white wine

1 to 2 tablespoons crème fraîche or sour cream

Heat the oven to 300 degrees and set the rack in the upper center. Choose a small cast-iron frying pan or other shallow pan that closely fits the size of the roast.

Using a very sharp knife, score the fat (or skin and fat) in a diamond pattern, cutting through just to the surface of the meat. Rub the cut sides of the garlic all over the surface. Cut the garlic into slivers and push them into the scored lines in the fat.

Make the rub by combining the sage, cumin, sugar, ginger, salt, mustard, cloves, and pepper. Rub this over all sides of the meat, using it up. Put the roast in the pan, fat side up. Pour the wine into the bottom of the pan, and put the roast in the oven.

Roast the meat for about 2½ hours (25 minutes per pound), basting it every 30 minutes with the liquid in the bottom of the pan. When the internal temperature registers 150 to 155 degrees on an instant-read thermometer, the roast is done.

Let the meat rest for 15 minutes or more before cutting it. Meanwhile, reduce the liquid in the bottom of the pan to a syrup, then remove it from the heat and add a little crème fraîche.

Serve the meat thinly sliced, napped with the gravy.

BURGUNDIAN MUSTARD

This is my adaptation of James Beard's recipe, which appeared in *James Beard's American Cookery*, and it is a revelation—who knew mustard could do tricks? One taster said it was "just like being in France!"

2 spears kosher dill pickle (½ whole pickle)

6 slices of bread-and-butter pickle

⅓ cup Dijon mustard

2 tablespoons brandy or cognac

Using a small food processor fitted with the steel blade, whirl all the ingredients together into a smooth paste. Scrape the mustard into a decorative bowl and serve. **Makes about ½ cup**

Jacob's Cattle Bean Soup with Berkshire Ham Bone

*T**he bone from a good smoked ham, along with all the meat clinging to it, fills a bean soup with fine flavor. I like burgundy-speckled Jacob's Cattle beans because they are also a heritage food (in this case from New England), but you could use any other member of the white bean family, or even dried (peeled) fava beans. Be sure to factor in the time you'll need to soak the dried beans before making the soup.*

SERVES 8

2 cups (¾ pound) dried
Jacob's Cattle beans

2 tablespoons extra-virgin
olive oil

1 onion, chopped

1 stalk celery, chopped

2 carrots, chopped

2 bay leaves

1 large pastured ham
bone with scraps of meat
attached

Salt and freshly ground
black pepper

For the garnish:

Freshly grated Parmigiano-
Reggiano

Extra-virgin olive oil

Sherry or wine vinegar

Put the beans in a pot with enough water to cover them by 2 inches and soak them overnight, or parboil and soak them for 1 hour. Rinse the soaked beans and reserve them.

Heat a large Dutch oven or other heavy soup pot over medium-low heat. Add the olive oil, and when it is thinned and fragrant, sweat down the onion, celery, and carrots until they are soft and slightly browned. Add the drained beans and the bay leaves, along with enough cold water to cover the contents by about 1 inch. Add the ham bone.

Bring the soup to a simmer, occasionally using a fine-mesh strainer or spoon to skim off the scum that rises to the top. (Skimming eliminates any muddy flavors.)

Lower the heat and cook the soup, with the lid positioned so that some steam is allowed to escape the pot, for 2 to 3 hours, until the beans are meltingly soft and the house is filled with the heady perfume of the soup. Remove the ham bone, cut off and reserve any bits of meat still clinging to it, and discard the bone. Taste the soup for salt and correct the balance, if necessary. Add pepper to taste.

If you want a thicker soup, use a potato masher or an immersion blender to partially or entirely purée the beans. If you are happy with the texture, leave it alone. Stir in the reserved bits of meat from the bone.

Serve with good bread on the side and a sprinkling of grated Parmigiano-Reggiano on top. Add a drizzle of fragrant olive oil and a drop of sherry or wine vinegar to each bowl.

Dressing Bean Soups

The flavor of a bowl of bean soup becomes more vivid when drizzled with robust extra-virgin olive oil and a few drops of sherry vinegar. These, along with salt and freshly ground black pepper, finish a soup that would taste flat if you didn't complete this final step.

Corn Chowder with Ham

've always loved corn, and when it's in season here in Vermont, I try to eat it daily. I also freeze as much as I can. Happily, even if I don't manage to freeze enough, frozen corn is one of the best things you can buy in a supermarket. The organic frozen corn I buy at my co-op works just fine for this recipe. The slivers of left-over ham add lots of character to this hearty soup. Chowders are usually served hot, but I like this one cold, too.

SERVES 2 TO 4

1 tablespoon extra-virgin olive oil

1 onion, chopped

1 cup leftover cooked pastured ham, cut into sticks or cubes

1 pound frozen kernel corn

Generous pinch of sugar

½ teaspoon sea salt

3 cups whole milk

Freshly ground black pepper

Chopped fresh tarragon or cilantro

Heat a Dutch oven or other heavy soup pot over medium heat, then add the olive oil. Sweat the onion pieces down to softness, and add the ham, turning it with the onion and oil to coat. Add the corn, sugar, and salt, and continue to stir to coat the corn with flavor and to cook off some of the moisture. When the corn smells fragrant and has just started brown-ing, add the milk and a generous grinding of pepper.

Cover the pot, bring it to a slow simmer, and cook for 10 minutes. Using an immersion blender, thicken the soup by partially blending the corn and ham, leaving some texture.

Serve hot or cold, garnished with tarragon or cilantro to taste.

Melon and Ham

here's something about the combination of sweet and salty that has a special allure. While many people may know of the plea-sures of prosciutto con melone (prosciutto with melon), they may be less familiar with an American variation—melon and smoked ham. Using an electric knife is by far the easiest way to cut the ham slices thinly for this recipe.

SERVES 6

1 ripe melon such as cantaloupe

6 thin slices of baked smoked pastured ham, at room temperature

1 lime, cut into 6 wedges

Sea salt

Cut the melon in half, scoop out the seeds and pulp, and divide each half into 3 wedges.

Serve each melon wedge on a plate with a slice of ham draped over it, accompanied by a wedge of lime and a small bowl of salt. Your guests will need a sharp knife, as well as a fork, for cutting the melon and ham.

SHANKS AND HOCKS: Filled with collagen, slow-cooked shanks and hocks add jellied texture and deep flavor to soups and stews, whether smoked or fresh. Alternatively, the meat can be shredded and used in a pasta sauce, in a main dish, or as a filling for anything from tacos to Chinese buns.

Black Bean Soup with Smoked Hocks and Sherry

Elegant and subtle, this double-puréed soup transcends its humble ingredients. I've written the recipe for an hour-long boil-and-soak for the beans rather than an overnight soak, but you can do that instead if you have time. The soup takes about 6 hours from start to finish, and it's easy to multiply to feed a crowd, or so that you'll have enough to freeze for later. This soup can also be made with a good smoked ham bone instead of the trotters.

SERVES 8

2 smoked pastured ham hocks

2 cups dried black beans

2 tablespoons extra-virgin olive oil

1 large onion, roughly chopped

2 stalks celery, roughly chopped

2 bay leaves

Kosher salt and freshly ground black pepper

½ cup dry sherry

2 tablespoons balsamic vinegar

For the garnish:

Sour cream, crème fraîche, or full-fat Greek yogurt

Chopped hard-boiled egg

½ cup minced fresh flat-leaf parsley

Rinse the ham hocks and blot them dry. Set these aside to return to room temperature as you start the beans.

Measure the beans onto a sheet pan—this makes it easier to pick out any stones or other foreign matter. Using a strainer and a bowl, rinse the beans very well. Put them in a large enameled soup pot or Dutch oven, and add enough cold water to cover them by a good 3 inches. Bring the water to a boil, turn off the heat, and let the beans sit in the cooling water for 1 hour.

Drain the beans, discarding the water, and return them to the pot. Add enough fresh water to again cover them by 3 inches. Cook the beans at a slow simmer over medium-low heat for 1½ hours, or until they are just starting to become tender.

Heat a frying pan or sauté pan over medium heat, then add the olive oil. When the oil has thinned and become fragrant, sweat down the onion and celery pieces until they begin to soften, but not brown. Add them to the beans, along with the ham hocks, bay leaves, about 1 teaspoon salt, and a grinding of pepper. Cover and simmer over very low heat for 3 hours, or until the beans are completely tender.

Remove and discard the bay leaves. Remove the ham hocks and let them cool on a cutting board. Use an immersion blender to purée the soup in the pot, adding a little boiling water if it is too thick.

When the ham hocks are cool enough to handle, pick through them and remove all the bits of meat, cutting the meat into a fine dice or shreds. Discard the bones and gristle. Return the meat to the soup pot and purée the soup again to incorporate the meat.

Stir in the sherry and vinegar. Set the pot over low heat to bring the soup up to serving temperature. Taste for seasonings and correct, if needed. To serve the soup, swirl sour cream on top and sprinkle on the egg and parsley.

PORK   SHANKS AND HOCKS

Ham Hock Stock

A quart or two of this stock, stashed in the freezer, makes for nearly instant bean soups later on, and it's especially useful for quick-cooking ones like lentil soup. If you have the freezer space, you may wish to make several batches to get you through the chilly soup season. The soft cooked meat shreds left after you strain the stock can be used in salads or added back into bean soups.

MAKES 3 TO 4 QUARTS

2 whole cloves

1 onion, cut in half

2 smoked pastured ham hocks

2 large carrots, cut into large chunks

3 cloves garlic, smashed

2 stalks celery, leaves and all

Stick a clove into each onion half, then put all the ingredients into a large stockpot and cover generously with cold water. Simmer for about 3 hours, or until the meat is falling off the bones and the stock is flavorful and rich.

Strain the stock and discard the vegetables, but save the meat for another use. If you do not plan to use the stock immediately, chill it and remove the fat that collects on top.

How to Cook Cracklings

Cut the pig skin into small squares or strips, using a utility knife or box cutter if necessary, and render/fry it over low heat for about half an hour until it is crisp and all the fat has rendered into the pan. Cracklings are great sprinkled on salads or floated on the surface of soups.

Lentil Soup with Smoked Ham Hock Stock

One great thing about lentils is that they don't need to be soaked, and they cook rapidly compared to most other dried beans. This soup ups the flavor ante by using stock made from ham hocks, along with sprigs of thyme and sage. Once you've got the stock made, this cooks in under an hour.

SERVES 8 TO 10

1 tablespoon extra-virgin olive oil

2 onions, finely chopped

3 cloves garlic, chopped

1 carrot, finely chopped

1 parsnip, finely chopped

½ cup red or white wine

2 tablespoons tomato paste

Pinch of sugar

1 bay leaf

1 teaspoon chopped fresh or dried thyme

1 teaspoon chopped fresh or dried sage

1 teaspoon grainy mustard

8 cups Ham Hock Stock (see page 237)

2 cups brown lentils

For serving:

Red wine vinegar

Extra-virgin olive oil

Sour cream or crème fraîche

Chopped fresh chives

Chopped hard-boiled egg

Heat a heavy enameled cast-iron casserole or soup pot over medium-low heat and add the olive oil. When it is thinned and fragrant, add the onions and sauté them until they begin to wilt. Add the garlic, carrot, and parsnip and continue to sauté until they are fragrant. Add the wine, tomato paste, and sugar, and let this stew for 5 to 10 minutes. Stir the bay leaf, fresh herbs, and mustard into the vegetable mixture until blended. Add the ham stock and lentils and bring the soup to a boil. Immediately reduce the heat to low, partially cover the pot, leaving a gap for steam to escape through, and simmer the soup until the lentils are soft and cooked through, 30 to 40 minutes.

To serve, swirl in a little red wine vinegar and olive oil to taste, ladle the soup into bowls, and finish with a dollop of sour cream, a few chopped chives, and a sprinkling of egg.

Grilled Pork Shank, Char Siu Bao Style

char siu bao are steamed buns filled with barbecued pork that are sold by street vendors, sidewalk lunch places, and the kind of meat shops that display whole barbecued ducks dangling in the window (the char siu bao will usually be in the steamer on the back counter). Here in Vermont, far from the cities with bustling Chinatowns, char siu bao are not easy to find, so making them myself is worthwhile. If you don't want to make the buns (recipe follows), you can simply serve the shredded meat as an entrée along with rice or beans and tortillas or corn bread. Note that you marinate the meat all day or overnight before cooking.

MAKES ENOUGH FOR 2 DOZEN STEAMED BUNS OR 4 ENTRÉES

1¾ to 2 pounds bone-in pastured pork shank

For the marinade:

3 tablespoons honey

2 tablespoons dark sesame oil

2 tablespoons hoisin sauce

2 cloves garlic, finely chopped

½ teaspoon Chinese Five-Spice Blend (see page 32)

3 tablespoons thin soy sauce

3 tablespoons Chinese rice wine or sherry

For the barbecue glaze:

¼ cup honey

2 tablespoons thin soy sauce

2 tablespoons Chinese rice wine or sherry

Blot the meat dry and place it in a large bowl. Mix the marinade ingredients together, coat the meat with them, and cover the bowl and refrigerate overnight or all day. When you are ready to cook the meat, bring it to room temperature, while heating a good amount of real hardwood charcoal in a covered grill such as a Weber or Big Green Egg.

When the coals are ashed over and hot, move them all to one side of the grill and put a disposable foil roasting pan on the empty side, to catch the drippings. Replace the grate, and position the marinated meat (shaking off any clinging marinade) over the foil pan. Discard the leftover marinade. Use an oven thermometer or the thermometer on the grill to maintain a temperature of 300 degrees in the grill as you cook the meat for 3 hours.

(Alternatively, roast the marinated meat in the middle of a 300-degree oven, basting as noted below. While you can't add smoke flavor, you can place a water-filled pan on the floor of the oven to help the meat cook to moist tenderness. Top off the water level in the pan as needed.)

At about the 2-hour mark, start mopping the meat with the glaze every 30 minutes or so. Keep cooking until the internal temperature of the meat registers 150 degrees on an instant-read thermometer.

Let the meat rest for at least 20 minutes before slicing, shredding, and serving it as an entrée. If you are making char siu bao, let the meat cool completely before shredding it.

Char Siu Bao

These little pork-stuffed buns make great party food, fun to put together with friends in the kitchen. You'll need a steamer of some kind; the tiered style of bamboo steamer and the large perforated metal disk steamer that fits in a pot are both available in Chinese cookware stores. You can also use a conventional steamer insert that fits like a double boiler on top of a saucepan. Char siu bao keep well, too: The finished buns can be frozen and defrosted in a steamer when you need them.

MAKES 24 STEAMED BUNS

For the buns:

¼ cup warm water

Sugar

1 package active dry yeast

4 to 4¼ cups unbleached all-purpose flour

2 tablespoons rendered pastured pork lard (see page 250) or strained pastured pork bacon fat (see page 257)

1 cup milk, heated to lukewarm

Oil, for greasing the bowl

For the filling:

1 recipe Grilled Pork Shank, Char Siu Bao Style (see page 239)

2 tablespoons oyster sauce

3 tablespoons light brown sugar

2 teaspoons sesame oil

For serving:

Hoisin sauce

Cut 24 pieces of parchment paper or waxed paper about 2 inches square.

Put the warm water in a bowl and sprinkle a pinch of sugar and the yeast on top. Let the yeast sit for 5 minutes—you should see a foam develop on top.

Place 4 cups of the flour in the bowl of a food processor fitted with the steel blade. Using the feed tube and pulsing with each ingredient, add the lard in 2 or 3 pieces and ½ cup sugar, then the milk and the yeast mixture. Process steadily (without pulsing) until the dough comes together to form a ball.

Knead the dough on a floured board until it is smooth and satiny. Pour a bit of oil into a large bowl and turn the ball of dough in it to coat. Cover the dough with plastic wrap and leave it in a warm (70 degrees is ideal), draft-free place to rise. After an hour or so, the dough should have doubled in size.

Meanwhile, combine the shredded meat, oyster sauce, brown sugar, and sesame oil. If the meat is not evenly shredded, briefly pulse all the filling in the bowl of a food processor with the steel blade until it forms a coarse purée with some texture. Set aside.

Roll the dough into a long, fat snake and divide it into 4 parts. Roll each quarter into a log again, and divide it into 6 parts. Roll all 24 pieces into balls and cover them with a slightly damp cloth as you work.

Using a rolling pin, flatten each ball into a flat disk roughly 4 inches in diameter. Put about 1 teaspoon filling in the center of each disk and gather the edges together to make a purse of dough. Twist the pleats to hold in the filling, pushing the bunched edges into the bun like an inverted belly button. Place a square of parchment under each little purse, then place it, paper side down, on a baking sheet. Leave a little distance between buns—they will rise a bit as they sit. Keep the finished buns covered with a cloth and let them rest for 30 minutes at warm room temperature.

When you are ready to cook, fill the bottom of a steamer with water and heat it to boiling. Put the buns, paper side down, about 1 inch apart on the steamer rack. Steam the buns for 15 minutes, in batches if necessary.

Serve the steamed buns warm, with a little hoisin sauce on the side, for dipping.

OFFAL AND ODD BITS: The insides of pigs form the basis for many of the world's best-loved dishes. The trick with cooking offal is to go from freezer to cooking fairly rapidly, with a short brine en route to reveal and excise any silverskin or membranes. After that, low slow-cooking and then (sometimes) breading and frying make for delectable entrées and appetizers.

Stir-Fried Pork Liver with Asparagus, Mushrooms, and Fried Garlic Chips

ere is another contribution from my friend Tuk Long. This recipe is instructive because Tuk soaks the strips of liver in many changes of cold water to remove the blood before she cooks them. This yields meat with a mild flavor that marries well with vegetables. Thin soy sauce is not very salty and is right for this dish; if all you have is regular soy sauce, dilute it by half with water. Start your rice as you begin cooking, and it'll be ready when you are.

SERVES 4

1½ pounds pastured pork liver

3 tablespoons peanut or canola oil

5 cloves giant elephant garlic, thinly sliced (about ¼ cup)

¼ cup thin soy sauce

2 tablespoons water

1 teaspoon cornstarch

¼ teaspoon freshly ground black pepper

1 cup snow peas, tops and tails removed

½ cup sliced white button mushrooms

2½ cups asparagus, cut on the diagonal into 4-inch lengths

1 fat carrot, thinly sliced (about ½ cup)

3 scallions, cut lengthwise into quarters, then sliced into 2-inch shreds

Wash the liver in cold water and cut it into ½-inch slices. Soak these in a bowl of cold water, draining them in a colander and replacing the water as soon as it begins to look murky. It will take about 30 minutes and perhaps 6 changes of water before the water begins to stay fairly clear. Drain the liver and set aside.

Using a small frying pan or saucepan, heat 2 tablespoons of the oil and fry the garlic slices until they are crisp and golden, to make garlic "chips." Drain on paper towels and reserve.

Combine the soy sauce and water, then sprinkle the cornstarch and pepper on top. Set this mixture aside.

Heat a wok or large frying pan and add the remaining 1 tablespoon oil. Swirl it around to coat the hot pan, and immediately add the vegetables, one kind at a time, so that there is a satisfying sizzle each time. Cook the snow peas first, then the mushrooms until they are translucent but firm, then add the asparagus, carrot, and scallions and stir until they are steaming.

Transfer the vegetables to a bowl, and add the drained liver strips to the pan. Stir-fry them over high heat until they are seared on the outside and pink within. Return the vegetables to the wok and stir to integrate. Push the ingredients to the outer edges, leaving an empty space in the hot center of the wok, and add the sauce mixture. Use a spoon or chopstick to stir this as it cooks. As soon as the sauce starts thickening, after about 1 minute, stir in the liver and vegetables to coat them, and turn off the heat.

Serve immediately with a scattering of garlic chips on top.

Pork Stew Five Ways:
A Mixed Braise of Pig Heart, Kidneys, Liver, and Sausage Cooked in Lard

ooking a number of innards together yields enough stew for a hearty and satisfying winter meal—you get such small amounts of offal with a half pig that you can't really make separate dishes with each. This homey dish is loosely based on one from Stéphane Reynaud's Pork and Sons, *and it is a kind of culinary souvenir from a time when each farmer processed his own pig for the season, cooking up the fresh innards in home-rendered lard.*

SERVES 6

2 to 3 links pastured pork sausage

¾ pound pastured pork heart

2 pastured pork kidneys (about ⅓ pound each)

½ pound pastured pork liver

¼ cup kosher salt

4 cups water

⅓ cup rendered pastured pork lard (see page 250) or 5⅓ tablespoons unsalted butter

2 onions, thinly sliced

6 Yukon Gold potatoes, peeled and thinly sliced

Salt and freshly ground black pepper

⅓ cup cognac or red wine

For the garnish:

1 cup fresh flat-leaf parsley, chopped

3 cloves garlic

Panfry or gently poach the sausage links—the object is to have them fully cooked before proceeding. Let them cool, then slice them into rounds.

Bring the rest of the meat to room temperature and rinse it well. Put the heart, kidneys, and liver in a brine made from the salt and the water and let them rest for about 30 minutes. Rinse them well and blot them dry. Cut the heart, kidneys, and liver into cubes about 1 inch square, removing and discarding any fat, white tendons (in the center of the kidneys), and membranes.

Melt half the lard over medium-high heat in a saucepan large enough to hold all the ingredients. Sauté the onions until they start to get limp, about 6 minutes; then add the potato rounds, sprinkle them with a little salt and pepper, and cook for about 15 minutes, or until they begin to turn golden. Remove the onions and potatoes from the pan and reserve.

Deglaze the pan with the cognac, scraping to incorporate the browned bits into the sauce. Pour it over the onions and potatoes.

Melt the rest of the lard in the saucepan over medium heat. Add the meat cubes and brown them well, then add the cooked sausage and return the onions and potatoes to the pan. Cook over the lowest possible heat, tightly covered, for 30 minutes (or more if you wish). If there is not enough liquid in the pan to maintain a moist atmosphere, add a little water to keep it wet.

While the stew simmers, make the garnish: On a cutting board or in the bowl of a food processor fitted with the steel blade, finely chop the parsley and garlic together. Just before serving, remove the stew from the heat, salt and pepper the contents, and add the parsley and garlic to the pan. Serve warm.

Red-Cooked Pork Hearts

*R*ed-cooking" is the Chinese term for a slow braise cooked with sugar, garlic, star anise, soy sauce, and Shaoxing wine—and in my view, all red-cooked meats taste wonderful. I tried red-cooking 2 pork hearts to tenderness, and the result was worth the 5-hour time investment. Since this dish needs lots and lots of time to mellow into tenderness, it is an excellent candidate for a slow cooker if yours can maintain a low temperature. If you are going to a Chinese grocery for ingredients, pick up some chow fun noodles to serve with this. Otherwise, any good egg noodle will do. Rice, of course, is the usual accompaniment. If you enjoy this, do have a look at Kiam Lam Kho's Web site, Redcook.net, for lots of wonderful red-cooking recipes.

SERVES 4

3 tablespoons peanut oil or coconut oil

2 tablespoons sugar

2 pastured pork hearts (½ to 1 pound), rinsed, blotted dry, and cut into 1-inch cubes

3 cloves garlic, smashed

3 whole star anise

2 tablespoons dark soy sauce

¼ cup Shaoxing wine or sherry

1½ cups chicken stock, preferably homemade (see page 303)

Noodles or rice, for serving

Put the oil and sugar in an enameled cast-iron casserole or other braising pot and heat until the sugar begins to color and caramelize (it will stay distinct from the oil). When the sugar is a nice golden brown, add the pieces of pork heart and turn them to coat. Keep cooking until they begin to brown, at least 8 minutes.

Add the garlic, star anise, soy sauce, rice wine, and chicken stock to the pot. Cover with a piece of parchment paper just touching the meat and then put the lid on top. Simmer at the lowest possible heat for 5 to 6 hours (depending on the toughness of the meat). This can be done on the stovetop, in a 275- to 300-degree oven, or in a Crock-Pot set on low. Aim for very slow bubbles.

When the stew is done, let it rest (preferably overnight in the refrigerator to develop the flavors, but 15 minutes will do). Reheat as needed and serve warm with noodles or rice.

Mixed Greens with
Shaved Pork Tongue, Sliced Radishes,
and Blue Cheese Dressing

Tongue, whether beef, lamb, or pork, is cooked the same way— at a long, slow simmer until tender. When peeled and trimmed, it's ready for the next step. This can mean breading and frying to make crispy tidbits (see Lenguas de Cordero Salteadas in the lamb chapter, page 175), slicing and accompanying with a piquant sauce (see Beef Tongue with Sweet-and-Sour Sauce, page 121), or cutting the tongue into very, very thin "shavings" to enrich a salad, as here.

SERVES 2 TO 4

1 pastured pork tongue
(about ½ pound)

¼ cup distilled white
vinegar

4 cups water

4 cups assorted baby salad
greens (mesclun)

1 bunch radishes

¼ cup Leslie Newman's
Blue Cheese–Buttermilk
Dressing with Bacon Fat
(see page 255)

Bring the tongue to room temperature and rinse it. Dissolve the vinegar in the water in a large saucepan and immerse the tongue. Bring this to a slow boil and then reduce the heat to a slow simmer. Simmer the tongue, partially covered, for 30 minutes. Discard the vinegar water and replace it with fresh water. Simmer the tongue, turning it in the water every once in a while, for another 60 minutes, or until it is tender when pierced with a knife.

Let the tongue cool in its liquid. Remove the tongue, and using a sharp knife, peel off the skin and discard it.

If you have a mandoline or Benriner cutting tool, this is a good time to take it out. If not, use a thin, sharp knife to shave the tongue into extremely thin slices, cutting at an angle (much like flank steak) across the tongue. Set these slices aside.

Wash and dry the salad greens and slice the radishes paper-thin. Arrange the salad in a bowl, and toss it with the radishes and shaved tongue slices. Add the dressing just before serving, toss well, and serve at once.

Romaine Salad with Grapefruit, Coconut, Mint, and Pig Ear Lardoons

aste this, and you'll see why pig ears are so good—they are like crisp yet chewy pork crunchies. I learned how to braise them flavorfully from Appon's Thai Food blog (Khiewchanta.com). Then I improved on an already good thing by slicing them into matchsticks and deep-fat frying them. Served over a Thai-inspired salad adapted from Nancie McDermott's book Quick and Easy Thai, *this is a terrific, summery light dinner or first course.*

**SERVES 2 AS A DINNER SALAD,
OR 4 AS A FIRST COURSE**

For the pig ear:

1¾ cups water

Kosher salt

⅓ cup sugar

2 tablespoons light or thin soy sauce

1 tablespoon dark soy sauce

2 teaspoons ground cinnamon

1 pastured pork ear, cleaned and cut into 1-inch pieces

4 cups rendered pastured pork lard (see page 250) or vegetable oil, for deep-frying

For the salad:

1 pink grapefruit, peeled

Freshly grated zest and freshly squeezed juice of 1 lime

1 tablespoon sugar

1 tablespoon fish sauce

1 teaspoon finely chopped green chile

3 tablespoons shredded dried coconut

½ cup chopped fresh mint leaves

1 head romaine lettuce, washed and spun dry

Bring the water to a boil in a 3- to 4-quart saucepan, and dissolve 1 tablespoon salt, the sugar, and both soy sauces in it. When there is no visible salt or sugar, lower the heat and stir in the cinnamon. Add the pieces of pig ear, and maintain the heat at a slow simmer, partially covered, for 1½ hours.

Remove the pig ear pieces from the braising liquid with a slotted spoon and put in a colander. Rinse, drain, and dry them well. Put the meat on a cutting board and slice it into fine shreds about ⅛ inch wide. (The tinier the shred, the more delicious the crisp will be.)

Heat the lard in a deep-fat fryer to 375 degrees. Working in batches, use a slotted spoon to put a third of the meat into the hot fat. Fry for a minute or two, until the meat is browned and crisp. Don't worry if the meat sticks together in the fryer—you will be able to tease it apart once it is cool and dry. Transfer the fried bits with a slotted spoon to paper towels to drain. Repeat twice more, until all the meat is fried. Salt the drained meat to taste.

Segment the grapefruit over a large salad bowl to catch any juices. Add the segments to the bowl, then add the lime zest and juice, sugar, fish sauce, chile, coconut, and mint.

When you are ready to serve, add the lettuce on top of the other ingredients and toss everything together. Sprinkle the fried pig ear batons on top and toss again. Serve at once.

Yellow Split Pea Soup with Ras El Hanout and Fried Pig Ear Slivers

This is my riff on a Fergus Henderson theme, because his Pea and Pig's Ear Soup in The Whole Beast *is so wonderful. I wanted to take it further, so I've paired yellow split peas with the richly flavorful and fragrant North African spice blend* ras el hanout.

Pig ears make a deliciously chewy and crunchy garnish, but because they cook in the soup for about 3 hours before being fried, they also give the soup lots of gelatin and body.

This soup can be made ahead and served the next day. If you plan to do this, go ahead and fry the pig ear pieces while you're reheating the soup. You can store them in a refrigerator container overnight. The next day, spread them out on a baking sheet and recrisp them in a hot oven for 5 or 10 minutes before using them.

MAKES 6 CUPS

4 cups chicken stock, preferably homemade (see page 303)

About 4 cups water

2 cups yellow split peas, well rinsed and drained

2 pastured pork ears, cleaned and cut into pieces 3 to 4 inches square

2 whole onions

1 tablespoon kosher salt

Freshly ground black pepper

4 cups vegetable oil or rendered pastured pork lard (see page 250), for deep-frying

Leaves from 6 sprigs fresh thyme

1 teaspoon Ras El Hanout spice blend (see page 32)

In a large pot, bring the chicken stock and 2 cups of the water to a boil and add the split peas, cut-up pig ears, and the onions. The meat should be submerged; if it is not, cut it into smaller pieces or add more water. Lower the heat to a very slow simmer and keep the pot partially covered, skimming any foam that rises to the top during the first 15 minutes. At about the 2-hour mark, add the salt and pepper to taste. Simmer for a total of 3 or 4 hours, adding water as necessary to keep the meat covered, until the split peas are soft and the meat is very pliant and essentially tender.

Remove and discard the onions. Remove the pieces of pig ears, rinse and drain them well, pat them dry, and then cut them into thin slivers about ⅛ inch wide (the thinner, the better). Dry them further on paper towels while you heat the oil for frying.

Add the thyme and *ras el hanout* to the soup and cook for about 10 minutes. Use an immersion blender or stand blender to purée the soup to a thick, even consistency. Keep it warm.

Fry the slivers of pig ears in 3 batches for about 3 minutes per batch, or until the meat is crisp and brown. Drain the pieces on paper towels.

Serve the soup hot, garnished with the crisp pig ear slivers.

Pig Ears

Most recipes for pig ears start out with instructions to clean the ears thoroughly and shave off any hair with a disposable razor. I am happy to tell you that the Berkshire pig ears I ordered from Heritage Foods arrived completely clean and needed no further treatment.

I've found, after cooking a number of pig ears different ways, that every recipe starts with a braise. I discovered the fastest and best method is to first cut the ear into 1-inch pieces, which shortens the cooking time by half, and allows the meat to absorb flavorings more efficiently. The meat can then be rinsed, cooled, and further slivered before being fried into a deliciously chewy lardoon or garnish for all kinds of dishes, from salads to soups.

Until I got to pig ears, I had been happy to fry on the stovetop using a deep saucepan and a thermometer. But I'd read many stories about how messy frying pig ears could be, because they hold so much moisture that they pop all over. I even read one story in which the frying fat flew all the way up to the ceiling! That did it. I went out and bought an electric fryer to keep it all contained, and it worked—no muss, no fuss, and the temperature was perfect after 10 minutes. It made deep-frying incredibly easy.

Braised Pig Cheeks with Fennel, Garlic, Olives, and Parsley

This makes a great dinner party meal if you can get enough meat. I bought my pig cheeks from Heritage Foods when I couldn't find any locally—if they'd come with my pig, I would have had only 2 cheeks to play with, just a fraction of what I needed. The stuffed tomato is the perfect acidic yet sweet foil for the lush meat, so don't omit it. This dish is a simplified version of one from Pork and Sons, *by Stéphane Reynaud. Among other things, I've changed it so that it can be made over 2 days, if you wish, to provide the added oomph that an overnight rest gives most braises.*

SERVES 4 TO 6

12 pastured pork cheeks (about 2 pounds)

Kosher salt

¼ cup extra-virgin olive oil, plus more for drizzling

1 cup white wine

4 cloves garlic

1 bunch fresh flat-leaf parsley

4 to 6 ripe tomatoes (1 per diner)

4 bulbs fennel, fronds removed and discarded

¾ cup pitted black Greek olives

Rice or couscous, for serving

Salt and freshly ground black pepper

Rinse the meat and blot it dry. Sprinkle lightly with salt and let it come to room temperature.

Heat the ¼ cup olive oil in a braising pot or Dutch oven over medium-high heat, and cook the pig cheeks until they are browned all over, about 10 minutes. Pour the wine into the pan and stir, scraping to incorporate any browned bits into the liquid. Simmer over very low heat, covered, for 1 hour, or until the meat is tender. (At this point, the dish can be refrigerated overnight, if desired. If you do this, be sure to reheat the cheeks and their liquid in a Dutch oven very gently over the lowest possible heat before proceeding.)

Heat the oven to 325 degrees. Chop 2 cloves of the garlic and half of the parsley together on a board.

Use a sharp paring knife to cut the stalk end of each tomato in a circle around the core. Cut out the core so that you have a nice cavity for stuffing; try not to pierce the tomato at the bottom. Stuff the tomatoes with the garlic and parsley mixture. Put them in a gratin or other ovenproof dish, drizzle with 1 or 2 tablespoons olive oil, and bake for 30 minutes. If your tomatoes are not dead ripe, they may need more time—they should look soft, slightly collapsed, and wrinkled when done.

While the tomatoes roast, cut each fennel bulb lengthwise in half, then lay the flat side down on the board and cut it in half again lengthwise to form 2 wedges.

Bring a pot of water mixed with 2 tablespoons kosher salt to a boil, blanch the fennel wedges for 15 minutes, and drain them.

Chop the remaining 2 cloves garlic, the remaining parsley, and the pitted olives together to make a chunky and very roughly textured blend.

Add the fennel and the garlic, parsley, and olive blend to the meat. (This is the right time to make the rice or couscous.) Taste the stew and adjust for salt and pepper.

Serve the stew on deep plates or in shallow bowls, on top of a bed of rice or couscous, placing a roasted stuffed tomato at the side of each plate.

Pig's Tail with Crunch

This adaptation of Fergus Henderson's recipe for Crispy Pig's Tails is enough for deliciously greasy nibbles with drinks for 4 sophisticated and adventuresome eaters. First, the meat is braised to softness and then it is breaded and ultimately oven-fried. Sliced and served speared on toothpicks, it's the perfect accompaniment to a very dry martini or a bitter and orangey Negroni.

SERVES 4

1 pastured pork tail

About 4 cups water

1 tablespoon kosher salt

1 tablespoon Shaoxing wine or sherry

1/3 cup sugar

3 tablespoons thin soy sauce

2 teaspoons ground cinnamon

1 cup unbleached all-purpose flour

2 eggs, beaten

2 cups homemade bread crumbs or panko (Japanese bread crumbs)

2 tablespoons Dijon mustard

1 tablespoon unsalted butter

1 bunch watercress, washed and dried

1 teaspoon red wine vinegar

Rinse the pig's tail and blot it dry. Bring the water to a boil and add the salt, wine, sugar, soy sauce, and cinnamon. Add the pig's tail to the pot, along with more boiling water, if needed, to completely cover the meat.

Cover the pan tightly—use an inner sheet of parchment paper if your lid is not a tight fit—and lower the heat to a bare simmer. Cook for 3 hours.

When the meat is soft and cooked through, remove it from the liquid and let it cool. Discard the braising liquid. Refrigerate the meat overnight.

The next day, heat the oven to 425 degrees. Fill 3 shallow bowls with the flour, beaten egg, and bread crumbs, respectively. Coat the meat with the mustard, using the back of a spoon or a rubber spatula. Next, dredge the meat in the flour (shaking off any excess), then in the egg, and finally in the bread crumbs.

Heat a cast-iron or other ovenproof frying pan large enough to hold the tail over high heat. Melt the butter in the pan, and lowering the heat to medium, brown the tail on all sides. Put the pan in the oven for 10 minutes so that the tail will continue to crisp in the hot butter.

Remove the pan from the oven and let the meat rest for 5 to 10 minutes. Cut small bits off the tail and set them on a platter lined with the watercress; sprinkle the red wine vinegar over all; and serve. Provide toothpicks for spearing the meat, and lots of napkins.

A Pig's Tail

I had thought a pig's tail would be a long, curling object, but it is instead a more peculiar thing—the stump of a tail centered on a butterfly-shaped portion of the surrounding flesh, which is surprisingly fatty. In fact, the whole experience is about fat rather than flesh, although there are some delicious gnawing opportunities on the bony tail bits.

PORK FAT: Pork fat is a precious commodity, and it's worth asking your processor to give you all of it, labeled if possible. Lard can be rendered from nearly any fatty portion of the pig, including the shoulder, ham, and flank, although most people assume it is from the back (back fat). Cubes of back fat are good additions to bean soups, or used as a fat for sweating down onions for tomato sauce. Back fat is also used for making lardo, a cured Italian delicacy from Tuscany. Delicate leaf lard (best for pastry) comes from the fat that surrounds the kidneys. Bacon fat, rendered when bacon cooks, is a useful ingredient in its own right, flavored with smoke. Caul fat is lacy, and is used to hold together mixtures that might fall apart while cooking. It melts in as it cooks and adds flavor.

Lard

The lard you make, in contrast to commercial lard you can buy in the supermarket, is pure, unhydrogenated, and without preservatives. Because it's made from pastured pork fat, it has the positive attributes of any traditionally raised animal, including omega-3 fatty acids. From a cook's perspective, lard is a valuable ingredient for frying, and for making flaky and long-keeping pastries.

CUT SHEET ALERT: Ask for all the back fat, as well as for the leaf lard from the kidneys, too.

MAKES ABOUT 4 CUPS

2 ½ pounds pastured pork back fat
or pure white fat without meat

1 cup water

Defrost the fat and chop it into 1-inch cubes, using a sharp knife. The smaller and more consistent the cubes are in size, the more efficiently the fat will render.

Pour the water into a 5-quart heavy pot such as a sand pot or Dutch oven. Put the fat cubes on top of the water, partially cover the pan, and turn on the heat to low. Let the fat melt, stirring every now and then. Don't be alarmed by the occasional pop, just give the meat another stir. After a while, you may begin to see small bits of pork (cracklings) in the mix. Keep in mind that, as time goes on, you need to stir more frequently to prevent sticking on the bottom. It is important not to overcook the rendered fat, but do not be alarmed that the liquid fat looks golden. It will whiten as it cools.

Eventually, after 3 or 4 hours of occasional stirring, much of the fat will have rendered into a liquid, the cracklings and other solids will have fallen to the bottom or be floating on the liquid, and the water will have evaporated. At this point, pour the mixture through a fine sieve or double layers of cheesecloth to remove the solids, and pour the liquid fat into a sterile jar. If there is any remaining water, it will show up as a visible layer in the jar, and you'll be able to pour it off.

Return the solids to the pot, along with fresh water, and continue to cook them down. The goal is to render as much fat as possible. Each time you pour off the liquid fat, strain it into a sterile jar, then, let it cool on the counter before refrigerating. After the jar is chilled, it can be frozen for about 1 year. Kept in the refrigerator, the lard will be good for 3 months or so.

Apple and Raisin Pie in the World's Best All-Leaf-Lard Pie Crust

*T*his crust sets records for crispness ("Like a potato chip!" said one taster) and all by itself is sufficient reason to render leaf lard. Don't overcook the lard—keep it pale. A dark lard will taste porky. The original recipe came from the grandmother of friend and fiction author Jessie Haas, but we tweaked it by substituting low-gluten Wondra flour (it's found in a can in supermarkets and most commonly used for gravy). This marriage of antique and mid-twentieth-century modern produced a remarkable texture that is, I believe, the Platonic ideal of pie crust.

What filling is worthy of this crust? Try your own favorites. We chose heirloom apples and plump raisins. Use a good mix of baking apples that won't dissolve into applesauce. Resist the temptation to cut into the hot pie. Letting it cool will keep the crust's wonderful crispiness and keep the filling from oozing. (The first time we made this pie, we were so eager for a taste that we nestled the hot pie in a snowbank just outside the front door to cool it faster!)

MAKES A 10½-INCH DEEP-DISH PIE TO SERVE 8 TO 10

For the crust:

2 cups Wondra flour

1 teaspoon kosher salt

1 tablespoon sugar

½ teaspoon ground cassia (preferably Korintje cassia) or ground cinnamon

¾ cup rendered pastured pork leaf lard (see page 250), broken up into crumbles and chilled

4 to 5 tablespoons ice water

Unbleached all-purpose flour, for rolling the dough

For the filling and pie assembly:

¼ cup plus 2 tablespoons sugar

¼ cup tapioca, ground to flour in a spice grinder

½ teaspoon ground cassia (preferably Korintje cassia) or ground cinnamon

¼ teaspoon freshly grated nutmeg

Freshly grated zest of 1 lemon

6 cups peeled, cored, and halved assorted heirloom apples, such as Empire and Cortland

Freshly squeezed juice of ½ lemon

¼ cup raisins

2 tablespoons cognac

2 tablespoons unsalted butter, chilled or frozen and cut into tiny pieces or grated on a box grater

1 egg white, beaten

Pie Crust Aid

I've learned from my culinary guests that many people are afraid of pie crust. With a food processor, putting together a great dough is truly as easy as pie—the issue seems more to be a fear of rolling. There's a remedy for this: a plastic gadget called a "pie crust maker" or a "pie crust aid." Resembling a large, round, double-sided shower cap with a zipper, it works by containing the dough during shaping. This way, the crust is easy to control and doesn't stick to the plastic as long as you've used enough flour. Then, just unzip and invert the finished dough into the pie plate for baking.

Pie crust makers come in two sizes, one for pies up to 9½ inches across, and one for larger pies. They're available from the Baker's Store at the King Arthur Flour Web site (see Sources, page 371), as well as at kitchen specialty shops.

Working by hand or using a food processor fitted with the steel blade, mix the Wondra, salt, sugar, and cassia together. Cut in the crumbled lard by hand, or pulse it briefly in the food processor. When the mixture looks like cornmeal, begin to add the ice water, a spoonful at a time, stirring or pulsing, until the dough just begins to come together (and long before it rides the blade). Turn the dough out onto a lightly floured board, and form it into 2 disks. Wrap each one in waxed paper, slip them both into a plastic bag, and place them in the freezer for 45 minutes.

Heat the oven to 425 degrees and set a rack in the center. Remove one of the disks of dough, dust it with flour, beat it gently with a rolling pin to flatten it further, and roll it to fit a 10½-inch deep-dish pie pan. As you roll, work from the center outward, turning the dough between rolls to make it even. Fit the dough into the pan without stretching it, leaving the edges rough (they will be sealed later with the top crust). Put the pastry-lined pie pan in the freezer while you make the filling.

In a bowl large enough to hold all the filling ingredients, combine the ¼ cup sugar, the tapioca flour, cassia, nutmeg, and lemon zest.

Cut the apples from pole to pole into even ¼-inch slices. Place them in a second bowl, and sprinkle them with the lemon juice, stirring to coat the slices. Mix in the raisins and cognac. Toss the apple mixture in the bowl with the dry ingredients, then let this mixture sit for 10 to 15 minutes to draw off the liquid. Meanwhile, roll out the remaining dough to form the pie's top crust.

Reduce the oven temperature to 400 degrees. Remove the chilled bottom crust from the freezer and use a slotted spoon to transfer the filling into it. Dot the apples with the chilled or frozen butter morsels. Paint the edges of the lower crust with cold water. Lay the top crust over all, pressing down and folding the edges under to seal them into a double layer of dough. Go around the edges once more, decoratively crimping the dough with your fingers or the tines of a fork. Paint the whole top of the crust with the egg white, taking care not to let the egg drip between the crust and the pan. Sprinkle the top with the 2 tablespoons sugar, and cut vent slashes to allow steam to exit.

Put the pie on a cookie sheet, and bake it for 20 minutes, then further reduce the heat to 325 degrees and cook until the filling is bubbling, about 30 minutes more. The crust should be deeply golden and crisp on top.

Let the pie cool completely on a rack or in the refrigerator (or in the snow) before cutting it. It is best eaten the day it is made, but it will keep at room temperature, covered, for another day or two.

Molasses Cookies with Crunch and Snap

Adapted from a recipe in Beat That! *by Ann Hodgman, these molasses cookies illustrate the difference that homemade lard makes in baked goods. Mixing the dough a day ahead so that it can rest before baking makes it much easier to handle. If you like strongly spiced cookies, you may find these very hard to resist. Note, too, that some people make molasses cookies with bacon fat (see page 257) instead of lard.*

MAKES 5 DOZEN COOKIES

1¼ cups rendered pastured pork lard (see page 250), at room temperature

3 cups sugar

2 eggs

½ cup molasses

3¾ to 4 cups unbleached all-purpose flour

¼ cup baking soda

½ teaspoon kosher salt

2 tablespoons ground cinnamon

2 tablespoons ground ginger

1 tablespoon ground cloves

1 tablespoon ground nutmeg

Cream the lard and 2 cups of the sugar together in the bowl of an electric mixer until the mixture is fluffy. Add the eggs and molasses, and beat well.

In another bowl, mix together 3¾ cups flour, the baking soda, salt, and spices, using a whisk to aerate them (or a sifter, if you prefer). Thorough mixing is very important here; otherwise, some of the cookies may have the unpleasant taste of baking soda.

Add the dry ingredients to the molasses mixture, beating until the dough is well blended. If it seems wet, gradually add another ¼ cup of flour. If it is stiff and cracks when you try to form a ball with a pinch of dough, beat in water by the ¼ teaspoon to slightly dampen it. When the dough is pliable, scrape it into a refrigerator container, or roll it into a log and double-wrap it well with plastic wrap or waxed paper. Refrigerate overnight.

When you are ready to bake, heat the oven to 375 degrees and put a rack in the center. Line a couple of baking sheets with parchment or silicone liners. Whirl the remaining 1 cup sugar in a food processor fitted with the steel blade to give it a finer texture, and pour it into a shallow bowl.

Roll the dough into 1-inch balls, dip the tops into the sugar, and put the dough balls on the cookie sheets 2 inches apart, sugar side up. Bake for 10 to 12 minutes, until the cookies are fragrant, soft in the middle, and have a fine, crackled crust on top. Remove the cookies with the paper or liner immediately to cooling racks or the counter. When cool enough to handle, remove them from the paper and store in a closed container.

Leslie Newman's Blue Cheese–Buttermilk Dressing with Bacon Fat

don't know Leslie Newman, but I have been a fan of her cookbook Feasts *for years. This dressing, which is cleverly flavored with bacon fat rather than the traditional bacon bits, is something of a staple in my refrigerator. I drizzle it on romaine and other salads, of course, but I also spoon it onto leftover steamed vegetables and occasionally on chicken breasts before broiling them. Don't even think of putting low-fat mayonnaise in this dish (first of all, it's an abomination, and second, you're using bacon fat, after all). If I'm not using homemade mayo, I choose Hellmann's. Unlike Leslie, I make this in a food processor.*

MAKES ABOUT 2 CUPS

⅔ cup good mayonnaise, preferably homemade

1½ cups buttermilk

3 to 4 tablespoons pastured pork bacon fat (see page 257)

1 tablespoon red wine vinegar

1 clove garlic, sliced

⅓ cup blue cheese such as Roquefort, Maytag, or Saga (you can even use the precrumbled kind)

Big pinch of cayenne pepper or hot paprika

Salt and freshly ground black pepper

Put all the ingredients in a food processor fitted with the steel blade, slicing or crumbling the cheese into chunks as you add it. Process until the mixture is very well blended and has only tiny chunks of cheese.

Pour the dressing into a jar and refrigerate it, shaking it well before each use. It keeps for about 1 week.

Potato Cake with Smoked Salt and Bacon Fat

A large, thin potato cake cooked in flavorful bacon fat and dusted with smoked salt is a side dish worth waiting for, although, to tell the truth, we sometimes make dinner of it, adding nothing more than a salad or cooked greens. Serve it with a dollop of sour cream, goat cheese, or plain yogurt if you like a little creaminess with your potatoes. This is best cooked on a flat griddle, if you have one.

SERVES 2 TO 4

¼ cup pastured pork bacon fat (see box below)

2 to 3 large Yukon Gold potatoes, peeled or not

1 teaspoon smoked salt flakes or other good coarse salt

Freshly ground black pepper

¼ cup sour cream, goat cheese, or Greek yogurt (optional)

Melt the bacon drippings in a flat griddle or large frying pan over low heat.

Using a food processor fitted with the shredding blade or a box grater, finely shred the potatoes. Increase the heat to high under the bacon drippings until they are hot, and when a shred of potato is tossed into the pan, it sizzles. Pour the potatoes into the fat, spreading them evenly over the griddle's surface and packing them down tightly.

Reduce the heat to medium-low, dust the top of the potato cake with ½ teaspoon of the smoked salt flakes, and cook, uncovered, for 5 to 8 minutes, until the bottom of the cake is browned and set.

Using a large pot lid or a plate, carefully invert the pan and potato cake onto the lid. Ease the reversed cake back into the pan, uncooked side down. Salt the top with the remaining ½ teaspoon smoked salt and give it a good grinding of black pepper.

Cook for another 7 minutes, or until cooked through. Serve hot, cut in wedges, with or without a topping of sour cream, goat cheese, or yogurt.

Saving Bacon Fat

Whenever you finish cooking bacon, pour the fat through a fine mesh metal strainer (to catch the meaty bits) set over a sterile wide-mouthed glass jar. Keep the jar in the refrigerator, and continue to add strained fresh bacon fat to the jar as it is rendered. This way, you will always have a good supply of clean white bacon fat to use for recipes.

Popcorn with Bacon Fat, Bacon, and Maple Syrup

*S*o wicked it should be illegal, this sinful dish should be saved for the evening after you've shoveled snow all day and can feel virtuous eating such an indulgence. Or invite a crowd to share at movie night chez vous. Smoked salt flakes will make an even more incredible taste. If you come across them, buy them for this recipe alone. Keep in mind that 1 pound of bacon yields ¼ cup bacon fat.

MAKES 12 CUPS

4 strips of pastured pork bacon

2 tablespoons unsalted butter, plus more as needed

½ cup popping corn, preferably organic

¼ cup maple syrup

Coarse salt (preferably smoked salt flakes), as needed

Heat a cast-iron or other heavy frying pan over low heat and cook the bacon slowly. This will take about 15 minutes per side if the heat is low enough. Transfer the cooked bacon to a folded paper towel, leaving the fat in the pan, and drain the bacon until cool. Crumble it into a bowl and reserve.

Carefully pour the bacon fat into the bottom of a 3-quart heavy saucepan with a tight-fitting lid. You need at least 1 tablespoon bacon fat. If you don't have enough, melt a bit of butter to make up the difference.

Heat the pan and fat over high heat and pour in the corn, clapping on the cover. Shake the pan and listen for the sound of the corn popping. Once it begins to pop furiously, lower the heat to medium and leave the pan alone until it is quiet and popped corn begins to push at the cover from beneath. Turn off the heat and let the residual heat finish cooking the corn, or move the pan to another burner and cook over low heat until all the corn is popped.

In the meantime, melt the 2 tablespoons butter in the microwave or on the stovetop. Measure out the maple syrup, get the bowl of crumbled bacon, and set a large bowl on the counter to receive the popped corn.

Pour the popped corn into the bowl, drizzle it with the maple syrup and melted butter, and pour the bacon bits on top. Toss the mixture rapidly and stir well to combine. Taste for salt and correct the seasonings, tossing again. Serve at once, providing plenty of napkins.

Raising Rabbit

Raising rabbit for meat doesn't require much land—they thrive in small spaces, and are prolific breeders. They eat moderate amounts of fresh grasses, grains, and vegetables, and recycle them into lean meat and fertilizer. They can be raised humanely, either in cages with their young, or in colonies within shelters attached to outdoor pens. They are easy to process, with the additional benefit of needing no resting or aging before cooking. In addition to their meat, rabbit pelts can be used to make warm hats and mittens.

Common meat breeds include New Zealand Whites, Californians, and Satins, and it should be noted that these are not the same breeds as are used for pets. A breeding rabbit can supply 80 pounds of usable meat in one year, spread over five litters of eight each.

All in all, sustainably farmed rabbit is a wonderful thing—high in protein, low in fat, delicious, and easy to raise well—what's to object to? Plenty, say those who think of rabbit as an adorable Thumper. My daughter Lizzie, who had a couple of pet rabbits during her childhood, was appalled when she learned I was cooking them. She said, "It's like you're cooking *kittens*," to bring her horror home.

I have to say that I like to eat rabbit, and I'm glad to have the chance to add another locally raised meat to my repertoire.

RABBIT ANATOMY

Rabbit is versatile and can be cooked the same way as most chicken braises, although it requires additional fat to keep it tender. In this section, I offer some of my favorite rabbit recipes to showcase the appeal of this lesser-known meat.

I met my local rabbit dealer at the farmers' market several years ago. Having created a demand for their products, they now sell directly to consumers, who can order fresh rabbit on a weekly basis. Their rabbit is custom processed, and they offer whole rabbits, or pieces, or their own homemade rabbit sausage in casings.

Understanding Rabbit Anatomy

Rabbits, like chickens, are normally sold whole or cut into pieces. The usual cutting pattern for rabbit is five pieces: the saddle (whole), the two front quarters, and the two back quarters. Some people prefer to split the saddle in two. While in Italy rabbits are always sold with the head as the sixth piece, here in America the head is rarely included.

In *The Zuni Café Cookbook*, Judy Rodgers proposes an unconventional cutting pattern that leaves some parts boneless and takes into account the different cooking and timing requirements of each part. When you follow her cut pattern, you can then cook each set of parts separately, but, of course, you need to start with a sufficient number of rabbits at one time to yield enough parts to make many different dishes. As most of us don't have this opportunity, I mention it here for those who are thinking of raising rabbits for meat, or considering buying them fresh in bulk.

Cooking with Rabbit

Rabbit does benefit from an overnight brine (just like chicken; see page 284). Alternatively, it can be pre-salted and left uncovered overnight in the refrigerator, or it can be rubbed with a salt and spice cure (such as the one on page 30) to absorb even more flavor overnight. However, this step is *not* essential—I find that even if I don't brine or salt ahead, local rabbit will cook into delectable tenderness when slowly braised. The key, as is so often the case with lean meats, is to cook very slowly over the lowest possible heat.

Fowl Mtn Farm & Rabbitry
PO Box 83
West Dummerston VT 0____
802-254-3601

Proc on __

Wgt _____ Pr___ ___12(B); Not I___

Exempt per 6___

RABBIT RECIPE

BRAISED

BRAISED: Perhaps the best way to cook rabbit is to braise it slowly, either whole or cut into pieces. As is usual with all lean meats, keep the words "low and slow" in mind while cooking.

Lapin à la Moutarde

lassic and delicious French home food, this recipe is easy to prepare. I depart from the traditional method by using grainy mustard, but if you prefer smooth Dijon, you will be making it the way rural Frenchwomen have done for centuries. If you put the bouquet garni in a large mesh tea ball and submerge that in the pot, it's much easier to remove than loose herbs.

SERVES 6 TO 8

2 tablespoons unsalted butter

1 small onion, minced

½ cup grainy mustard

1 sustainably farmed rabbit, cut up, saddle split into 2 pieces

1 cup dry white wine

Salt and freshly ground black pepper

1 or 2 sprigs flat-leaf fresh parsley, plus ¼ cup minced fresh parsley for garnish

3 to 4 sprigs fresh thyme

1 bay leaf

¼ cup crème fraîche

Melt the butter in an enameled cast-iron Dutch oven or a wide, heavy sauté pan with a tight-fitting lid. When the butter is foaming and fragrant, add the onion and lower the heat to sweat the pieces to translucency. While the onion is cooking, smear the mustard on the rabbit pieces, covering all sides. Before the onion begins to color, add the meat to the pot and brown it on all sides until it is deeply golden. Transfer the meat to a platter.

Add the wine and deglaze the pot, scraping and stirring to incorporate all the browned bits into the liquid. Let the wine cook for a minute or two to evaporate the alcohol. Return the meat to the pot; add salt and pepper to taste.

Make a bouquet garni with the parsley and thyme sprigs and the bay leaf (if using a mesh tea ball or cheesecloth) and add it to the pot, or put the herbs in loose. Clap the cover onto the pot and simmer slowly at the lowest possible heat for 45 minutes to 1 hour, until the meat pulls away from the bones and the kitchen is fragrant. Remove and discard the bouquet garni herbs.

Transfer the meat to a platter, and off the heat, stir the crème fraîche into the juices in the pot. Return the meat to the pot, coat it with the sauce, and serve, garnished with the minced parsley.

Rabbit and Prunes Marinated in Red Wine

You can tell how much I like dried plums and other fruits with meat—there are a number of such recipes in this collection. The red-wine-and-prune combo is a well-known French one, and exemplifies French rural cookery to me. This version is based on Anne Willan's recipe in The Country Cooking of France. All braises and stews improve with age, so try to make it a day or two ahead of time. Note also that the meat marinates for a day before cooking.

SERVES 4

1 bunch flat-leaf fresh parsley

2 teaspoons dried thyme or about 10 sprigs fresh thyme

2 cups red wine

1 small onion, cut into chunks

1 carrot, roughly chopped

Salt and freshly ground black pepper

1 sustainably farmed rabbit, cut into pieces

About 1 tablespoon extra-virgin olive oil

About 1 tablespoon unsalted butter

2 tablespoons unbleached all-purpose flour

1 cup chicken stock, preferably homemade (see page 303)

3 cloves garlic

1 cup pitted prunes

Remove almost all the leaves from the bunch of parsley, chop them, and set them aside (reserve 3 tablespoons in another container). Place the parsley stems in a lidded storage container large enough to hold the rabbit. Add 1 teaspoon of the dried thyme or half of the thyme sprigs, along with the wine, onion, carrot, salt and pepper, and rabbit pieces. Cover and shake to combine; marinate the meat, covered and refrigerated, overnight or for up to 24 hours. Every once in a while, give the container another shake to redistribute the marinade, and open it to turn the pieces of meat.

Remove the rabbit from the marinade and blot it very dry. (Reserve the marinade.) Melt the olive oil and butter in an enameled cast-iron Dutch oven or braising pot over medium-high heat. Cook the rabbit pieces, turning them as they brown on each side. Remove the pieces from the pot as they are done. This will take about 15 minutes, depending on the pot and the heat of your stovetop. Cook in batches, if necessary.

Strain the marinade or use a slotted spoon to fish out the carrot and onion pieces, still reserving the liquid, and cook the vegetables in the hot pot until they start to become soft. Add more fat, if you need to. Sprinkle on the flour and stir it in until it begins to brown, 1 to 2 minutes. Add the marinade liquid and the chicken stock, stirring and scraping to incorporate any browned bits stuck to the pan, and bring the mixture to a boil. Let this simmer for a few minutes. Add the garlic, the remaining thyme, and half of the reserved chopped parsley leaves. Lower the heat, add a little salt and pepper, and return the rabbit to the pot. Cover the pot, putting an inner parchment-paper cover under the lid to keep in the moisture, and cook over the lowest possible heat for 30 minutes.

Look at your prunes—if they are dry and leathery, rehydrate them by soaking them in boiling water to cover while the rabbit simmers. If they are glossy and pliant, do nothing.

At the end of 30 minutes, add the prunes (draining them first if rehydrated) to the pot. Cook for another 30 minutes or so, until the rabbit is falling off the bones.

Scoop out and discard any loose stems and herbs, and taste the stew for seasonings. At this point, you can refrigerate the dish for a day or two.

When you are ready to serve, reheat the stew slowly over low heat. Serve it with a shower of the reserved fresh parsley on top.

Cider-Braised Rabbit with Apples

A perfect autumn or winter dish, this rich yet delicately flavored braise combines fresh cider, Calvados, and panfried apples. Both a terrific "company" dish and a weeknight possibility (since it cooks in under an hour), try serving rice, noodles, dumplings, or steamed potatoes with it to sop up the gravy.

SERVES 4

1 sustainably farmed rabbit, cut into pieces

4 tablespoons (½ stick) unsalted butter

1½ cups diced shallots

Leaves from 6 to 8 sprigs fresh thyme, chopped

Salt and freshly ground black pepper

¼ cup Calvados or other apple brandy

1¾ cups fresh apple cider (not pasteurized apple juice)

2 tart apples, peeled and cored

1 to 2 tablespoons heavy cream

Blot the rabbit pieces dry and set them aside. Melt 2 tablespoons of the butter in a wide, shallow braising pot or frying pan with a lid, and brown the rabbit on both sides, 6 to 8 minutes over medium heat. Remove the meat to a plate. Add the shallots and thyme to the pot and cook gently over the lowest possible heat, covering the pot to steam/cook the shallots into tenderness, 2 to 3 minutes. Add salt and pepper.

Pour in the Calvados and carefully flame it, keeping the pot lid handy. The alcohol should burn off immediately. Pour in the cider, stir, return the meat to the pot, and simmer slowly, partially covered, for 35 to 45 minutes. The meat should shrink from the bones. Remove the cover and continue cooking over low heat to concentrate the sauce.

In another frying pan, melt the remaining 2 tablespoons butter. Cut the apples into wedges or thick slices. Sauté the apples until they are soft and slightly caramelized on the edges. Remove the rabbit from the pot and arrange it on a serving dish along with the cooked apples. Strain the pan sauce to remove any solids, stir in the heavy cream, and pour this over all. Serve at once.

Red Rabbit Stew with Red Peppers, Garlic, and Chorizo

R eal Spanish chorizo—air-dried, ruddy and intense—is newly available in this country; these days I find it in quite a number of Vermont groceries. I hope that's true everywhere, because, along with smoky sweet pimentón, it adds authentic flavors and color to this gutsy Spanish dish. Try this with bomba rice and a bottle of Spanish red wine to taste Spain without leaving home. Note that this recipe uses two pots—one to fry and one to braise.

SERVES 4

1 sustainably farmed rabbit, cut into pieces

½ cup extra-virgin olive oil

1 medium onion, finely chopped

1 (14-ounce) can diced tomatoes

Salt to taste

1 tablespoon sweet (*dulce*) pimentón de la Vera (smoked Spanish paprika)

4 cloves garlic, chopped

1 link Spanish chorizo (about half a 200-gram package or about 8 ounces)

1½ cups diced red bell peppers (about 2 large)

2 tablespoons chopped fresh thyme

For serving:

Cooked rice

Fresh thyme sprigs, for garnish

Blot the rabbit pieces dry and set them aside. Heat ¼ cup of the olive oil in a large braising pot or a 5-quart Dutch oven. Cook the onion over low heat until it is soft, about 10 minutes. Add the tomatoes and their juices, along with salt to taste, and cover. Simmer gently.

In a skillet over medium heat, heat the remaining ¼ cup olive oil and cook the rabbit pieces to golden brown, about 10 minutes. Stir in the pimentón, garlic, and chorizo. Transfer this mixture to the braising pot with the tomatoes, leaving the cooking oil in the pot

In the now-empty skillet, cook down the bell peppers in the fat that remains in the pan, using medium heat and stirring as needed, until the peppers are soft, slightly charred, and fragrant, about 15 minutes. Stir in the thyme, and add the skillet contents to the braising pot.

Stir, cover the braising pot, and simmer gently for about 40 minutes, or until the rabbit is cooked through and shrinking from the bones.

Serve over rice to show off the red juices, garnished with a few fresh thyme sprigs.

Sicilian Rabbit Agrodolce

S̶weet and sour flavors are prized in southern Italy, and this dish is the kind of home-style favorite that you'd find on Sunday tables in every rural area. Serve it with couscous, dusted with the grated zest of an orange.

SERVES 4

1 sustainably farmed rabbit, cut into pieces

2 tablespoons extra-virgin olive oil

1 onion, finely chopped

2 tablespoons unbleached all-purpose flour

Salt and freshly ground black pepper

1 cup white wine

4 whole cloves

2 bay leaves

½ cup chicken stock, preferably homemade (see page 303), plus more as needed

2 tablespoons sugar or honey

½ cup cider vinegar

¼ cup raisins

½ lemon, peeled and thinly sliced

¼ cup pine nuts

For the garnish:

½ cup finely chopped flat-leaf parsley

Finely grated zest of 1 orange or lemon (optional)

Blot the rabbit pieces dry and set them aside. Heat 1 tablespoon of the olive oil in a braising pot over medium-low heat until thinned. Add the onion and sweat it down. Meanwhile, mix the flour with salt and pepper, and dredge each piece of meat through the mixture. Set the meat on a plate.

Using a slotted spoon, remove the onion from the pot, turn the heat up to medium-high, and add the remaining 1 tablespoon olive oil. When it is hot, add the floured meat. Brown this until golden on both sides, in batches if necessary, about 8 minutes in all. Remove the meat from the pot, turn off the heat, and deglaze with the wine, scraping the pot, incorporating the browned bits into the liquid.

Add the cloves and bay leaves, stock, sugar, and vinegar, and cook over low heat until the sugar is dissolved. Return the onion and meat to the pot; the liquid should come halfway up the side of the meat—add more stock if necessary. Position an inner parchment cover so that it touches the meat before putting on the pot's lid to create a double seal. Cut off any paper that overlaps the lid so that there is no danger of fire. Simmer over the lowest possible heat for 1 hour. The meat should shrink from the bones, and be cooked through and tender.

Transfer the meat to a deep platter or bowl. Strain the sauce to remove all the solids. Taste the sauce and correct the seasonings, cooking it down further to reduce it, if desired. Add the raisins, lemon slices, and pine nuts to the sauce and cook for a few minutes longer. Just before serving, add the chopped parsley if desired, along with grated orange zest.

Serve the meat and sauce together.

Orange Rabbit Fricassee

A vintage recipe from my Australian friend Jill Hulme's grandma Tot, this delicious dish harks back to a surfeit of wild rabbits in southern Australia. Well worth cooking with today's sustainably farmed rabbit, serve it as Tot did, with orange segments and fragrant rice such as basmati or jasmine.

SERVES 4

1 sustainably farmed rabbit, cut into pieces

2 tablespoons unbleached all-purpose flour

Salt and freshly ground black pepper

2 tablespoons extra-virgin olive oil

2 slices of pastured pork bacon, cut into batons

1 onion, finely chopped

1 carrot, finely chopped

¼ cup red wine

2 cups chicken or turkey stock, preferably homemade (see page 303 or page 318)

Juice and grated zest of 2 oranges

¼ cup red currant jelly

To finish:

2 cups cooked rice

Grated zest of 2 oranges, peeled and segmented

Heat the oven to 325 degrees, and place a rack in the center. Blot the rabbit pieces dry and set them aside. Season the flour with salt and pepper, and roll each piece of meat in the mixture. Set them aside on a plate.

Heat a braising pot or Dutch oven over medium heat, and add 1 tablespoon of the olive oil. When it's thinned and fragrant, add the bacon batons. Lower the heat and render the bacon fat. When most of the fat has rendered (after 5 minutes) add the onion and carrot and cook them down slowly, stirring as needed, until tender (another 5 minutes).

Using a slotted spoon, remove the bacon and vegetables from the pot and add the remaining 1 tablespoon olive oil. When it is thinned and fragrant, arrange the floured meat on the bottom of the pot in one layer. Increase the heat to medium, and brown the rabbit pieces on both sides, 6 to 8 minutes. Remove the meat from the pot, turn off the heat, and deglaze the pot with the wine, scraping up the browned bits to incorporate them into the liquid. Let the wine reduce by half, using the heat left in the pan. Add the stock, then the orange juice and zest, and the jelly. Turn the heat to low and cook until the jelly melts.

Return the bacon and vegetables to the pot, along with the meat. Cover tightly, using an inner parchment cover as well as the pot's lid, and bake for 1 hour.

Serve with rice, sprinkling on grated orange zest, and arranging the orange segments around the perimeter of the platter.

Braised Rabbit with Porcini, Tomatoes, and Thyme

*B*ecause rabbit is lean, every rabbit recipe requires added fat. This one uses duck or goose fat, which adds a welcome unctuous texture to the braise. If you don't have rendered poultry fat (any bird will do), try bacon fat or butter.

SERVES 4

5 dried porcini mushrooms

1 tablespoon rendered pastured duck or goose fat (see page 331)

1 large onion, finely chopped

2 cloves garlic, chopped

Kosher salt and freshly ground black pepper

1 sustainably farmed rabbit, cut into pieces

½ cup white wine

1 (14-ounce) can diced tomatoes

1 heaping tablespoon chopped fresh thyme

For serving:

Roasted or steamed potatoes

Rehydrate the mushrooms by pouring 1 cup boiling water over them to cover and setting them aside for at least 15 minutes.

Meanwhile, choose a wide, shallow braising pan and melt the fat. Sauté the onion and garlic together over medium-low heat until they begin to color and are limp, about 6 minutes. Remove them to a bowl and reserve.

Salt and pepper the rabbit pieces on both sides, add them to the pan, and brown them over medium-high heat, turning them as needed, about 6 to 8 minutes in all. Remove the meat to a plate. Deglaze the pan with the wine, scraping to incorporate the browned bits. Add the tomatoes and their juices into the liquid; stir in the thyme.

Return the onion and garlic, along with the meat to the pan. Remove and discard the stems from the mushrooms, and reserve the soaking liquid. Chop the mushroom caps into a coarse dice and add them to the pan. Strain the mushroom water through a paper coffee filter, and add ½ cup of this to the pan.

Cover the pan (adding an inner parchment-paper cover if possible), reduce the heat to the lowest possible setting, and simmer gently for about 45 minutes, or until cooked.

Serve warm in deep plates, with potatoes.

ROASTED: Because this meat is so lean, adding fat while roasting is especially important. Bacon-wrapping is the usual solution because it adds both fat and flavor, and is an easy way to insure that the fat cover stays on for the full period of cooking.

Roasted Rabbit with White Wine and Black Olives

*A*n example of Italian home cooking at its simplest, this easy recipe yields a dish with lots of oomph for little labor. You just give the meat a brief toss with herbs, white wine, and olive oil, then pop it into a hot oven with a bit of bacon atop each piece.

SERVES 4 TO 6

¼ cup extra-virgin olive oil

1 tablespoon chopped fresh thyme, or
2 tablespoons dried

1 tablespoon chopped fresh rosemary

1 tablespoon kosher salt

½ teaspoon crushed red pepper flakes

8 cloves garlic, smashed

1 sustainably farmed rabbit, cut into pieces

1 slice of pastured pork bacon

1 cup white wine

1 cup oil-cured black olives, pitted

Choose a shallow pan such as a large gratin dish, sheet pan with sides, or lasagna pan large enough to hold all the rabbit pieces in one layer. Combine the oil, herbs, salt, red pepper, and garlic, and pour the mixture over the rabbit pieces in the pan, shaking the pan so that the meat is coated with the marinade. Set this aside at room temperature for 10 to 15 minutes while the oven heats.

Set the oven temperature to 450 degrees, and position a rack in the upper third. Cut the bacon slice into as many pieces as you have rabbit pieces. When the oven is hot, put a bit of bacon on top of each rabbit piece and roast the rabbit for 20 minutes; the rabbit should be browned.

Turn the rabbit pieces over and pour the wine into the pan. Cook for another 8 to 10 minutes. Scatter the olives over the pan and cook for 15 to 20 minutes longer, until the meat is cooked through.

Let the meat rest for 5 to 10 minutes before serving.

Roasted Rabbit in a Bacon Blanket

This simple oven roast, with each piece wrapped in bacon to add fat and flavor, has to marinate overnight before roasting. While that might put it in the weekend-only category, it does really take only a half hour to cook, so it's practical to make the marinade one night after dinner to serve the next night. I've adapted this from a Pete Wells recipe that appeared in the New York Times. *His version was stronger and more sour than I prefer, so I decreased the amount of vinegar and added good-quality sherry instead.*

SERVES 4 TO 6

1 tablespoon kosher salt

½ teaspoon coarsely ground black pepper

1 teaspoon fennel seeds

1 teaspoon coriander seeds

2 bay leaves

1 tablespoon fresh thyme

8 cloves garlic, smashed

¼ cup sweet sherry

¼ cup sherry vinegar

1 sustainably farmed rabbit, cut up saddle split into 2 pieces

8 to 10 slices of pastured pork bacon

Using a mortar and pestle, grind and break the salt, pepper, fennel, and coriander a little until the seeds release their flavor and are bruised. Crumble in the bay leaves and thyme, and add the garlic to the mortar, then carry on for another minute or two to blend all the flavors. (If you don't have a mortar and pestle, put all these ingredients in a resealable plastic bag and bash away with the bottom of a heavy frying pan.)

Choose a glass or other nonreactive refrigerator dish large enough to hold the rabbit and marinade (or a large resealable plastic bag). Pour in the contents of the mortar, the sherry, and the vinegar. Give these ingredients a good stir or shake to blend them, then add the rabbit pieces, dragging or shaking each one in the marinade to coat it well. Refrigerate, covered, overnight or for up to 24 hours.

When you are ready to cook, heat the oven to 450 degrees and set a rack in the upper third. Choose a sheet pan or other rimmed large pan. Remove the rabbit from the marinade and blot each piece quite dry. Wrap each piece with a slice of the bacon, and put it, seam side down, on the baking sheet. (Any flat pieces, such as the flap attached to the ribs, can be rolled along with the bacon.)

Roast the meat for about 30 minutes, or until the bacon is crisp and the rabbit is no longer pink in the center. Serve warm.

GROUND RABBIT: Whether made into loose sausage or put in casings, ground rabbit is a versatile ingredient. Serve links accompanied by eggs, or with beans or sauerkraut. Alternatively, rabbit sausage can be sliced and sautéed with vegetables as part of a pasta sauce. When rabbit meat is ground for sausage, a good proportion of fat is ground in at the same time to add succulence.

Penne with Rabbit Sausage, Celery, and Onion

idia Bastianich makes a similar quick-cooking dish with pork sausage and fennel, and while I love Lidia's version, I find rabbit sausage is equally delicious, especially when paired with celery and ground fennel. Here, I use Lidia's technique of browning single ingredients and pushing them to one side of the pan while the next ingredient cooks in the center. It's a very efficient system. Use the biggest sauté or frying pan you have, as you'll be tossing the pasta and sauce in it at the end.

NOTE: This recipe also works well with ground pastured turkey.

SERVES 4 AS A MAIN COURSE

2 tablespoons extra-virgin olive oil

1 pound loose sweet Italian sustainably farmed rabbit sausage (or plain ground rabbit), removed from the casings if necessary

1 large onion, thinly sliced

6 stalks celery, cut into ¼-inch slices

1 teaspoon ground fennel or wild fennel pollen

½ teaspoon crushed red pepper flakes

1 (14.5-ounce) can diced tomatoes

1 cup boiling water

Salt and freshly ground black pepper

1 pound penne

1 cup freshly grated Romano cheese or Parmigiano-Reggiano

Heat a large, heavy sauté pan over medium heat and add the olive oil. When it thins and becomes fragrant, crumble the meat into the pan, and cook it until it begins to brown, 2 to 3 minutes. Push the meat to one side of the pan and add the onion slices, stirring often, until they start to wilt, about another 2 minutes. Toss the onion with the meat and push them to one side. Add the celery to the empty side of the pan, and cook for another 2 to 3 minutes. Push the celery toward the meat mixture and add the ground fennel. Stir to mix everything together, then push the contents to one side again, and toast the red pepper in the open part of the pan for 30 seconds. Mix this in.

Add the tomatoes along with their juices and the boiling water. Add salt and pepper. Mix everything in the pan together and bring it to a boil, then lower the heat, partially cover the pan, and let the flavors come together for about 10 minutes while the pasta cooks.

Cook the pasta in copious amounts of well-salted boiling water. When the pasta is al dente, use a spider or pasta scoop to remove it from the pot and transfer it to the pan with the sauce. Carefully stir the pasta into the sauce and let it cook for about 1 minute more.

Pour the sauced pasta into a serving bowl or deep platter and stir in the cheese. Serve at once.

OFFAL AND ODD BITS: When I buy rabbits, they always come with their livers, heart, and kidneys. I separate and save these parts until I have enough to make something from them. I find that the livers of six rabbits weigh about a pound, enough for a generous batch of pâté. Kidneys and hearts from the same number of rabbits are just enough to make nibbles to serve as an appetizer (see Panfried Rabbit Hearts and Kidneys, page 279).

Rabbit Liver Pâté

Try this with brandy, as written, or use port for a fruitier taste. You could also add chopped pistachios or grated orange zest to vary it further. Let this pâté age for a day or two before serving.

SERVES 10 TO 12

1 pound sustainably farmed rabbit livers

8 tablespoons (1 stick) unsalted butter

1 large shallot or small onion, finely chopped

2 cloves garlic, finely chopped

1 bay leaf

1 heaping tablespoon chopped fresh thyme

1 tablespoon brandy

1 tablespoon heavy cream

Salt and freshly ground black pepper

For serving:

Fresh thyme sprigs, for garnish

Freshly grated orange zest, for garnish

Warmed baguette slices

Cornichons

Blot the livers dry. In a medium frying pan, over medium-low heat, melt the butter until it is foaming and fragrant. Add the shallot and garlic, stirring often, until they are limp.

Add the rabbit livers, bay leaf, and thyme, and continue to cook slowly until the livers are only just cooked through and still slightly pink in the center, turning the pieces as needed. Add the brandy and turn off the heat. Let the livers continue to cook very slowly in the heat left in the pan. After 20 minutes, remove the bay leaf and pour the contents of the pan into a food processor fitted with the steel blade.

Process the pâté until it is very smooth, add the cream toward the end, along with a generous amount of salt and pepper. Scrape the pâté into a bowl or terrine, and cover it closely with plastic wrap, pressing the wrap onto the surface. Refrigerate for a day before garnishing it with thyme sprigs and a sprinkling of orange zest. Serve it with slices of warm baguette, accompanied by cornichon pickles.

Panfried Rabbit Hearts and Kidneys

erve these speared on toothpicks with a dipping sauce of Burgundian Mustard (see page 233) or very thinly sliced on a bed of greens as a modest first course. Either way, they are hard to stop eating.

SERVES 2

3 to 4 ounces mixed hearts and kidneys (from 6 sustainably farmed rabbits)

1 tablespoon unbleached all-purpose flour

Salt and freshly ground black pepper

1 tablespoon extra-virgin olive oil

Blot the hearts and kidneys dry. Season the flour with salt and pepper and toss the meat in the mixture to coat each piece. Heat a frying pan over medium-high heat and add the olive oil. When the oil is thinned and fragrant, add the meat and panfry for about 4 minutes, shaking the pan to brown all sides. These are done when they are only slightly pink in the center. Let cool for 10 minutes before serving.

POULTRY

Pastured Poultry

The range of birds raised sustainably by farmers includes chicken, duck, goose, pheasant, turkey, and guinea fowl. All such poultry is full of flavor, has real texture, and is vastly different from its industrial counterpart, even when the bird in question is exactly the same breed. It's a real demonstration of the difference that true free-ranging offers.

What is "false" free-ranging, then? It's when the birds have theoretical access to a small patch of green, but never actually go there, or are allowed outdoor time for only brief portions of a day. Quite a number of supermarket and specialty store chickens labeled organic fall into this category, and they are the birds I refer to as "reasonable-quality birds." They are fed organic grain, sometimes supplemented with organic greens. They are both tastier and more sustainable than industrial birds, who are fed appalling substances and live under much more inhumane conditions, but they do not have the flavor of real free-ranged or pastured chickens, nor do they generally cost as much. I may buy these reasonable-quality birds whole to brine, or in parts like leg-and-thigh combinations to use for braises. True pasture-raised chickens are the ones I cook reverently as whole roasts, saving their bones for rich stock.

Note that pasture raised can mean that the birds walk around the farm freely during the day and are cooped at night to protect them from predators. It can mean that they are "day ranged"—that is, kept in portable "chicken tractors" that allow them to always be on grass but to be moved daily from one part of a pasture to another while remaining inside the pen. They may be in "eggmobiles" that allow them out into various fenced portions of a pasture by day. They can be cooped at night but allowed to spend their days in an outdoor fenced chicken run. The main factor in all of these examples is that the birds have regular and prolonged contact with dirt, green growing things, and insects for most daylight hours. If you visit a farm with pastured chickens, you'll hear contented clucking and see visibly happy birds, busily exploring every blade of grass.

These days in Vermont and some other states, farmers are allowed to bypass USDA processors to slaughter and sell a limited number of uninspected birds from the farm. (In Vermont, the regulation allows up to 1,000 birds per year, labeled as farm raised and uninspected, and sold from the farm to retail customers and chefs.) Such birds profit from the fact that they have not been transported or stressed prior to processing. Look for these superb birds at farmers' markets, where they are sold fresh or frozen. (If you buy a fresh one, give it a day or two in the coldest part of the refrigerator before you cook it, as these birds need to "relax" before they are good eating.)

When you encounter a poultry seller at a farmers' market or farm store, here are some of the questions to ask:

- Are the birds pastured?
- If so, how much of the time?
- What else do you feed them?
- Are the grains organic or local or grown by you?
- How are the birds processed—on the farm or in a USDA facility?

Even though pastured chickens are processed at a very young age (just like industrial birds), and even though they are usually exactly the same breed of meat bird, their flesh has much more texture and a fine deep flavor.

Understanding Poultry Anatomy

Even when a bird is whole, it has some additional parts. While most birds bought at retail come without heads or feet, their necks are often included even though they are no longer attached to the body. Similarly, some of the offal—the gizzards, liver, heart—are also routinely included in packages inside the bird. Traditionally, the neck is reserved for stock-making, while the liver, gizzards, and heart can be used in stuffing.

When buying pastured birds, while you may get all of the above parts, you can't count on it. It pays to ask what is included with a bird you buy directly from the farmer, and to let him know if there are other parts you want. It's not easy, for example, to get a pound or two of chicken livers from pastured birds unless you've either special-ordered them or participated in the processing. The same goes for gizzards, hearts, feet, and necks, so if you are interested in cooking all of your bird, you'll have to let your producer know.

When cutting up a raw bird at home to use as parts, the usual pattern is to cut it into eight pieces, as follows: Each leg and thigh quarter is cut from the body in one piece, and then the drumstick is removed from the thigh at the joint. Then the backbone is removed, cutting through each side of the

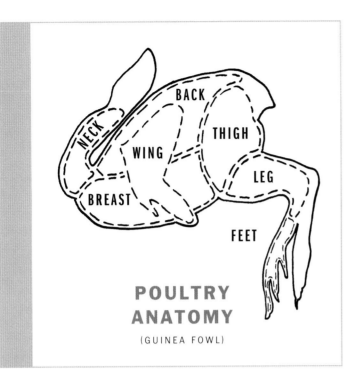

POULTRY ANATOMY

(GUINEA FOWL)

spine to free it. The breast portion is divided into two, cutting through the breastbone, and then the wings are removed.

When carving a whole cooked bird, particularly a large one like a roasting chicken or turkey, the pattern is somewhat different because you usually want to slice the breast meat rather than serve it as a large part. In this case, start by removing the legs and thighs, cutting them first as one, and then dividing them into each part. Arrange them on a serving platter, then remove the wings and add them to the platter. Slice the white meat on either side of the breastbone, allowing the knife to follow the curve of the body to create even slices. The back can be cut into two pieces, or it can remain in the kitchen to use for stock, along with the neck.

Cooking Chicken

When you have paid twenty-five dollars or more for a whole chicken, and bought it from the person who raised it, you want to make that bird the best it can be by using appropriate cooking techniques. You can salt or brine the bird overnight, marinate it in spices and oil, slow-cook it to melting tenderness, or simply roast the whole bird while paying close attention to its internal temperature. Brining or pre-salting always adds succulence, but is perhaps less essential with pastured birds than with supermarket organic birds.

If you can buy sustainably raised chicken in parts or cut one up yourself, the meat will make one of the most memorable chicken braises you will ever taste. And if you are lucky enough to come across a stewing hen (usually older birds that are no longer laying eggs), snap it up and make any of those braises again (only cook it for much longer—up to 5 hours) to discover a depth of chicken flavor you've probably never had the chance to experience before. My source of "old hens" is a local organic egg farm—they process the old girls when they stop laying regularly, and they always have a good supply of old hens in the freezer of the farm store. There may be similar sources local to you.

Capons are castrated roosters, and they used to be commonly available, but they are hard to find now. They are worth seeking out because fixing the birds makes them gain weight—they average about 10 pounds a bird, which is perfect for entertaining or festive events. These days, the only national source I know of for organic free-range capon is D'Artagnan, which is also the source for *poussin*, or baby chickens. These weigh about a pound and a quarter, and are a tender delicacy. If you find a local producer who is raising chickens for meat, you can ask if they offer capon or *poussin*, and encourage them to consider this if they haven't done so already.

Cooking with Poultry Fat

Chicken fat is a time-honored cooking medium now fallen out of favor, but worth paying attention to nonetheless. Like many animal fats, it's not as bad for you as you may think. A tablespoon of rendered chicken fat has 120 calories, of which 117 are from fat. This fat is about 30 percent saturated, with about 10 mg of cholesterol; it includes palmitoleic acid, an antimicrobial, and its relatively small amounts of omega-3 and omega-6 are in a good ratio, if the chickens were raised pastured. I use pastured chicken fat for cooking potatoes, and I leave a little of it in the chicken stock I make.

Goose fat is culinary gold, lending its flavor to potatoes, red cabbage, and confits of all kinds. It has a smoking point of 375 degrees, so it's good for frying. It is lower in saturated fat than butter or lard, and is "heart healthy" because it's high in monounsaturated fat and rich in the kind of oleic acid that appears to lower cholesterol. Sealed in an airtight, sterile glass container (such as a screw-top jar that has just gone through the high-temperature cycle of the dishwasher or that has been boiled in a kettle of water), rendered goose fat will keep for several months in the refrigerator, and it can be frozen for even longer.

Traditionally, there are two kinds of goose fat: "white" fat, which is rendered slowly on top of the stove from skin and lumps of fat removed prior to cooking the bird; and "brown" fat, which is what is poured out of the roasting pan as a goose cooks (see page 331). In reality, the color of the two can be fairly similar, ranging from snow to cream.

I think the distinction has more to do with ease and flavor—it's much easier to pour off fat as you cook a bird than it is to pull it off a raw bird and render it slowly. But the fat that comes off a cooking bird, while plentiful, has a meaty flavor and so may be less suitable for pastry. It is, however, quite wonderful for basting meat, cooking potatoes, making savory tarts, and other nondessert uses.

Duck fat contains about 35 percent saturated fat and 45 to 50 percent monounsaturated fat (which are high in linoleic acid), and nearly 14 percent polyunsaturated fats (which is where the omega-6 and omega-3 essential oils are). Duck fat has even more linoleic acid than goose fat. Like goose fat, it can last, rendered and stored in a sterile jar in the refrigerator for months at a time. Dr. Serge Renaud, director of research at France's National Institute of Health and Medical Research, and the originator of the term "the French paradox" was quoted in the *New York Times* on November 17, 1991, suggesting that goose and duck fat may improve cardiovascular health. He says (and chemists agree) that "goose and duck fat are closer in chemical composition to olive oil than to butter and lard." From frying to roasting, whether used for cooking meat or vegetables, duck fat makes food taste wonderful.

Our homemade portable chicken tractor

POULTRY RECIPE

BRAISING CHICKEN PARTS: Slow-cooked, falling-off-the-bone braises are the height of home-cooking. Chicken braises are particular favorites because they're easy to put together with (slightly esoteric) pantry ingredients. These recipes work with both "reasonable quality" chicken parts and (given more time) older or chewier real pastured birds.

Provençal Chicken with Tomatoes, White Wine, Black Olives, and Herbs

The only tricky thing about this recipe is pitting the olives— either use a small knife to slice away the flesh from the pit or flatten them with the side of a large knife and watch the pits pop out. If you really object to pitting, this dish can be made with unpitted olives—just warn your guests so that they eat carefully.

SERVES 4 TO 6

4 skin-on pastured chicken leg-and-thigh combinations

Sea salt and freshly ground black pepper

3 tablespoons extra-virgin olive oil

2 large onions, thinly sliced

2 cups white wine

1 cup canned fire-roasted whole tomatoes, with their juices

1 cup good aged black olives, pitted

3 tablespoons Herbes de Provence Blend (see page 32)

Blot the chicken and salt and pepper it. Heat a wide, shallow frying pan with a lid or an enameled cast-iron Dutch oven over medium-high heat and add 2 tablespoons of the oil. When the oil is thin and fragrant, brown the chicken pieces on both sides well, 7 to 10 minutes in all. Transfer the chicken to a plate to rest.

Pour off the accumulated fat, add the remaining 1 tablespoon olive oil, and reduce the heat to medium-low. Slowly sweat the onions until they are wilted and translucent, but not browned, 3 to 4 minutes. Add the wine and deglaze the pan, stirring and scraping with a wooden spoon to incorporate any browned bits into the liquid. Add the tomatoes and their juices, the olives, and herbs. Return the browned chicken to the pan, cover, and lower the heat to a slow simmer. Cook for about 1 hour, or until the chicken is falling off the bones.

Serve warm.

Braised Chicken Thighs in Red Wine with Porcini

When made with four bone-in chicken thighs, this darkly delicious mahogany-colored dish cooks in 30 to 40 minutes in an enameled cast-iron Dutch oven, but it is even better when it is made a few days ahead and left to mellow in the refrigerator. In other words, this is a great dish to make on a weekend for dining on later in the week. Serve it with a robust starch such as quinoa to sop up the juices. Note that a paper coffee filter and a filter holder will be useful when draining the rehydrated mushrooms, and a fat-separating pitcher will improve the sauce.

SERVES 2 TO 4

4 skin-on, bone-in pastured chicken thighs

¼ cup dried porcini mushrooms

1 tablespoon unsalted butter

3 bay leaves

2 sprigs fresh rosemary

About 1 cup red wine

Salt and freshly ground black pepper

Blot the chicken dry with a paper towel on both sides and leave the pieces on a bed of folded paper towels to air-dry a little more at room temperature while you proceed.

Soak the dried mushrooms in a small bowl with enough very hot water to cover by 1 inch.

Melt the butter in a cast-iron frying pan and turn the heat to medium, adding the bay leaves and rosemary. Give the herbs a swirl in the butter and let them stew gently for a few minutes to perfume the fat.

Put the chicken, skin side down, into the hot butter, and brown it over medium-high heat. When they no longer stick to the pan, turn the pieces to brown on the other side.

Remove the rehydrated mushrooms from the soaking liquid, squeezing them to remove extra moisture, and set them aside. Place a paper coffee filter in a holder, and pour the mushroom liquid through it to remove any dirt. Pour this clarified liquid into a large measuring cup. Add enough red wine to make the total liquid 1½ cups.

When the chicken is darkly golden, pour in the wine-and-mushroom-liquid mixture and deglaze the pan, stirring with a wooden spoon to incorporate any browned bits into the sauce. Add the reserved mushrooms, as well as salt and pepper to taste. Cook, uncovered, over medium-low heat (the liquid should simmer slowly) turning the meat occasionally for about 30 minutes, or until the meat is falling off the bones. Remove and discard the bay leaves.

Serve with the pan sauce (which may be poured through a fat separator first).

Sicilian Chicken Thigh Stew with Capers

dapted from Nancy Harmon Jenkins's Cucina del Sole, *this is another winter dinner favorite that comes together with pantry ingredients (if your pantry runs to salt-packed capers). It improves over time, so making this dish a day ahead is a benefit, although not essential.*

SERVES 2 TO 4

2 tablespoons extra-virgin olive oil

1 onion, thinly sliced

4 skin-on, bone-in pastured chicken thighs

3 tablespoons white wine or champagne vinegar

⅓ cup salt-packed capers, well rinsed

¼ cup finely chopped flat-leaf parsley

Salt and freshly ground black pepper

Heat an enameled cast-iron Dutch oven or other 3-quart braising pan over medium heat, and when it is hot, add 1 tablespoon of the olive oil to the pan. When the oil is thin and fragrant, sweat the onion slices until soft, but not colored. Remove them from the pan and add the remaining 1 tablespoon olive oil. Brown the chicken pieces by adding them, skin side down, to the hot pan. When one side no longer sticks to the pan, turn the chicken and brown the other side. Remove the browned pieces from the pan.

Pour off the accumulated chicken fat. Put the vinegar in a measuring cup and add enough water to make 1 cup of liquid. Pour this into the hot pan and deglaze with a wooden spatula, scraping the pan to incorporate the browned bits into the sauce. Add the capers and parsley. Return the chicken to the pan, along with a little salt and pepper to taste. Cover the pan and cook for 1 hour, either at a slow simmer on top of the stove or in a 350-degree oven. The chicken should be falling off the bones. Taste for salt and adjust.

Serve warm.

Thai Green Curry Chicken

We've been making this curry for nearly fifteen years in our household, ever since I took a Thai cooking class. Over time, this fast curry has become a weeknight staple for its speedy delivery of spicy comfort. You can find small bottles of fish sauce and Thai green curry paste (and red and yellow) in most grocery store ethnic aisles. Each color has a different flavor. You can start cooking the rice when you begin making the curry—they'll finish about the same time.

SERVES 4

4 boneless, skinless pastured chicken thighs

1 (14-ounce) can whole coconut milk, preferably organic

1 heaping teaspoon Thai green curry paste, or more to taste

1 tablespoon Thai fish sauce

2 tablespoons light brown sugar

$\frac{1}{2}$ cup water

$1\frac{1}{2}$ cups any *one* of the following vegetables:
- frozen green peas
- zucchini or winter squash, finely diced
- green beans, trimmed and cut into 1-inch lengths
- eggplant, finely diced

For serving:

Steamed jasmine rice or Coconut Rice (see page 365)

$\frac{1}{4}$ cup chopped fresh cilantro, for garnish

Bring the chicken to room temperature, blot it, and cut the meat into 2-inch pieces.

Heat a heavy enameled cast-iron casserole or other heavy saucepan gently over low heat. Open the can of coconut milk, spoon out the thick cream on top, and melt it in the pan over low heat until it just begins to bubble at the edges. Stir in the curry paste with a wooden spoon. Simmer the mixture for about 3 minutes.

Add the chicken pieces and turn them in the paste, then pour in the thin coconut milk remaining in the can, taking care to scrape the can clean with a rubber spatula. Add the fish sauce, brown sugar, and water. Add the vegetable of your choice.

Cover the pan and simmer the stew over medium-low heat for 15 to 20 minutes, until both the chicken and the vegetable(s) are cooked through. Serve in bowls over rice, sprinkled with the chopped cilantro.

ROASTING CHICKEN PARTS: High-heat oven-roasting of spice-rubbed chicken parts is another way to coax flavor from "reasonable quality" birds.

Roasted Cardamom, Oregano, and Garlic Chicken Thighs

dapted from a recipe by Greg Malouf in Artichoke to Za'atar, *this dish roasts to a crisp at high heat. While it cooks, the perfume of cardamom and garlic infuses the kitchen. You can find green cardamom pods at any good spice purveyor and (far less expensively) at Indian and Middle Eastern groceries. Please don't use ground cardamom—you need the crunch of the tiny seeds, which are much more intensely flavored. Similarly, if you can get intensely flavored wild Greek oregano (found hanging upside down in bunches in some Greek markets), use it here. Be sure to leave time for the marinating—at least 4 hours. If you like, make a batch of rice to saok up fragrant juices.*

SERVES 4

¼ cup whole green cardamom pods or 1 to 2 tablespoons whole black cardamom seeds out of the pods

2 cloves garlic

1 tablespoon kosher salt

¼ cup fresh or dry oregano

¼ cup plus 2 tablespoons olive oil

4 to 6 large skin-on, bone-in pastured chicken thighs

Freshly ground black pepper

Select a shallow pan that will hold the thighs closely in one layer, such as a quarter sheet pan, cast-iron lasagna pan or frying pan, or gratin dish.

Using a mortar and pestle, or a heavy resealable plastic bag and the back of a cast-iron frying pan, pound the cardamom pods until they split. Discard the husks, and bruise the tiny black seeds by pounding them a little to release their oils. Add the garlic, salt, and oregano, and bash away a bit more to make a rough paste. Transfer the mixture to a bowl, then stir in the olive oil to thin the paste.

Arrange the thighs, flesh side up, in the pan and massage half the paste onto the flesh; turn them over and do the same on the skin side with the remaining paste. Allow the meat to marinate, covered and refrigerated, for at least 4 hours or overnight before bringing it back to room temperature. Grind black pepper over the thighs.

Heat the oven to 450 degrees, and set a rack at the top of the oven, just under the heating element (although you are not broiling, this exposes the skin to more heat for crispness). When the oven is good and hot, roast the chicken for 45 minutes, turning the meat over halfway through the cooking.

When done, the skin should be beautifully crisp and the flesh completely cooked through. Pour off the fat in the pan and arrange the pieces on a serving platter. Serve warm or at room temperature with rice.

BRAISING WHOLE BIRDS: Since pastured birds can be chewy, moist slow cooking is a wonderful way to showcase their flavor while tenderizing their flesh.

Römertopf Lemon Chicken Braised with Beer, Paprika, and Cumin

A *Römertopf is an unglazed clay pot made for braising meats, fish, or vegetables without added fat. The pot is immersed in cold water for 10 minutes, drained, then filled with the ingredients and placed in a cold oven that is then brought to temperature (this is important, to avoid cracking the clay of the pot). The dish cooks without any further attention until done, and tastes like you've slaved over the stove for hours!*

SERVES 4 TO 6

1 (3-pound) pastured chicken

Sea salt and freshly ground black pepper

2 lemons, rinsed and thinly sliced

1 teaspoon sweet (*dulce*) pimentón de la Vera (smoked Spanish paprika) or other smoked paprika

1 teaspoon ground cumin

½ teaspoon salt

½ cup beer

1 tablespoon maple syrup or honey

Rinse the chicken inside and out with cool water. Blot all the surfaces well with paper towels, salt and pepper the interior, and set it aside. Immerse the Römertopf for 15 minutes in cold water in the sink.

Empty the Römertopf of water, and line the bottom with some of the lemon slices. Put the remaining slices inside the chicken. Blend the spices and ½ teaspoon salt and sift them over the bird. Place the chicken in the pot, breast side down. Add the beer, pouring it down the side of the pot.

Cover the Römertopf and set it in the cold oven. Turn the heat to 480 degrees and cook for 2 hours. At that point, using tongs, turn the bird over, and pour the maple syrup over the breast, spreading it with a brush or the back of a spoon. Return the pot to the oven, uncovered, for an additional 10 minutes to brown and crisp the chicken.

Remove the bird from the pot with tongs and let it rest. Transfer the juices into a saucepan (the Römertopf can't take direct stovetop heat) and reduce them over high heat to a thick and concentrated sauce.

Cut up the chicken, arrange it on a platter or individual plates, and serve it with the sauce.

Old Hen Stewed in Red Wine
(Coq au Vin)

As you can see from the French name, this richly colored dish was originally devised for cooking rooster, but hens work just as well! You'll be amazed; the braising liquid that results from this long, slow cooking turns to aspic overnight in the refrigerator. Make this one day and reheat it the next to achieve this classic's ideal flavor.

SERVES 4 TO 6

About 8 cups chicken stock, preferably homemade (see page 303)

3 slices of good pastured pork bacon, cut crosswise into ¼-inch batons, or about 1 ounce finely chopped pastured pork belly, skinless fatback, or bacon fat (see page 257)

2 tablespoons unsalted butter

1 (2½-pound) pastured stewing hen, rinsed and blotted dry, innards removed

Kosher salt and freshly ground black pepper

¼ cup cognac

1 (750 ml) bottle red wine

½ teaspoon tomato paste

2 cloves garlic, finely chopped

1 teaspoon dried or fresh thyme leaves

3 bay leaves

3 tablespoons unbleached all-purpose flour

For serving:

Steamed rice or cooked egg noodles

Chopped fresh flat-leaf parsley, for garnish

Bring the stock to a boil in a small saucepan. Heat a 5-quart oval or round enameled cast-iron Dutch oven over medium-low heat and render the bacon or pork belly fat with the butter over low heat. When the fats are liquid, move the bacon or any meat to the edges of the pan, and add the chicken, seasoning it lightly with the salt and pepper and turning it in the fat to coat it on all sides.

Cook the chicken, turning it as necessary, until it begins to look more intensely colored, but is not yet browned, about 15 minutes. Add the cognac and let it cook down for a few minutes. Add the red wine and enough of the boiling stock to just cover the chicken. (If your bird is large, remove it from the pot with tongs and cut it into smaller pieces so that the meat will be submerged.) Stir in the tomato paste, garlic, thyme, and bay leaves.

Bring the chicken and liquid mixture to a slow simmer, lower the heat, cover the pot tightly, and cook for 4½ hours, or until the meat is falling off the bones.

Remove the chicken from the liquid and refrigerate it. Ladle or pour the cooking liquid through a strainer to eliminate all the solids. You should have about 4 cups liquid. Refrigerate it overnight.

The next day, remove the white fat that has solidified on top of the liquid (the stock itself should have turned to jelly). Set the fat aside. Remove the cooked chicken from the refrigerator and let it begin to come to room temperature. Reheat the stock in a saucepan and slowly bring it to a boil.

Again using the Dutch oven, melt 2 tablespoons of the reserved chicken fat over low heat and whisk in the flour all at once to make a roux. Ladle in the boiling stock in ½-cup portions, mixing each addition well with the roux, until you have added all the stock and created a thickened sauce.

Return the chicken and any gelatin it has exuded to the pot, reheating everything slowly to serving temperature. Taste for salt and adjust. Serve with rice or egg noodles, and garnish with plentiful amounts of chopped parsley.

Stewing Old Chickens

There is a depth of gamy flavor to old hens that is unknown to most of us because we were raised on young factory birds. Stocks and braises made with such hens yield an appreciable amount of gelatinized protein, which makes the dishes that contain them even more delicious, and nutritious (and they're perfect for use in chicken dumplings; see box on page 303). These are the birds that such classic dishes as coq au vin and poule au pot were created for, and using the kind of stewing birds those recipes were meant for creates authentic flavors you just can't duplicate with younger birds.

Spanish-Style Pastured Chicken Pot Roast

A dapted from a recipe in Spain: A Culinary Road Trip, *by Mario Batali and Gwyneth Paltrow, this pot roast of whole pastured chicken is a revelation in long, low, slow, moist cooking. It is the perfect method for a pastured bird, which can tend to toughness as well as gigantism, or an old hen that needs long cooking. You may need to cook the bird breast-side-down to get it to fit under the lid of a close-fitting oval enameled cast-iron pot or a Römertopf.*

Aside from the time involved (as many as 12 hours!), this is an easy dish to prepare, and it works well if made ahead. If you do that, let the dish cool to room temperature, then refrigerate it until an hour or two before dinner. Then bring it slowly back to serving temperature in a low oven. (Just don't refrigerate it inside a Römertopf, because the clay can't withstand thermal shock.) Serve the chicken with its juices, accompanied by a wonderful Spanish rice such as bomba to soak up the juices, and good, garlicky cooked greens (see page 362).

SERVES 6 TO 8

1 (4- to 5-pound) pastured chicken

½ cup diced pastured pork bacon or pancetta, cut into ¼-inch cubes

¼ pound Loose Pork and Fennel Sausage, (see page 197) or sweet Italian pastured pork sausage, casings removed (if necessary) and meat crumbled

3 to 4 cups chicken stock, preferably homemade (see page 303)

Salt and freshly ground black pepper

Heat the oven to 200 degrees and choose an enameled cast-iron pot that will closely fit your chicken, or immerse a Römertopf pot in cold water to soak for 15 minutes, and start the roasting process in a cold oven. Bring the chicken to room temperature, rinse it, and blot it dry.

Combine the bacon and sausage meat and stuff the mixture firmly into the chicken's cavity.

Put the chicken in your chosen pot, add the chicken stock, and sprinkle salt and pepper on top of the bird. Cover the pot, adding foil or parchment paper if necessary to maintain a tight seal on a cast-iron pot.

Place a cast-iron pot in the already hot oven, or put a Römertopf into the cold oven and turn the heat to 200 degrees. Cook for 8 to 12 hours—longer cooking makes the bird more succulent (just add more chicken stock or water as necessary to keep the liquid level high).

Serve the chicken whole or in shreds, drizzled with the rich stock.

ROASTING WHOLE BIRDS: When I buy whole pastured chickens from a farmer, I tend to roast them for festive dinners and use the bones for stock (see pages 303 and 308). Brining always adds succulence.

Roasted Maple-Glazed Brined Chicken with Ancho Chile Rub

ecause this chicken is brined, it is juicy. When rubbed with ancho chile powder and then glazed with real maple syrup, the combination of heat, salt, and sweet is unforgettable. Try cooking this on a bed of potato wedges mixed with garlic cloves, or cook it plain, as it is here. I've written this recipe for an indoor oven, but it can easily be made on a covered gas or charcoal grill, using a cast-iron frying pan and thermometers to check the temperatures of the grill and the bird.

SERVES 4 TO 6

1 (3-pound) pastured frying chicken	1 teaspoon kosher salt
	1 to 2 tablespoons water
3 tablespoons ancho chile powder	2 tablespoons maple syrup

Brine the chicken all day or overnight, then rinse and blot it dry, as described in the box below.

When you are ready to cook, heat the oven to 425 degrees.

Combine the ancho chile powder and salt, and rub the mixture over all sides and the interior of the chicken. Let it sit at room temperature for 15 to 20 minutes.

Put the bird, breast side up, in a cast-iron frying pan or shallow roasting pan. Push the wing tips behind the neck area of the chicken, so that the bird is in a "sunbathing" position. Tie the legs loosely together using kitchen twine.

Pour the water in the pan and put the chicken in the oven, feet first. Roast for 1 hour, or until the bird's internal temperature registers 160 to 165 degrees on an instant-read thermometer.

Drizzle the maple syrup over the chicken, spreading it with a brush or the back of a spoon, and roast the chicken for another 5 minutes, or until the skin is golden and crisp.

Let the chicken rest at room temperature for 15 minutes before carving it.

Brining Chicken

I brine nearly every whole chicken because the process adds flavor and produces a juicy bird. I find that even free-range pastured birds can also profit from it because they can be tough. Although some people add flavorings to their brine—brown sugar, peppercorns, cloves, juniper berries, cinnamon sticks—the only additions I ever use are 1 tablespoon of sugar and 1 tablespoon of cider vinegar.

Use a plastic food-safe 5-quart bucket with a lid and add ½ cup non-iodized kosher salt. Dissolve the salt in a little hot water, and fill the bucket halfway with cold water, adding sugar and vinegar if desired. Rinse the chicken inside and out, removing any innards or dangling bits of fat. Submerge it in the bucket, neck first, allowing the cavity to fill to keep the bird from floating. Top off with more cold water to cover. Close tightly and refrigerate all day or overnight.

When ready to cook, remove the bird and rinse it well before blotting dry and proceeding with a recipe.

Roasted and Glazed Lemon Chicken

M *arcella Hazan, in* More Classic Italian Cooking, *calls this* pollo al limone *the essence of Italian cooking, because it is so very simple and so delicious. You need a hot oven (don't use convection because it will make a smoky mess), a good lemon or two (depending on the size of your bird), some excellent salt and pepper, and a reasonably good bird. I like to brine mine overnight (in a brining solution with sugar added), but even an hour in the brine will help make a juicier bird. The bird is then stuffed with lemon and "sewn" closed with wooden toothpicks. When the toothpick suture works and keeps the cavity closed, the chicken swells up like a balloon from all the interior juices! But even if it leaks and doesn't swell, the meat always tastes fabulous. I've simplified Marcella's recipe by not turning the bird, but I've made it slightly more complicated by adding a sweet glaze at the end, which makes for incredibly delicious and deeply colored skin. Finally—the true secret to the great taste of this dish—be sure to squeeze the juice from the hot lemon over the sliced meat before you serve it.*

SERVES 4 TO 6

1 (2½- to 3-pound) pastured frying chicken

Sea salt and freshly ground black pepper

1 or 2 lemons, rinsed, rolled, and each pierced all the way through with a skewer 30 times

Maple syrup, honey, or slightly diluted pomegranate molasses

Brine the chicken for at least 1 hour or as long as overnight in a brining solution with ½ cup sugar added, then rinse and blot it dry as described in the box on page 297.

Heat the oven to 375 degrees.

Sprinkle a good amount of salt and pepper on the chicken, massaging them into the surface and interior. Put 1 or 2 lemons in the cavity of the bird (remember that there needs to be room for the juices to swell during cooking), and seal the opening tightly with toothpicks, piercing in, out, and in, as if you were sewing, to keep it closed. Tie the legs loosely together to keep the skin on the thighs from cracking as it cooks, and put the wings behind the neck in "sunbathing" position.

Put the chicken in a roasting pan or cast-iron frying pan and roast it, legs facing the back wall of the oven, for 45 minutes. Turn the heat up to 425 degrees and cook for another 15 to 25 minutes, until the juices run clear when you pierce the bird at the thigh with the tip of a sharp knife.

Spread the glaze of your choice over the bird and allow it to cook and melt for the last 5 minutes of the cooking time. Because all these glazes are high in sugar, they will make the bird brown fast, so keep a close eye on the oven.

Let the bird sit for about 10 minutes before carving. I first slice off the wings, thighs and legs, then slice the breast into thin slices, much like a turkey. (An electric knife is invaluable.) Arrange all the meat on a platter. Remove the lemon from the cavity, and using tongs, squeeze the hot lemon juice over the sliced meat before serving.

How Can You Roast Chicken So Many Different Ways?

I have come to the conclusion that there is no one right way to roast a chicken! Surprisingly, you can make great roast chicken by cooking it low and slow, by flash-roasting it at high heat pretty rapidly, or by following a middle path and using a high heat/low heat formula. Remarkably, all of these methods produce succulent birds, although they do not taste the same. Try all the different methods (there is at least one example of each in this book) and see what you prefer.

Mustard Roast Chicken

've always loved meat and poultry with a grainy mustard crust, so I created this recipe to satisfy that yearning. This chicken starts at high heat and then cooks the rest of the time at a lower heat to give it both crispness and succulence.

SERVES 6 TO 8

2½ pounds new potatoes, cut into 2-inch chunks

1 (5-pound) pastured chicken

Salt and freshly ground black pepper

1 head garlic, separated into cloves, papery skins left on

1 bunch fresh rosemary

1 cup grainy mustard

¼ cup extra-virgin olive oil

2 tablespoons thin soy sauce

½ cup white wine

2 tablespoons heavy cream

Heat the oven to 450 degrees. Choose a ceramic, glass, or metal roasting pan large enough to hold both the chicken and the potato pieces, and fill it with the potato. Rinse the chicken and blot it dry. Remove any lumps of chicken fat and put them among the potato pieces, then place the bird on top of the potatoes. Salt and pepper the bird (inside and out), as well as the potatoes, arrange the garlic cloves over all, and put some of the rosemary sprigs inside the bird and between the chunks of potatoes.

Remove and chop enough of the leaves from the remaining rosemary sprigs to make ¼ cup. Using a food processor fitted with the steel blade, or mixing by hand in a bowl, blend the chopped rosemary with the mustard, olive oil, and soy sauce to make a paste. Scrape this over the chicken, smoothing it on with a spatula to make a thick crust.

Bake the chicken and potatoes for 30 minutes, then reduce the heat to 350 degrees for another 60 to 75 minutes, until the internal temperature of the bird registers 160 to 165 degrees when an instant-read thermometer is inserted in the thigh.

Put the bird on a carving board to rest for 15 minutes before carving. Using a slotted spoon, transfer the potatoes to a serving dish and keep them warm. Make a sauce with the liquids left in the pan by first running them through a fat-separating pitcher, then cooking down the defatted liquid with the white wine in a saucepan until the volume is reduced by half.

Remove the sauce from the heat and stir in the cream; pour the sauce into a gravy boat.

Put the carved chicken on a platter and serve it along with the potatoes. Pass the gravy at the table.

Air-Dried Slow-Roasted Pastured Whole Chicken

Air-drying overnight in the fridge helps chicken skin to tighten and then crisp in the oven. Slow-roasting and pre-salting create unbelievable succulence. Combine these approaches, and you're in chicken heaven, but take note—just like getting into heaven, this requires time! Figure on about 3 hours of cooking in addition to all the preparation, making this a dish you start one day with the air-drying and then cook the next afternoon. An accurate thermometer that lets you read the internal temperature outside the oven is very helpful.

SERVES 6 TO 8

1 (5-pound) pastured chicken

Sea salt and freshly ground black pepper

1 lemon, preferably organic, washed and quartered

1 bunch fresh thyme

1 head garlic, separated into cloves, papery skins left on

2 tablespoons honey

¼ cup extra-virgin olive oil

1 cup fruity white wine

Reserve any innards such as the liver, neck, and heart and freeze them for another use. Rinse the chicken inside and out, then carefully blot it dry on all surfaces. Generously salt and pepper the bird, both outside and in the cavity. Put the bird on a cooling rack set on a plate, and place it in the refrigerator, uncovered, for up to 24 hours to allow the skin to dry further and tighten.

When you are ready to cook, allow the bird to come to room temperature for 30 minutes. (If you can, aim a fan of some kind at it to further dry its surface.) Heat the oven to 250 degrees and position a rack in the center.

Put the lemon quarters, thyme sprigs, and garlic cloves into the cavity of the chicken, tucking in any flaps of skin or fat to help keep them inside.

Arrange the bird, breast side up, on a V-rack or other roasting rack set into a broiler pan, or roast the chicken without a rack in a heavy gratin dish or an ovenproof cast-iron frying pan. Put the chicken in the oven with its feet facing the back wall.

Roast the chicken for 3 hours, turning the pan halfway through, or until the internal temperature registers 155 to 160 degrees when an instant-read thermometer is inserted in the thigh. Remove the roasting pan from the oven while you increase the oven temperature to 475 degrees. Stir together the honey and olive oil.

When the oven has reached that temperature, rub half of the honey and oil-mixture onto the breast of the bird using the back of a spoon. Insert an ovenproof thermometer probe into the chicken, pour the wine into the pan, and return the chicken to the oven. Cook for another 10 minutes, or until the thigh temperature reads 160 degrees and the skin is browned. Using tongs, carefully turn the bird, coat the underside with the remaining glazing mixture, and return it to the oven for a further 5 to 10 minutes.

Let the chicken rest for 15 minutes before carving it. Meanwhile, remove the garlic from the cavity and arrange it around the edges of the serving platter for those who like to squeeze out the flavorful insides. Squeeze the cooked lemon wedges into the pan juices.

Use the pan drippings to make a sauce by cooking them down to a syrupy consistency, stirring occasionally to incorporate the browned bits stuck to the bottom of the pan. Pour the liquid through a fat-separating pitcher and pour the pan sauce into a gravy boat.

Carve the bird (an electric knife is ideal for this) by first cutting off the legs and thighs and setting them on the platter. Do the same with the wings, and then cut the breast meat into slices and arrange them on the platter and serve. Pass the gravy boat at the table.

Slow-Roasted Pastured Chicken with Pimentón and Cumin Rub

It's easy to see how much I like pimentón, that smoky, sweet Spanish paprika. If you don't yet have it in your pantry, try substituting Hungarian paprika or chili powder (but only if you like the heat!) and using smoked salt in place of the kosher salt to add a smoky flavor.

This big chicken is cooked low and slow, a bit like barbecue, but in the oven. Since pastured chicken can be chewier than the industrial birds you may be used to, this is a good way to make the chicken meltingly tender. Believe me, it's worth the effort and time. Be sure to save the carcass for a very flavorful stock, so that none of that pastured goodness goes astray.

SERVES 6

2 teaspoons sweet (*dulce*) pimentón de la Vera (smoked Spanish paprika)

½ teaspoon freshly ground black pepper

1 heaping teaspoon fresh or dried thyme

½ teaspoon ground cumin

1 teaspoon kosher salt

1 (3½- to 4-pound) pastured roasting chicken

2 tablespoons extra-virgin olive oil, plus more for the pan

1 onion, cut into 6 wedges

Choose a nonreactive glass or stainless-steel bowl or refrigerator dish large enough to hold the whole chicken. Blend the pimentón, black pepper, thyme, cumin, and salt.

Rinse the chicken inside and out, and blot it dry. Rub the chicken all over with the olive oil. Spoon about half the spice blend into the cavity and add the onion wedges. Tuck the legs into the skin to hold them, or tie them loosely together with kitchen twine.

Put the bird in the bowl, and rub the remaining spice blend all over the back, breast, and front. Cover the bowl with a double layer of plastic wrap and refrigerate the chicken for 8 to 12 hours, or overnight.

When you are nearly ready to start cooking, let the bird come to room temperature for about 30 minutes. Heat the oven to 275 degrees.

Lightly oil the bottom of a roasting pan and place the chicken in it, breast side up. Roast the chicken, uncovered, with the feet facing the back wall of the oven. After 2 hours, loosely tent the breast with foil to protect it from drying out. Continue to cook the chicken for a total of 4½ hours, or until the dark meat is meltingly tender.

Let the bird rest for a good 15 minutes before carving it, and serve it with the pan juices poured over the white meat.

The Taste of Pastured Chicken

Chickens ranging freely on grass develop strong thighs, and unless they are Cornish Crosses, their breast meat may be meager. That means that while they are full of flavor and satisfying texture, they can be a very different eating experience than a supermarket bird. Longer, slower cooking, added fat and spices, and a good pan sauce all complement the deep taste of naturally raised poultry.

Roast Chicken with Apples, Sausage, and Cider

In autumn, our basement is stuffed with baskets of heirloom apples, and I'm always looking for ways to incorporate them into dinner dishes. This roast chicken feels like apple squared, thanks to the bit of cider that accompanies the roasted apples. It's one of our favorites. With the tasty sausage and onion, we think of it as stuffing without the bread.

SERVES 4

2 links sweet Italian pastured pork sausage

1 (2½-pound) pastured or organic chicken

1 tablespoon fresh thyme leaves

2 tablespoons unsalted butter, softened

Kosher salt and freshly ground black pepper

1 tablespoon extra-virgin olive oil

3 assorted heirloom apples

1 onion

½ cup apple cider

1 tablespoon heavy cream

Heat the oven to 400 degrees, and position a rack in the middle.

Gently prick the sausage links with a toothpick. Pour cold water into a frying pan, submerge the sausage links, and bring the water to a simmer. Poach the meat for 10 to 15 minutes, until it is cooked through. Remove the sausage from the pan to cool and dry.

Rinse the chicken thoroughly and blot it dry inside and out. Mix the thyme leaves and butter together with a fork. Using your hands, carefully detach the skin from the flesh of the chicken breast to make a pocket, and press the butter-herb mixture into it to make an even layer over the breast. Salt and pepper the chicken inside and outside.

Choose a roasting pan only slightly larger than the chicken, such as a small cast-iron frying pan or gratin dish. Coat the pan with the olive oil.

Peel, core, and cut each of the apples into 4 wedges. Cut the onion into 8 wedges. Distribute the apple and onion wedges in the pan. Cut the sausages into ½-inch slices and mix it in as well. Put the chicken on top, and sprinkle salt and pepper over all. Pour the apple cider into the pan.

Insert a probe thermometer between the leg and thigh of the chicken, taking care not to hit the bone. Roast the chicken with its feet facing the back wall of the oven for 1 to 1½ hours, until the internal temperature is 160 to 165 degrees.

Let the chicken rest for 15 minutes, loosely draped with foil, before you carve it.

Meanwhile, using a slotted spoon, remove all the solids from the pan, put them in a serving dish, and keep them warm. Defat the juices, if you wish, using a fat-separating pitcher. Put the pan with the juices on the stove over medium heat, scraping to incorporate any caramelized bits into the sauce. Reduce the liquid by half, until it begins to be syrupy, stirring as needed.

Remove the sauce from the heat and stir in the heavy cream. Serve the chicken drizzled with the sauce, with the roasted apples, sausage, and onion alongside.

Every Week Chicken Stock

I like to roast a chicken every weekend or two, and I never throw away the carcass, because that's the basis of this stock—obviously, I make it often. It's wonderful to have in the freezer for making risotto, soups, any recipe or sauce that calls for stock. I buy quart freezer containers in bulk so that I always have some ready to fill. I don't add salt to stock because I can always do that when I use it. The onion peel adds color.

MAKES ABOUT 4 CUPS

1 pastured chicken carcass after carving off the meat

1 onion, unpeeled

1 whole clove, stuck in the onion

1 carrot, unpeeled, cut into large chunks

1 stalk celery, cut in half

5 whole peppercorns

1 bay leaf

Fill a large stockpot with all the ingredients, covering them with water by at least 5 inches. Bring the pot to a slow boil, uncovered. Immediately turn the heat down to the slowest simmer; you will need to skim foam from the top from time to time during the early part of the cooking. Continue simmering the stock for a few hours, or until it is concentrated, fragrant, and golden.

Strain the stock through a colander or sieve to remove the solids. Press down on the vegetables to extract their juices, then discard the solids and let the stock cool. Ladle the cooled stock into a freezer container and chill it overnight. Remove the fat from the top and freeze the stock. It will last for several months. Bring it back to a slow boil for 10 to 15 minutes before using in a recipe.

Ten Ideas for Leftover Chicken

First of all, reserve the carcass and bones for stock (see above and page 308). Then use any of the following ideas to create a new meal with the leftover chopped, shredded, or chunked meat:

1. Chicken Salad—with grapes and almonds, served on slices of challah or brioche.
2. Chicken Potpie—with purchased or homemade pie crust or puff pastry on top.
3. Chicken Shepherd's Pie—with homemade mashed potatoes on top.
4. Chicken Dumplings/Ravioli/Pot Stickers—ground in a food processor with ricotta, cooked greens, and Parmigiano-Reggiano (or scallions, tofu, and soy sauce), wrapped in wonton skins.
5. Shredded Chicken Wrap—using nori as the wrapper, and adding chopped salad; or rolled in flatbread, pita, or naan along with pieces of grilled red bell pepper and onion.
6. Chicken Pasta Sauce—mixed with tomato sauce, garlic, and oregano.
7. Chicken à la King—shredded chicken mixed with onions, cooked in butter and cream, and served on rice.
8. Chicken Tortillas—with lettuce, salsa, and sour cream.
9. Chicken–Black Bean Soup—stirred into beans and broth with onion, garlic, and chili spices, served with a dollop of sour cream.
10. Quick Chicken Curry—with yogurt and grapes.

GRILLED CHICKEN: Whether outdoors on charcoal or gas, or indoors in a grill pan, grilling exposes meat to high heat, making food crisp on the outside and tender within.

Grilled Rosemary Chicken Under Bricks

This is classic Italian summer fare. You butterfly a chicken so that it lies flat and then press it down on the grill with bricks. This always yields a tasty bird that cooks rapidly. When that chicken has been brined and then rubbed with a paste of garlic, rosemary, and salt, dinner is even more memorable. Try cooking this outside on the grill or inside on hot cast iron. I keep two foil-wrapped bricks near my grill just for this dish, but you could also weight down the bird with a heavy cast-iron pot. Putting foil on the bottom will ensure that it is easy to clean.

SERVES 4

1 (3-pound) pastured chicken

2 teaspoons sea salt

½ cup fresh rosemary leaves

¼ cup extra-virgin olive oil

2 cloves garlic

1 lemon, cut into wedges

Brine the chicken, then rinse and blot it dry, as described in the box on page 297.

Heat a charcoal or gas grill to 435 to 450 degrees. If your grill does not have a thermometer, heat it to high heat. If you are cooking indoors, heat a cast-iron grill pan or other heavy frying pan over high heat. Wrap 2 bricks or the bottom of a heavy cast-iron pan with foil to use as a weight and have it at hand near your cooking area.

Butterfly the bird by putting it, breast side down, on a cutting board and cutting out the backbone with a knife or poultry shears. Open the chicken so that it lies flat, slightly breaking the breastbone to flatten it.

In a food processor fitted with the steel blade, or in a mortar and pestle, process the salt, rosemary, olive oil, and garlic to a paste. Rub the paste all over the chicken, front and back, on skin and flesh, inserting a little under the skin (try not to tear the skin as you do this).

Put the chicken, skin side down, on the hot cooking surface, and immediately weight it with the bricks or heavy pan. Cook for about 12 minutes, or until the skin is golden and crisp. Using oven gloves, remove the bricks carefully, turn the bird over, and replace the weight. Cook for another 12 minutes, or until an instant-read thermometer registers 160 to 165 degrees when inserted into the fleshy part of the thigh. Let the chicken rest for 5 to 10 minutes before cutting it.

Serve the bird as follows: Remove the legs, thighs, and wings and put them on a platter. Divide each breast portion in two to make 4 more pieces. Serve with the lemon wedges.

CHICKEN OFFAL AND ODD BITS: Less-familiar innards from chickens include hearts, gizzards, and feet; they are appreciated as much for their texture as for their flavor. Chicken feet enrich stocks with gelatin, which aids in relieving stiff joints. Gizzards may aid digestion, while hearts offer satisfying chewing. Livers, perhaps the most familiar of offal, offer velvet texture to spreads and pâtés.

Stir-Fried Gizzards with Ginger and Black Mushrooms

Gizzards from pastured birds are at least twice the size of commercial ones, and offer lots of satisfying chewiness. This perfect winter entrée was unexpectedly delicious to me, and offered the further benefit that its ingredients may help boost the immune system. It is perfect to serve with rice.

SERVES 4

1 pound pastured chicken gizzards

2 ounces (about 4 inches) peeled fresh ginger stalk

½ cup dried Chinese black mushrooms

1 large clove garlic

1 small "bird" hot pepper

½ cup thin soy sauce

Pinch of sugar

¼ cup water

2 tablespoons vegetable oil

2 scallions, chopped

Clean the gizzards of any loose fat and wash them thoroughly in cold water. Using a sharp chef's knife with a thin blade, slice the gizzards at a slight angle into ¼-inch slices, cutting through the tough membrane and meat.

Slice the ginger very thinly and cut each slice into thin shreds. Set aside.

Reconstitute the dried black mushrooms in a little boiling water to cover for about 10 minutes, or until they are tender. Remove them from the water, discarding the liquid. Chop the mushrooms into ¼- to ½-inch pieces, put them in a small bowl, and set aside.

Chop the garlic and the hot pepper into a fine dice; put them in a bowl and set aside.

Mix the soy sauce, sugar, and water. Line up all the ingredients near the stove.

Heat a wok over high heat and add the oil, swirling it to coat the pan. Add the garlic-pepper mixture (it should sizzle) and stir-fry for 1 minute. Add the gizzards and stir-fry them, using a wooden spoon to move them around, until they are browned and half-cooked, about 1 minute. Add the chopped mushrooms and cook, stiring, for another 3 to 4 minutes. Add the soy sauce mixture, cover the pan, and cook for another 4 to 5 minutes, until the meat is cooked. Add the ginger and scallions, and stir-fry them in. Serve immediately.

Stir-Fried Chicken Hearts and Liver with Chiles and Garlic

Spicy and hearty, this is a dish to serve with jasmine rice or boiled chow fun noodles to balance the flavors. Like all stir-fried dishes, most of the work is in the preparation of the ingredients—the cooking takes almost no time at all. Chile peppers vary in their heat according to the season; they are hotter in summer than in winter. In terms of heat, of the three most common Mexican chile peppers, the strongest is the habanero, next comes the serrano, and then comes the jalapeño. Know your own palate, and choose accordingly.

SERVES 4

1 onion	¼ cup water
1 red bell pepper	½ cup thin soy sauce
1 green bell pepper	Pinch sugar
1 cup (half a can) bamboo shoots	Freshly ground black pepper
3 large cloves garlic	1 tablespoon cooking oil, peanut oil or canola oil
1 or 2 chile peppers	¼ cup water
½ pound (1 cup) pastured chicken hearts	
5 ounces pastured chicken liver	

Cut the onion in half and slice thinly. Reserve it in a small bowl. Cut the red and green bell peppers in half, reserve half of each pepper for another use, remove the seeds and membrane from the other half, and slice thinly. Put them in another bowl. Drain and measure out 1 cup of bamboo shoots and reserve, saving the rest for another dish.

Slice the garlic thinly, and remove the inner membranes and seeds of the chile peppers before dicing them. Using a mortar and pestle, pound the garlic and chile pepper together to make a rough, fragrant paste.

Rinse and drain the hearts. Slice each open (like a book, horizontally), and reserve in a bowl. Rinse, drain, and slice the chicken livers into 2-inch pieces, and reserve in another bowl. Mix the water, soy sauce, black pepper and sugar and set aside.

Heat a wok and add the oil. Fry the chile pepper and garlic paste, stirring, for 30 seconds. Add the onion slices and stir-fry them until they are coated with the paste and softened, about 1 minute. Add the hearts and stir-fry them until they are colored and slightly cooked. Add the bamboo shoots and the soy sauce mixture and stir. Cover the wok and cook for 4 to 5 minutes, until the hearts are nearly cooked through.

Remove the cover and add the livers, stir-frying to cook them for a minute or two. Add the red and green bell peppers, and cook for another 3 minutes, or until the livers are cooked but slightly pink on the inside. Serve at once.

Coconut Soup with Chicken Feet

hen the feet are attached to a living chicken, they look so prehistoric that it's not hard to imagine that dinosaurs and chickens have a common relative. But when they're detached, inverted, and in the kitchen, those same feet have a startling likeness to a human hand. That likeness becomes even more distracting when you start to prepare them for cooking, because it's necessary to slice the "palm" to make it cook evenly. It's worth persevering, however, because cooked feet offer great gnawing opportunities, and this soup is really good. Since chicken feet from pastured birds are tougher than feet purchased at an Asian or other ethnic grocer, they are cooked here for 25 minutes instead of the more usual 10 to 15 minutes. Fresh galangal root, lemongrass stalks, and Kaffir lime leaves are available from Thai and Asian grocers.

SERVES 4

8 pastured chicken feet

1 large shallot

1-inch-piece fresh galangal root

4 stalks lemongrass

4 to 6 Kaffir lime leaves

3 or 4 chile peppers (see headnote, page 306)

1 (13.5-ounce) can coconut milk

½ pound white button mushrooms

2½ tablespoons fish sauce

¼ cup fresh lime juice

1 teaspoon light brown sugar, or as needed

1 bunch fresh cilantro

Wash the feet thoroughly under running water. Set a large pot of water to boil, and blanch the feet for 1 minute to loosen the skin. Remove them to a bowl of ice water, then drain. Lay each foot on a cutting board, and use a cleaver or knife to whack off the ends of the feet, removing and discarding the toenails. Using a paring knife, peel off the loose skin and discard. Use a sharp knife to sever the tendon on the "palm" between the "thumb" and "forefinger," slicing deeply into the meat to cut through the deep callus, which is actually the ball of the foot.

Finely chop the shallot and put it in a bowl. Peel and cut the galangal root into ¼-inch slices and add this to the bowl. Using the side of a chef's knife, smash the base of each lemongrass stalk to expose the inner white core. Slice this finely and reserve in the same bowl.

Put the chicken feet, 3 cups water, and the shallot, galangal, and lemongrass mixture in a soup pot. Tear off and discard the central stalk of each lime leaf, and add the leaf sections to the pot. Remove and discard the inner membranes and seeds from the chile peppers, cut them into ½-inch pieces, and add the pieces to the pot. Bring this to a boil, then lower the heat to a simmer, and cook, partially covered, until the meat is tender, about 25 minutes for pastured chicken feet.

Keeping a low simmer, add the coconut milk, mushrooms, and fish sauce, rinsing the coconut milk can with ½ cup water, and adding that to the pot as well. Cook for another 5 minutes. Add the lime juice off the heat and stir it in. Taste for balance, and add brown sugar if necessary.

Chop the cilantro leaves finely.

Serve at once, putting 1 or 2 chicken feet in each bowl, garnished with the fresh cilantro. Eat the soup by holding a chicken foot in your hands, and gnawing. Spoon out the rest of the soup.

Chinese Chicken Super Stock

To make this stock, I buy packages of Misty Knoll Vermont-raised chicken backs and wings, save those same parts (along with necks) when I cut up chickens for other dishes, or use a whole old hen. I find that this stock demands a good quantity of meat and bones—more than just the carcass left over from one great roast chicken dinner. When I have them, I add chicken feet or duck feet (or both) to the mix for gelatin and extra flavor.

This stock is the basis in soup dumplings (see page 194), but you'll find many other uses for it as well, including (in our family, at least) curing a cold—a big bowl of this steaming broth makes anyone feel better nearly immediately. Try cooking fresh or frozen stuffed wontons in it, too (see box on page 303).

Put all the chicken parts and the water in a big pot and bring it to a boil, then reduce the heat to a fast simmer. Skim off the foam that forms during the first 15 minutes. When the liquid begins to stay relatively clear, add the remaining ingredients and lower the heat to maintain a slow simmer, partially covered. Simmer the stock for 3 to 4 hours, until it has reduced by half and is strong and richly flavored.

Let the stock cool and strain it through a colander or sieve; discard the solids. Chill the stock and remove any fat that rises to the top.

When you are ready to use the stock for soup, heat it to the boiling point and simmer it for 10 to 15 minutes before proceeding.

MAKES ABOUT 4 CUPS

12 cups water

3 pounds pastured chicken backs, wings, necks, and scraps

6 to 10 pastured chicken or duck feet, cleaned (see page 307)

1 bunch scallions (white part only)

1 (2-inch) knob fresh ginger, peeled

2 dried shiitake mushrooms

1 clove garlic, smashed

1 tablespoon soy sauce

1 tablespoon Shaoxing wine

Be Thoughtful with Chicken Stock

Chicken stock is a perfect growing medium for bacteria. If you have rapidly cooled and refrigerated your stock, there is little to worry about. But if your cooling has left the stock at room temperature for an hour or more, I suggest you bring it back, after refrigeration, to a slow boil for a good 10 to 15 minutes before using it in a dish to ensure that there are no bacteria lurking.

PHEASANT: Farmed pheasant is surprisingly affordable, and is an even leaner alternative to chicken. Try braising it into tenderness, or brine it before roasting or grilling it to succulence. Pheasants are small; one bird will feed two people as a main course or four as part of a larger, multicourse meal.

Pheasant Braised with Green Cabbage and Garlic with Sherry

This is a straightforward way to cook pheasant, using added fat, time, and a rich braising liquid to flavor and tenderize the bird. It is based on a recipe published by Simon Hopkinson in The Independent, *and the beauty of it is that it can be the template for any number of variations—a Provençal version could feature winter greens with tomatoes, black olives, and capers, while an Asian take could include bok choy with rice wine, soy sauce, and star anise. I like this version because there is something about new green cabbage that sings of spring to me, and I find this the perfect home-style April dinner, served with steamed potato wedges to mix into the gravy.*

SERVES 4

1 pastured pheasant (about 1½ pounds)

Salt and freshly ground black pepper

2 tablespoons unsalted butter

1 tablespoon pastured pork bacon fat (see page 257) or pastured chicken fat (see page 331)

8 cloves garlic, smashed

¼ cup sherry

4 cups chicken stock, preferably homemade (see page 303)

4 sprigs fresh thyme

1 small green cabbage, fresh and tightly furled, outer leaves discarded

4 Yukon Gold potatoes, cut into wedges

Heat the oven to 275 degrees and put a rack in the center. Bring the pheasant to room temperature and lightly salt and pepper it.

Melt the butter and fat in an enameled cast-iron Dutch oven or other heavy braising pot that's not too much bigger than the pheasant. Brown the bird on all sides in the fat—this will take at least 15 minutes over medium heat. Use tongs to transfer the bird to a plate.

Add the garlic cloves to the pot and cook them in the fat until they begin to turn a little golden, then add the sherry and stock and stir with a wooden spatula, scraping the bottom of the pot to incorporate the browned bits into the sauce. Add the thyme and let simmer slowly.

Meanwhile, prepare the cabbage: Cut the head in half and remove the core. Slice down the center to form 4 wedges from each half. Add all 8 wedges to the pot and stir them in. Return the pheasant to the pot, breast side up, moving the cabbage aside to let the bird nestle in the center of the pot.

Cut a piece of parchment paper slightly larger than the pot and push it down onto the surface of the food. Clap the pot lid on top and put the pot in the oven to cook slowly for about 1 hour. You'll know the pheasant is cooked when the meat on the shanks starts to shrink away from the bones and all the meat begins to shred and is completely tender to the touch.

Let the bird sit in the pot, covered, for 20 minutes to allow the flavors to settle. While the bird cools, steam the potatoes in a stovetop steamer, and serve them on the platter with the pheasant and its pan juices.

Pheasant in Lemon Cream Sauce with Nutmeg

*M*any of the flavors that make lemon pasta so delicious can also be used to make a sauce for roasted pheasant. Do brine the pheasant before cooking it to ensure that it won't be dry or tough. I cook this in a heavy oval Dutch oven because it holds a bird well without much wasted space, but if you don't have an oval pot, a round one will also do.

This is an elegant dish, suitable for a romantic dinner for two or a special meal with friends. Serve it with rice to absorb the sauce, and surround it with a good assortment of side vegetables.

SERVES 2 TO 4

1 (3-pound) pastured pheasant

Salt and freshly ground black pepper

4 thin slices (3 to 4 ounces) of pastured pork pancetta or bacon

2 tablespoons extra-virgin olive oil

2 tablespoons unsalted butter

½ cup fruity white wine such as Viognier

Finely grated zest and juice of 1 lemon

¼ cup heavy cream

¼ to ½ teaspoon freshly grated nutmeg

Brine the pheasant overnight, rinse it, and blot it dry according to the instructions in the box on page 297.

Salt and pepper the cavity of the bird and layer the pancetta or bacon onto the breast, securing it with kitchen twine wound around the bird.

Melt the olive oil and butter together in an oval or round enameled cast-iron pot over medium-high heat. Brown the pheasant in the hot fat. When the bird is browned on all sides, remove it from the pot and discard most of the fat.

Setting the heat to low, deglaze the pot with the wine, stirring and scraping with a wooden spatula to incorporate any browned bits into the sauce. Add the lemon zest. Return the bird and its juices to the pot, and cook, covered, for about 30 minutes, or until the internal temperature of the bird registers 150 degrees on an instant-read thermometer and the juices are beginning to run clear when the skin is pierced.

Add the cream and a good dusting of nutmeg to the pot and cook over low heat for another 15 minutes, covered, or until an instant-read thermometer registers an internal temperature of 160 degrees. Remove the bird from the pot using tongs, and allow it to rest.

Meanwhile, add the lemon juice to the pot and reduce the sauce for 10 to 15 minutes, until it thickens.

Carve the pheasant and serve it napped with the sauce.

Fennel-Stuffed Grilled Pheasant

t's unusual to grill pheasant, but I find that if it is brined overnight, it stands up well to high heat and smoke and has lots of allure. Use the same procedure to brine pheasant as you use for chicken (see box on page 297). In terms of flavor, fennel pollen is an intense version of ground fennel seeds, but is more expensive and harder to find. If you have it in your pantry, this is a great time to use it. If you don't, regular ground fennel will also work well.

SERVES 2 AS A MAIN COURSE,
4 AS PART OF A MULTICOURSE MEAL

1 (2- to 3-pound) pastured pheasant, whole or butterflied

2 tablespoons ground fennel seeds or wild fennel pollen

2 tablespoons extra-virgin olive oil

Salt and freshly ground black pepper

2 tablespoons chopped mixed fresh herbs such as thyme, oregano, and tarragon

Brine the pheasant overnight, then rinse and blot it dry, as described in the box on page 297.

If the bird is whole, lay it on a cutting board, breast side down, and use a sharp knife or poultry shears to remove the backbone. Press with your hands to break the breastbone and flatten the bird. If you wish, you can also remove the breastbone and ribs, but this is not essential.

Heat a covered gas or charcoal grill to high. Prepare a weight by wrapping a brick or the bottom of a heavy cast-iron pan in foil.

Make a paste with the fennel, olive oil, salt and pepper to taste, and herbs, and put most of it between the skin and the flesh of the breast, taking care not to tear the skin as you work your hand under it. Smear all the remaining paste on the outside skin.

When the grill is hot, lay the bird, flattened, skin side down and position the weight on top. Cook for 7 to 10 minutes, then turn the pheasant over and cook for a similar amount of time.

Let the cooked pheasant rest on a cutting board for 10 minutes, then cut it into 4 pieces. Serve it right away, or let it cool a little before serving.

GUINEA FOWL: Guinea fowl are small and lean, with more dark meat than light, as is common with all birds that free-range. Because they have a slightly gamy edge, fruit complements them beautifully. They can be panfried, roasted, or stewed, whole or in parts. Because the breast meat cooks much more rapidly than the legs, remove the white-meat portion early when roasting or panfrying, or braise the whole bird slowly.

Roast Guinea Fowl Stuffed with Apple, Almonds, and Thyme

*S*tuffing a bird with fruit is always a good idea, whether it is chicken and lemons, duck and oranges, or guinea fowl and apples. Here I've also used an herb butter rub for the breast meat (between the skin and flesh). This is a useful technique for keeping chicken and turkey moist, too, but it is especially important for lean birds like guineas and pheasant.

SERVES 2 EASILY, BUT CAN STRETCH TO 4

1 (2-pound) pastured guinea fowl	2 tablespoons slivered almonds, toasted
Salt and freshly ground black pepper	2 tablespoons fresh thyme leaves
Extra-virgin olive oil	Freshly grated zest of 1 lemon
4 or 5 potatoes, cut into smallish chunks	1 tablespoon unsalted butter, softened
1 firm apple such as Honeycrisp, Fuji, or Granny Smith	¼ cup white wine

Bring the bird to room temperature. Remove the fat from the cavity, along with any innards. Rinse the bird, blot it dry, and rub the inside with salt and pepper.

Heat the oven to 350 degrees. Choose a small cast-iron frying pan, a baking dish, or gratin dish that will hold the bird snugly, and film it with a spoonful of olive oil. Scatter the potato chunks over the bottom of the dish.

Peel, core, and chop the apple into a fine dice. Mix this with the almonds, 1 tablespoon of the thyme, and the lemon zest. Spoon the mixture into the cavity of the bird, packing it in to fill it. Close the cavity by pulling the skin over the opening and securing it with a toothpick. If there is any stuffing left over, scatter this in with the potato chunks.

Mix the remaining 1 tablespoon of thyme with the butter to make a paste, using either a fork and a bowl or a mini food processor. Carefully inserting your fingers under the skin of each half of the breast, open a pocket, and smear the herb butter inside. Loosely tie the legs together with kitchen twine, and drizzle a little more olive oil over all. Pour the white wine into the bottom of the pan.

Roast the guinea fowl for 1 to 1¼ hours, until the internal temperature, taken at the thigh, registers 160 degrees on an instant-read thermometer. Remove the bird from the oven, and transfer it to a board to rest for 5 minutes. Do not turn off the oven.

Transfer the potatoes and any stuffing in the pan to a dish. Cut the legs and thighs off the bird, return them to the pan, flesh side down, and roast them for 10 minutes longer. Let the breast continue to rest on the counter until the dark meat is done.

Carve the breast meat thinly, but leave the legs, thighs, and wings whole. Arrange the meat on a platter with the potatoes and stuffing, drizzling all with the pan juices (which can be defatted or not, as you wish).

Guinea Fowl Stewed with Wine and Pears

Here the guinea fowl is cut into pieces and braised in spiced white wine, while pieces of pear are poached at the same time. Finished with a squeeze of lemon and a small shot of sweetness, this dish is fragrant and satisfying. Once, when I served it to friends, one said with pleasure, "Oh . . . they're pears! I thought they were going to be potatoes."

SERVES 2 TO 4

1 (2½- to 3-pound) pastured guinea fowl, cut into pieces like a chicken

4 tablespoons (½ stick) unsalted butter

1 carrot, coarsely chopped

3 pears, peeled, cored, and cut into ½-inch dice

½ teaspoon ground cinnamon

½ teaspoon ground cardamom

¼ teaspoon ground aniseed (anise seed or ground anise)

1 tablespoon unbleached, all-purpose flour

1¼ cups white wine

1 cup chicken stock, preferably homemade (see page 303), or water

1 teaspoon dried or chopped fresh tarragon

Salt and freshly ground black pepper

1 teaspoon sugar

Freshly squeezed juice of ½ lemon

Steamed rice, for serving

Bring the guinea fowl to room temperature, rinse it, and blot it dry.

Using a heavy braising pot such as an enameled cast-iron casserole or Dutch oven, melt the butter over low heat. Slowly cook the carrot and pear pieces along with the spices, stirring as necessary, until the spices are softly fragrant and the carrot and pears start to become limp, 7 to 10 minutes.

Remove the carrot and pears from the pot with a slotted spoon, raise the heat to medium, and add the guinea fowl pieces. Brown them on all sides, and transfer them to a plate. Sprinkle in the flour and cook it in the fat in the pot until it starts to brown.

Add the wine and stir, scraping to incorporate into the liquid all the browned bits stuck to the pot. Add the stock and continue to cook the liquid down until it is reduced by a quarter. Add the tarragon, along with the reserved carrot and pears and guinea fowl, and salt and pepper to taste.

Reduce the heat to very low and simmer, covered, for 45 to 60 minutes, until the poultry is cooked through and tender. Mix in the sugar and lemon juice. Serve the guinea fowl with its sauce over rice.

Raising Guinea Fowl

I raised guinea fowl for the first time two years ago, primarily because they eat the deer ticks that carry Lyme disease. I kept them as part of a mixed flock that included turkeys, geese, ducks, and a few chickens. Enclosed in portable electric poultry netting, the whole crowd rotated onto pasture after the sheep had moved.

Although everyone I knew warned me about their noisiness (they respond like very vocal watchdogs to anything that comes into view), I found them endearing. First of all, they were beautiful, with lavender-gray speckled feathers. Second, they must have eaten every kind of tick on our land, because no one, not even the dog, came in with ticks from late spring to early autumn.

When it came time for processing, they were hard to catch (they are fast!), and easily panicked, which made caging them distressing. That first year, I brought them to the poultry processor in cages, and they were returned to me as neat shrink-wrapped packages. This year we processed them ourselves, and found it relatively easy to accomplish, particularly since the birds were already confined in their tractor when we were ready to process.

TURKEY: While pastured free-range turkeys can grow as large as 40 pounds, most growers process them earlier. Heritage breeds offer more flavor and texture than conventionally raised industrial turkeys, with well-developed thighs and smaller breasts, but even when a conventional breed is raised naturally, it will look and taste different. Adding fat in the form of a spice paste and finishing the bird with a rich sauce beautifully complements the flavor of whole roasted free-range turkey. Alternatively, birds can be cut up and ground to make a wide variety of different dishes from sausages to meat loaf, or left in parts to make other dishes such as rolled turkey loaf or braises.

Roast Turkey with Ancho Paste and Maple-Coffee Sauce

This unstuffed, straight-up roast turkey reaches new heights with chile and a deep maple-coffee sauce. The spice rub is liveliest if you grind the dried chiles and cumin seeds yourself. Try grating a dusting of bitter chocolate over all just before serving. Thanksgiving may never be the same.

SERVES 6

For the turkey:

1 (8- to 9-pound) pastured turkey

2 dried ancho chiles or 3 tablespoons ancho chile powder

3 teaspoons cumin seeds or 3 teaspoons ground cumin

3 tablespoons sweet paprika

1 tablespoon kosher salt

½ cup extra-virgin olive oil

¼ cup maple syrup or honey

For the sauce:

⅛ teaspoon ground cloves

2 tablespoons ancho chile powder

¼ cup light brown sugar

½ cup hot strong black coffee

1 tablespoon Worcestershire sauce

¼ cup grade-B dark maple syrup

4 tablespoons (½ stick) unsalted butter, cut into small pieces

1 tablespoon grated bitter chocolate (optional)

Bring the turkey to room temperature, rinse it, and blot it dry. Whirl the whole spices, paprika, and salt together in an electric spice grinder or combine the already ground spices with the salt. Stir the spices mixture with the oil to make a paste and rub it all over the turkey, inside and out. Massage it into every nook and cranny. Let the turkey sit at room temperature for about 1 hour to allow the flavors to penetrate.

Heat the oven to 325 degrees and set a rack in the lower third. Arrange a roasting rack inside a roasting pan large enough to hold the turkey, and put the bird on the rack, breast side down. Roast the turkey, feet facing the back oven wall, for about 1 hour, then turn the bird breast side up and roast it until the internal temperature registers 155 degrees on an instant-read thermometer inserted in the thickest part of the thigh. This should take about 2 hours and 20 minutes in total. If the bird starts browning too much on the breast, tent it loosely with silver foil. Baste the turkey as needed, using the fat and juices in the pan.

When the bird hits 160 degrees, increase the oven temperature to 375 degrees and pour the maple syrup over the breast to give the skin a sweet glaze. Cook for another 10 minutes, check to be sure the internal temperature has reached 165 degrees, then remove the bird from the oven and let it rest.

Meanwhile, prepare the sauce. Mix the spices and the sugar, coffee, Worcestershire sauce, and maple syrup together in a saucepan and heat to a boil, stirring. Immediately remove the pan from the heat and whisk in the butter. Keep the sauce warm over the lowest possible heat until you are ready to serve, or leave it, covered, off the heat in a warm kitchen. Whisk the sauce again before drizzling it over the turkey or passing it at the table, grating the bitter chocolate over the meat on a serving platter, if desired.

Brown Turkey Stock

urkey stock can usually substitute for chicken stock in recipes, so it's always a good base to have on hand. When you've paid a lot for a pastured turkey, every bone and bit of meat is a precious resource. When strained and greatly reduced, and with the addition of a roux made with fat and flour, this stock turns into succulent gravy (see below).

If you want a faster stock, or one that is not so brown, you can omit the roasting step. To remove the fat, chill the stock overnight so that it solidifies.

MAKES ABOUT 4 CUPS

4 tablespoons (½ stick) unsalted butter

1 pastured turkey carcass with meat clinging to the bones, plus the neck, gizzard, heart, and wings

Salt and freshly ground black pepper

1 onion, unpeeled

4 or 5 whole cloves, pushed into the onion

3 carrots, unpeeled, cut into rough chunks

2 stalks celery, cut into rough chunks

2 bay leaves

1 teaspoon black peppercorns

1 cup dry sherry

Preheat the oven to 375 degrees. Melt the butter. Put the turkey parts in a roasting pan and salt and pepper them all over lightly. Brush the turkey parts with butter, and roast them at 425 degrees for 1 to 2 hours, basting frequently with the fat, until the bones and meat are darkly fragrant.

Put the entire contents of the roasting pan into a large pot, along with the onion and cloves, carrots, celery, bay leaves, and peppercorns. Deglaze the roasting pan with the sherry on the stovetop over high heat, stirring and scraping to incorporate any caramelized bits into the pan juices. Add this to the stockpot along with enough cold water to cover the bones by 2 to 3 inches, and cook the stock at a slow simmer, partially covered, for 4 to 6 hours.

When the stock is rich and richly colored, pour it through a strainer and discard the solids. Let it cool, and then pour it into refrigerator containers (the 1-quart size are most practical for soups), and refrigerate it for several hours or overnight. Remove the fat that collects at the top (you can use this fat for making gravy, see below).

Turkey Gravy

ulia Moskin's story on gravy, which appeared in the New York Times, *introduced me to using turkey fat for a roux-based gravy. Gravy made this way simply sings with all-turkey notes. If you don't have reserved turkey fat, however, butter is a good substitute.*

MAKES 1 CUP

1 tablespoon chilled pastured turkey fat or butter

1 tablespoon unbleached all-purpose flour

1 cup strong reduced Brown Turkey Stock (see above)

Salt and freshly ground black pepper

1 tablespoon unsalted butter or heavy cream

Melt the turkey fat in a skillet over medium-high heat. Sprinkling with one hand and whisking with the other, add the flour gradually and incorporate it into the hot fat. Cook this roux for 1 to 2 minutes, until it turns golden and fragrant. Reduce the heat to medium-low.

Add the stock ¼ cup at a time, thoroughly incorporating it into the roux after each addition. Add salt and pepper to taste. Cook at a low simmer, continuing to whisk, until thick. Add the butter or cream and serve.

Kenji's Turkey Sausage

Fortunately, Kenji and I had hog casings in the refrigerator and pork fat in the freezer when we set out to make this sausage. You can always make sausage without casings, but extra fat is essential. A good grinder also makes a big difference, as does partially freezing the meat and fat, along with the grinding and stuffing attachments.

The basic sausage formula is 80 percent lean meat, 20 percent fat. These percentages are by weight, so I computed it in grams for ease of mathematics.

MAKES 8 FAT LINKS, 5 INCHES LONG AND 3 INCHES AROUND

800 grams lean pastured turkey meat from the legs and thighs, cut into rough cubes

200 grams pastured pork fat, cut into rough cubes

1 pastured turkey liver

20 grams kosher salt

1 teaspoon sweet (*dulce*) pimentón de la Vera (smoked Spanish paprika)

½ teaspoon ground coriander

½ teaspoons ground cumin seeds

½ teaspoon freshly ground black pepper

½ teaspoon ground red pepper

3 cloves garlic, smashed or finely minced

1 long hog casing

Combine the meat and fat with the liver, salt, spices, and garlic. Chill in the freezer, along with the grinding and sausage-stuffing attachments, a small sheet pan, and a medium-sized metal mixing bowl, for at least 30 minutes.

Rinse the hog casing in running water and reserve it in a bowl of fresh water.

When you are ready to proceed, assemble the grinder. Force the meat mixture through the grinder, using the pushing pestle, allowing it all to fall into the chilled mixing bowl. (If you want a finer texture, you can grind the meat a second time.) Use a crumpled paper towel to push any remaining meat through the grinder by pushing it down with the pestle into the shaft while the grinder is on. Turn off the machine before grinding the paper through it.

Return the bowl of ground meat briefly to the freezer while you prepare for stuffing. Remove the grinding attachment and put on the sausage-stuffing attachment.

Put the hog casing onto the stuffing horn, evenly pushing it into place with your hands. Leave a small end drooping off the horn and tie a knot in it. Position the chilled sheet pan so that it can catch the newly cased sausage.

Using the pushing pestle, push the ground meat through the hopper with one hand while guiding the casing with the other as it fills with meat. Your goal is to prevent air bubbles, so push the meat through at a steady pace. Make one very long sausage, winding it into a coil onto the chilled sheet pan as it grows. At the very end of the process, with the pestle, again push a crumpled paper towel into the hopper to force out all the meat that remains. Turn off the machine before you grind the paper.

When all the meat has been fed into the casing, tie a knot in the open end. Holding the sausage in your hands, create links by twisting a few times every 5 inches or so. Make your twists in opposite directions each time (first twist toward yourself, then for the next one, twist the other way).

Lightly puncture the sausage links all over with a toothpick.

Fill a deep frying pan or sauté pan halfway with water and gently poach the sausage, uncovered, over medium-low heat for 5 to 8 minutes, until it is cooked through. Keep the water at a very low simmer the whole time. Remove the sausage from the water and let it cool.

At this point, if you will not be using it right way, the sausage can be wrapped for refrigeration or shrink-wrapped (or otherwise tightly wrapped) for freezing. It will keep for several days in the refrigerator or up to 3 months in the freezer.

Turkey Sausage Tapas

Use your homemade turkey sausage (see page 319) as an appetizer by frying it crisp and serving it on a platter with good mustard and sweet relish or chutney.

SERVES 4 TO 6

3 to 5 Kenji's Turkey Sausage links (see page 319)

1 to 2 tablespoons extra-virgin olive oil

3 tablespoons grainy mustard

3 tablespoons green tomato relish, mango chutney, or other sweet salsa

Cut the poached sausage into ½-inch-thick slices, and panfry the slices in olive oil until they are browned and crisp. Serve them as an appetizer with a small bowl of the mustard and another of the sweet relish or chutney for dipping. Provide toothpicks so guests can spear the sausage pieces.

Turkey Meat Loaf with Tarragon and Sweet Tomato Glaze

Whether you grind your own turkey or buy it already ground (I buy Vermont-raised ground turkey from either Misty Knoll Farms or Stonewood Farms at my local co-op), you will have the best success if your blend is comprised of equal parts light and dark meat. This is a very moist and flavorful meat loaf that makes a great family meal as well as hearty sandwiches, but it is also excellent to serve for entertaining.

SERVES 8

1 tablespoon plus
1 teaspoon extra-virgin
olive oil

4 pastured eggs

1 large onion, cut into
chunks

1 clove garlic

1 carrot, cut into chunks

½ pound mushrooms

1 teaspoon kosher salt

Freshly ground black
pepper

1¼ pounds ground
pastured turkey

2 teaspoons
Worcestershire sauce

½ cup fresh chopped
parsley

1 tablespoon fresh or dried
tarragon leaves

¼ cup ketchup

½ cup cooked oatmeal

1 tablespoon honey

Heat the oven to 400 degrees and set a rack in the upper middle. Lightly brush a standard metal bread pan (4 x 7½ x 3 inches) with the 1 teaspoon olive oil and set it aside.

Cook 2 of the eggs by putting them into cold water, bringing the water to a boil, and then turning off the heat, covering the pot, and letting the eggs sit for 10 minutes. Put the eggs into ice water for a few minutes and then peel them and cut them in half lengthwise. Reserve. Beat the remaining 2 eggs in a small bowl, and set them aside.

Using a food processor fitted with the steel blade or a chef's knife, chop the onion, garlic, carrot, and mushrooms together into small pieces, pulsing if you are using a food processor to maintain separate textures and prevent turning the mixture into a paste.

Heat a sauté pan or frying pan and add the 1 tablespoon olive oil over medium-low heat. When the oil has thinned and become fragrant, add the vegetables and stir them very occasionally, cooking them slowly until they are darker and fragrant, about 15 minutes. Transfer the mixture to a large mixing bowl.

Add the 1 teaspoon salt and pepper to taste, along with the turkey, Worcestershire sauce, parsley, tarragon, 2 tablespoons of the ketchup, the cooked oatmeal, and the reserved beaten eggs. Mix this all together with your hands or a rubber spatula. It will be very wet and gloppy.

Scrape half of the turkey mixture into the prepared pan. Lay the hard-boiled egg halves in a row down the length of the pan, yolk side up. Scrape the rest of the turkey mixture on top. Mix the remaining 2 tablespoons ketchup with the honey and spread this over the top.

Put the loaf pan on a cookie sheet (in case it overflows), and roast the loaf for 1 hour, or until the internal temperature registers 160 degrees on an instant-read thermometer. Let the meat sit and settle for 5 to 10 minutes before serving, or serve it at slightly warmer than room temperature an hour or so later.

Roasted Turkey Breast Roll

This is a homemade version of the kind of round turkey roll you see at the deli. It's perfect to serve both as a roast and as a filling for fine sandwiches. It is absurdly easy to make, and you will never have to buy those additive-rich, water-plumped industrial cold cuts again! It is very beautiful when sliced, as the crosswise pattern shows up on each piece. Gravy made from homemade turkey stock (see page 318) is an ideal accompaniment to this roll when it's served for dinner.

MAKES ENOUGH FOR MANY SANDWICHES, OR A DINNER ENTRÉE FOR 6

1 skin-on pastured turkey breast (about 3 pounds)

2 tablespoons Red Barn Spice Rub (see page 32)

Extra-virgin olive oil (for entrée only)

Heat the oven to 275 degrees and set a rack in the center.

To separate the turkey breast from the bone, first remove the skin in one piece and reserve it. Using a fillet or boning knife, cut off one side of the breast and then the other by carefully cutting along the breastbone, following the bone toward the wing and back again to free the meat.

You should have two large breast halves. Rub each with the spice blend on both sides. Lay one boneless, skinless breast half on top of the other, matching the thick side of one with the thin side of the other so that they form an even block.

Cut 8 lengths of kitchen twine about 18 inches long and lay them in a vertical pattern on a cutting board 2 to 3 inches apart.

Put the reserved skin on the cutting board and lay the block of breast meat on top, aligning a long end of the meat with one long end of the skin. Starting at a long end, roll the meat and skin together, using the skin to hold and keep the roll tight. Secure the roll by tying each length of string into a knot around it, taking care to keep the roll tightly constrained. Tie a longer piece of string around the roll lengthwise to make everything a little more secure.

Set the meat, seam side down, into an oval cast-iron gratin dish or a small cast-iron frying pan. Roast for 1 to 1½ hours, until the meat's internal temperature registers 150 degrees on an instant-read thermometer. Remove the meat from the oven and let it rest for 15 minutes, or until its internal temperature rises to 160 degrees.

To use the roll for cold cuts, let it cool to room temperature, wrap it very well, and refrigerate it until it's needed. Slice the chilled roll very thinly all at once or as needed.

To use the roll as a dinner entrée, rest it before cutting it into ⅓- to ½-inch slices. Panfry each slice over high heat in a little olive oil until crisp on the edges, and serve warm.

Raising Turkeys

When I first raised turkeys, I started out with six birds, but ended up with four, thanks to predators. Although I ordered Broad–Breasted Bronze birds, I received conventional White turkeys instead. (Apparently it's not unusual to get different breeds of birds from the one you ordered, especially when they are ordered from large stores, such as my local Agway, rather than directly from specialty hatcheries. (I could have refused them, but then I wouldn't have had turkeys to raise.) The Bronze birds I had hoped for have beautiful marked feathers, and these were the feathers of choice for Native American headdresses.

The turkeys lived, along with the rest of the mixed flock, in a mobile poultry tractor within portable fencing. They grew from tiny birds to full processing size in 5 months, subsisting on nothing but small amounts of organic grain, fresh water, and whatever they found in the pasture.

DUCK: Cooking my own Rouen pastured duck was revelatory—it was tasty, but also lean and chewy. There was plenty of duck fat that rendered as it cooked, turning the potatoes layered under the bird to delectable morsels—but the amount of fat rendered was less than half the amount from a conventionally raised Pekin duck.

Roast Duck à l'Orange

Don't think, "Ho hum," and turn the page—this is the real thing, made with fresh orange, not with one of those nasty packets filled with sweet sludge. I use Nela Rubinstein's unique massage method from Nela's Cookbook, *and I've been serving this duck recipe for nearly twenty-five years with great pleasure. Give it a try, and you'll understand why the combination of rich duck and acid oranges is a match made in heaven. If you use a Pekin duck, you'll also harvest about a pint of duck fat to use for other dishes.*

SERVES 3 OR 4

1 (4- to 5-pound) pastured duck

Kosher salt and freshly ground black pepper

4 juice oranges such as Valencia (not navel)

⅓ cup sugar

1 tablespoon orange liqueur such as Grand Marnier or triple sec

Rinse the duck inside and out, blot it dry, and bring it to room temperature. Heat the oven to 325 degrees and set a rack in the center. Choose a pan that will hold the duck fairly closely but with some room to hold the fat it will exude. A shallow pan is much better than a deep one (which will steam the duck as it cooks). Choose a clean pint jar to hold the duck fat you'll be saving.

Using lots of pressure, massage the duck, the breast area especially, to begin to break up the fat. Give it a good 3 to 5 minutes of massage, even though you may feel silly doing it.

Using a fork, prick the skin all over, taking care not to penetrate the flesh. (The bird should be heavily speckled with pricks.) Lightly salt and pepper the duck inside and out. Put it in the pan, breast side up, and place it in the hot oven, feet facing the back wall. Roast for 45 minutes.

Pour the fat from the pan into the clean jar. Return the duck to the oven, raise the temperature to 350 degrees, and roast for another 45 minutes, removing the fat with a bulb baster as necessary during this time.

Use a pointed knife to slash the skin (but not the flesh) at the junction of thigh and body, and prick the whole breast and thigh area again with a fork. Return the duck to the oven for another 30 minutes.

Start the sauce by first zesting and then juicing the oranges. If you are not using a Microplane zester, peel off the zest (carefully excluding the white pith) and chop it into fine slivers. Put the fresh juice, the zest, and the sugar in a small saucepan and bring it to a boil. Add the orange liqueur. Reduce the heat to low and cook the mixture for about 10 minutes, or until it is reduced and slightly syrupy.

Pour this sauce over the duck as it cooks and continue to baste the duck with the sauce while cooking it for a final 30 minutes. (The total time for the duck is about 2½ hours, or until the internal temperature registers between 160 and 165 degrees on an instant-read thermometer.)

Transfer the duck to a platter to rest for 15 minutes. Meanwhile, cook down the contents of the pan, scraping to incorporate all the crusty browned bits into the sauce. If you have been removing the fat as it cooks, this liquid will not be fatty at all! Just before carving the duck, pour any juices it has released back into the pan sauce. Pour the sauce into a gravy boat and serve it alongside the duck.

Pan-Sautéed Duck Breast
with Rose Petal Jam

or those who can buy Pekin duck in pieces, this is a simple dish that's both flavorful and exotic. The traditional way to use duck pieces is to cook the breast like steak and to use the legs and thighs for confit. If you can't buy duck in pieces, you can easily cut several up to make packages of different parts, freezing some for later. Rose petal jam is available in fancy food stores, and dried rose petals are found in Middle Eastern stores (or in a nearby garden, perhaps, as long as they are unsprayed). In place of the rose petal jam, you could use any delicately flavored jam or good honey instead—lavender honey works equally well (when I use that, I garnish the dish with a scattering of dried lavender flowers).

This is my idea of a great romantic dinner. Duck is the red meat of the poultry world, and eating it is like eating a great steak.

SERVES 2

2 large pastured duck breast halves	6 tablespoons rose petal jam
2 teaspoons sea salt	1 tablespoon white wine
2 teaspoons freshly ground black pepper	Dried rose petals, for garnish
4 teaspoons finely chopped fresh thyme leaves	

Using a sharp knife, score the skin through the fat, cutting a diamond pattern, but do not cut the meat. Season the breasts with the salt, pepper, and thyme, and let the meat rest for about 1 hour.

Heat a cast-iron skillet over medium heat, and place the duck fatty skin side down, immediately lowering the heat to prevent burning. As you cook, a lot of fat will be rendered from the duck skin; pour it off and save it as it gets excessive.

Cook the duck until browned, about 4 minutes, then turn it and cook the other side for the same amount of time. Top each breast with a couple of teaspoonfuls of the jam and gently spread it onto the meat. Cook for another minute, then repeat the process on the other side. Remove the duck to a cutting board and let it rest for at least 5 minutes before cutting it on the bias into ¼-inch slices and arranging them on a platter.

While the meat is resting, add the wine to the pan juices, and deglaze the pan, stirring and scraping with a wooden spatula to incorporate any browned bits into the sauce. Drizzle the sliced meat with the pan juices and garnish with dried rose petals.

Serve warm.

Leaving Food Alone

Because I have the pleasure of cooking with a number of culinary guests every year, I am able to see where people sometimes can go wrong in the kitchen. One thing I've observed is that it is often hard for folks to leave the food they're cooking alone—they nudge it and turn it and poke it, and so it never gets a chance to develop a crust or *fond* (that's the tasty browned bits that form and then stick to the bottom of the pan, to be scraped up when you deglaze). Flavors unfold and develop slowly as foods cook in their own juices, and they must be left undisturbed in order to do this. It is always a good idea to keep a watchful eye on things, but don't fiddle with them unnecessarily.

Duck Breast with Gingered Cinnamon Peaches

his uses a large whole magret *breast from a Moulard duck.* Magret *is both larger and fattier than the more common Pekin duck breast, and it will easily feed four to six people. Trim off as much fat as possible (and save it to render) before massaging and scoring the skin. Serve this with something wonderful, such as an orzo salad (see page 364) or wild rice. It is a rich and celebratory dish, worthy of an anniversary or birthday dinner party. The cooking takes under an hour altogether and offers a bonus yield of at least a cup of rendered duck fat. It is also a great way to use underripe peaches, if that's all you can find.*

SERVES 4 TO 6

1 (2¾- to 3-pound) pastured *magret* duck breast	2 fresh peaches, each with an X cut on the bottom
Salt and freshly ground black pepper	2 tablespoons unsalted butter
1½ teaspoons ground ginger	1 tablespoon honey
	1 tablespoon brandy
¾ teaspoon ground cinnamon	
Zest and juice of 1 lemon	

Split the breast in two and trim it of any excess fat along the side edges (not under the skin), and put the fat pieces aside for rendering. Massage the breast halves with your fingertips fairly vigorously to break down the fat. Using a sharp knife, carefully score the halves in a diamond pattern, cutting through the skin and fat but not into the meat.

Combine salt and pepper to taste, 1 teaspoon of the ginger, ½ teaspoon of the cinnamon, and the lemon zest, and rub this mixture over the meat on both sides. Cover the meat with plastic wrap, and refrigerate for at least 1 hour, turning once.

Prepare a bowl of ice water. Boil a large pot of water and put the whole peaches in it. When they bob to the surface with split skins, transfer them immediately to the ice water. Drain the peaches and peel off and discard the skins. Cut the fruit into small pieces over a bowl to catch all the juices. Set aside.

When ready to cook, choose a cast-iron frying pan large enough to hold both halves of the breast and heat it until it is very hot. Lay the meat in, skin side down. Immediately reduce the heat to low, and brown the meat very slowly. You should cook it for about 25 minutes on the skin and fat side, and about 20 minutes on the flesh side. The goal here is medium-rare meat—it will be pink in the center, like steak. The lower heat helps the fat to render while the meat and skin still cook. As the fat accumulates in the pan, pour it off into a jar through a strainer to eliminate bits of crust. When the duck is done, transfer it to a plate to rest while you begin making the sauce.

After pouring off all but 2 tablespoons of the fat from the pan, gently sauté the peach pieces over medium heat until they are fragrant, soft, and jammy, about 3 minutes. Stir in the butter, lemon juice, honey, and brandy, and add the remaining ½ teaspoon ginger and ¼ teaspoon cinnamon. Simmer, stirring, until the sauce is slightly reduced, 3 to 5 minutes. Remove the pan from the heat and set it aside.

Cut the duck breast halves on the bias into thin slices, and add any juices that have accumulated on the plate to the sauce. Arrange the slices on a platter, spoon the sauce over each slice, and serve warm.

Duck Breeds

Most of the duck you can buy at retail is Pekin duck, usually sold as whole birds. It's possible to find duck parts in some specialty stores and on the Web, and in these venues you can find other breeds of duck such as Moulard (when this duck has been raised for foie gras, the meat is called *magret*). It's quite a different experience to cook a *magret* breast than the breast meat from a Pekin. *Magret* takes nearly three times longer to cook—it's much larger and much fattier, and (I think) even more delicious.

DUCK POULTRY

Duck Leg Confit

Confit

Confits are a very old and traditional way of keeping food, and were used on ships as well as on land to preserve food for months at a time. I've cooked a number of confits, including pork and vegetable ones, but preserving duck legs (and wings) is the classic application; the breast is usually eaten immediately.

The method is simple: The duck legs and thighs are first salt-and-herb-cured for a few days in the refrigerator, then the salt is brushed off and they are cooked very slowly in the oven in a pot with rendered fat for about 3 hours. (Sometimes, as in my recipe, they are browned first before fat-cooking.) You can use duck fat or goose fat to make your confit; the flavor is slightly different with each but not dramatically so.

When the meat is cooked through, it is removed, the fat is strained, and the legs and thighs are put in a sterile wide-mouthed jar and covered with the strained fat. This mixture will last as long as 3 to 6 months, refrigerated. (Note that you can make confit without doing the salt cure or browning first, but the shelf life will be much shorter.)

When you are ready to use a confit, heat the jar in a bowl of hot water and pour out the contents (so as not to tear the meat by pulling it). Lay each piece of meat, skin side down, in a hot cast-iron skillet over medium-high heat to crisp the skin. Serve the crisped and heated confit of duck shredded on salads, add it whole or in chunks to long-cooked bean dishes (such as cassoulet), or serve the whole pieces hot and crisp on a bed of watercress or arugula, or on a potato cake made with duck fat (see page 331) or bacon fat (see page 257). You can also glaze the duck with a sweet sauce such as preserved fruit, maple syrup, or honey, by putting it in a 450-degree oven for 10 to 15 minutes, then present it as an entrée with rice or another starch.

This is a proper confit, made with meat that has been salt cured, then browned, and then cooked in fat. If you want to use the confit right away, you can jump straight to the fat-cooking without the two initial steps—they are mostly for preserving. But if preserving is what you are after, bear in mind that you need to salt and spice the meat at least overnight, then to wipe it down very well before proceeding to brown the meat in the oven, and then to cook it through, very slowly, in fat. Unless you have been saving goose or duck fat for quite a while, it's likely that you'll have to purchase most of the fat you need, but you can reuse it for up to 6 months, provided it has been kept clean and strained, sealed in a sterile jar, and well-chilled.

NOTE: You will need to sterilize the jar for the confit just before you fill it, either by submerging it in boiling water or putting it through the "high-temperature" cycle of your dishwasher. Once cooked and put into the jar, this confit will keep for up to 6 months in the refrigerator.

MAKES 1 HALF-GALLON JAR FILLED WITH DUCK CONFIT AND DUCK FAT

4 skin-on pastured duck legs and thighs (about 4 pounds)

½ cup kosher salt

1 tablespoon crushed juniper berries

Freshly ground black pepper

4 dried bay leaves, crushed

1 tablespoon fresh thyme leaves, crumbled

For more flavor (optional):
- 1 teaspoon ground cumin
- 1 teaspoon ground coriander
- 1 teaspoon ground cinnamon
- 1 teaspoon ground cloves

- 1 teaspoon ground allspice
- 1 teaspoon ground ginger

6 to 8 cups rendered duck or goose fat (see page 331), at room temperature

Take the duck out of the refrigerator, rinse it, and blot it dry.

Mix or pound together in a mortar and pestle the salt, juniper, pepper, bay leaves, thyme, and other spices, if using. Rub this over the duck pieces on both sides (don't miss the little flap near the leg), put them in a covered dish, and refrigerate them at least overnight or up to 2 days.

When you are ready to proceed, bring the duck to room temperature and carefully wipe off all the salt and spices with paper towels. Clean off every nook and cranny, aiming for a completely clean piece of meat. (This is important, because confit can easily turn out too salty if the rub is left on.)

Heat the oven to 425 degrees and position a rack in the upper third. Put the duck, skin side up, in the pan, and brown it for 15 minutes in the oven. Afterward, let it cool slightly in the pan, then remove the duck and the fat from the pan and reserve separately.

Reduce the oven heat to 275 degrees and move the rack to the middle position. Choose a heavy ovenproof pot with sides high enough to hold the meat along with 6 to 8 cups of melted fat to cover it. You could use a clay casserole such as a Chinese sand pot, an enameled Dutch oven, or a braising pan.

Put the duck in the pot, and pour or scoop the fat over it to cover the meat. (If a little bit of bony leg end sticks out, don't worry.) Put the pot in the 275 degree oven on the middle shelf, and let the duck cook for 2 to 2½ hours, until the meat is pulling off the bones.

While the duck slow-cooks, pour the fat left from browning through a paper coffee filter to strain out the solids. Pour the strained fat into a jar for another use (such as Paris chicken; see page 332) and refrigerate it, labeled. (This fat, which has cooked at a relatively high heat, will taste different from the low-temperature fat used to make the confit).

When the duck is ready, use tongs to transfer the pieces to the sterile jar. Pour or ladle the hot fat over them so that all the meat is covered, topping off the jar with additional fat to make a seal. Age the confit in the refrigerator for at least 1 week or up to 3 months before using.

Raising Ducks and Geese

When we lived in Denmark twenty years ago, duck and goose were readily available and became some of our favorite meats. They are both much harder to find here in New England, especially in free-range pastured form. That's why, for the first time two summers ago, I raised my own. I chose two French breeds: small bronze Rouen ducks and beautiful gray Toulouse geese.

Raising waterfowl on a small scale is simple—they need only a little wading pool to swim in, lots of good grass, fresh water, and a portion of grain pellets, along with waterfowl companions and the odd windfall apple to nibble on,

Our duck and goose, who each lost its mate to a fox after a brief walk in the woods, became inseparable companions. After it became clear that complete free-ranging was too dangerous, and we put them inside electric poultry netting with the other birds, they never left each other's sides.

I grew so fond of them that I didn't want to process them, but they didn't get along with the laying hens (who had the only winter-proof housing), so we reluctantly concluded that we had to stick to our original plan. I processed them sadly, and cooked them with respect.

Poultry-Processing Workshop

One mild November day, NOFA (Northeast Organic Farming Association) sponsored an on-the-farm processing workshop for poultry, and I brought my waterfowl to learn how to process them. Until that day, I had had my fowl processed at a commercial processor, delivering live birds and coming back a week later to pick up neat vacuum-sealed packages. I wasn't sure if I wanted to actually wield the knife, pluck, or eviscerate my own birds, but I wanted to learn how it was done.

The process was remarkably quiet, respectful, and efficient, although I stayed firmly in the onlooker camp. Chickens, turkeys, and my goose and duck were each dispatched in turn, and many of the participants took an active role in each step of the process.

Here is how it is done:

Before processing, birds are not fed for 24 hours, and have only water to drink to cleanse their systems.

The first step is bleeding. The bird is set, upside down, into a killing cone (either manufactured for the purpose or a homemade version constructed from a plastic bucket). The bird's head is drawn down through the hole, its beak is weighted with a weight on a hook, and the neck is swiftly cut with a very sharp boning knife, first on one side of the trachea, then on the other. A bucket set on the ground below collects the blood, which is later composted.

When the bird has stopped moving, it is removed from the cone, and the head is cut off completely. The body is then scalded, or placed in a large pot of water heated to 140 degrees (for chickens and turkeys) or 150 degrees (for waterfowl; there is also a little dish-washing liquid in this water to dissolve the oil on the feathers). The birds are swished around in the hot water until a gentle tug on their feathers indicates that they are ready to be plucked—this takes mere minutes per bird if the water was at a proper temperature.

At the workshop, we tried three different methods for plucking—hand plucking, an electric rotary tabletop plucker, and a much larger electric barrel plucker called a Whizbang. While the electric versions were indeed faster and easier, it was not too hard to do it by hand, either. The feathers were collected in a bucket to compost.

Eviscerating is the part of the process that demanded the most skill. First the feet and neck were cut off. Laying the bird on its back and using a sharp knife, a V-shaped incision was made around the vent (the bird's anus), and it was removed and discarded. This cut revealed a cavity familiar to anyone who has ever cooked a chicken.

Reaching into the bird's cavity, one could feel all the internal organs. A careful swipe and turn with one hand was often sufficient to dislodge everything. If not, a bit more light scraping emptied the bird. On the board, we could see the liver, heart, gizzard (which needs to be carefully cut at the seam and inverted before being skinned), lungs, and arteries. When we processed old hens, we found as many as twenty unlaid eggs of various sizes, all without shells and brilliantly yellow. Such unborn eggs can be layered in salt in a jar until dry and hard, and then grated over pasta or salads for a yolky treat.

Once the bird was clean and the offal separated and packaged, the birds were washed and set in a cooler filled with ice and water for chilling. At the end of the afternoon, workshop participants took their own birds home to package and freeze. (It's never a good idea to cook a bird the same day it has been processed—it needs at least 24 hours to rest before cooking.)

It was a remarkable experience to learn these skills. I have since practiced them this past season with my own chickens and guinea fowl, and I like the idea that I can learn to take my birds from chick to table without anyone's help, using low-technology methods.

GOOSE: Geese have high arched breasts, large cavities, and meager wing meat, so the best part of the goose (aside from its valuable fat and liver) tends to be breast and thigh meat, along with crisp skin. A 10-pound goose easily feeds six people, and can be stretched to eight with sufficient accompaniments. Such a bird will yield about a cup and a half of fat after straining.

Beer-Braised Goose with Apples

Adapted mostly from Anne Willan's French Country Cooking, *this method of roasting a goose starts at a high temperature and then finishes at a moderate temperature, producing a bird with a crisp skin and rendering plenty of great goose fat. I like to serve goose in the Danish Christmas manner, alongside red cabbage braised in goose fat and caramelized potatoes (see pages 334 and 365).*

SERVES 6 TO 8

1 (10-pound) pastured goose

Kosher salt and freshly ground black pepper

5 assorted tart heirloom apples

8 ounces dark beer

1 cup white wine, vermouth, or apple cider

1 tablespoon heavy cream

Bring the goose to room temperature, rinse it, and blot it dry inside and out. Using both hands, massage the breast with a good amount of pressure to break up the fat under the skin. Use a fork to prick the skin all over, taking care not to pierce the flesh.

Season the goose with a generous amount of salt and pepper, inside and out. Let it sit at room temperature for 1 hour. Meanwhile, set an oven rack in the center and heat the oven to 450 degrees—give it plenty of time to get entirely to temperature.

Peel and core the apples, leaving them whole. Stuff them into the cavity of the goose, and secure the vent with toothpicks. Tie the legs together with kitchen twine. Have a bowl ready to hold the fat that renders as you cook.

Choose a roasting pan only slightly bigger than the goose (this helps to keep the fat from burning), along with a rack that fits inside it. Put the goose, breast side up, on the rack. Pour the beer over the goose, and put the bird in the oven, feet toward the back wall. Roast it for 40 minutes. The skin will have started browning and crisping by this stage.

Remove the goose from the oven and take it off the rack for a moment so that you can pour the accumulated goose fat into the bowl. Return the goose to the rack, this time with the back facing up. Prick the skin again, taking the usual care not to pierce the flesh. Using a turkey basting tool or a brush or spoon, baste the back of the bird with the fat and pan juices and return it to the oven. Reduce the heat to 350 degrees and cook for 1 hour longer, basting every 15 minutes with the juices from the pan.

Remove the goose from the oven and the rack, and again pour off the accumulated goose fat. Return the goose to the rack, breast side up; prick the skin again; and roast it for a further 30 to 40 minutes, until it is deeply browned and crisp. The juices that flow when you prick the skin at the thighs should run clear, and an instant-read thermometer inserted deeply in the thigh should register 170 degrees. Transfer the goose to a tray and let it rest for 20 minutes.

Pour all the remaining fat into your bowl and reserve for another use. Put the roasting pan on a burner on top of the stove and deglaze it with the wine, vermouth, or cider, stirring and scraping to incorporate any caramelized bits into the sauce. Reduce the liquid by half and remove it from the heat. Stir in the cream and keep the sauce warm over very low heat until you are ready to serve—do not allow it to boil. Just before serving, transfer it to a gravy pitcher.

Carve the legs and thighs off the goose and set them on a platter, then do the same with the wings. Cut the breast meat into thin slices and set them on the platter, along with the cooked apples from the interior of the bird. Serve as soon as the meat is carved, along with the gravy.

Stuffed Goose Neck

When we farm-processed the goose I raised, I saved the neck and liver and froze them. I remember my grandmother talking about eating goose neck with pleasure, and I wanted to try it for myself. Although she never gave me the recipe, I invented this one based on my memory of her memories. The neck is boned and stuffed with a forcemeat made from bread crumbs, egg, cheese, and liver. It is then rolled inside a cabbage leaf—actually, I meant to use the skin, but it was accidentally shredded—and poached in stock. It's served sliced, with salsa verde and potatoes.

The salsa—essentially a salad dressing with extras—works well with any mix of greens or potatoes. For those who don't want to attempt stuffing a poultry neck or don't have those ingredients available, let me tell you that salsa verde with boiled potatoes is a great treat in its own right.

SERVES 4 TO 6 AS A FIRST COURSE

1 pastured goose neck

½ cup finely chopped flat-leaf parsley

1 clove garlic

1 pastured goose liver

⅓ cup bread crumbs, preferably homemade

1 egg, beaten

2 tablespoons freshly grated Parmigiano-Reggiano

Salt and freshly ground black pepper

1 large cabbage leaf

About 6 cups water

1 carrot, cut into large chunks

1 stalk celery, cut into thirds

½ onion, unpeeled

1 clove, stuck into the onion half

1 to 2 pounds small new potatoes

For the salsa verde:

½ cup fresh flat-leaf parsley leaves

2 tablespoons salt-packed capers, well rinsed

2 salt-packed anchovies, rinsed and filleted

2 hard-boiled eggs, sliced

3 tablespoons extra-virgin olive oil

1 tablespoon red wine vinegar

Using a sharp knife, slice along the length of the neck and slowly and carefully detach from the vertebrae the flesh (and the skin, if you can), using your fingers and scraping with the knife to remove the whole neck bone. Reserve the skin, and discard the bone or save it for stock.

Make the stuffing by combining the parsley, garlic, and liver, finely mincing them with a chef's knife or pulsing them in a food processor (taking care not to go too far in the direction of a purée). Mix in the bread crmbs, egg, cheese, and salt and pepper.

Lay the meat out on the cabbage leaf arranged flat on a board and top with the stuffing. (If you have been able to save the skin in one piece, you can use it in place of the cabbage.) Roll the leaf (or skin) around the stuffing so that it makes a neat, firm cylinder, folding in the sides as you go, the way you roll a burrito. Secure the roll with kitchen twine using the same method used to tie a stuffed and rolled roast (see page 26), and put the neck roll in a medium-sized saucepan.

Add at least 6 cups water and the carrot chunks, celery, and the onion with the clove, and bring the water slowly to a boil. Reduce the heat to the lowest temperature at which the water makes slow bubbles, and poach the neck roll at a simmer for 40 minutes, or until the juices run clear when it is pricked with a knife.

Meanwhile, boil the potatoes and prepare the salsa verde. Using a chef's knife, chop the parsley, capers, anchovies, and eggs together, or carefully pulse them in a food processor (working to keep a chunky texture rather than a purée). Add the oil and vinegar and mix in gently.

Remove the roll from the pan and let it cool. (Strain and save the stock for soup.) Remove and discard the twine. Cut the roll into ½-inch rounds and arrange several of these on each plate along with a spoonful or two of potatoes. Spoon the chunky salsa over all.

POULTRY FAT: Goose fat can be "brown," or poured from the roasting pan as a goose cooks, or it can be "white," which means it was deliberately rendered slowly from lumps of fat. Brown fat is great for cooking savory dishes, while white fat is good for anything, but is best for pastry. It takes a number of birds to collect enough fat to render "white" in one session.

Rendering Poultry Fat

Whether chicken, goose, or duck fat, rendered poultry fat is immensely useful in roasting and frying because it adds flavor, and has a high smoke point (about 375 degrees, in contrast to butter's 350 degrees). Any crisp bits left in the pan as the fat renders are deliciously crunchy additions to salads (see Gribenes *below). When preparing a bird for the oven, tear off any lumps of fat and set them aside in a labeled plastic freezer bag. When you've collected several cups, it's time to slowly render the fat into culinary gold. After rendering, be sure to sterilize your jar before filling it to insure the fat will last as long as possible.*

MAKES ABOUT 1 CUP

1 pound pastured goose, chicken, or duck fat, cut into small pieces

About 2 cups water

Put the fat pieces in a deep, heavy pan (a Dutch oven or a ceramic Chinese sand pot are both good choices) and cover them with the water. Cook the fat over very low heat for about 2 hours.

The water insulates the fat and protects it from browning as it melts. Check its level occasionally to make sure it does not evaporate too quickly. Eventually, during about the last 30 minutes of the cooking time, it will all boil away, leaving clean, perfectly rendered fat. As the cooking time ends, watch the fat closely and take it off the heat before it starts to color. Any water that is left will be visible after cooling and can be easily discarded. It is far better to have a little water mixed in than to have browned and strongly flavored fat.

Pour the hot fat once or twice through a paper coffee filter or several layers of cheesecloth to remove any impurities. Then put it into the sterile glass jar and store it in the refrigerator.

Gribenes

Gribenes are the cooked and crispy bits of chicken skin left over when you strain rendered chicken fat (see above)—the word means "scraps" in Yiddish. They are wonderful sprinkled on salads (much like crisp bits of bacon), and are a cherished cook's snack in the kitchen.

However, select the chicken you use to make *gribenes* carefully—a friend told me about the unpleasant taste of *gribenes* he made from "reasonable quality" chicken parts. He said they tasted strongly of fish! That makes sense to me, because many commercial chickens are fed fish meal both to increase the omega-3 levels in their eggs and to make the flesh more nutritious. Of course, whatever is in a chicken's feed will show up in the taste of the fat.

Paris Street Market Chicken Basted with Goose Fat

If you love golden, crunchy chicken skin and have fond memories of meals in Paris, this recipe is for you—it tastes just like the chickens you buy from the rotisserie stand at the Marché rue Cler. The chicken is brined and then slow-roasted for 3½ hours; it's so memorable that it inspires cravings!

SERVES 6 TO 8

1 (6- to 7-pounds) large pastured roasting chicken

3 tablespoons pastured goose fat (see page 331), melted

Kosher salt and freshly ground black pepper

Brine the chicken for several hours (or, ideally, overnight), rinse, and blot dry, according to the instructions in the box on page 297.

When you are ready to cook, heat the oven to 300 degrees and set a rack in the center. Choose an oval gratin dish, a cast-iron frying pan, or other shallow ovenproof dish that closely fits the shape of the chicken.

Place the chicken in the dish, breast side up. Using a brush, paint it with as much of the melted fat as it can hold. Reserve the balance to add as the bird cooks. Generously salt and pepper the chicken, and put it in the oven, feet facing the back wall.

Roast for about 3½ hours, basting every 30 minutes or so, first with the fat you have left over from the initial brushing, then with the fat from the pan; a bulb baster is helpful.

Remove the chicken when an instant-read thermometer inserted between the thigh and the leg (and without touching bone) registers 165 to 170 degrees. Let the bird rest for 15 minutes before carving.

Save the accumulated fat in the pan—when it's cool, pour it through a paper coffee filter or cheesecloth and store it in a sterile jar. This chicken-and-goose-fat blend is a wonderful medium for basting meat and for cooking potatoes and vegetables, or even for your next Paris chicken.

Paris Chicken Redux

I had a "natural" chicken, unbrined and straight from the supermarket. With less than 2 hours till dinnertime, I craved the impossible: slow-cooked, shatteringly crisp Paris chicken, which is brined overnight and roasts for a good 3-plus hours. I went for it anyway, layering thin slices of Yukon Gold and sweet potatoes on the bottom of a gratin pan, and salting and then basting the bird with goose fat. (The goose fat wasn't melted either—I just massaged it in with my hands straight from the refrigerator.)

I put the chicken in the center of a 450-degree oven with its feet facing the back wall, basted a couple of times, and hoped for the best. Done after an hour and a half, it was delicious—not as juicy as the slow version, but still crisp and satisfying, the potatoes full of the rich flavors of goose fat and chicken.

Diced Rosemary and Garlic Potatoes

If you like crispness, these are heaven on a plate. Finely dice the potatoes for even, quick cooking, bearing in mind that you don't have to peel them if you don't want to.

SERVES 4 AS A SIDE DISH

3 tablespoons pastured goose fat (see page 331)

1½ to 2 pounds Yukon Gold potatoes, cut into ½-inch dice

2 to 3 cloves garlic, chopped

2 heaping tablespoons chopped fresh rosemary

Sea salt and freshly ground black pepper

Choose a big cast-iron frying pan and melt the goose fat over medium-high heat. When adding a potato cube causes a sizzle, add the garlic, potatoes, and rosemary, shaking the pan so that the potatoes stay in one layer and are coated with fat and flavorings. Cook for 3 to 4 minutes, then add a little salt and pepper.

Cover the pan and shake every few minutes to redistribute the potatoes; they should start to brown, and it should take about 10 minutes to cook them to tenderness.

Uncover the pan, raise the heat to high, and cook for a minute or two longer, shaking or stirring, until the potatoes reach a perfect stage of crispness. Remove them with tongs or a slotted spoon and drain them on paper towels. Serve hot with more salt as needed.

Red Cabbage with Apples and Cranberries

Another take-off on a traditional Danish Christmas dish, this cabbage cooks slowly for a few hours to a melting texture. It is also wonderful the next day, especially when reheated with morsels of leftover roast goose or pork. If you don't have goose fat or duck fat saved, substitute butter.

SERVES 6 TO 8

⅓ cup pastured goose fat (see page 331)

1 cup sugar

1 small head red cabbage, cored and slivered

2 apples, peeled, cored, and cut into cubes

⅔ cup apple cider

1 (12-ounce) bag cranberries

Zest and juice of 1 lemon and 1 orange

In a large, heavy Dutch oven or a flameproof ceramic pot with a cover, melt half the goose fat over medium heat. Sprinkle on 1 teaspoon of the sugar, and add the cabbage shreds and apples. Turn the cabbage in the fat until it glistens.

Add the apple cider and lemon and orange zest and juice along with the cranberries and the rest of the sugar, stir, and cover the pot. Reduce the heat to low and continue to cook, covered, for 2 to 3 hours, checking every now and then to make sure there is still some liquid in the bottom of the pot and the cabbage is steaming.

When the cabbage is very limp and cooked down, stir in the remaining goose fat. Taste for balance—add more lemon juice for tartness or a little sugar for sweetness.

Serve warm or at room temperature.

Schmaltzy Chopped Chicken Liver

My grandmother would recognize this dish because although it is different from the one she served, it has the same rich, chunky quality. If you don't have any chicken fat, you can substitute duck or goose fat. Choose a heavy pan that can hold the livers closely in one layer—a 9-inch cast-iron frying pan is perfect.

MAKES 1¼ CUPS

3 eggs

1 onion

2 tablespoons pastured chicken fat (see page 331)

1 pound chicken liver, rinsed and blotted dry

1 teaspoon kosher salt

Freshly ground black pepper

Leaves from 8 to 10 fresh parsley sprigs

1 tablespoon dry sherry

1 teaspoon crunchy and flavorful salt such as smoked salt flakes or Maldon salt

Put the eggs in a small pot of water and bring the water to a boil. Turn off the heat (moving the pan to a cold burner, if necessary) and let them sit for 10 minutes. Fill a bowl with ice and water and put the eggs in the water to chill rapidly.

Coarsely chop the onion into ½-inch pieces (they will be chopped further in the food processor later). Heat a heavy medium-sized frying pan over medium-low heat and melt 1 tablespoon of the chicken fat in it. When the fat is hot, lower the heat and add the onion, shaking the pan to coat the onion pieces with fat. Let fry until wilted but still with some bite, 4 to 5 minutes. Remove most of the onion from the pan, but don't worry if some onion shreds remain, as they add a little crunch if they are cooked more.

Rinse the livers in a strainer under running cold water and shake them dry. Melt another tablespoonful of chicken fat in the pan and when it is hot, add the chicken livers. Reduce the heat to low, add salt and pepper, and shake the pan often to distribute the meat evenly. Turn the livers, using a fork or tongs, when they are lightly browned, but not seared, about 5 minutes. Cook on the other side for another 3 minutes, or until they are cooked but still pink in the middle.

Using a food processor fitted with the steel blade, put the livers and onions in the bowl. Peel the hard-boiled eggs and coarsely slice them into the bowl. Add the parsley and sherry. Pulse in about 12 very short bursts, aiming for a chunky texture (not a paste). Scrape into a serving bowl and finish with the crunchy flavorful salt.

Serve with pieces of matzoh, crackers, or bread.

EGGS

A Year in Poultry

APRIL

I've ordered two sets of birds from two different sources—a batch of chickens for eggs (the Rainbow Layers) and another batch of mixed fowl (ducks, geese, turkeys, guinea fowl) for meat.

There has been such an unprecedented demand for baby chicks and other poultry this year that all the hatcheries are backed up! Our second set of birds will be a month late. I'm thinking we'll coop the laying hens in a real henhouse with access to the outdoors every day to free-range, and put the guinea fowl, turkeys, ducks, and geese in a home-made day-range setup within an electric fence that follows the ruminants, à la Andy Lee and Joel Salatin.

OCTOBER

Summer is over, and much of the meat flock has been processed. The turkeys are in the freezer, as are the guinea fowl. The surviving goose and duck (their mates were eaten by predators) have formed a close relationship and live together in the pen last used by sheep, awaiting their fate as featured stars in a farm-processing workshop next week.

The fourteen Rainbow Layer laying hens (and one speckled rooster) live in the henhouse, going outside by day and locked safely in at night. After five and a half months, the chickens are finally beginning to lay eggs just as the days get shorter. I'm getting two eggs a day, and am thinking about putting in a light to keep the chickens laying all winter. I'm told they need twelve hours of light "sufficient to read by" in order to keep on laying. I like thinking of the hens with glasses perched on their beaks and a good book held tight in their feathers.

JANUARY

The electric light has helped the hens to keep on laying, although sometimes there are only one or two eggs a day. They perch up on the rafters most of the time, and seem very bored. I gave them a whole cabbage one day, and it was playtime for chickens—they just loved rolling it and pecking it and generally having a good time. I am going to be more assiduous about bringing a bucket and picking up the organic vegetable culls from the Coop that they throw away every day. I know the chickens will enjoy the variety.

APRIL

The chickens go out every morning now, and can range inside and out all day long. When it starts to get dark, they all roost up in the rafters of the henhouse, and one of us goes out to lock the door against predators. We are averaging eight to ten eggs a day, but we have found broken eggs and shells, indicating cannibalism (which we are told is very hard to stop once started). I'm hoping that once it's warm enough for the chickens to range on new grass, they'll stop breaking and eating their own eggs.

It's time to order the meat birds for this summer. I am planning on Label Rouge chickens, a new-to-the-U.S. breed from France that is well-suited to grazing on pasture. The problem with ordinary meat birds—Cornish Crosses—is that they've been bred to be so big-breasted that their legs can't support them! Like Dolly Partons of the poultry world, they're so well-endowed that they fall and break their legs.

MID-APRIL

Today was our first whole-dozen-in-a-day egg bonanza! And one was a double-sized blue egg with two yolks (twins!) inside.

And three days later we got to a regular rhythm of fourteen eggs a day, one per hen! I also found that feeding the hens oyster shells for calcium, in addition to the crushed granite we feed them for grit, took care of the cannibal problem—they were just starving for calcium, and their own shells were the only place they had to find it! Smart birds. Stupid farmer.

Cooking with Pastured Eggs

Eggs from pastured free-range birds that scratch in dirt are visibly different from grocery-store eggs—their yolks are a bright and vibrant deep orange, and they sit high on the whites. They taste different, too—they have profound flavor—and they are high in omega-3 fatty acids. While you can buy DHA-enriched eggs at almost any grocery store, local free-range eggs will be naturally high in DHA, thanks to the birds' diet of greens. (Commercial DHA or high-omega-3 eggs may have been fed fish meal, which can be polluted or high in mercury, unless the fish have been screened for heavy metals or otherwise specified as clean.) It is for this reason, among others, that I most prefer local eggs from free-range pastured chickens that have been fed organic grain, to avoid pesticides. The best eggs I've tasted (besides my own) come from a farmer who feeds her chickens sunflower seeds in addition to their natural diet of bugs, llama poop (they share a pasture), grass, and organic grain.

As a beginning egg farmer myself, I can attest to the high price of organic grain and supplements, as well as to the difficulties of keeping baby chicks alive and safe from predators. Babysitting chicks from the time they are one day old until they reach the age of five months (when they finally begin to lay) is a process that requires dedication and care. As a result, I've gone from being shocked at the sight of eggs that cost five dollars per dozen to feeling like that's a bargain.

Once you begin to pay real money for good eggs, it only makes sense to use them as an important ingredient. I now prefer to use my own eggs as a main ingredient for dinner, or for special desserts, as the recipes that follow attest.

EGG RECIPES

Blue Cheese and Toasted Walnut Custards

Made in a mini-muffin tin, these little custards are best eaten warm. Serve three or four of them per person for a weeknight dinner, along with a big salad, or offer them at a party as an accompaniment to drinks. Either way, their adorable size makes them very appealing. The leftover ramekin's worth of filling will make an excellent lunch for another day.

MAKES 24 LITTLE CUSTARDS, PLUS A (½-CUP) RAMEKIN; A LIGHT DINNER FOR 4, OR DRINKS FOR 6 TO 8

½ cup walnut halves

¾ cup crumbled blue cheese

¼ cup grated Parmigiano-Reggiano, freshly grated

1 cup heavy cream

4 pastured eggs, at room temperature

Heat the oven to 350 degrees. Butter and flour all 24 depressions in a mini-muffin tin *very* thoroughly. Butter a half-cup ramekin as well. (As an alternative to butter and flour, use an oil-and-flour baking spray such as Baker's Joy.)

Using a dry cast-iron skillet, toast the walnuts over medium heat, stirring and shaking the pan as needed to prevent burning. When the nuts become fragrant, tip them onto a plate to cool. Chop into ¼-inch pieces.

Using a food processor or blender, or working by hand with a whisk, beat the cheeses, cream, and eggs together. Stir in the chopped walnuts and pour the mixture into a pitcher. Divide the batter evenly in the pan, filling each cup ⅔ full, and pour the remainder into the ramekin.

Bake for 40 minutes, reversing the position of the pan halfway through baking. The custards are done when they are golden, slightly cracked on top, and cooked through. Let them cool slightly before removing them from the pan and serving.

Stracciatella

This Roman egg-drop soup is proof that sometimes the simplest things are the best. A practically instant dinner, the dish depends on good-quality ingredients: Use the best homemade stock and the freshest local pastured eggs you can find. The key to making the eggs look authentic—like rags rather than curds—is to use a big spoon and stir fairly slowly in one direction as you add them.

SERVES 4 TO 6

6 cups homemade chicken stock, such as Every Week Chicken Stock (see page 303)

2 eggs, at room temperature

¼ cup freshly grated Parmigiano-Reggiano or Grana Padano

½ teaspoon freshly grated nutmeg

2 tablespoons finely chopped fresh flat-leaf parsley

Salt and freshly ground black pepper

In a deep pan, bring the stock to a slow boil over medium-high heat.

Choosing a medium bowl, beat the eggs with the cheese and add the nutmeg. Hold a cooking spoon in one hand, and the bowl of beaten eggs in the other, then pour the eggs into the simmering stock while stirring the soup slowly and continuously in one direction. The eggs will instantly form "rags." Turn off the heat and add the parsley, and salt and pepper. Give the soup one more slow stir, and ladle it into bowls to serve at once.

Spinach, Red Pepper, and Asparagus No-Crust Quiche

Bake this easy dinner in a 9-inch porcelain quiche pan for an elegant presentation, or use a glass or ceramic pie pan instead. If you want to add meat, pieces of cooked bacon, sliced ham, leftover cooked chicken, or shreds of braised beef or pork would be good additions to the basic mix. If you add more mix-ins, increase the eggs to four. And, of course, if you'd like to encase the custard in a crust, any of the ones in this book will work; "blind" bake the crust before adding the filling (see box).

SERVES 8

½ cup chopped fresh or cooked spinach

6 to 8 stalks fresh asparagus, cut into ½-inch lengths

3 tablespoons chopped red bell pepper (about ¼ pepper)

1 cup heavy cream

3 pastured eggs, at room temperature

4 ounces feta cheese, drained and crumbled

¼ cup freshly grated Parmigiano-Reggiano

1 teaspoon unbleached all-purpose flour

¼ cup fresh basil leaves, sliced

Heat the oven to 325 degrees, and set a rack in the upper third. Grease a quiche pan.

Arrange the chopped spinach, asparagus, and bell pepper pieces across the bottom of the pan.

Using a food processor or blender, or working by hand, combine the cream, eggs, cheeses, flour, and basil. Pour this over the vegetables so that the custard covers all. Place the pan on a baking sheet and bake for 50 minutes, or until the top is golden, the sides are cooked through, and the center is only slightly soft.

Let cool on a rack for about 10 minutes before serving warm.

Baking "Blind"

To prebake pie crusts, prick them all over with a fork (so that they don't puff up), and line them with parchment paper weighed down with beans or pie weights. After baking for 15 minutes in a 350-degree oven, the paper and weights should be removed. At this point, the crust can be baked for 10 minutes longer to brown it, or it can be filled for the final bake.

Eggs Poached in Tomato Sauce on Couscous with Oregano and Parsley

omatoes and eggs have a great affinity, and this dish combines them with couscous to make a hearty dinner entrée. If you like, you can substitute canned or home-cooked white, red, or black beans for the couscous, or serve the poached eggs over cottage cheese when the weather is hot.

SERVES 4 TO 6

3 tablespoons extra-virgin olive oil

1 onion, chopped

2 cloves garlic, chopped

Salt

1 tablespoon Greek oregano

1 (28-ounce) can whole peeled tomatoes

Freshly ground black pepper

⅔ cup couscous

4 to 6 pastured eggs, at room temperature

¼ cup freshly grated or shredded Grana Padano or Parmigiano-Reggiano

3 thick slices artisanal white or whole wheat bread, cut into cubes

⅓ cup finely chopped fresh flat-leaf parsley

Heat a wide saucepan or deep frying pan over low heat and add 1 tablespoon of the oil. When it is thinned and fragrant, add the onion and sweat it down over low heat until the pieces are translucent. Add the garlic and season with salt, and stir them in for a minute or so. Crumble in the oregano and grind a generous amount of black pepper over all. Stir this in over low heat for another minute or two.

Add the tomatoes and their juices to the pan, breaking up the tomatoes with a spatula. Increase the heat to create little bubbles at the edges, then lower the heat to maintaining a steady, slow simmer for 10 to 15 minutes.

Meanwhile, make the couscous: Heat 1 tablespoon of the remaining olive oil in a saucepan over medium heat, and when it is hot, add the couscous. Stir it around in the oil; add 1⅓ cups water and salt to taste. Cover the pan, and cook until all the water is absorbed, about 8 minutes. Uncover and fluff the couscous grains with two forks.

Crack the eggs one at a time into the simmering tomato sauce, spacing them evenly around the pan. Sprinkle the grated cheese over the surface and cover the pan. Poach the eggs for 10 minutes on medium-low heat, or until the whites are set and the yolks are creamy.

As the eggs cook, make croutons: Using a cast-iron frying pan, heat the remaining 1 tablespoon olive oil and fry the croutons over medium-high heat until they are crisp and golden on all sides, turning them as necessary. Remove these to a paper towel to drain.

To serve, fill shallow bowls with the couscous, then spoon on some tomato sauce and one of the eggs. Add more salt to taste; scatter croutons and the chopped parsley on top.

Creamy Double-Boiler Eggs with Chèvre and Cooked Arugula

*S*low-cooking scrambled eggs in a double boiler is transformative—the eggs retain a loose, creamy consistency even when they are entirely cooked. This dish takes 15 minutes to make, and can serve as a festive breakfast, celebratory brunch, or breakfast for dinner entrée.

SERVES 2

1 teaspoon extra-virgin olive oil

3 ounces (two loose handfuls) arugula, washed, but not dried

2 tablespoons unsalted butter

3 or 4 pastured eggs, at room temperature

1 teaspoon dried tarragon

¼ cup heavy cream

¼ teaspoon kosher salt

Freshly ground black pepper

2 ounces fresh goat cheese, crumbled

2 slices good white bread such as brioche, challah, or Swiss peasant bread, toasted

Using a saucepan or frying pan with a lid, heat the olive oil over medium heat and add the wet arugula. Shake the pan or use a spoon to briefly toss the greens with the warm oil, and then cover the pan. Cook for about 5 minutes, or until the greens are wilted. Turn off the heat and uncover the pan to cook off any excess liquid using the heat left in the pan.

Fill the base of a double boiler so that the bowl-like top portion sits above but not in the water. Heat to a boil. Melt the butter in the top portion. Using a whisk or a blender, beat the eggs, tarragon, cream, salt, and pepper together. Whisk or beat in the crumbled soft cheese so that it is well-blended. Have a heatproof silicone spatula or other tool ready to stir the eggs as they cook.

Pour the egg mixture into the melted butter, then gently and constantly stir the eggs as they cook, forming into soft curds. As you stir, work from the outside in and the base upward, dislodging any cooked curds and making room for the still liquid mixture to cook. It will take 10 minutes for all the egg to cook in this manner.

To serve, layer the greens on the toast and top with the eggs.

Nori Scrambled Egg Roll-Up

I have always found packages of nori, or pressed sheets of dried seaweed, in the Asian section of my local food co-op or grocery store. Such plain nori sheets can be lightly toasted over a hot flame or high heat. I do this directly over fire, but with an electric stove you would have no choice but to hover over the hot burner using tongs. However, I've recently discovered a new nori product at a giant Asian supermarket in Queens: Assi seasoned seaweed. This nori has been salted and fried in olive oil with green tea powder, corn oil, perilla oil, and sesame oil. Delicious, and ready to eat without further toasting, it serves as a wrapper for all kinds of foods.

MAKES 1 SERVING (MULTIPLY AS NEEDED)

1 sheet nori, plain or seasoned and toasted

1 or 2 pastured eggs, at room temperature

1 teaspoon extra-virgin olive oil, unsalted butter, or virgin coconut oil

Lay the sheet of nori on a plate. If it is regular nori, lightly toast first over a flame or in a dry cast-iron frying pan, heating both sides until fragrant and pliable.

Beat an egg or two to blend the yolk and the white. Heat an omelet pan and add the oil or butter. Pour in the beaten egg and lightly scramble over low heat, drawing up the cooked egg and tilting the pan to allow the uncooked egg to cook. Turn to cook the other side, if necessary, and slide the scrambled egg onto the nori sheet. Roll the nori around the hot egg and serve.

Deviled Eggs with Fresh Basil and Pimentón

Few can resist the charm of deviled eggs when they are among the appetizers at a buffet. These are special, partly because pastured eggs are so incredibly yellow, but also because of the basil and pimentón. Here I've used the picante version, but if all you have is dulce, or plain paprika, feel free to use that instead.

MAKES 12 DEVILED EGGS

6 pastured eggs at room temperature

2 tablespoons white vinegar

2 tablespoons salt

2 tablespoons sour cream

1 tablespoon Dijon mustard

2 tablespoons diced onion

¼ teaspoon hot (picante) pimentón de la Vera (smoked Spanish paprika)

1 tablespoon unsalted butter

1 teaspoon extra-virgin olive oil

⅓ cup fresh basil leaves

Put the eggs in a saucepan and fill it with enough cold water to cover them. Add the vinegar and salt—this helps the eggs to peel more easily. Bring the water to a boil, cover the pot, and turn off the heat under it for 10 minutes, or move the pot to a cool burner.

Meanwhile, prepare an ice-water bath. Remove the pan from the heat, and shock the eggs in the ice water. Peel them and cut them in half. Gently remove the yolks and put them in the bowl of a food processor fitted with the steel blade.

Add the sour cream, mustard, onion, pimentón, butter, olive oil, and basil leaves to the yolks. Process the mixture, scraping down the sides of the bowl as necessary, until the mixture is a purée.

Arrange the egg white halves on a platter, and spoon or pipe the yolk mixture into the cavities. Cover the platter with plastic wrap and chill for at least 1 hour before serving.

Tamagoyaki

This slightly sweet, layered Japanese rolled omelet is flavored with soy sauce and mirin. The trick with cooking tamagoyaki *is to keep folding and rolling successive very thin layers of egg as the mixture cooks. I don't have the distinctive square-edged pan that's traditionally used, but I find that a small round cast-iron frying pan works well.*

SERVES 2

1 tablespoon vegetable oil

3 pastured eggs, at room temperature

2 teaspoons thin soy sauce

1 teaspoon mirin

1 teaspoon sugar

Choose a small frying pan or flat skillet that is about 6 inches in diameter. Heat the pan and add the oil.

Using a fork or small whisk, beat the eggs with 2 tablespoons water, the soy sauce, mirin, and sugar. Scrape this mixture into a pitcher or measuring cup with a spout. Pour a quarter of the mixture into the hot pan. Let this cook into a thin layer, tipping the pan as necessary to cook all the egg in one layer, scraping up and incorporating any cooked bits into the mass to make room for the excess to cook on the bottom of the pan. Use a spatula to roll the egg over itself into a thin roll at the far end of the pan, tilting the pan to help facilitate the process.

Add another quarter of the egg mixture to the near (open) end of the pan, and tilt the pan so that the mixture goes under the roll at the far end. Let this layer cook, and tilting as before, tilt the pan toward you, nudge the cooked roll onto the new layer, and roll the egg toward you, so that the new layer wraps around the already rolled egg. You will now have a larger roll in the part of the pan closest to you.

Repeat with the next quarter of the egg mixture, making the roll end up at the far end of the pan. Repeat with the last bit of egg. You will end up with one roll of egg. Remove it from the pan.

Cut the omelet in half—you should be able to see layers. Serve each half on a plate, further sliced or not, as you wish.

Bringing Eggs to Room Temperature

If you have cold eggs fresh from the fridge, put them in a bowl of hot tap water. They will heat up in about 5 minutes, and they'll expand in volume when whipped just as if they had come to room temperature slowly.

Leek and Potato Gratin with Chèvre, Blue Cheese, and Shirred Eggs

*D*inner *in one dish is always easy, and although this bakes for an hour and a quarter, it is really very little work to put together. It's a good way to use up any little bits of soft cheeses that may be left over, and almost any mix of good-tasting cheeses will add great flavor to the gratin.*

SERVES 2 TO 4

2 tablespoons extra-virgin olive oil

1½ pounds leeks (1 or 2 fat leeks)

2 russet potatoes

1 to 2 ounces chèvre and blue cheese, or other soft cheeses, mixed

1 tablespoon unsalted butter

½ cup heavy cream

Salt and freshly ground black pepper

4 pastured eggs, at room temperature

Heat the oven to 350 degrees, and position a rack in the upper third. Pour the oil into a 4-cup capacity oval or other shallow gratin dish (or even a glass or metal brownie pan) and use it to coat the sides.

Cut the potatoes into very thin ¼-inch slices and arrange them on the bottom of the dish, slightly overlapping. They should form a nearly solid layer.

Cut off and discard the root end and most of the green end of the leeks. Slice in half lengthwise, and clean them under cold running water, opening the layers (like turning pages in a book) under the stream of water to rinse all the dirt out. Drain slightly, then cut the leeks crosswise into ¼-inch slices, and scatter them on top of the potatoes.

Dot the leeks with crumbles of the soft cheese, and then with tiny bits of butter. Pour the cream over all and add salt and pepper. Break the eggs on top, spacing them as evenly as possible.

Cover the dish tightly with aluminum foil, set it on a baking sheet, and bake for 1 hour. Remove the aluminum foil, return the dish to the oven, and bake for another 15 minutes, or until the whites are firm and the yolks are slightly shaky. Serve warm or at room temperature.

Baked Eggs with Arugula, Fresh Tomato, and Cheese

This is a quick weeknight dinner at my house, and I recommend it for yours. The preparations take about 5 minutes, the baking another 20, so dinner is on the table in less than half an hour. You need only good bread to round out the meal. Use any leftover cheese you've got in the house, although a runny one with lots of flavor is the best way to punch up the dish.

SERVES 2 TO 4

2 tablespoons extra-virgin olive oil

1 onion, finely chopped

Salt

4 ounces arugula or spinach

1 large fresh tomato, chopped, juices saved

4 pastured eggs, at room temperature

Freshly ground black pepper

1 tablespoon leftover cheese, preferably a runny one such as St. Marcellin

2 to 3 tablespoons freshly grated Parmigiano-Reggiano

Heat the oven to 325 degrees and position a rack in the top third. Grease a 1-quart ceramic or glass gratin dish with a little of the olive oil.

Heat a skillet over medium heat and pour in 1 tablespoon of the oil. When it thins and becomes fragrant, sweat down the chopped onion with a little salt until the onion pieces are translucent. Pour them into the gratin dish.

Put the skillet back over the heat, add the remaining olive oil, and cook down the arugula with a little salt, covered, for about 2 minutes, or until it is wilted. Add this to the onion in the gratin dish.

Layer in the chopped tomato and its juices on top of the arugula. Break the eggs over the dish, and layer them onto the tomato, trying to distribute them evenly. Shower the eggs with a little more good salt and grind on plenty of pepper to taste.

Pour the leftover cheese over the eggs, or, if your cheese is not runny, slice or shave it to make this layer. Finish by sprinkling on the Parmigiano-Reggiano.

Bake the dish, uncovered, for 20 minutes, or until the eggs are cooked and not wobbly. Serve at once with good artisanal bread.

Vermont Cheddar Soufflé

ompletely foolproof, and much easier than you may think, cheese soufflé makes a wonderful supper when accompanied by a salad and good bread (I like to serve it with Sweet and Salty Bacon Corn Bread, page 224). Don't be put off by the length of this recipe—all those details are there to ensure you won't fail.

I find the soufflé tastes best when made with four-year-old Grafton cheddar. If you can't find that, look for a sharp cheddar and you'll get similar results.

Using a real ceramic soufflé dish makes a difference here and is not a big investment. Note that the dish is first buttered and coated with cheese, then chilled while you prepare the rest of the ingredients. This helps the soufflé to rise impressively. To ensure that everyone gets a good view of your expertise, call folks to the table before you take the soufflé out of the oven!

SERVES 4 TO 6

3 tablespoons unsalted butter

½ cup finely grated Parmigiano-Reggiano

3 tablespoons unbleached all-purpose flour

1 cup whole milk

1 cup sharp cheddar cheese, grated on the biggest holes of a box grater

Sea salt and freshly ground black pepper

1 teaspoon finely chopped fresh tarragon or dried tarragon

6 pastured eggs

Pinch of cream of tartar

Heat the oven to 400 degrees. Using your fingers or a bit of the butter wrapper, grease the bottom and sides of the soufflé dish well with 1 tablespoon of the butter. Dust the sides and bottom of the dish with the Parmigiano-Reggiano, turning the dish and shaking it so that the surfaces are well-coated. Put the dish in the refrigerator to chill.

Melt the remaining 2 tablespoons butter in a saucepan. When it is bubbling, whisk in the flour to make a roux. Cook the paste for 1 minute, then slowly add the milk, whisking or stirring constantly, and bring the mixture to a boil. The paste will become thick; continue to cook for another full minute— it should be smooth and glossy. Remove the pan from the heat and add the cheddar, stirring to help it to melt. Season with salt and pepper, and add, stirring, the tarragon. Allow the mixture to cool slightly.

Separate the eggs into yolks and whites, using two bowls. Add ⅓ of the yolks to the cooling sauce mixture and whisk rapidly. Add the sauce mixture back into the rest of the yolks and continue to whisk. Return the mixture to the pot, and using the lowest possible heat, bring the enriched sauce to a simmer, stirring constantly for no more than a few seconds (I count to 10). Pour the sauce into a clean bowl to stop it from cooking further, and let it sit for 10 minutes.

In a spotlessly clean and grease-free bowl, beat the egg whites with the cream of tartar until they are very stiff, using a stand mixer, hand mixer, or balloon whisk. The peaks should easily hold their form when cut with a beater or knife. Pour about a third of the egg white mixture into the cooled sauce and stir together to lighten the sauce. Now, carefully, fold in the remaining whites, using a silicon spatula and a light folding motion to ensure that you don't deflate the bubbles. Err on the side of underfolding—inflation is more important than thorough mixing.

Scrape the mixture into the prepared soufflé dish and run your thumb around the edge of the dish, creating a trough along the side of the soufflé dish (this will help it to rise). Put the soufflé in the oven, close the door, and immediately turn the heat down to 375 degrees. Bake for 30 minutes and serve at once.

Middle Eastern Fried Eggs

oth a great Sunday breakfast and an equally good evening meal, these fried eggs are made with garlic, salt, and a little za'atar (a Middle Eastern spice containing sumac that is available in specialty grocery stores and spice shops). If you don't have za'atar, you can make a similar dish using Moroccan Spice Blend (see page 31) instead, or even just using cumin. Of course, the flavors will be different, but the eggs will still taste very good. Pair them with Merguez Sausages (see page 148) and pita, naan, or even English muffins to round out the plate.

MAKES 1 SERVING (MULTIPLY AS NEEDED)

1 teaspoon extra-virgin olive oil

2 pastured eggs at room temperature

½ clove garlic, minced

⅛ teaspoon kosher salt

½ teaspoon za'atar

Freshly ground black pepper

METHOD 1

Heat the olive oil in a small frying pan until it is thinned and fragrant, but not hot enough to smoke, and gently slip in each egg. Immediately lower the heat and layer the garlic, salt, za'atar, and pepper onto the egg. Cook one side for about 2 minutes, then turn the egg, spice side down, and continue cooking to your preference.

METHOD 2

I also like to make these eggs in a steamer specially designed for poaching—one of those frying pans with little ramekins set over boiling water and made to steam-cook eggs on the stovetop. When I cook them this way, I put all the ingredients except the eggs in the ramekins in the order given and break the eggs on top. Then all I have to do is put on the cover and cook until the yolks are no longer runny.

Baby Chicks, Day 1

The day-old chicks in the Rainbow Layer collection arrived yesterday morning; the post office called at 6:45 to say they were there (and urgent cheeping in the background confirmed it). I dashed in to pick up the perforated cardboard box filled with tiny babies, cranked up the car heat to low oven temperature, and brought them home. We had already made a brooder out of a large clear plastic container, with a cutout in the top fitted with firmly bolted screening to provide fresh air and keep cats out. I lined it with newspapers, added a thermometer, set up a Gatorade-like drink dispenser in an inverted mason jar feeder, and put in the chicks. Setting a desk lamp fitted with an infrared bulb over the opening to keep them warm, I checked the temperature and then sat down to watch chicken TV.

Twenty-four hours later, I'm still entranced, as are my two cats. We sit on the window seat opposite the kitchen island and watch the birds move around, peck each other and their food, walk all over other sleeping chickens, and cuddle. They have more than doubled in size since yesterday morning! They are fascinating and charming, emitting soft cheeps that are a pleasure to live with. Each looks and acts differently from the other. There are several "chipmunk" chickens with brown stripes down the centers of their backs; there's a leopard chick with spots; there's a soft, pale gray chick that likes to perch odalisque fashion as if she is sitting for a Matisse drawing; there are big golden fluff balls and two paler yellow ones, along with a number of black and gray birds with yellow butts or white faces. I never knew you could fall in love with chickens, but now I get it. I find myself thinking about keeping one or two in an aviary in the house, as they are such a nice presence. Before, when I read about pet chickens, I thought they sounded pathetic. It took me less than a day to turn around completely. Because their brooder box is transparent, we can watch them, and (most surprisingly) they seem to like to watch us. In fact, I felt quite self-conscious making an egg for breakfast this morning in front of them.

Cardamom Popovers with Pearl Sugar

ry these popovers as an accompaniment to a dinner of carrot or parsnip soup. Pearl sugar adds a nice crunch and is available from specialty baking stores. One technical note: Because the cardamom seeds are infused in hot milk, you'll need to have whole green cardamom pods to start with and allow time for the milk to cool.

MAKES 12 POPOVERS

10 whole green cardamom pods

1 cup whole milk

1 cup unbleached all-purpose flour

1 teaspoon kosher salt

3 pastured eggs, at room temperature

3 to 4 teaspoons pearl sugar, if available, or granulated sugar, if necessary

Heat the oven to 425 degrees (if you have a convection setting, use it without reducing the temperature) placing a rack in the upper third. Put a muffin pan in the oven to heat. Let the oven and pan preheat for at least 20 minutes.

Using a mortar and pestle, pound the cardamom pods to release their inner black seeds. Discard the green papery husks and slightly bruise the seeds with the pestle. Put the milk in a saucepan and add the seeds. Heat until the milk is warm, but not boiling, then turn off the heat and let the infusion sit until it has cooled to slightly warm.

Whisk or sift the flour and salt together.

Using a stand mixer or handheld electric mixer, beat the eggs on high speed until they are lemon colored, foamy, and expanded, about 3 minutes. Gradually add the cardamom milk to the bowl, beating on high. Add the flour and salt mixture very slowly, using the lowest speed or mixing by hand.

Transfer the batter to a container with a spout (there will be 4 cups batter). Working quickly, remove the hot muffin pan from the oven, set it on a baking sheet, and spray each cup with an oil-and-flour baking spray such as Baker's Joy. Fill each cup about half full. Sprinkle each top with pearl sugar, if using.

Bake the popovers for 15 minutes, then reduce the heat to 350 degrees for another 10 minutes. (Don't open the oven until the full baking time is up.) The popovers should be tall and golden without, and airy and custardy within. Carefully remove them from the pan and serve at once.

Lavender Crème Brûlée

You can find culinary lavender in the bulk spice section of many health food stores and at specialty spice purveyors. Among other things, it's an ingredient in Herbes de Provence Blend (see page 32), but it is also lovely as a single-flavor note. While it is wonderfully easy to flame crème brûlée with a kitchen blowtorch if you've got one, it's not hard to do under the broiler either.

SERVES 6

2 cups heavy cream

⅓ cup plus 6 tablespoons sugar

1 tablespoon culinary lavender buds

1 tablespoon pure vanilla extract

6 pastured egg yolks at room temperature

Heat the oven to 325 degrees and set a rack in the center. Choose 6 dishes with a capacity of about ½ cup—little Pyrex bowls, ceramic ramekins, or shallow crème brûlée dishes (these provide more surface area for the burnt sugar). Put them in a broiler pan or rimmed sheet pan (or use 2 pans, if necessary) suitable for serving as a water bath when you bake the custards.

Using a heavy saucepan, heat the cream and the ⅓ cup sugar over medium heat until the sugar dissolves. Reduce the heat to low, add the lavender buds, and continue to cook for 10 minutes to infuse the cream with flavor. Taste the cream and see if it is infused to your liking. If not, continue to steep, off the heat, for another 15 to 30 minutes. Strain out and discard the lavender. Put the warm cream in a bowl with a pour spout, and stir in the vanilla.

Whisk the yolks together in a medium bowl and then slowly drizzle in the hot cream, whisking constantly to prevent curdling. When both are blended, pour the custard into the ramekins.

Carefully pour boiling water into the broiler pan so that it comes halfway up the sides of the ramekins. Bake for 35 minutes, or until the custard is set.

Remove the ramekins and let cool on a rack. When the custards are cool to the touch, cover them with plastic wrap and chill for a few hours or overnight.

Several hours before serving, heat the broiler and set an oven rack at the highest position. Sprinkle 1 tablespoon of the remaining sugar over the top of each ramekin. Arrange the ramekins on a sheet pan and put the pan in the oven as close as you can to the broiler—almost, but not quite, touching the element. If you need to, set the filled sheet pan on top of another inverted sheet pan to raise it up higher. Broil the custards for 2 to 5 minutes, watching very closely, to brown the tops. The timing will depend on how close you've been able to get to the heat. The sugar should form a golden, caramelized crust that will become fragrant as they finish (but be careful not to let them catch fire or carbonize). Let the crème brûlées cool on a rack until they are warm to the touch.

Cover and refrigerate the crème brûlées for 2 to 4 hours, until the custard is cold and firm (longer chilling may make the topping soft). Serve cold.

Spiced Brod Torte with Chocolate, Almonds, and Currants

I love old-fashioned German-Jewish bread crumb cakes, and today's artisanal multigrain breads make them even better—I use an eight-grain bread for mine. Thinly slice and darkly toast the bread on an oven rack, then use a blender or food processor to pulse it into fine crumbs. You can grate the chocolate in the blender or processor, too, after first cutting it into small bits. All the fat in this easy cake comes from egg yolks, almonds, and cocoa butter, so it's lovely served with whipped cream.

SERVES 10 TO 12

¼ cup dried currants or raisins

¼ cup dry sherry

10 pastured eggs, separated, at room temperature

2 cups sugar

½ teaspoon pure almond extract

1 teaspoon pure vanilla extract

1¾ cups toasted multigrain bread crumbs

1 cup grated good-quality dark chocolate

1 teaspoon ground cinnamon

1 teaspoon ground allspice

½ teaspoon freshly grated nutmeg

¼ teaspoon ground cloves

¼ cup chopped almonds or almond meal

2 teaspoons baking powder

For serving:

Confectioners' sugar

Whipped cream

Heat the oven to 350 degrees, and position a rack in the upper third. Have an ungreased springform pan ready. Put the currants and the sherry in a small saucepan and bring the mixture to a boil. Immediately turn off the heat and let the fruit soak in the hot wine.

Beat the egg yolks and sugar together until the mixture is very yellow and thoroughly combined. Stir in the almond and vanilla extracts, and the fruit and sherry mixture.

In another bowl, combine the bread crumbs, chocolate, spices, almonds, and baking powder. Mix these dry ingredients into the yolk mixture. The batter will be very stiff.

Beat the egg whites into stiff peaks. Stir about a third of the egg whites into the batter to lighten it. Then fold in the rest of the beaten whites, trying not to deflate them. Scrape the batter into the springform pan.

Bake the cake for 50 minutes to 1 hour, or until the top is springy and just dry. Let it cool on a rack before removing the sides of the pan. Dust the cake with confectioners' sugar, and serve it with a dollop of whipped cream on top.

Rosewater Lemon Meringue Pie

Lemon meringue pie is a diner staple, but no diner I know adds rosewater and orange blossom water to the filling, nor do they cut the sugar to manageable levels. This pie crust recipe, very simple to make in a food processor, is a sure winner for any kind of pie. When I'm not using lard for pie crust, I use Earth Balance Natural Shortening, which is not hydrogenated and is available in health food stores and natural retailers. Orange blossom water and rosewater are available from specialty retailers, Middle Eastern markets, and some supermarkets. Make this pie a day ahead.

MAKES ONE 9-INCH PIE

For the crust:

1¼ cups unbleached all-purpose flour, plus more for dusting

¼ teaspoon kosher salt

6 tablespoons (¾ stick) very cold unsalted butter

2 tablespoons very cold vegetable shortening

2 tablespoons ice water, plus more as needed

For the filling:

4 pastured egg yolks, at room temperature

¾ cup sugar

2 tablespoons cornstarch

¼ teaspoon kosher salt

1 cup water

½ cup whole milk

1 tablespoon unsalted butter, cut into tiny pieces if cold

Freshly grated zest and freshly squeezed juice of 1 lemon

¼ teaspoon orange blossom water

¼ teaspoon rosewater

For the meringue topping:

4 pastured egg whites

¼ teaspoon cream of tartar

¼ teaspoon kosher salt

2 tablespoons sugar

To make the crust, combine the flour and salt in a food processor fitted with the steel blade. Cut the chilled butter and shortening into a small dice, working quickly so that they don't warm up. Put everything in the processor bowl and whirl it around until the mixture looks like coarse meal, about 1 minute.

While the processor is running, drizzle the first tablespoonful of ice water through the feed tube. When it has been absorbed, about 20 seconds, drizzle in the second tablespoonful the same way. The dough should immediately start clumping and cleaning the sides of the bowl, forming a lump that rides the blade. If this doesn't happen, drizzle in a *tiny* amount of additional ice water until it does—do not overmix. As soon as the dough comes together, stop the machine. Form the dough into a thick disk. Lightly flour it and wrap it in waxed paper. Chill it for at least 30 minutes.

Roll out the chilled dough on a floured board (or in a floured plastic pie crust maker, see page 252) to an inch or so larger than your standard 9-inch pie plate. Lay the dough into the pie plate without stretching it, crimp the edges, and prick the surface all over with a fork. Chill the crust for another 30 minutes or more.

Heat the oven to 425 degrees and set a rack in the upper center. Lay a sheet of parchment or waxed paper over the bottom crust and pour beans, rice, or pie weights on top (this prevents puffing). Bake the crust for 15 minutes, remove the paper and weights, and bake for another 5 to 8 minutes, until the crust is golden. Let it cool on a rack.

To make the filling, in a medium bowl, briskly beat the egg yolks together with a fork.

In a heavy saucepan over low heat, combine the sugar, cornstarch, and salt. Add the water and milk, and whisk until the dry ingredients dissolve. Increase the heat to medium and cook, whisking, until the mixture comes to a boil. Remove the pan from the heat.

Slowly pour about 1 cup of the hot milk mixture into the yolks to temper them, whisking. Then pour the yolk mixture into the saucepan, continuing to whisk.

Set over medium heat and cook, still whisking, for about 3 minutes, or until the mixture is thick. Stir in the butter and remove the pan from the heat. Stir in the lemon zest and juice, along with the orange blossom water and rosewater.

Scrape the filling into a clean bowl and cover it with plastic wrap placed directly on the surface of the filling to prevent a skin from forming. Chill the filling until you are ready to use it.

When you are ready to assemble the pie, heat the oven to 350 degrees.

Using an electric hand mixer or a stand mixer, beat the egg whites with the cream of tartar on low to medium speed until they start to form peaks. Sprinkle on the salt and very gradually add the sugar, beating at high speed until stiff peaks form. (Don't overbeat—the whites will deflate.)

Pour the lemon filling into the pie shell, using a spatula. Using a clean spatula, scrape the meringue mixture onto the top of the filling, forming it into swirls that cover the surface to the edges.

Bake the pie for about 15 minutes, or until the meringue is golden. Let cool completely on a rack, then cover and chill before serving. (For the best flavor and cleanest cuts, refrigerate it overnight.)

Poached Kumquats in Syrup

I am always very happy to see kumquats in the market, and happier still when California friends send me a shoe box full from the tree in their yard. I make kumquats in syrup and always have a jar in the refrigerator to pull out for chocolate desserts, especially soufflés. They are also wonderful with good Greek yogurt, ice cream, or with pound cake.

MAKES 4 CUPS

4 cups kumquats

6 cups water

1¾ cups sugar

Wash the kumquats, cut them in half lengthwise, and pick out and discard the seeds.

Boil the water and sugar together until dissolved, then lower the heat to a slow simmer. Add the prepared kumquats to the slowly bubbling syrup, and cook them gently until they begin to look transparent on the edges and to collapse a little (about 10–15 minutes).

Meanwhile, sterilize a 1-quart jar by boiling it in water or running it through the high-temperature cycle of a dishwasher.

Remove the fruit with a slotted spoon and put it in the jar. Set the jar on a folded dish towel (to prevent thermal shock on contact with the cool countertop) and pour the hot syrup over the fruit. Put the lid on and let the jar cool completely.

Refrigerate the kumquats until you are ready to use them. They will keep for 3 to 4 months, chilled. (If, at the end of 4 months, they are still in your refrigerator, reboil them for 10 minutes and pour into a newly sterile jar before cooling and refrigerating them again.)

Mini Chocolate Soufflés with Kumquats in Syrup

oth quick and easy, this dessert soufflé uses remarkably little butter and eggs, so it is actually a rather low-fat, low-cholesterol dessert. I make it in 8 mini soufflé dishes, which are available in 3 to 4 ounce sizes. You could use straight-sided ramekins or ceramic custard cups instead.

If you'd like, you can work ahead through the step where you mix the egg yolks with the chocolate, then stop for an hour or two to serve dinner. Resume the process by whipping the egg whites. That way, you can put the soufflés in the oven at the end of the meal (perhaps while clearing the table and serving coffee), as they take a scant 12 minutes to cook and must be served immediately. The kumquats offer a tart and yet sweet contrast to the airy chocolate, but if you don't have kumquats, use the grated zest of an orange or half of a grapefruit to add that citrus counterpoint when you mix the soufflé ingredients.

SERVES 8

4 tablespoons (½ stick) butter, cut into small pieces, plus more for each soufflé dish

Sugar, for each soufflé dish

1 tablespoon strong black leftover coffee or espresso

3 ½ ounces high-quality sweet chocolate, such as Black and Green's milk chocolate, or 4 ounces good-quality bittersweet chocolate such as Ghirardelli

4 pastured eggs, at room temperature, separated

1 teaspoon pure vanilla extract

Pinch of salt

Poached Kumquats in Syrup (see page 358)

Heat the oven to 450 degrees if making immediately, and set a rack in the bottom third of the oven. Butter 8 mini soufflé dishes and dust them with sugar to coat, tapping out any excess. Refrigerate the dishes until you are ready to fill them.

Put the coffee, chocolate, and 4 tablespoons butter in a microwave-safe dish, layered in that order, and heat them for 20 seconds. Stir the mixture well, and microwave it for 20 seconds longer. Stir again.

In a large mixing bowl, gently whisk the egg yolks together, then slowly add a little yolk to the chocolate-and-butter mixture to temper it. Next reverse the process, by adding all the chocolate mixture to the yolks, whisking as you pour. Stir in the vanilla.

Add the salt to the egg whites and beat them at medium-high speed until they just hold a peak (they should not be dry). First fold one-third of the whites into the chocolate mixture to lighten it. Then fold the chocolate mixture into the whites, working as gently and swiftly as possible. Don't worry if specks of white remain in the mix—this doesn't have to be perfectly combined.

Pour the soufflé into the prepared dishes (they should each be about two-thirds full), and bake for 7 minutes. Reduce the heat to 400 degrees, and bake 5 minutes longer. The soufflé should be a bit jiggly in the center. Serve it at once, with a few poached kumquats in syrup on top.

SIDE
DISHES

These are some of the dishes I use to round out a meal. Many of them are particular favorites, such as the orzo salad on page 364, while others seem to be perfect complements to meat stews or roasts, like Coconut Rice (see page 365). Others are master recipes for dishes we make often, like wilted greens, or polenta.

Wilted Greens with Garlic and Olive Oil

Whether you are cooking spinach, Swiss chard, kale, dandelion greens, collards, or other sturdy greens, this is the master recipe. The only difference between one kind of green and another is the time it may need to wilt and relax and the degree to which the stems need removal.

Greens with thick, stiff stems such as Swiss chard and kale can be folded lengthwise and the stems cut out from the spine. You can chop and cook the stems with the leaves, or save them for another night. Once the leaves are stemless, roll them into a cigar shape and cut them crosswise into a fine shred (or chiffonade, in cookspeak). They'll cook very rapidly and well.

With more tender greens such as spinach or dandelion, you don't need to cut out the stems, nor do you need to cut the leaves into chiffonade. Whatever the green, careful washing in several bowls of clean water is essential to remove grit and dirt. Drain them casually, as the water clinging to the leaves is part of the cooking process.

Prepare the greens as directed above and set them in a colander.

Heat a large, heavy frying pan or sauté pan with a lid, or a Dutch oven, over medium heat, and add the olive oil. When it is thinned and fragrant, reduce the heat to medium-low, add the garlic pieces, and turn them in the hot oil for 1 minute.

Add the greens, give them a quick turn in the oil, then clap on the lid, tightly. Keeping the heat low, let the greens wilt in the fragrant oil until they are cooked down. This will take 5 to 7 minutes. If you are cooking collards, chard, or kale, you may want to add the water or chicken stock to provide a little more cooking liquid, but I find this necessary only when these greens are not very fresh. Shake a little hot pepper onto the greens, if you like bite. Add salt and pepper, and serve.

SERVES 2 TO 4

1 bunch greens (about 1 pound)

2 tablespoons extra-virgin olive oil

2 cloves garlic, smashed

¼ cup water or chicken stock, if needed

Crushed red pepper flakes (optional)

Salt and freshly ground black pepper

Orzo with Slivered Almonds, Currants, and Mint

Cold pasta dishes offer hot weather refreshment, and this rice-shaped-pasta salad is especially good with grilled meats. Although it's called a cold salad, serve it at room temperature along with a big green salad or with vegetables you've thrown on the grill alongside the meat.

SERVES 8

1 tablespoon unsalted butter

½ cup slivered almonds

½ pound orzo (also called riso)

1 tablespoon extra-virgin olive oil

½ cup Zante currants

2 tablespoons finely chopped fresh mint

Drizzle of balsamic vinegar

Salt and freshly ground black pepper, as needed

Using a small cast-iron frying pan, melt the butter until it is fragrant and beginning to color, and add the almonds. Cook, stirring, until the nuts brown lightly. Set aside.

Cook the orzo in salted boiling water until it is al dente. Drain it, put it in a serving bowl or platter, and toss it with the olive oil.

Add the currants, browned almonds, and mint. Toss well and drizzle with balsamic vinegar. Taste for salt and pepper and serve at room temperature.

Clementine, Fennel, and Olive Salad

Now one of our favorite salads, I made this for the first time in Sicily, where I was working in a kitchen surrounded by orange and lemon and olive trees. Once I got home, I discovered that this is wonderful paired with a slow-cooked chicken dish, or a pork dish. If you have a mandoline or Benriner slicer, this is a good time to use it. I've also used navel oranges and blood oranges to good effect.

SERVES 4 TO 6

3 clementines or other good oranges

2 tablespoons extra-virgin olive oil

2 tablespoons freshly squeezed lemon juice

2 tablespoons chopped fresh flat-leaf parsley

2 tablespoons honey

Salt and freshly ground black pepper

2 large fennel bulbs, trimmed and washed

½ cup salt-cured black olives, pitted

Juice one of the oranges, and combine the juice with the olive oil, lemon juice, parsley, and honey. Season the mixture with salt and pepper to taste and set it aside.

Peel the remaining oranges and divide them into sections. Add the sections to a salad bowl (they look very pretty in a glass one).

Cut the fennel bulbs in half lengthwise, from top to bottom. Make a V-shaped incision to remove the hard cores and discard them. Cut the remaining fennel into very thin slices, using a mandoline or Benriner, or a sharp knife. Add the slices to the salad bowl.

Toss in the olives, add the dressing, and toss well again. Serve at once.

Coconut Rice

oconut is a great accompaniment to many of the dishes in this book, and this rice is one of my favorite ways to showcase its flavors. (I buy my virgin coconut oil and shredded dried coconut from Tropical Traditions.) Upping the sugar and adding more milk and eggs turns this into coconut rice pudding; leaving it unchanged but adding sliced mangoes makes it into a traditional Thai dish.

SERVES 4 TO 6

1 tablespoon virgin coconut oil	½ teaspoon salt
1 (14-ounce) can coconut milk	1 teaspoon sugar
1½ cups jasmine rice	3 tablespoons shredded dried coconut, for garnish
1¼ cups water	

Using a heavy saucepan with a tight-fitting lid, heat the coconut oil over low heat. (If the coconut milk has separated in the can, add the heavy creamy part of the contents, and let that melt in the saucepan.) Otherwise, add the whole can.

Add the rice and turn it in the liquid, then add the remaining coconut milk (if there is any), the water, salt, and sugar. Increase the heat to medium high, then stir occasionally to prevent the rice from sticking as it comes to a boil.

Once the liquid boils, immediately reduce the heat to low. Put the lid on the pan, slightly ajar to allow steam to escape. Cook for about 15 minutes, or until nearly all of the water is absorbed.

Cover the pot tightly, and turn off the heat. Let the rice continue cooking in the residual heat of the pan, moving the pan to a cold burner if necessary. It will stay warm for about half an hour if the pan is sturdy.

When you are ready to serve, fluff the rice with a fork and sprinkle it with the dried coconut.

Danish Caramelized Potatoes

raditionally served only during the week between Christmas and New Year's, these potatoes are rolled in caramelized sugar and melted butter to glaze them with sweetness. Some people dust them with chopped parsley, but I prefer them plain, in all their candied glory. They are often served with roast goose or pork.

SERVES 6

24 to 36 small, round red or yellow potatoes	2 tablespoons unsalted butter
½ cup sugar	

Steam or boil the potatoes until they are cooked through and can be pierced with a skewer. Allow them to cool.

In a heavy skillet large enough to hold all the potatoes in one layer, melt the sugar over medium heat until it is liquid and just beginning to color. Add the butter to the pan, and when it is melted, add the potatoes. Turn them in the sugar-and-butter mixture until they are coated on all sides. Immediately transfer them to a serving dish and serve.

Polenta Two Ways

I like polenta. I like it hot and freshly made, and I like it the next day, cut into squares and sautéed or grilled. I make it two different ways, depending on the time available and my inclination.

Neither of these methods is the way an Italian would make polenta, but they are easy. Traditional polenta has hazards—it can be lumpy if not done correctly. These two methods are foolproof.

Polenta is good plain or served under any kind of stew or meat braise that has lots of sauce. It is also good with cheese cooked in, with a drizzle of extra-virgin olive oil, or with a strong honey such as chestnut honey, for breakfast.

DOUBLE-BOILER POLENTA

I learned this method from Deborah Madison's book *Vegetarian Cooking for Everyone*, and I use it because it is very easy—very little stirring!—although it takes about an hour and half.

SERVES 6 TO 8

8 cups boiling water
1 heaping tablespoon kosher salt
2 cups coarse stone-ground cornmeal or Italian polenta (not instant)
2 tablespoons unsalted butter

Bring a few inches of water to a boil in the bottom of a double boiler, and set the top pan over the water. Lower the heat to maintain a slow simmer in the bottom pot.

Pour the 8 cups boiling water and the salt into the top pan. Slowly add the cornmeal in a steady stream, whisking as you pour. Once all the cornmeal is mixed in, leave it alone to cook slowly. Give it a stir every now and then when it looks crusty, but otherwise leave it alone. The polenta should bubble and occasionally erupt, but as long as it simmers slowly, it will cook perfectly.

After 90 minutes, when the polenta is thick and stiff, stir it vigorously. If it is slightly glossy, it is done. Take it off the heat and stir in the butter. Serve it hot, or ladle it into a flat dish or quarter sheet pan to cool. When the polenta is cool, cover the pan with plastic wrap and refrigerate it overnight before cutting it into squares to grill or sauté.

COLD-WATER POLENTA

This method is the way I make polenta in a hurry. It takes 20 minutes, although longer cooking and stirring will improve it.

SERVES 4 TO 6

5 cups cold water
1½ cups coarse stone-ground cornmeal or Italian polenta (not instant)
1 teaspoon kosher salt

Pour the cold water into a saucepan and whisk in the cornmeal and salt. Slowly bring this to a boil, whisking. Turn the heat to medium-low so that the mixture simmers, and continue to cook it, stirring often, until it is very thick and glossy, about 20 minutes over low heat. If the polenta starts to become too dry during cooking, you can dribble in more water, whisking furiously.

Stir it vigorously as it finishes cooking to give it more gloss. Serve it hot, or pour it into a greased sheet pan or lasagna pan and let it cool. When the polenta is cool, cover the pan with plastic wrap and refrigerate it overnight before cutting it into squares to grill or sauté.

Persian Wedding Polow with Orange Peel

Adapted from Najmieh Batmanglij's extraordinary book Silk Road Cooking, *this is the dish I make for special occasions. You can collect orange peel as you eat oranges, storing the peel in the refrigerator after parboiling and draining it. I found this home-made peel tasted much better than purchased dried orange peel. Orange blossom water can be found in Middle Eastern stores.*

SERVES 4

3 cups white basmati rice

8 tablespoons (1 stick) unsalted butter, melted

Seeds from 2 green cardamom pods

1 (4-inch) cinnamon stick

1 onion, thinly sliced

2 carrots, cut into thin strips with a vegetable peeler

1 cup orange peel, white pith removed, cut into slivers

1 cup sugar

4 cups cool water

½ cup unsalted pistachios

½ cup almonds, toasted

1 tablespoon kosher salt

½ teaspoon saffron threads

2 tablespoons hot water

1 tablespoon orange blossom water

Wash the rice under running lukewarm water, picking out and discarding any stones. Soak the rice in a bowl, agitating it with your hands to bring the starch to the surface. Change the water until it finally runs clear (usually about 5 times). Soak the rice in the clear water for about 10 minutes.

While the rice soaks, heat 4 tablespoons of the butter in a deep pot over medium heat until it is very hot. Add the cardamom seeds and cinnamon stick and fry them for a moment or two, until their aroma is strong. Add the onion and fry it, stirring, until it becomes golden. Add the carrots and cook them, stirring, for another 2 minutes. Add the orange peel, sugar, and 1 cup of the cool water and bring this to a boil. Reduce the heat to low, and simmer for about 15 minutes. Remove the pot from the heat and add the pistachios and almonds.

In a heavy pot with a tight-fitting lid such as an enameled Dutch oven, combine the remaining 3 cups water, the salt, 2 tablespoons of the remaining butter, and the washed and soaked rice. Cover the pot tightly and cook over medium heat for 15 minutes.

Meanwhile, soak the saffron threads in the hot water.

Add the orange-and-carrot mixture to the rice, give it a good stir, and drizzle the remaining 2 tablespoons butter, the orange blossom water, and the dissolved saffron and its water over the rice. Reduce the heat to the lowest possible setting, cover the pot very tightly (wrapping the lid with a tea towel, if necessary), and cook for another 30 minutes.

Set a damp tea towel on the counter or on a board. Remove the covered pot from the heat and let it cool without removing the lid, setting it on the damp towel (this helps to loosen the bottom crust, the most desirable portion of the rice).

When you are ready to serve, invert the rice onto a serving platter so that the browned crust is on top.

AFTERWORD

When I became a ranch owner I realized that I had to make a very important choice. I had to decide if my ranch would be driven only by economics or by social responsibility.

If I chose to run my ranch based on economics, my challenge would be to produce as many cows as possible at as cheap a cost as possible. This would mean fattening up cows with grain and administering antibiotics and hormones, and force-feeding them in industrial grain-based feedlot operations, which require intensive consumption of fossil fuels, produce higher levels of environmental pollutants, and provide terribly inhumane treatment to the cows.

If I opted instead to run La Cense Montana in a socially responsible way, I would be putting my choices to love animals and people, and to respect the land through a commitment to sustainable ranching, ahead of financial gain. For me, the decision was simple. I opted to practice natural and grass-feeding methods that would be sustainable and profitable at the same time.

I teamed up with a great man, Bud Griffith, who already had thirty years of ranching and livestock experience. Together we explored how to raise cows properly through all-natural grass feeding, and how to provide the cow a low-stress, quality life, thus producing healthy, tender, and delicious meat for the end consumer. I was challenged by many skeptics who thought I could only achieve my goals of nurturing the cows and land by keeping my operation small. I was told this could not work if you own an 88,000-acre ranch. Through study, research, and experimentation, however, we were able to accomplish our objectives on a large scale.

We started the program with fifty cows, and trained cowboys and staff who not only had extensive ranch experience, but also showed a real compassion and respect for our cows. We then developed and implemented a series of grass-fed beef practices and protocols that would be audited by a third party. Eventually we became the first grass-fed beef ranch to receive USDA certification, validating our ability to source and age-verify our beef, and testifying to the fact that our cows are exclusively grass fed and that we do not use hormones or antibiotics in raising them.

At La Cense we developed rotational and Intensive Grazing practices that work well for the larger-scale herd, and take advantage of the natural herding instincts of grazing animals. These cattle have evolved from prey animals, and find security and comfort in belonging to groups. By grazing our livestock in groups we are better able to manage the pastures. It allows us to split one very large pasture into twenty-five to thirty individual pastures. Each day the cattle enter a new, lush pasture that is 12–14 inches tall and graze it down to 5–6 inches. This allows for even grazing of all grasses and allows the pasture to rest and regrow for approximately twenty days before another grazing. We defer grazing some of our pastures for use in the fall and winter months. These grasses are lower in quality than they would be in the growing seasons but work very well. We also stockpile some baled grass and forage to ensure that the animals' nutritional requirements are being met in the event of a harsh winter storm. All of these practices serve to make the ranch carbon positive.

At La Cense we also use time-honored animal husbandry practices and blend them with low-stress handling facilities. Because we limit the animals' stress, the herd gains weight more efficiently and produces a higher-quality meat. The most important stress-reducing measure we take is to let the cow dictate the speed of the process, during pasture moves, for instance. We train our cowboys to understand the natural behavior of the cattle, which includes understanding the flight zone (personal space) of the animal.

A gentle animal's flight zone can be different from that of a more excitable or younger animal. The cow needs to be left to do what it wants, as opposed to forcing it to do what you want. Since not all cows respond to humans in the same manner, it is also important that the cowboy move slowly and quietly and train the animal to be comfortable around him. Again, it's about letting the cow dictate the pace.

Each year, the children from our local 4-H come before the local community to showcase the cows that they were given the chance to feed and nurture. The children talk about the learning experience that comes with raising the animals, including how they got to know the cows' personalities, and they describe the time and care they gave to the cows every day. When I attend these gatherings and see the joy in the children's eyes and souls, it is a reminder of how fortunate I

am to be a part of the sustainable ranching tradition, and its responsibility for our world community, including the cows, the people, and mother nature. As a U.S. citizen who came to this country from France twenty-five years ago, I am very fortunate to have created a successful business that continually honors the land and our global community. The La Cense story shows that, even on a grand scale, it is possible to raise cattle in a way that upholds tradition and maintains a good quality of life for each living creature.

WILLIAM KRIEGEL
owner, La Cense Montana

SOURCES

To learn more about the vacations I host, visit www.culinaryvermont.com and www.italyonaplate.com. To follow what I'm working on, see deborahkrasner.blogspot.com.

The Web is a wonderful and overwhelming source of information, contacts, products, and resources. Each of the sources below will direct you to many more if you follow their links. Especially, do not miss the links on Eatwild, which maintains perhaps the most thorough list of related articles, organizations, and resources anywhere on the Web on the subject of traditionally raised, grass-fed, and pastured food.

National Resources

- **Slow Food USA** (www.slowfoodusa.org) is the American wing of an extraordinary international organization devoted to linking the pleasures of food with the community and the environment. Local chapters across the country offer members a chance to organize, celebrate, and connect with farmers, cooks, educators, students, and everyone who cares about food and their environment.
- **The American Grassfed Association** (www.americangrassfed.org) is a national organization dedicated to protecting and promoting grass-fed producers and products.
- **American Livestock Breeds Conservancy** (www.albcusa.org). A nonprofit membership organization working to protect over 150 breeds of livestock and poultry from extinction; the pioneer organization in the U.S. working to conserve historic breeds and genetic diversity in livestock.
- **Eatwild** (www.eatwild.com) is indeed, as they themselves say, the number-one site for grass-fed food and facts. You can click on your state to see what is available locally; you can also find farms that will ship to you. Read the articles; follow the links to other studies and sites—this is an incredible resource!
- **LocalHarvest** (www.localharvest.org) is a compendium of local farmers, CSAs, and other local resources, listed state by state.
- **Organic Grass Fed Beef Info** (www.organicgrassfedbeefinfo.com) offers clearly written and attractively presented information about grass-fed beef.

Other Resources

On the Issue of Sustainability

- **Center for Food Safety** (www.truefoodnow.org) is an activist group aimed at promoting organic and other forms of sustainable agriculture.
- **Community Food Security Coalition** (www.foodsecurity.org) is an umbrella organization for more than 300 member organizations dedicated to building strong, sustainable local and regional food systems.
- **Cool Foods Campaign** (www.coolfoodscampaign.org) aims to educate the public about how food choices can affect global warming.
- **Eating Green Calculator** (www.cspinet.org/EatingGreen/calculator.html). This interactive site allows you to calculate the environmental impact of a week's meals.
- **Factory Farm** (www.factoryfarm.org). This is an advocacy group devoted to sustainable food production that is healthful and humane.
- **Farm Aid** (www.farmaid.org) works to keep family farmers on their land to build a family-farm-centered system of agriculture.
- **Food & Water Watch** (www.foodandwaterwatch.org) is a nonprofit group that works to ensure clean water and safe food.
- **FoodRoutes** (www.foodroutes.org) is dedicated to encouraging consumers to buy local, sustainable, grass-fed, and organic products.

Periodicals

- *Small Farmers Journal* (www.smallfarmersjournal.com)
- *Stockman Grass Farmer* (www.stockmangrassfarmer.net)

Sustainable Meat Sources

Of course, it is always preferable to obtain your food as locally as possible, and there are producers now in every state who sell direct to consumers. However, below is a selection of meat producers who ship and sell by the cut or quarter. They may offer cuts you can't find elsewhere or breeds that are not available locally, or they may age their meat in a way that is more to your liking.

Sources for Assorted Products

- **Heritage Foods** (www.heritagefoodsusa.com). Retail food products from heritage and traditionally raised animals. They offer grass-fed beef, pork from hard-to-find breeds, and other food in their capacity as the sales and marketing arm of Slow Food.
- **D'Artagnan** (www.dartagnan.com). Retail duck and a great many other products, including hard-to-find meat breeds and duck fat.
- **Preferred Meats** (www.preferredmeats.com) is Bill Niman's new company, which offers Boer goat meat, grass-fed beef, pork from Berkshire and Duroc pigs, and poultry.

Sources for Grass-Fed Beef

- **La Cense Beef** (www.lacensemontana.com and www.lacensebeef.com) is nationally available, certified grass-fed beef. There is even a La Cense burger truck that sells grass-fed beef burgers on the streets of New York City. La Cense Beef offers individual cuts and packages of cuts.
- **Grassland Beef** (www.grasslandbeef.com) sells grass-fed and pastured meat nationally, by the cut.
- **Slanker's Grass-Fed Meats** (www.texasgrassfedbeef.com)
- **AmericanGrassFedBeef** (www.americangrassfedbeef.com)
- **Alderspring Ranch Grass-Fed Beef** (www.alderspring.com)
- **Organic Prairie** (www.organicprairie.coop)
- **Meadow View Farm** (www.meadow-view-farm.com)
- **Lasater Grasslands Beef** (www.lgbeef.com)
- **Grass-Fed Traditions** (www.grassfedtraditions.com)

Sources for Pastured Pork

- **Caw Caw Creek** (http://cawcawcreek.com)
- **Flying Pigs Farm** (www.flyingpigsfarm.com). Pork is sold at their farm, online, and through Lobel's Meats, in New York City.

Sources for Pastured Poultry

- **Earth Shine Farm** (www.earthshinefarm.com)
- **Good Shepherd Poultry Ranch** (www.reeseturkeys.com)

Sources for Pastured Lamb

- **Jamison Farm** (www.jamisonfarm.com)
- **Lava Lake Lamb** (www.lavalakelamb.com)

Sources for Rabbit

- **Fresh Tracks Game and Poultry** (www.vermontqualityrabbits.com)

Other Web Sites of Interest

- **Centre français d'information des viandes** *(CIV)*, or **French Meat Information Center** (www.civ-viande.org/uk). Offers an English-language copy of part of their terrific French meat Web site, which describes meat parts and provides recipes for each part.
- **Civil Eats** (http://civileats.com) promotes critical thought about sustainable agriculture and food.
- **Eat Local Triangle** (http://slowfoodtriangle.org/eatlocal) is a project of North Carolina's Slow Food Convivium, with links to local CSAs and meat producers.
- **Institute for Agriculture and Trade Policy** (www.iatp.org) is a Minnesota-based organization that defines its mission "to create environmentally and economically sustainable rural communities and regions through sound agriculture and trade policy."
- **Leopold Center for Sustainable Agriculture** (www.leopold.iastate.edu). This Iowa-based center works to reduce the negative impacts of agriculture on natural resources and rural communities.
- **Local Fork** (www.localfork.com) is a food guide for New York City.
- **The Meatrix** (www.themeatrix.com) is a terrific flash movie about meat.
- **Polyface** (www.polyfacefarms.com). Joel Salatin's Web site, offers information about the food he produces, his books and methods, talks, visits, and more.
- **The Sustainable Table** (www.sustainabletable.org) celebrates sustainable food by educating consumers on food issues, aiming to build community through food.
- **Wilson College Robyn Van En Center** (www.wilson.edu/wilson/asp/content.asp?id=804) will help you find a CSA near you.

Product Sources

- **Penzeys Spices** (www.penzeys.com) sells a large selection of spices in bulk.
- **Vanns Spices** (www.vannsspices.com) is another large bulk spice seller.
- **Global Palate** (www.globalpalate.com) sells their spices already packaged in tins.
- **Specialty Bottle** (www.specialtybottle.com) is a good source of containers of various kinds; I get my spice tins here.
- **Lee Valley Tools** (www.leevalley.com) sells the "low-profile mortar and pestle" I like for smashing garlic.

- **King Arthur Flour** (www.kingarthurflour.com) sells all sorts of baking supplies, including the handy "pie crust aid" for rolling out pie dough.
- **Thai Supermarket** (http://importfood.com). This online market sells Thai ingredients and a great mortar and pestle.
- **Kalamala** (http://kalamala.com) offers a great selection of Persian ingredients.
- **Kalustyan's** (www.kalustyans.com), which has a store in New York City, also has an online store, which offers Indian ingredients and other unusual and bulk foods.

Animal Husbandry Sources

- **McMurray Hatchery** (www.mcmurrayhatchery.com) was the source of my Rainbow Layer hens, as well as the Toulouse goose, Rouen ducks, and guinea fowl.
- **J. M. Hatchery** (www.jmhatchery.com) was the source of my meat chickens, the "colored range chicks," which are bred to thrive on pasture, as well as the larger French guinea fowl I raised this year.
- **Ledgewood Farm Icelandics** (www.ledgewoodfarmice landics.com) is where I get the sheep I raise for meat and fleece.

Canada Sources

For all of Canada, province by province: www.eatwild.com/products/canada.html

Toronto
The Healthy Butcher
www.thehealthybutcher.com
The Healthy Butcher specializes in offering completely organic food. They're a "good old-fashioned butcher."
565 Queen Street West, Toronto, ON M5V 2B6, Canada
T: 416-703-2164

Quebec
Ferme Morgan
www.fermemorgan.com
They will deliver to a drop-off point in Montreal, and offer a bulk discount for those who have freezer space to buy half a cow.
1 Van Horne, Montreal, Quebec H2T 2J1
T: 819-687-9021

Donava Angus
www.donava.ca
100 percent grass-fed beef and lamb, and pastured pork from Black Angus cattle, North Country Cheviot lamb, and heritage breed Tamworth pigs.
T: 450-264-3395

Ferme Borealis Inc.
www.fermeborealis.com
They specialize in breeding grass-fed bison and pure-bred Highland cattle.
236, Lisgar Ulverton, Québec J0B 2B0
T: 819-826-2056

Saskatchewan
Triple H Beef
www.triple-h-beef.com
Triple H Beef sells wholes and sides as well as cuts of 100 percent grass-fed beef.
Box 222, Dysart, Saskatchewan, S0G 1H0
T: 306-432-4583

Manitoba
Country Quarters
www.countryquarters.com
Country Quarters is a working beef farm that strives for low-impact and sustainable agriculture.
Box 26, Arborg, Manitoba, Canada R0C 0A0
T: 1-888-376-2369

BIBLIOGRAPHY

Aidells, Bruce, and Denis Kelly. *Bruce Aidells' Complete Sausage Book*. Berkeley: Ten Speed Press, 2000.

———— *The Complete Meat Cookbook*. New York: Houghton Mifflin, 1998.

Aidells, Bruce, with Lisa Weiss. *Bruce Aidells's Complete Book of Pork*. New York: HarperCollins, 2004.

Barrett, Judith, and Norma Wasserman. *Risotto: More Than 100 Recipes for the Classic Rice Dish of Northern Italy*. New York: Charles Scribner's Sons, 1987.

Basan, Ghillie. *The Middle Eastern Kitchen*. New York: Hippocrene Books, 2004.

Bastianich, Lidia Matticchio. *Lidia's Italy: 140 Simple and Delicious Recipes from the Ten Places in Italy Lidia Loves Most*. New York: Knopf, 2007.

Batali, Mario. *Molto Italiano: 327 Simple Italian Recipes to Cook at Home*. New York: Ecco Press, 2005.

Batali, Mario, with Gwyneth Paltrow. *Spain: A Culinary Road Trip*. New York: Ecco Press, 2008.

Batmanglij, Najmieh. *Silk Road Cooking: A Vegetarian Journey*. Washington, DC: Mage Publishers, 2004.

Beard, James. *James Beard's American Cookery*. Boston: Little, Brown, 1972.

Benoit, Jehane. *Mme. Jehane Benoit's Complete Heritage of Canadian Cooking*. Toronto: Pagurian Press Ltd., 1976.

Berry, Wendell, with contributions by Daniel Kemmis and Courtney White. *The Way of Ignorance: And Other Essays by Wendell Berry*, Berkeley: Counterpoint, 2005.

Bittman, Mark. *How to Cook Everything: Simple Recipes for Great Food*. New York: Macmillan, 1998.

Bsisu, May S. *The Arab Table: Recipes and Culinary Traditions*. New York: William Morrow, 2005.

Child, Julia, Louisette Bertholle, and Simone Beck. *Mastering the Art of French Cooking*. New York: Knopf, 1967.

Claiborne, Craig. *Craig Claiborne's Kitchen Primer*. New York: Knopf, 1969.

Clark, Samuel, and Samantha Clark. *Casa Moro: The Second Cookbook*. London: Ebury Press, 2004.

———— *Moro East*. London: Ebury Press, 2007.

———— *Moro: The Cookbook*. London: Ebury Press, 2001.

Corriher, Shirley O. *BakeWise: The Hows and Whys of Successful Baking with Over 200 Magnificent Recipes*. New York: Scribner, 2008.

———— *CookWise: The Secrets of Cooking Revealed*. New York: William Morrow, 1997.

Enig, Mary, and Sally Fallon. *Eat Fat, Lose Fat: The Healthy Alternative to Trans Fats*. New York: Plume, 2006.

Fearnley-Whittingstall, Hugh. *The River Cottage Cookbook*. Berkeley: Ten Speed Press, 2008.

———— *The River Cottage Meat Book*. Berkeley: Ten Speed Press, 2007.

Friend, Catherine. *The Compassionate Carnivore: Or, How to Keep Animals Happy, Save Old MacDonald's Farm, Reduce Your Hoofprint, and Still Eat Meat*. Cambridge, MA: Da Capo Press, 2008.

Forbes, Leslie. *Remarkable Feasts: Adventures on the Food Trail from Baton Rouge to Old Peking*. New York: Simon and Schuster, 1991.

Giobbi, Edward. *Italian Family Cooking*. New York: Random House, 1971.

Grandin, Temple, and Catherine Johnson. *Animals in Translation: Using the Mysteries of Autism to Decode Animal Behavior*. New York: Scribner, 2005.

Green, Aliza. *Field Guide to Meat: How to Identify, Select, and Prepare Virtually Every Meat, Poultry, and Game Cut*. Philadelphia: Quirk Books, 2005.

Grigson, Jane. *Charcuterie and French Pork Cookery*. London: Grub Street, 2001.

Gyngell, Skye. *A Year in My Kitchen: A Collection of Recipes Inspired by the Seasons and Based on a Culinary Toolbox of Inventive Flavorings*. London: Quadrille, 2006.

Halpern, Daniel, and Julie Strand. *The Good Food: Pastas, Soups, and Stews*. New York: Viking, 1985.

Hatkoff, Amy. *The Inner World of Farm Animals: Their Amazing Social, Emotional, and Intellectual Capacities*. New York: Stewart, Tabori & Chang, 2009.

Hayes, Shannon. *The Farmer and the Grill: A Guide to Grilling, Barbecuing and Spit-Roasting Grassfed Meat . . . and for Saving the Planet One Bite at a Time*. Richmondville, NY: Left to Write Press, 2007.

———— *The Grassfed Gourmet Cookbook: Healthy Cooking and Good Living with Pasture-Raised Foods*. Bala Cynwyd, PA: Eating Fresh Publications, 2004.

Hazan, Marcella. *Marcella Cucina*. New York: HarperCollins, 1997.

————*Marcella Says . . . : Italian Cooking Wisdom from the Legendary Teacher's Master Classes, with 120 of Her Irresistible New Recipes.* New York: HarperCollins, 2004.

Helou, Anissa. *Mediterranean Street Food: Stories, Soups, Snacks, Sandwiches, Barbecues, Sweets, and More from Europe, North Africa, and the Middle East.* New York: HarperCollins, 2002.

Henderson, Fergus. *The Whole Beast: Nose to Tail Eating.* New York: HarperCollins, 2004.

Henderson, Fergus, and Justin Piers Gellatly. *Beyond Nose to Tail: A Kind of British Cooking Part II.* New York: Bloomsbury USA, 2007.

Hill, Kate. *A Culinary Journey in Gascony.* Berkeley: Ten Speed Press, 2004.

Hopkinson, Simon. *Roast Chicken and Other Stories.* New York: Hyperion, 2006.

————*Second Helpings of Roast Chicken.* New York: Hyperion, 2008.

Jenkins, Nancy Harmon. *Cucina del Sole: A Celebration of Southern Italian Cooking.* New York: HarperCollins, 2007.

Jenkins, Sara. *Olives and Oranges: Recipes and Flavor Secrets from Italy, Spain, Cyprus, and Beyond.* New York: Houghton Mifflin, 2009.

Kafka, Barbara. *Roasting: A Simple Art.* New York: William Morrow, 1995.

Kamman, Madeleine. *When French Women Cook: A Gastronomic Memoir.* Berkeley: Ten Speed Press, 1976.

Kander, Mrs. Simon. *The Settlement Cook Book.* Milwaukee, WI: The Settlement Cook Book Company, 1944.

Katzen, Mollie. *Moosewood Cookbook.* Berkeley: Ten Speed Press, 1977.

Kingsolver, Barbara, with Steven L. Hopp and Camille Kingsolver. *Animal, Vegetable, Miracle: A Year of Food Life.* New York: HarperCollins, 2007.

Krasner, Deborah. *The Flavors of Olive Oil: A Tasting Guide and Cookbook.* New York: Simon and Schuster, 2002.

————*From Celtic Hearths: Baked Goods from Scotland, Ireland, and Wales.* New York: Viking Studio Books, 1991.

La Place, Viana, and Evan Kleiman. *Cucina Rustica: Simple, Irresistible Recipes in the Rustic Italian Style.* New York: William Morrow, 1990.

Lawson, Jane. *The Spice Bible: Essential Information and More Than 250 Recipes Using Spices, Spice Mixes, and Spice Pastes.* New York: Stewart, Tabori & Chang, 2008.

Lee, Andy W., and Patricia Foreman. *Chicken Tractor: The Permaculture Guide to Happy Hens and Healthy Soil.* Buena Vista, VA: Good Earth Publications, 1998.

————*Day Range Poultry: Every Chicken Owner's Guide to Grazing Gardens and Improving Pastures.* Buena Vista, VA: Good Earth Publications, 2002.

Lo, Eileen Yin-Fei. *The Dim Sum Book: Classic Recipes from the Chinese Teahouse.* New York: Crown Publishers, 1982.

Madison, Deborah. *Local Flavors: Cooking and Eating from America's Farmers' Markets.* New York: Broadway Books, 2002.

————*Vegetarian Cooking for Everyone.* New York: Broadway Books, 1997.

Malouf, Greg, and Lucy Malouf. *Artichoke to Za'atar: Modern Middle Eastern Food.* Berkeley: University of California Press, 2008.

————*Turquoise: A Chef's Travel's in Turkey.* San Francisco: Chronicle, 2008.

McCullough, Fran. *The Good Fat Cookbook.* New York: Scribner, 2003.

McDermott, Nancie. *Quick and Easy Thai: 70 Everyday Recipes.* San Francisco: Chronicle Books, 2004.

McLagan, Jennifer. *Bones: Recipes, History, and Lore.* New York: HarperCollins, 2005.

————*Fat: An Appreciation of a Misunderstood Ingredient, with Recipes.* Berkeley: Ten Speed Press, 2008.

McWilliams, James E. *Just Food: Where Locavores Get It Wrong and How We Can Truly Eat Responsibly.* Boston: Little, Brown, 2009.

Mettler, John J., Jr. *Basic Butchering of Livestock and Game.* North Adams, MA: Storey Publishing, 1986/revised 2003.

Midkiff, Ken. *The Meat You Eat: How Corporate Farming Has Endangered America's Food Supply.* New York: St. Martin's Press, 2004.

Nathan, Joan. *The Foods of Israel Today.* New York: Knopf, 2001.

Nestle, Marion. *What to Eat.* New York: North Point Press, 2007.

Newman, Leslie. *Feasts: Menus for Home-Cooked Celebrations.* New York: HarperCollins, 1990.

Niman, Bill, and Janet Fletcher. *The Niman Ranch Cookbook: From Farm to Table with America's Finest Meat.* Berkeley: Ten Speed Press, 2008.

Pépin, Jacques. *La Technique.* New York: Pocket Books, 1978.

Picard, Martin. *Au Pied de Cochon: A Cookbook from the Celebrated Restaurant.* Vancouver, BC: Douglas & McIntyre Ltd., 2008.

Planck, Nina. *Real Food: What to Eat and Why.* New York: Bloomsbury USA, 2007.

Pollan, Michael. *The Omnivore's Dilemma: A Natural History of Four Meals.* New York: Penguin, 2007.

Portale, Alfred. *Alfred Portale's 12 Seasons Cookbook.* New York: Broadway Books, 2000.

———*Simple Pleasures: Home Cooking from the Gotham Bar and Grill's Acclaimed Chef.* New York: William Morrow, 2004.

Reynaud, Stéphane. *Pork and Sons.* New York: Phaidon Press, 2007.

——— *Terrine.* New York: Phaidon Press, 2008.

Robinson, Jo. *Pasture Perfect: The Far-Reaching Benefits of Choosing Meat, Eggs, and Dairy Products from Grass-Fed Animals.* Vashon, WA: Vashon Island Press, 2004.

——— *Why Grassfed Is Best: The Surprising Benefits of Grassfed Meat, Eggs, and Dairy Products.* Vashon, WA: Vashon Island Press, 2000.

Roden, Claudia. *Arabesque: A Taste of Morocco, Turkey, and Lebanon.* New York: Knopf, 2006.

Rodgers, Judy. *The Zuni Café Cookbook: A Compendium of Recipes and Cooking Lessons from San Francisco's Beloved Restaurant.* New York: W.W. Norton and Company, 2002.

Rombauer, Irma S., and Marion Rombauer Becker. *Joy of Cooking.* Indianapolis: Bobbs-Merrill, 1971.

Rubinstein, Nela. *Nela's Cookbook.* New York: Knopf, 1983.

Ruhlman, Michael, and Brian Polcyn. *Charcuterie: The Craft of Salting, Smoking, and Curing.* New York: W. W. Norton, 2005.

Salatin, Joel. *Family Friendly Farming: A Multigenerational Home-Based Business Testament.* Swoope, VA: Polyface, 2001.

——— *Holy Cows and Hog Heaven: The Food Buyer's Guide to Farm Friendly Food.* Swoope, VA: Polyface, 2005.

——— *Salad Bar Beef.* Swoope, VA: Polyface, 1996.

Schlesinger, Chris, and John Willoughby. *How to Cook Meat.* New York: William Morrow, 2000.

Schlosser, Eric. *Fast Food Nation.* New York: Harper Perennial, 2007.

Schwartz, Arthur. *Arthur Schwartz's Jewish Home Cooking: Yiddish Recipes Revisited.* Berkeley: Ten Speed Press, 2008.

Scripter, Sami, and Sheng Yang. *Cooking from the Heart: The Hmong Kitchen in America.* Minneapolis: University of Minnesota Press, 2009.

Simopoulos, Artemis P., and Jo Robinson. *The Omega Diet: The Lifesaving Nutritional Program Based on the Diet of the Island of Crete.* New York: HarperCollins, 1999.

Slater, Nigel. *The Kitchen Diaries: A Year in the Kitchen with Nigel Slater.* New York: Gotham Books/Penguin, 2006.

Sortun, Ana. *Spice: Flavors of the Eastern Mediterranean.* New York: Regan Books/HarperCollins, 2006.

Stevens, Molly. *All About Braising: The Art of Uncomplicated Cooking.* New York: W.W. Norton, 2004.

Tanis, David. *A Platter of Figs: And Other Recipes.* New York: Artisan Books, 2008.

Time-Life Books Editors. *The Good Cook: Variety Meats.* New York: Time-Life Books, 1982.

Torode, John. *Beef: And Other Bovine Matters.* Newtown, CT: Taunton Press, 2008.

Willan, Anne. *The Country Cooking of France.* San Francisco: Chronicle Books, 2007.

Wolfert, Paula. *The Cooking of Southwest France: Recipes from France's Magnificent Rustic Cuisine.* Hoboken, NJ: John Wiley and Sons, 2005.

——— *Couscous and Other Good Food from Morocco.* New York: William Morrow, 1973.

CONVERSION CHARTS

Weight Equivalents

The metric weights given in this chart are not exact equivalents but have been rounded up or down slightly to make measuring easier.

AVOIRDUPOIS	METRIC
$1/4$ oz	7 g
$1/2$ oz	15 g
1 oz	30 g
2 oz	60 g
3 oz	90 g
4 oz	115 g
5 oz	150 g
6 oz	175 g
7 oz	200 g
8 oz ($1/2$ lb)	225 g
9 oz	250 g
10 oz	300 g
11 oz	325 g
12 oz	350 g
13 oz	375 g
14 oz	400 g
15 oz	425 g
16 oz (1 lb)	450 g
$1^1/2$ lbs	750 g
2 lbs	900 g
$2^1/4$ lbs	1 kg
3 lbs	1.4 kg
4 lbs	1.8 kg

Volume Equivalents

These are not exact equivalents for American cups and spoons but have been rounded up or down slightly to make measuring easier.

AMERICAN	METRIC	IMPERIAL
$1/4$ tsp	1.2 ml	
$1/2$ tsp	2.5 ml	
1 tsp	5.0 ml	
$1/2$ Tbsp (1.5 tsp)	7.5 ml	
1 Tbsp (3 tsp)	15 ml	
$1/4$ cup (4 Tbsp)	60 ml	2 fl oz
$1/3$ cup (5 Tbsp)	75 ml	2.5 fl oz
$1/2$ cup (8 Tbsp)	125 ml	4 fl oz
$2/3$ cup (10 Tbsp)	150 ml	5 fl oz
$3/4$ cup (12 Tbsp)	175 ml	6 fl oz
1 cup (16 Tbsp)	250 ml	8 fl oz
$1^1/4$ cups	300 ml	10 fl oz ($1/2$ pint)
$1^1/2$ cups	350 ml	12 fl oz
2 cups (1 pint)	500 ml	16 fl oz
$2^1/2$ cups	625 ml	20 fl oz (1 pint)
1 quart	1 liter	32 fl oz

Oven Temperature Equivalents

OVEN MARK	F	C	GAS
Very cool	250–275	130–140	$1/2$–1
Cool	300	150	2
Warm	325	170	3
Moderate	350	180	4
Moderately hot	375	190	5
	400	200	6
Hot	425	220	7
	450	230	8
Very hot	475	250	9

INDEX

(Page references in *italic* refer to illustrations.)

GOOD MEAT